Flowers into art

Floral motifs in

and decorative arts

Exhibition in the Kunstindustrimuseet
Copenhagen, Denmark, 5 October to 2 December
1990

Organization
Vibeke Woldbye
Associate
Maria Fabricius Hansen
Secretariat
Ella Jull Kjærulff

Editor Danish catalogue
Vibeke Woldbye
Assistant editor
Maria Fabricius Hansen
Consultants
Hanne Westergaard, Assistant Curator,
Statens Museum for Kunst, Copenhagen
Peter Wagner, Assistant Professor, Botanisk Central
Bibliotek, Copenhagen
Graphic design of Danish catalogue
Sunna and Ruben Blædel

English translation
David Hohnen
Hanne Westergaard, pp. 25-36
Peter Wagner, pp. 9-27, 93-100 and catalogue entries
Monique M. Kennedy and Thomas E. Kennedy
Maria Fabricius Hansen, pp. 74-81
Mary Höcker
Winfried Baer, pp. 82-92
Katja Johansen
Jørgen Hein, pp. 101-106
Kenneth Kindall
Charlotte Christensen, p.p. 107-115
Charlotte Paludan, pp. 116-126
Jane Zuyl-Moores
Saskia de Bodt, pp. 57-73
Editors English catalogue
Kist Kilian Communications, Amsterdam
Cover design English catalogue
Alje Olthof, Amsterdam
Composition and mechanicals
Assist, Goes, Netherlands

CIP-DATA KONINKLIJKE BIBLIOTHEEK,
THE HAGUE

ISBN 90 6179 140 5

Flowers into art

Vibeke Woldbye *ed.*

Floral motifs in European painting and decorative arts

SDU PUBLISHERS

The Hague 1991

Lenders

INTERNATIONAL

Rijksmuseum, Amsterdam
Stedelijk Museum, Amsterdam
Schloss Charlottenburg, Berlin
Porzellansammlung Belvedere, Berlin
Gustavsbergs Museum, Gustavsberg
The Board of Trustees of The Victoria & Albert Museum, London
Musée des Arts Décoratifs, Paris
Museum Boymans-van Beuningen, Rotterdam
Statens Konstmuseer, Nationalmuseum, Stockholm
Linnémuseet, Uppsala
Centraal Museum, Utrecht
Burghley House, Stamford, Lincolnshire
Galerie Börjeson, Malmö
Julie Schafler Dale, Artisans' Gallery, New York
The Duke of Devonshire and the Chatsworth House Trust
S. Franses, London
Hubert de Givenchy, Paris
Helena Hernmarck, Ridgefield, Connecticut
Erik Mortensen, Paris
Marijke van Os, The Hague
The Duke of Westminster

DENMARK

Her Majesty Queen Margrethe of Denmark

Aarhus Art Museum, Aarhus
Botanisk Central Bibliotek, University of Copenhagen
The Danish National Library of Science and Medicine, Copenhagen
Nationalmuseet, Brede
The David Collection, Copenhagen
Det Nationalhistoriske Museum på Frederiksborg, Hillerød
Den kongelige Kobberstiksamling, Statens Museum for Kunst, Copenhagen
The Royal Collections, Rosenborg Palace, Copenhagen
Statens Museum for Kunst, Copenhagen
The Royal Theatre, Copenhagen
Baltica, Inc., Copenhagen
Torben Hardenberg, goldsmith, Copenhagen
Arje Griegst, goldsmith, Copenhagen

As well as a number of private collections in Denmark and other countries.

Table of contents

Vibeke Woldbye

Introduction

The organizers of an exhibition with a theme as rich as *flowers* naturally face many difficult choices. It may seem reckless even to attempt to tackle such a multifaceted subject. How to encompass such diverse subjects as Venus and the Virgin Mary, life and death, war and love, the flower garlands of poetry, the senses? Just to mention a few of the realms of which flowers are an intricate part.

Flowers have always been a motif in the history of art, whether as symbols, or simply serving as an inexhaustible source of inspiration for artists and craftsmen with their challenging beauty and evident decorative qualities. The selection for this exhibition was based on various conceptual, practical and economic criteria which naturally could have been replaced by others just as valid and relevant (or not). In short, several aspects have not been dealt with in this exhibition. We have limited ourselves geographically to the western world. However, this does not mean that the exhibition restricts itself only to western plants. After all, a busy exchange of seed and bulbs has been going on between East and West at least since the sixteenth century; the tulip is just one of many examples. Unfortunately, limitations of space have made it necessary to disregard the wealth of floral art from China, Japan and India.

Another choice was to focus almost exclusively on 'naturalistic' flowers. However, it is not always easy to make clear distinctions. Flowers tend to form patterns. When is a rose a rose, and when does it become a rosette? What is imaginary and what is real in the variegated bouquets of Delft faience, the decorative flower painting in European porcelain factories or the floral splendour of Lyon silks in the time of Madame de Pompadour? William Morris and other European artists from the end of the last century and beginning of the present century, with their renewed interest in craftsmanship, did not hesitate to mix real with imaginary flowers.

The exhibition does not aim at a chronological demonstration of floral art through five centuries, but focusses instead on those periods when, for various reasons, flowers were of crucial importance to people and thus found expression in art. For instance, this occurred when botanical science gained momentum during the sixteenth century and knowledge of flowers and plants, including many imported specimens from recently discovered continents, became widespread. This popularization was assisted by the appearance of richly illustrated botanical works, followed by the florigelia which found a ready market with wealthy citizens and provided inspiration to all branches of craftsmanship. Flower still lifes became an artistic specialty which, with their particular symbolic content, gave the genre a new dimension.

Flowers again gained currency during the 1730s up to about 1760-70 with Linnaeus' pioneering binomial system of scientific nomenclature of plants which suddenly made it possible for 'ladies' to classify plants. Gardens were laid out and described, flowers became fashionable, and particularly roses bloomed everywhere; on costumes, silverware, furniture and ceramics. This exuberance died down in the course of the eighteenth century; the swelling roses were reined in by lines and straight ribbons, and the tidy lily of the valley became an increasingly frequent sight.

Then came Romanticism, the 'golden age,' the Biedermeier period when flowers were loved and bred as never before. Flowers filled the window sills and flower tables. This was the great epoch of flower painters in Denmark and Europe; some of whom painted their floral designs on porcelain. The poets incorporated flower symbolism in their reflexions on love, and the language of flowers was understood by all sensitive souls.

Floral motifs continued their triumphant conquest, dominating the style known as Art Nouveau. The study of nature and 'natural' ornamentation became the starting point for design and decoration at all levels, from Eugène Gaillard's sumptuous metro entrances in Paris to Karl Koepping's delicate flower glasses. Craftsmanship flowered during a short, hectic period around the turn of the century, liberated from the conventions of historical styles and intoxicated by the possibilities inherent in the new style to create its own universe.

Not until our own time has the flower, with a few beautiful, entirely personal exceptions, again attained a visible place in the language of art with pop art's 'banal' flowers, the hippie culture's message of love, and the psychedelic imagery of the 1960s and 1970s. The symbols are viable on all fronts: the strong grip around the rose of the social democratic party, just to mention a single well-known example.

During the 1980s, industry has drowned us in flowers which are ingratiating, decorative and often banal. A new generation's need for nostalgia, romanticism and happy images has created a market for that which is lavish, facile and glossy. Flowers have become part of the addiction to security characteristic of our time. The interesting Dutch jeweller, Gijs Bakker, mocks this commercial pandering in his sensual necklace-rose, *Dewdrop*. It is the drop of dew which makes the 'cup runneth over.' New flowers will continue to appear on the horizon.

The essays included in this catalogue deal with very different aspects of the theme of flowers, and serve to supplement the exhibition. Warm appreciation is expressed to the authors, not only for their significant contributions to the range of topics covered in this exhibition, but for their sympathetic participation in the entire project. Particular thanks are due to Hanne Westergaard, curator at the Statens Museum for Kunst, Copenhagen, and Peter Wagner, Associate Professor at the Botanisk Centralbibliotek, University of Copenhagen, who never ceased to make available their vast knowledge and whose inspiration during the preparation of the exhibition was indispensable.

Vibeke Woldbye is, as a Curator of the Kunstindustrimuseet at Copenhagen, the organizer of the exhibition.

Peter Wagner

Flower gardens, flower fashions and illustrated botanical works

Observations on fashion from a botanist's point of view

During the last part of the fifteenth century some of the ancient Greek writers on natural science were translated into Latin, possibly because manuscripts were brought to Italy by Eastern Roman scholars who had fled from the Turks; this knowledge, thus, became available to the world of learning. A work by Theophrastus, generally regarded as the father of botany, was translated in 1451 (although the translation was not published until 1483), and a manual by the physician Dioscorides in 1478. During the fifteenth and sixteenth centuries, several scholars wrote commentaries on these authors as well as on the Roman naturalist Pliny the Elder. These commentaries were primarily medical, however there were sections attempting to identify Mediterranean plants (which had often been inadequately described in the classical sources) on the basis of known flora. In this work it is clear that many plants had never been described at all. For instance, Dioscorides mentions only those for medicinal use. When new, hitherto unknown plants began pouring into Europe from America and Asia as a consequence of exploration and early colonization, the shortcomings of the classical authors became evident. As a result, in-depth studies were conducted and modern botany emerged as a science.

This development was further facilitated by technical advances. In the early sixteenth century scholars discovered that plants could be pressed and dried, making it possible for them to exchange specimens in order to check their classifications. Moreover, they also began using drawings as an aid in classifying plants, profiting from the advances in naturalism made by illustrators and painters during the Renaissance. The first collections of drawings of plants and animals appeared in Italy during the fifteenth century. Dissemination of information was further helped when these drawings began to be printed in the course of the sixteenth century as a result of the refinement of the technique of wood engraving and the emergence of highly skilled craftsmen. In 1530 and 1542, Otto Brunfels (1488-1534) and Leonhard Fuchs (1501-1566) published works containing 135 and 550 woodcuts of plants respectively. Artists were accorded sufficient importance for their names to be mentioned. Brunfels's illustrator, Hans Weiditz, is praised in a poem in the book's introduction (fig. 1). The title of the book, *Herbarum vivae eicones*, also emphasizes the importance of the pictures: 'living portraits of plants.' Fuchs includes portraits of the contributing artists (fig. 3). Thanks to these illustrations, both books enjoyed a long life and were reprinted many times (fig. 2).

In the sixteenth century, botanical gardens also made their appearance. During the Renaissance, collections were founded and museums or *Kunst- und Wunderkammern* (collections of products of nature, curiosities and works of art) assembled. The actual process of collecting objects, particularly from the newly discovered, faraway regions of America and Asia, contributed further to undermining the authority of the classical authors. The impulse for the formation of these collections was a lack of faith in the authority of the classical authors and the impossibility of obtaining sufficient knowledge of the world and the self only by studying the Bible. The idea was that by examining all of creation, one could come to know God and thus oneself. The collection, museum, or study – whatever it might be – became the refuge of the scholar and was the basis for such knowledge as could be acquired: the macrocosm represented in the microcosm. In this connection the garden was regarded as an outdoor museum, that is, a collection of plants representative of the world as a whole. Also current was the notion that the Garden of Eden had not been destroyed by the Flood but rather that its plants had been dispersed. With the discovery of America the original garden could be recreated by col-

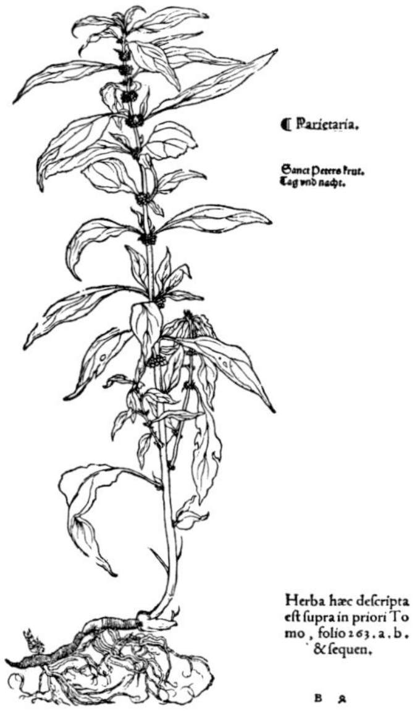

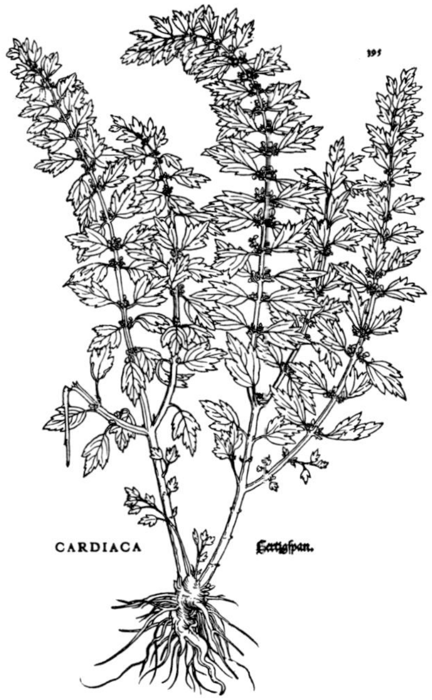

1 Otto Brunfels, *Herbarum vivae eicones*, Strasbourg 1530-36. Pellitory, *Parietaria officinalis*
Botanisk Centralbibliotek, Copenhagen (*cat. 61*)

2 Leonhard Fuchs, *De historia stirpium*, Basel 1542. Motherwort, *Leonurus cardiaca*
Botanisk Centralbibliotek, Copenhagen (*cat. 62*)

lecting all of the world's plants. This function, in turn, influenced the form of the garden. The old Persian gardens had been divided into four quarters, representing the four corners of the world. Now they came to represent the four continents instead (prior to the discovery of America only three had been known). This symbolism, together with many other symbolic ideas taken over from the Middle Ages, thus became embodied, not only in the layout of the gardens, but also in the way the plants were arranged. In some places, attempts were actually made to plant the vegetation of each continent in its respective quarter, though without success.[1]

These developments were not only fueled by new ways of apprehending God and the universe. It is significant that the oldest botanical gardens, linked to universities, were laid out in the Italian city states of Pisa and Venice. Their highly developed trade created not only an economic basis but also the possibility of obtaining plants from faraway places. The botanical garden in Padua, the university town of Venice, was especially renowned for its collection of plants from the Orient, which was Venice's sphere of interest. Another early botanical garden, in Leiden, was particularly rich in plants from the West and East Indies, the traditional trading posts of Holland. The botanical garden in Paris could boast of one of the oldest collections of American plants originating from Central America and to some extent from North America, where the French had colonies.

Plant collections thus became status symbols for states and princes as well as private families. The garden was not only essential to the pious scholar, but became the pride of the learned prince or merchant. It was simply *comme il faut* to follow scholarly pursuits – without necessarily earning a living from it.

During the sixteenth and especially the seventeenth century, the creation of gardens and plant collecting was influenced by the collector, whether botanist, merchant or prince. Plants were so diligently and ardently collected in fact, that the number of specimens described rose from about 500 in 1542 to about 6,000 in 1623. Furthermore, this practice was costly. The interest in exotic plants resulted in higher prices, allowing plants to be sought in increasingly distant places. Interest in bulbous plants in particular led to speculation; prices were driven up even higher, and when the tulip market collapsed in Amsterdam in 1637 many commercial enterprises faced financial disaster.

The prestigious nature of gardens and the fact that a great many people were both interested in and willing to spend money on their creation laid the foundation for publishing descriptions of gardens. These could vary from modest lists of plant names to expensive publications in which all (or nearly all) the flowers were illustrated by copperplate engravings. Ground plans might also be included, as was often the case with descriptions of botanical gardens. The largest work of this kind, *Hortus Eystettensis,* was published by Basilius Besler in 1613. This garden, which belonged to the prince-bishop of Eichstätt, was extensive, and the 374 copperplate engravings in the book depict more than 1,000 flowers. However, the illustrators and engravers sometimes sacrificed botanical accuracy in favour of decorative effect.[2]

This great interest in plants led to publications of collections of plant illustrations. The oldest anthology, or florilegium, was printed in 1608 and published by Pierre Vallet (b. 1575) who was employed at the French court. He dedicated the book to Marie de' Medici – Henry IV's queen. It is a reflexion of the interest in flowers at the time that the illustrations in the book were intended to serve as embroidery patterns (fig. 4).

Johann Theodor de Bry's (1562-1620) *Florilegium novum,* published in 1611 contains a number of copies from Vallet's book. The publication must have been a success because De Bry's son-in-law, Matthaeus Merian (1593-1650) published an enlarged

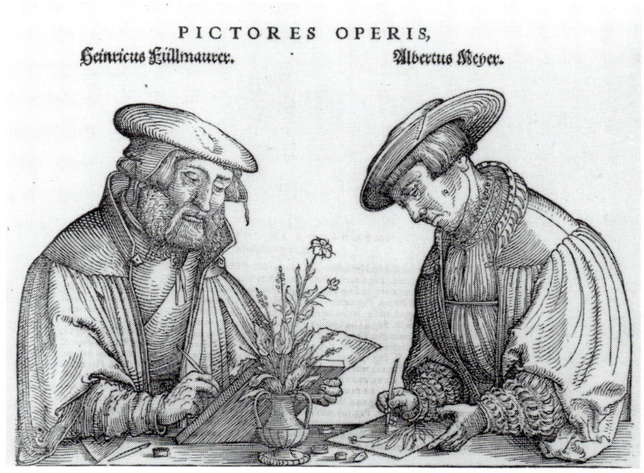

3 Leonhard Fuchs, *De historia stirpium*, Basel 1542. Portraits of Albert Meyer, who drew the plants, and Heinrich Füllmaurer, who transferred the drawings to wood blocks. Detail of plate
Botanisk Centralbibliotek, Copenhagen (*cat. 62*)

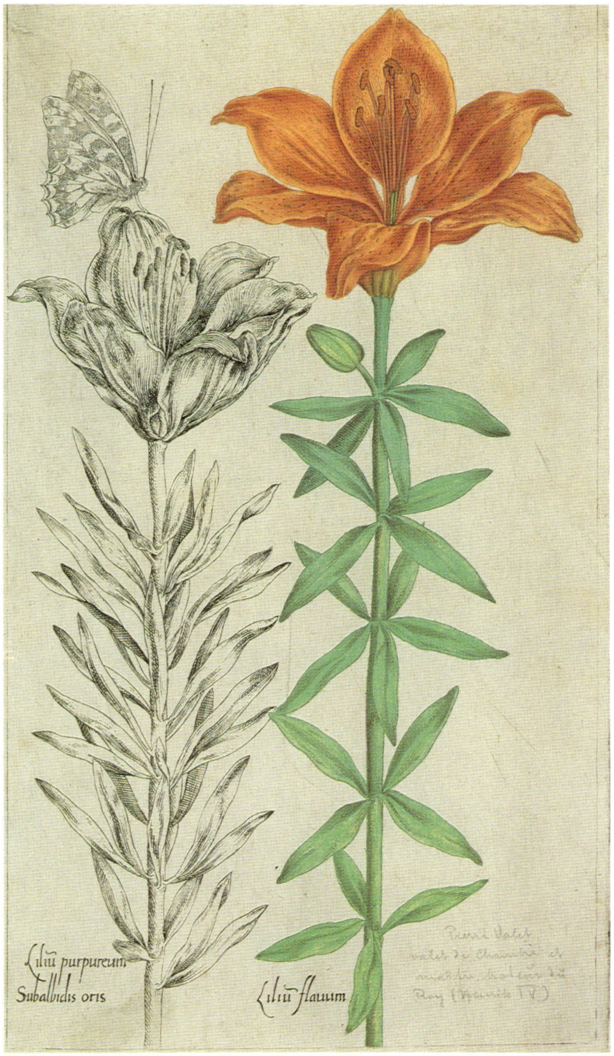

4 Pierre Vallet, *Lilium purpureum – Lilium flavum*. Woodcut. France ca. 1600. The names do not cover modern botanical species
Kunstindustrimuseet, Copenhagen (*cat. 63*)

edition in 1641 under the title *Florilegium Renovatum* (fig. 5).

The most famous florilegium is probably *Hortus floridus,* published by Crispin de Pas (1560-1637) in 1614. The plates are far more elegant than those in the florilegia mentioned above and the plants are depicted in the soil, together with butterflies, bees or birds (fig. 7).

A collection of flower pictures could also take the

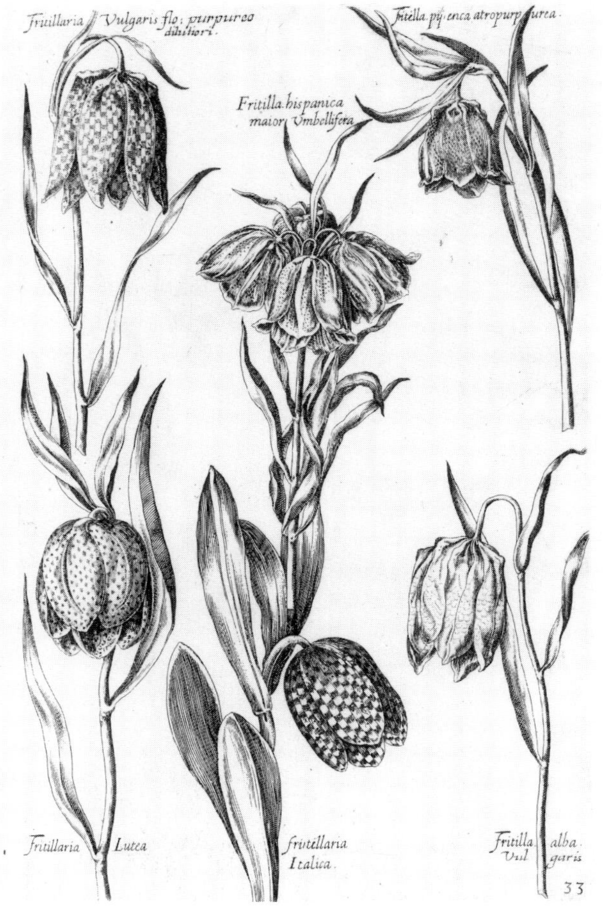

5 Matthaeus Merian, *Florilegium Renovatum et Auctum*, Frankfurt am Main 1641. Snake's head, *Fritillaria forms*
Botanisk Centralbibliotek, Copenhagen (*cat. 68*)

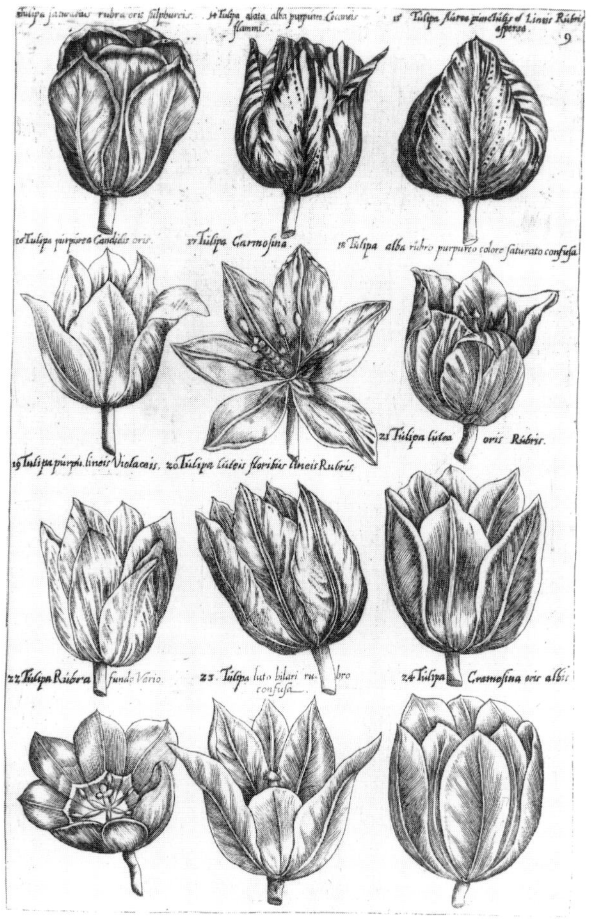

6◂Emmanuel Sweert, *Florilegium*, Frankfurt am Main 1612. Tulip sorts
Botanisk Centralbibliotek, Copenhagen (*cat. 64*)

form of a sales catalogue. The Dutch-born botanist and gardener Emmanuel Sweert had a florilegium printed in 1612. The plates are not very good and several of them have been copied from De Bry and Vallet. With the exception of a foreword there is no text, nor are any prices given. However, it is stated on the title page that the flowers can be purchased from the author in Frankfurt (fig. 6).

Many other books of flower pictures were published, but most were repetitions of known illustrations. A big publishing house like Plantin-Moretus in Antwerp had a large collection of woodcuts which were used over and over again for new books.

Plants were often very expensive and attempts to keep them alive or make them bloom often failed. This meant that a publication such as *Hortus Eystettensis* relied on illustrators depicting the plants when they were in bloom or bearing fruit. The oldest collections of plant drawings related to a particular garden are dated from around 1560 and, as might be expected, were made in a patrician garden in Venice. The memoirs of the physician, Otto Sperling, born in Hamburg, reveal that virtually every self-respecting owner of an important garden employed an illustrator. While studying in Padua, he was employed for a short time as superintendent of a garden belonging to a Venetian patrician. He relates that an illustrator, a gardener and an apprentice were also employed for the benefit of the garden.[3]

Louis XIV's younger brother, Gaston of Orleans, laid out a botanical garden in Blois that included a menagerie. He employed the artist Nicolas Robert (1614-1685), whose task was to execute a unique collection of pictures of the plants and animals at Blois. On Gaston's death, Louis XIV inherited this collection, which later became known as *Les velins du Roi.* During the Revolution, it was transferred to the Musée d'Histoire Naturelle, where it remains to this day. Louis XIV employed Robert as miniature painter to the court, enabling him to continue working on the flower illustrations. Until the Revolution in 1789, there were always flower illustrators attached to the Jardin du Roi; their duties included the execution of illustrations for *Les velins,* which steadily expanded. Contributors comprised some of the world's most admired flower illustrators, e.g., Claude Aubriet (1665-1742), Madeleine Basseporte (1701-1780), Gerard van Spaendonck (1746-1822) and Pierre-Joseph Redouté (1759-1840).[4]

As mentioned above, the illustration of rare and expensive plants from extensive gardens was a relatively common practice: examples can also be found in-Denmark. Duke Friedrich III of Schleswig-Holstein-Gottorp (1616-1659) was, as befitted a prince at that time, a very learned man who did everything within his power to turn his duchy into a centre of art, culture and learning. In 1651 he acquired a *Kunst- und Wunderkammer* and spent large sums on expanding the library founded by his father. He also wanted to establish a university in Kiel, a plan subsequently realized by his son, Christian Albrecht. Duke Friedrich had the gardens at Gottorp Castle replanted and

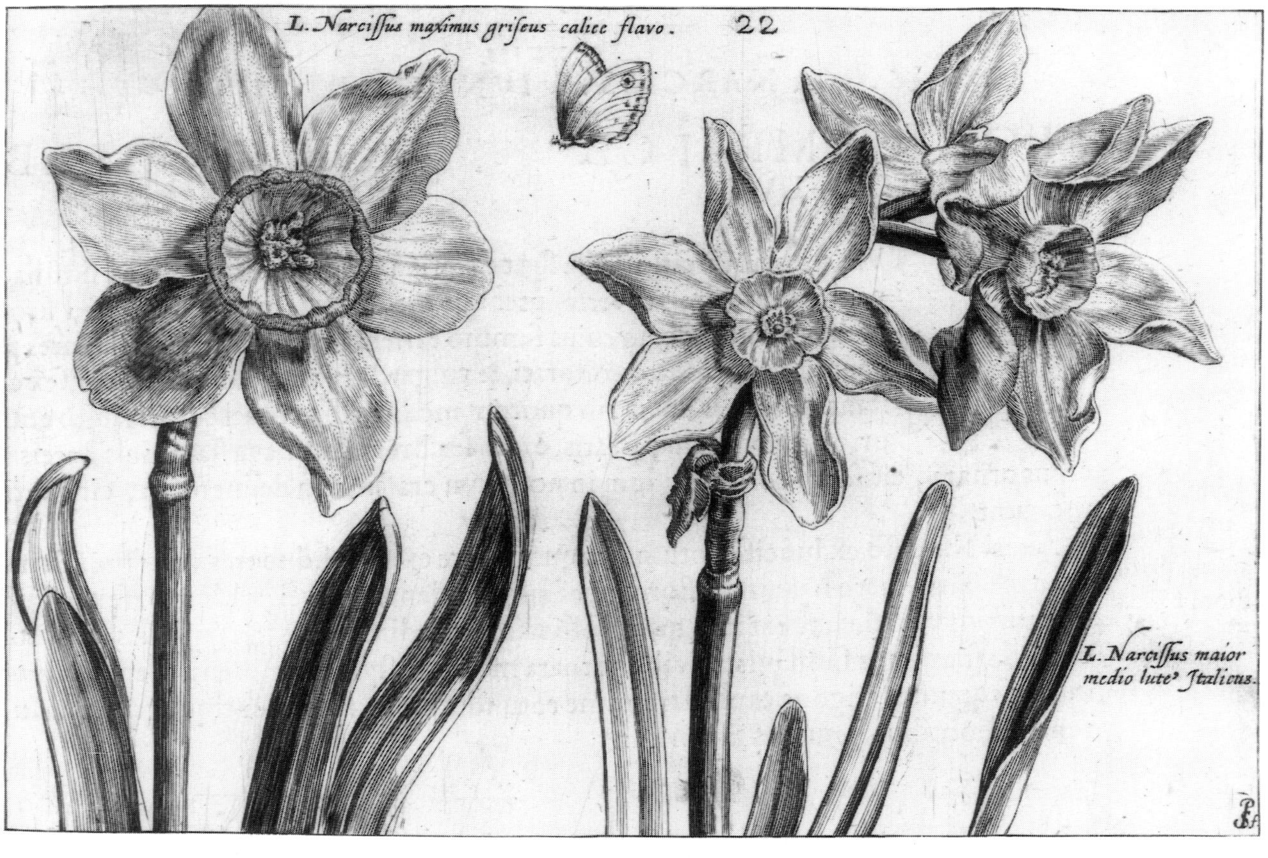

7 Crispin de Pas, *Hortus Floridus,* Arnhem 1614. *Narcissus*
Botanisk Centralbibliotek, Copenhagen (*cat. 67*)

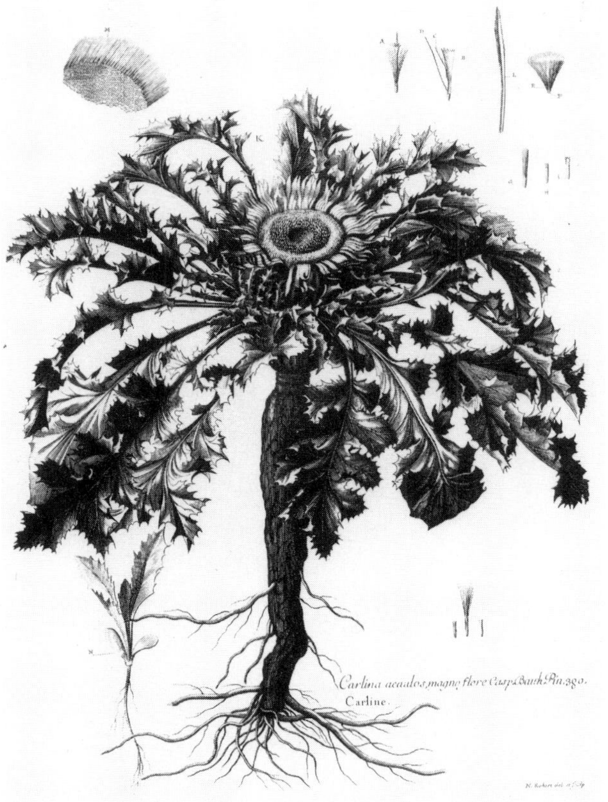

8 Nicolas Robert, *Recueil des plantes*, Paris 1701. Carline thistle, *Carlina sp.*
Botanisk Centralbibliotek, Copenhagen (*cat. 78*)

extended (he actually planted two new gardens) and spent large amounts of money on this as well as on importing rare herbs and trees.

From 1649 to 1659, the Hamburg flower painter Hans Simon Holtzbecker (d. 1671) was appointed to paint pictures of the garden. The result of his work, four volumes containing 363 plates and 1,180 pictures in gouache, was transferred to Copenhagen in 1713, after the Gottorps had been driven out of Schleswig-Holstein (fig. 9). A small florilegium containing 178 plates and 385 pictures possibly represents plants from the garden of Duchess Maria Elisabeth in Husum. These volumes, together with records of expenditure for the garden, and the painter, as well as lists of plants give a good idea of the importance attached to having a splendid collection of plants.[5]

Prior to the seventeenth century, botanical literature had consisted of herbals in which the selection of plants and their description were determined by their medicinal use. During the seventeenth century this literature became botanico-scientific works in the modern sense, to the extent that the descriptions of the plants and their placement in relation to each other depended more on the supposed mutual relationship than on their use. A clear division into medical, botanical and horticultural literature was ultimately established. Considerably more books on botany were published in the seventeenth century than before: in England, for example, five times as many as during the sixteenth century. In the course of the century, woodcuts were replaced by copper engravings which were more suitable for reproducing the details that had come to be regarded as necessary. However, they were also considerably more expensive.[6]

An example of the independent position which botany achieved was the decision taken by the French Academy of Sciences during the 1670s to publish a textbook for which Nicolas Robert, together with other engravers, was to provide the drawings and engravings. Because of Louis XIV's expensive wars, the work was finally published after considerable delay in 1701 – without text – under the title *Recueil des plantes* (fig. 8). The work was reprinted in 1788. Robert thus advanced from representations of curiosities and treasures to scientific illustration.[7]

Only a few books were published on botany and ornamental gardening on the Continent during the Thirty Years' War; in England publications during the Civil War were correspondingly modest. In the second half of the century the economic situation improved, making it possible to lay out larger gardens. The style of the gardens gradually changed from the geometric, symbolic patterns of the Renaissance to the architecturally conceived compartments of the Baroque. The garden lost its significance as a museum; the expensive bulbous plants were grouped in embroidery beds, and the closed garden was opened and extended into the landscape with long avenues emphasizing the dominance of the manor or palace over the region – a visible expression of society's hierarchical order. Curiously enough, the development of the Baroque garden in France and Ger-

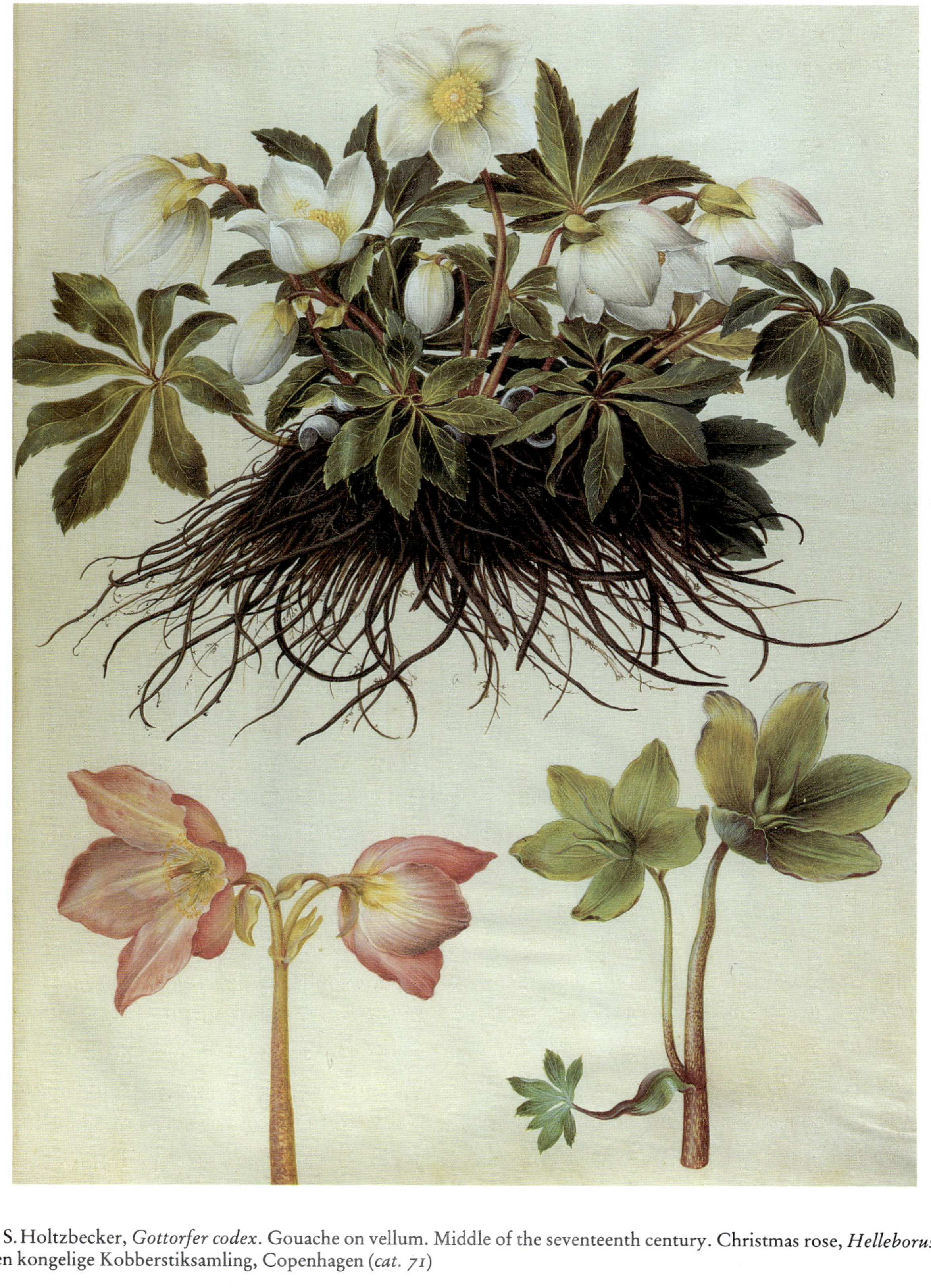

9 H. S. Holtzbecker, *Gottorfer codex*. Gouache on vellum. Middle of the seventeenth century. Christmas rose, *Helleborus*
Den kongelige Kobberstiksamling, Copenhagen (*cat. 71*)

many was promoted by the consolidation of the centralistic absolute monarchy and in England by the Whig aristocracy's victory over the central administrative power.[8]

The more architectural concept of the garden appeared not only in books on landscape gardening but also in botanical works. In J.C. Volckamer's *Nürnbergische Hesperides* (1708-14), which deals with fruit trees (also an important topic during the Middle Ages and the Renaissance) the plates show not only fruits, but also prospects of gardens and palaces in Germany, Austria and Italy.

New inspiration for lovers of gardens and flowers, particularly exotic kinds, came from another front as well. During the sixteenth century, the collecting botanist had predominated (it was he who had created the botanical garden), but during the seventeenth century this changed, not because collecting ceased – on the contrary, people collected more than ever – but because the botanist began to travel, also outside Europe. Earlier, travelling had been confined to Western Europe, though in rare instances extending to Russia, Turkey and the Middle East. Towards the end of the century expeditions were also undertaken to the new continents. This was made possible by the increase in trade that followed in the wake of colonization. In 1636, when Prince Maurits of Nassau travelled to the Dutch possessions in South America, he brought with him natural scientists and artists whose task it was to examine and depict the natural wealth of these colonies. The best-known results of this work in Denmark are the pictures painted by Albert Eckhout and given to Frederik III now in the Nationalmuseet, Copenhagen. They record not only native inhabitants and animals but also give very detailed and accurate pictures of plants, flowers and fruits.

One of the most famous travellers towards the end of the seventeenth century was Maria Sibylla Merian (1647-1717). She was the daughter of Matthaeus Merian, the son-in-law of Johann Theodor de Bry, whose florilegium Merian had republished. Maria married one of her art instructors, Johann Graff. From an early age she had taken an interest in insects and their transformations and in 1679 she published the first of three volumes on European insects. The copperplates show not only the insects but the plants

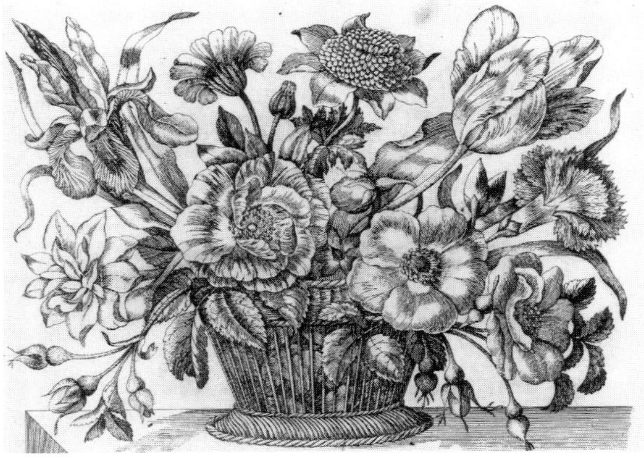

10 Maria Sibylla Merian, *Neues Blumenbuch*, Nuremberg 1680
Botanisk Centralbibliotek, Copenhagen (*cat. 69*)

on which they live as well. One year later (1680), Mrs. Graff published a florilegium intended to serve as patterns for embroidery (fig. 10) in which several of the flowers were redrawn after Nicolas Robert. In 1685 she left her husband and with her two daughters joined a religious sect to live in a kind of commune. Some years later, she travelled to Surinam (Guyana) to study insects. Together with her daughter, Dorothea, she stayed for two years in South America (1698-1700) collecting material for her book *Metamorphosis insectorum Surinamensium* which was published in 1705. Her eldest daughter, Johanna, then returned to Surinam to gather more material for the second edition. Here, too, the insects are depicted together with plants and other animals. Maria Sibylla Merian (she reverted to her maiden name after leaving her husband) also made a series of drawings in which she concentrated strictly on flowers; a large collection of these can be seen at Rosenborg Castle in Copenhagen (fig. 11).[9]

By this time flowers were not to be found only in books and gardens, they were also popular in homes. Stylized flowers as decoration had been used since antiquity on coins and included in coats of arms. Perhaps most famous were the roses in the escutcheons of the families of Lancaster and York. Fresh flowers were also used, for example, as table decorations. The cut flowers scattered over tables on festive occasions may have suggested patterns for the embroidered and woven tablecloths with flower motifs that came into fashion during the seventeenth century. In many cases, the patterns for the flowers on tablecloths were inspired by the above-mentioned florilegia, whether originally so intended (Vallet, Maria Sibylla Merian) or not (Sweert). The woven or embroidered flowers and fruits on these tablecloths are therefore naturalistic (fig. 47).[10]

Furniture was not immune to the charm of flowers, and was decorated with either intarsia or painted flowers. Jean Joubert, for example, Nicolas Robert's successor as royal miniature painter, is known to have decorated furniture. Flower painted furniture remained in fashion for a long time. In fact, the country chests of drawers of the nineteenth century featuring painted tulips were inspired by furniture made two hundred years earlier.

It also became fashionable to hang pictures of flowers on the wall. Dutch and Flemish flower painting is said to have been initiated by a Dutch lady of modest means who asked Jan Brueghel the Elder (1568-1625) to paint the flowers which she could not afford to buy. The story is unlikely to be true, even though prices of flowers reached such a high level that it became necessary to pass a law in the Netherlands in the 1630s prohibiting the price of a bulb from exceeding 6,000 guilders.[11] In fact, flower painting is older than Brueghel, the oldest example to be designated as such dating from about 1490 (by Hans Memling) and painted on the inside of a wooden panel. However, flower painting as an acknowledged genre did not appear until much later. Apart from Jan Brueghel, other early practitioners include Jacob de Gheyn (1565-1629), Georg Flegel (1563-1638) and Osias Beert the Elder (1580-1624). Jan Brueghel's school is represented by e.g. Ambrosius Boschaert the Elder (1573-1621), Daniel Seghers and Balthasar van der Ast (1563-1651) who were the first generation of flower painters (ca. 1590-1650). The second period is represented by e.g. Jan Davidz de Heem the Younger (1606-1683/84), Abraham Mignon, Willem van der Aelst (1627-1683) and his pupil Rachel Ruysch (1664-1750). The genre reached its zenith with Jan van Huijsum (1682-1749). Wilfrid Blunt, author of the standard work on botanical illustration, claims that a decline set in after Van Huijsum's death. Nevertheless, the same author admits that one of Van Huijsum's pupils, Gerard van Spaendonck, became arguably the world's best flower illustrator.

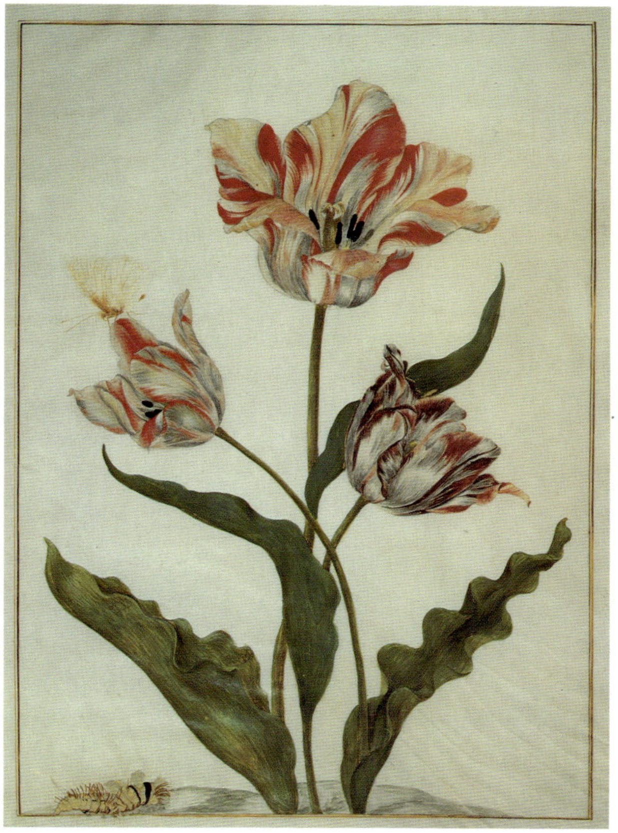

11 Maria Sibylla Merian, *Tulips*. Gouache on vellum. Germany before 1685
The Royal Collections, Rosenborg Palace, Copenhagen (*cat. 70*)

The flower painters did not make their paintings directly from nature, but constructed them from drawings and studies. Spring, summer and autumn plants are depicted in the same bouquet. The Swedish art historian I. Bergström has shown that identically drawn flowers appear in several pictures by the same artist, often with different colours. This is one of the reasons for separating flower painters from flower illustrators. The flower illustrator, working in watercolour or gouache on paper or vellum, can complete a picture very quickly (for example out in the country). A painter, on the other hand, needs more time, not only for the actual painting but because the paint has to dry. Most flower painters made studies for their paintings in which they varied and mixed the flowers.

The technical and artistic advances achieved by the flower painters were naturally of benefit to flower illustrators and vice versa.[12]

At the end of the seventeenth century and during the first half of the eighteenth century, botany experienced an explosive growth. The microscope made it possible to study different parts of a flower in greater detail, a fact which, together with the discovery of the mechanism of pollination (1696), resulted in a hitherto unparalleled interest in the structure of flowers and new ways of describing them. This led to a new concept of the generic relationship between plants. The first keys to indentification of plants were constructed in this period. Prior to this, extensive knowledge of the available literature was necessary (one had to know most of the genera by heart) in order to be able to name a plant. In the 1730s, Carolus Linnaeus (1707-1778) plucked the ripe fruit and created, by means of a sexual system and his reform of the nomenclature of plants, a method for determination and classification so simple that even 'ladies' could hope to learn it. A *Botany for Ladies* was actually published in 1782 by J. J. Rousseau, and translated into several languages, including Danish.[13]

At the end of the seventeenth and during the first half of the eighteenth century many florilegia were still being compiled for private patrons in England, the Netherlands and Germany. Several were made by Dutch painters (often engaged by rich Englishmen), and almost all of them contain only garden plants. An exception is a little florilegium by Richard Waller (1650-1715) who drew wild plants in England. Waller, an amateur artist, may have planned an illustrated flora.

The steadily increasing wealth enabling people to spend more on gardens and plants, created a continued economic basis for the publication of expensive works. In the Netherlands, magnificently illustrated works on the vegetation of the colonies appeared, i.e., Van Rheede tot Drakenstein, *Hortus Indicus Malabaricus* (1678-93) and Rumphius, *Herbarium Amboinense* (1741-55) and the flower catalogues were richly illustrated. Particularly famous is *Twelve Months of Flowers,* by Robert Furber, a sales catalogue in which the flowers are shown in lavish bouquets displayed in baskets or jars with their names but not profaned by prices. A characteristic feature of the times was that a catalogue would be reissued as patterns for embroidery, watercolour painting and intarsia work. One of the illustrators, Mark Catesby (ca. 1679-1749), became famous as a publisher of the first thoroughly illustrated natural history from North America, *Natural History of Carolina* (1730-47). A somewhat exceptional position is occupied by *Catalogus Plantarum* (1730), published by the Society of Gardeners in London whose members met once a month to decide which names were to be used for the plants they wanted to sell (bearing witness to the need for the nomenclature reform introduced by Linnaeus). This was to avoid doubt in their customers' minds about buying a plant they already might have under another name. The *Catalogus Plantarum* is beautifully illustrated by, *inter alia,* Jacobus van Huijsum (1687-1740), a younger brother of Jan van Huijsum. Printed florilegia were also published. The pharmacist Johann Weinmann in Regensburg published an eight-volume florilegium with more than 6,000 copperplate engravings, *Phytanthoza Iconographia* (1737-45).

Descriptions of flowers from large gardens were also continuously published. Jan and Caspar Commelin (1627-1692 and 1668/69-1731) commissioned a beautifully illustrated description of the botanical garden in Amsterdam, *Horti Medici Amstelodamensis Rariorim Plantarum Descriptio et Icones* (1697-1701) with illustrations by Johan and Maria Moninckx. The wealthy owners of large private gardens also commissioned prestigious deluxe editions. When Linnaeus was in the Netherlands as a young man he was employed by the very wealthy banker, Clifford, to supervise his garden at Hartecamp; the garden was provided with a rich collection of plants and contained four greenhouses for plants from each of the four continents. The result was *Hortus Cliffortianus,* the only deluxe work to have been written by Linnaeus.

The concept of the garden and its layout also changed in the course of time. During the Renaissance, a well-ordered garden was regarded as a way of counterbalancing the disorder in nature which, as a result of the Fall, was considered sinful. As mentioned above, the Garden of Eden could be recreated by gathering together the plants scattered by the Flood and arranging them in an orderly fashion. In the Baroque period, this idea was transformed and the orderly garden and its avenues represented a hierarchical order in the world and in society. During the eighteenth century both this idea and that of recreating the Garden of Eden were abandoned. It had become clear that there were far too many plants for one garden. It had also proved impossible to make them grow in the same place despite all efforts and expenditure. To a certain extent, the museum approach had to be abandoned and drawings of plants and dried specimens had to suffice instead. This is why the travelling botanist was much sought after during the eighteenth century. The most important change, however, was that nature itself was no longer considered sinful and was therefore allowed to enter into the garden. The strictly architectural-cum-spatial division of the garden was gradually replaced by a combination of open spaces and densely planted areas (representative of nature) with winding paths and felled passages providing 'views,' such as those as laid out by Bridgeman and Batty Langley. William Chambers and 'Capability' Brown developed this concept into the landscaped garden in which avenues disappeared, open spaces were bordered by trees and shrubbery and the whole area diversified by small groups of trees.[14]

This change coincided with a steadily increasing interest in flowers and flower pictures. Flower illustrators became celebrities who associated with members of high society (Louis XV was fond of watching Madeleine Basseporte paint) and they began publishing books themselves instead of merely illustrating those written by others. The first illustrator of this type was Georg Dionysius Ehret (1708-1770). Born in Heidelberg – the son of a gardener – he became a gardener himself, but like his father also made drawings of plants. His interest in drawing gradually took over, and he gave up working as a gardener to travel around Europe for some years as an illustrator. As far as is known, he received no other training than what his father was able to give him.

For a time he worked for Weimann (and was grossly underpaid), but soon came into contact with a wealthy Nuremberg physician, Christoph Jacob Trew (1695-1769). Trew became a life-long friend and buyer of his drawings and also helped him to find other patrons. Later in his travels, Ehret met Clifford and, through him, Linnaeus. Clifford bought many of his drawings and engaged him to illustrate *Hortus Cliffortianus*. Ehret drew up a tabular presentation of the botanical sexual system used by Linnaeus which proved quite lucrative. In 1736 Ehret went to England, where he remained for the rest of his life. He achieved distinction, becoming a member of the Royal Society (and the German Leopoldina) and a drawing teacher for several duchesses and other aristocratic and rich women. Many of his drawings and studies have been preserved. He made drawings for Weimann's *Phytanthoza Iconographia*, Trew's *Plantae selectae* (1750-73, fig. 12) and *Hortus amoenissimorum florum* (1750-86), *Hortus Cliffortianus* and numerous other books on natural science. He published *Plantae et Papiliones rariores* (1748-59). Ehret developed into an outstanding flower illustrator whose lifelike pictures, often with analytical drawings of flowers, have never been surpassed.[15]

The great interest in flower pictures which existed in England (along with plenty of money) attracted other flower illustrators from the Continent as well; at the same time England herself produced a great many illustrators.

In France too, flower drawing reached a climax during the eighteenth century. As already mentioned, the king employed a flower illustrator on a permanent basis. Claude Aubriet (1665-1742) began as an assistant to Joubert and later worked with the prominent botanist Tournefort, with whom he travelled to the Levant (1699-1702). He stayed in the Jardin du Roi for the remainder of his life drawing excellent if somewhat stiff pictures. His successor, Madeleine Basseporte, kept up the tradition. In 1780 she was succeeded by Gerard van Spaendonck (1746-1822) who as a member of Jan van Huijsum's school had made a name for himself in Paris. The first pictures he drew for *Les velins* are in gouache, but from 1783 onwards he used watercolour which lend his pictures an unusual grace. He only published a few drawings as engravings in *Fleurs dessinées d'après Nature;* however, Wilfrid Blunt calls it the most distinguished work of engravings ever to have been executed. Van Spaendonck's development of the watercolour as the best form of flower illustration was most convincingly exploited by Pierre-Joseph Redouté, probably the best-known illustrator of all. Born in 1759 into a Belgian family of flower painters, he was educated by

Tab. XCIII.

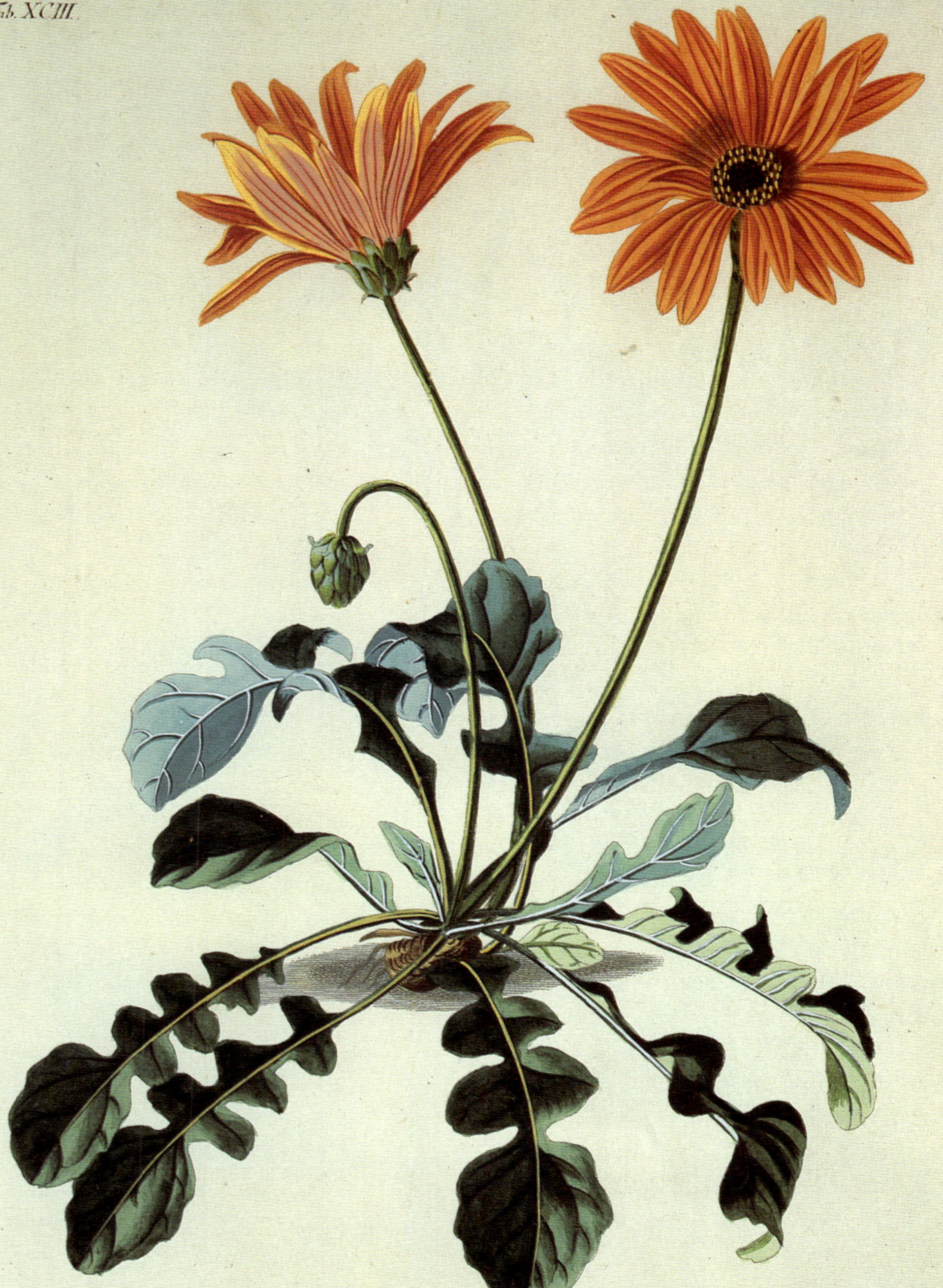

ARCTOTIS /: acaulis :/ pedunculis radicalibus, foliis lyratis.
Linn. Spec. 1306.

Joh. Jac. Haid, excud. Aug. V.

his father until he left home at the age of thirteen. On his travels he assiduously studied the Flemish masters, particularly Jan van Huijsum, for the next ten years. In 1782 he and his brother became scene painters in Paris. While studying flowers in the Jardin du Roi he met the wealthy amateur botanist L'Héritier de Brutelle who taught him botany and commissioned him to illustrate several botanical works: *Stirpes novae* (1784-85) and *Sertum Anglicum* (1788). In 1789, Redouté was appointed *Peinteur des Fleurs du Chambre de la Reine,* an appointment which had no practical consequences. Van Spaendonck encouraged and helped him, and in 1793 he was employed by the Jardin des Plantes (known before the Revolution as Jardin du Roi). He found an extravagant patroness in Joséphine Bonaparte. She spent enormous sums on buying and growing expensive plants and had Redouté draw them. He illustrated Ventenat's *Jardin de la Malmaison* (1803-05, fig. 13) and Bonpland's *Plantes rares cultivées à Malmaison et à Navarre* (1812-17). He drew the eight volumes of *Les liliacées* (1802-16, fig. 14) and, most famous of them all, *Les roses* (in three volumes, 1817-24), with a text by Claude Antoine Thory. Joséphine paid him well, and on Van Spaendonck's death in 1822 he became *Maître des dessins* in which capacity, just like Ehret, many distinguished women, including several princesses, became his pupils. Despite a good income and enormous diligence, he died relatively poor in 1840 at the age of eighty. He was not only an outstanding illustrator, he also improved the quality of copperplate engraving. By refining a technique in which the engraving is made with dots instead of lines he was able to shade and vary outlines much more delicately. In 1796 he invented a method for printing several colours from one plate so that the colouring became reminiscent of a watercolour; Louis XVIII subsequently rewarded him for this invention.[16]

Some outstanding artists, including P.J. Turpin (1775-1840) and P.A. Pointeau (1766-1854) worked close to Redouté and Van Spaendonck and sometimes with them. With the deaths of Redouté and Turpin in 1840, the golden age of French flower drawing is considered to have come to an end.

Allowing nature to enter into gardens in the course of the eighteenth century also led to a certain interest in domestic flora. The large deluxe editions and by far the majority of the florilegia (with the exception of Richard Waller's) were concerned almost exclusively with exotica. The botanists had admittedly compiled floras covering local districts – as a rule the surroundings of a university town – but in England, for example, a survey of the nation's plants had been published. However, these modest works were unillustrated. This changed during the 1750s. G.C. Oeder (1727-1791) proposed his plan for an illustrated flora of the twin kingdoms of Denmark-Norway, i.e., a flora limited not to a local region but to a polity. The plan was implemented in 1761-1883 and the idea was followed up because it created prestige; similar works were published in many countries.[17]

However, exotica were still the main interest, and the scientific expeditions made to foreign or little-known places were followed with great interest. From Denmark, for example, an expedition was made to Arabia Felix (1761-67) and G.W. Baurenfeind (1728-1763), who had also contributed to Trew's *Hortus,* took part as illustrator. From England, James Cook undertook his first circumnavigation of the globe with the scientists Joseph Banks (1743-1820) and Daniel Solander (1736-1782), a pupil of Linnaeus, and the illustrator Sidney Parkinson (1745-1771), who was a woollen draper by trade; he died during the voyage, and a number of his very beautiful drawings were completed by others.

Austria also participated in this development. The Dutch-born physician and botanist Nikolaus Joseph Jacquin (1727-1817) was employed at the newly established botanical garden at Schönbrunn, but prior to this had been sent to the West Indies and Central America to collect plants. When his dried plants were destroyed by insects, he began drawing them instead. He later became a professor in Vienna and an energetic publisher of numerous deluxe works. He drew many plates himself, but also taught others how to make correct botanical drawings. His pupils included Franz von Scheidel (1731-1801) and Johann Scharff

12 ◂ Cristoph Jacob Trew, *Plantae selectae*, Nuremberg 1750-73. *Arctotis acaulis.* Illustration by Georg Dionysius Ehret
Botanisk Centralbibliotek, Copenhagen (*cat. 75*)

(1765-1794). The results of the expedition to America were published in *Selectarum stirpium Americanarum Historia* (1763). A regional flora supplementing *Flora Danica* was *Flora Austriacae* [...] *Icones* (1773-78) published in five volumes; the last major deluxe work from a botanical garden in the eighteenth century was *Plantarum rariorum Horti Caesarei Schönbrunnensis Descriptiones et Icones* (1797-1804).[18]

Interest in local, i.e., European flora had grown, but was not great. William Curtis (1746-1799), publisher of *Flora Londinensis* (1777-87), the English counterpart of *Flora Danica,* was forced to realize that interest in local herbs was not sufficient to make a publication about them profitable. Instead, he began publishing pictures of exotic garden plants accompanied by a short text. This developed into a magazine, *Curtis's Botanical Magazine*, which is still published (now under the name *The Kew Magazine*). Illustrators such as William Kilburn (1745-1818) and James Sowerby (1757-1828), both of whom had worked on *Flora Londinensis,* contributed to it (fig. 15).[19]

That the eighteenth-century reading public could justify the publication of so many botanical works (and far from all have been mentioned) was due to an extraordinary interest which, during the Rococo period, exceeded all bounds. From about 1730 to 1760-70 it was fashionable to be interested in natural history. In France, this was undoubtedly due to the works of Abbé Pluche and G. L. L. de Buffon (1707-1788), and from here the fashion spread to other countries. In England, for example, *The Gentlemen's Magazine* devoted five times as many pages to aspects of natural history between 1745 and 1750 as during the preceding five-year period, and the tendency in-

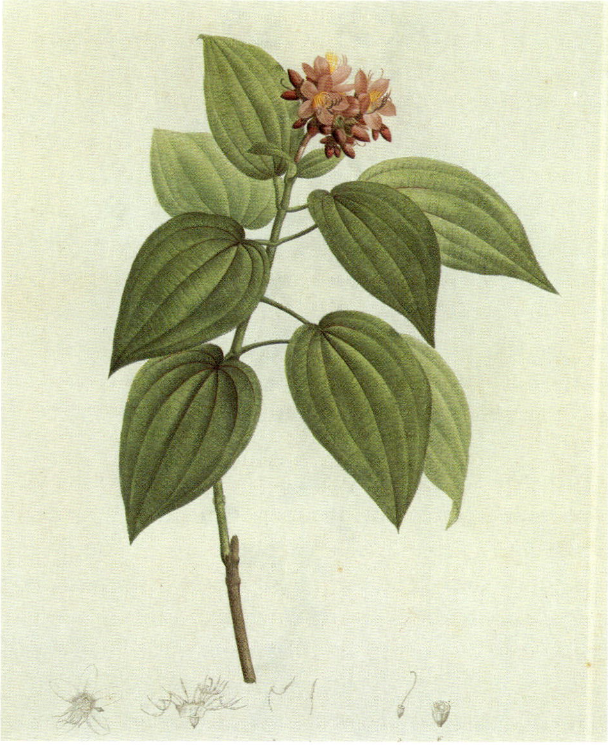

13 E. P. Ventenat, *Jardin de la Malmaison*, Paris 1803-05. *Melastoma cymosa*. Illustrated by P.-J. Redouté
Botanisk Centralbibliotek, Copenhagen (*cat. 80*)

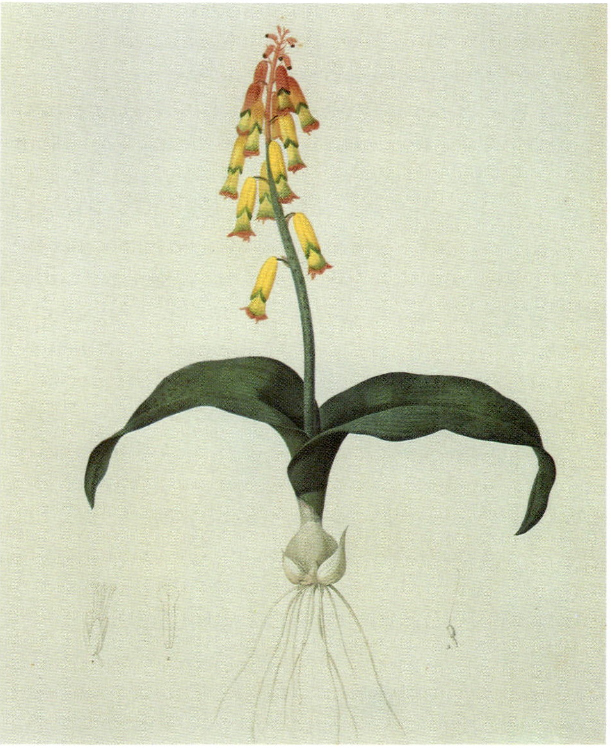

14 Pierre-Joseph Redouté, *Les liliacées*, Paris 1802-16. *Lachenalia bicolor*
Botanisk Centralbibliotek, Copenhagen (*cat. 79*)

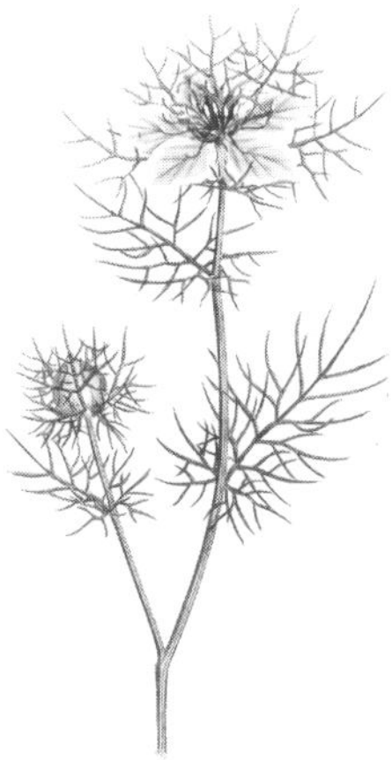

15 *Curtis's Botanical Magazine*, London 1787- . Love-in-a-mist, *Nigella damascena*
Botanisk Centralbibliotek, Copenhagen

creased during the 1750s. One of Linnaeus's correspondents in England wrote to him in 1746 that books on natural history subjects sold best.[20]

Mineralogy, zoology and botany in particular provided topics of conversation for cultivated people. Not all of it was idle talk. Economic theories of the time displayed great interest in the exploitation of natural resources and textbooks on mining, farming and gardening were read and discussed. This naturally left its mark on fashions. People liked to have pictures of flowers in their homes: overdoors and columns, for example, were ornamented with flower festoons, ceilings featured flower vines in stucco work; furniture was ornamented with fittings in the form of flower clusters and vines as well as intarsia work representing flowers or bouquets in vases. Gentlemen's jackets and waistcoats were embroidered with flowers, and ladies' dresses made of fabrics into which flowers were woven (cat. 286) and moreover decorated with an abundance of artificial flowers. Young ladies, as indicated above, took lessons in drawing or painting flowers. Small personal objects were also decorated with flowers. Van Spaendonck made a name for himself when quite young by decorating snuffboxes.

Many of the eighteenth-century examples of intarsia work, embroidery, etc., known to us are not strictly naturalistic. It was not always 'portraits' of certain species that were used, but types. One sees, for example, a rose type, a composite type, a dicotyledon type, an iris or lily type, etc. Sometimes, however, greater accuracy was observed, particularly in the middle of the century, when certain plants were bred as models. At the silk factory in Spitalfields, Anna Maria Garthwaite designed strictly naturalistic patterns. In 1743 she created patterns in which the auriculas, bindweeds, camomiles, and woodbines are depicted so accurately that they can be determined. She even included a rarity such as *Kalmia latifoli*. It is therefore assumed that she must have had access to a well-appointed garden (her brother-in-law and neighbour, who was a pharmacist, had one).[21]

By the end of the century interest seemed to have peaked. Deluxe editions of botanical works became more difficult to sell and several had to be halted before completion. Fashions, too, had changed. It was no longer *de rigueur* to have too many flower decorations in one's rooms. The Louis Seize and Adam styles did allow flower vines, but in a strict, stiff form more reminiscent of antiquity than of nature. Ladies still wore flowers on their dresses and in their hair, but gentlemen had abandoned their flower-embroidered waistcoats. Botanical books continued to be published, but the number of deluxe edition declined. Flower painting and drawing were also still practised, but as motifs for interior decoration the fun was over.

Only in one area did the flower fashion endure beyond the Rococo period. On porcelain, flower decoration remained fashionable throughout the following centuries.[22]

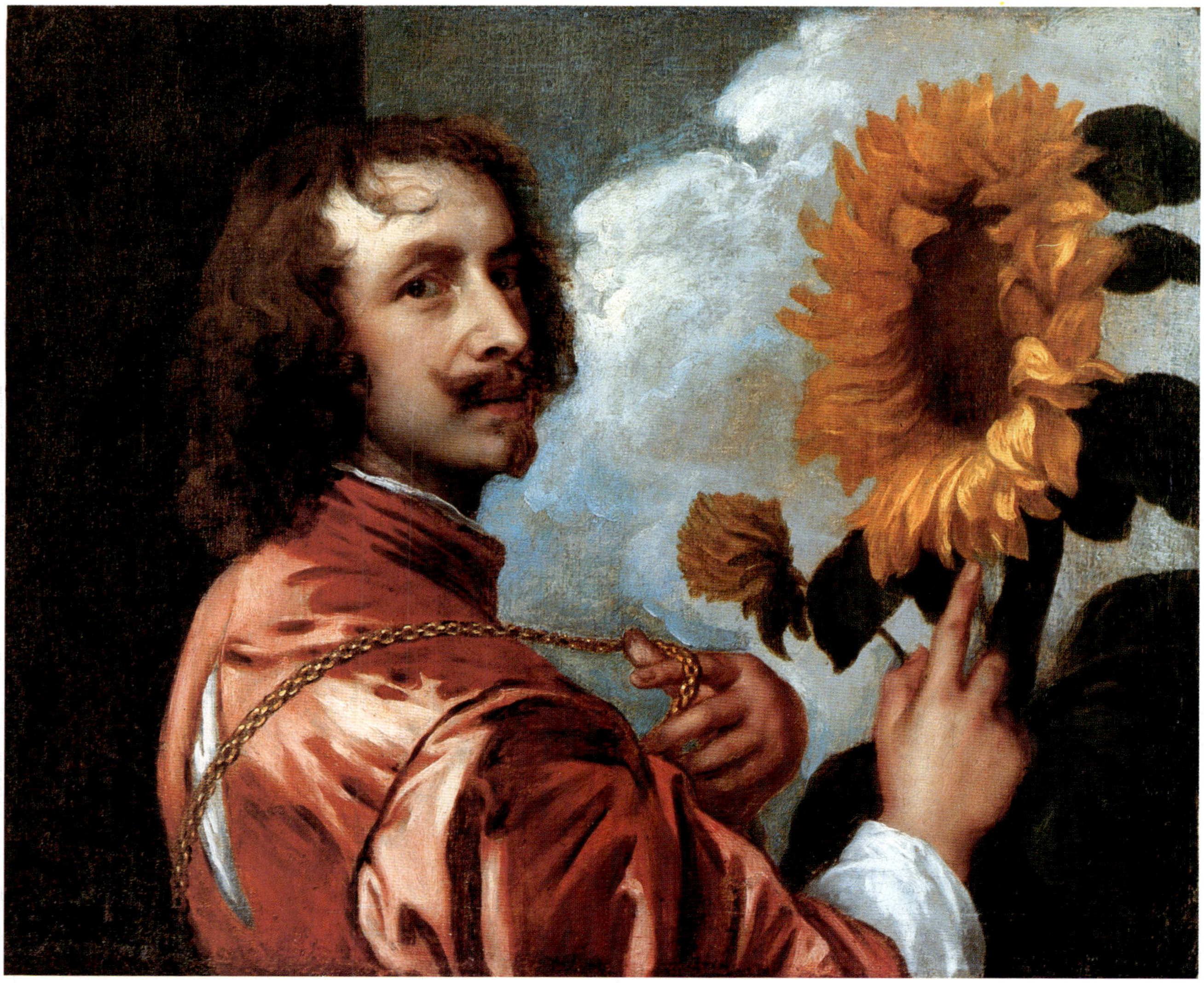

16 Anthony van Dyck, *Self-portrait with sunflower*. Oil on canvas. England ca. 1635-36
The Duke of Westminster, England (*cat. 2*)

Hanne Westergaard

The immortal motif

Human beings can, and always have been able to make flowers tell a story about man himself.

The Flemish painter Sir Anthony van Dyck lived in England from 1632 to 1641. He had already established his reputation on the Continent and, while working for Charles I, soon became the favourite portrait painter of the English aristocracy as well. Van Dyck had a special talent for lending distinction to his subjects: one only has to note his exquisitely painted silk fabrics, the posture, mien and slender, eloquent hands of his sitters in which blue blood beats imperceptibly. Charles I showed his appreciation by presenting Van Dyck with a portrait medallion of himself on a gold chain. The artist commemorated this great honour in a self-portrait in which he shows himself wearing the gold chain (fig. 16).

How did Van Dyck represent himself, and his position in society? It should be remembered that the artist's standing in the seventeenth century was quite different from what it was to become several centuries later. Van Dyck was a citizen who had received recognition equal to that of other courtiers, and it was as a courtier that he portrayed himself, almost half-length and wearing a magnificent, warm red, silk doublet. He depicted himself in profile, his face turned towards the beholder, lifting the chain around his neck with one hand and pointing to an enormous sunflower with the other. The flower is larger than his face and set off against the blue sky by a tremendous white cloud. There is a clear connection between the gold chain and the flower and, they are, in fact, the subject of this painting. Even Van Dyck's gaze, seeking the eye of the beholder, attempts to draw attention to these two objects – quite understandably, for the sunflower was the emblem of a ruler and protector.

Flowers symbolize transitoriness, but also immortality. More than a century after Van Dyck immortalized the sunflower as a symbol of power, Jean-Jacques Rousseau inspired people to appreciate nature as a means of refreshing the soul. A new era was ushered in when he wrote *La nouvelle Heloïse* (1761) and plucked flowers in England (1765-67) on outings with ladies. Walking in the countryside and consciously observing nature was in itself a novelty; to gather bouquets in memory of nature was revolutionary. Is has always been acceptable for women and children to pick flowers, but from this time on it was perfectly permissible for men to pick flowers as well. Sometimes aspects are found in literature which appear only later in the art of painting. Very few examples can be found in art of people walking in the countryside, picking flowers as a source of pleasure and consolation for the living and as a silent homage to the dead; the subject is universal, yet personal. One of these examples is Lafrensen the Younger's *Portrait of Baron Eric Magnus Staël von Holstein* (fig. 17), Swedish ambassador in Paris. Staël von Holstein is primarily known as the husband of Madame de Staël. Theirs was an unhappy marriage of convenience and they eventually divorced. Madame de Staël became one of the most celebrated women of her time and Staël von Holstein returned to Sweden where he enjoyed a great reputation. She might have been bitter about their marriage, but he had his regrets as well. Lafrensen portrayed him in 1792, sitting in front of a tomb in a garden laid out in the manner of the period in an imitation of nature. In one hand he holds his hat filled with flowers which he has picked and in the other a handkerchief. His eyes – exaggeratedly large in the taste of the times – are turned, glistening with tears, towards the tomb above which floats a halo of stars. He is sitting beside his son's grave. Even the seventeenth-century Dutch who never hesitated to

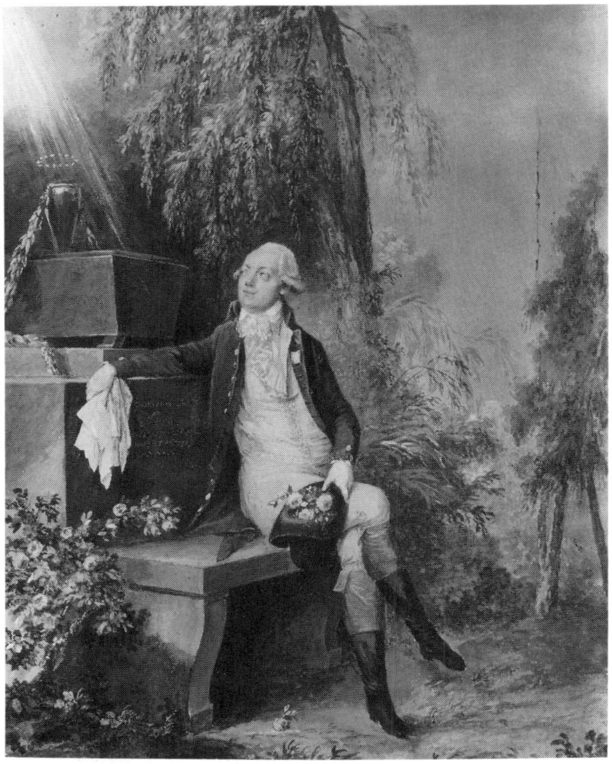

17 N. Lafrensen the Younger, *Ambassador, Baron Eric Magnus Staël von Holstein*. Gouache. Sweden 1792
Statens Konstmuseer, Nationalmuseum, Stockholm (*cat. 13*)

depict the realities of life, including the emotional ones, never came so close to rendering the intense emotions aroused by death as is shown here. Ambassador Staël von Holstein, dressed in a Werther costume, mourns his child; that he could do so is due to the emancipation ushered in by Rousseau and perhaps Madame de Staël as well. While manners, customs and tastes changed towards the end of the eighteenth century, it is difficult to pinpoint the precise cause for this. From the costumes that have been preserved we can see that the abundance of double roses sprinkled over the full court dresses of Marie Antoinette and her contemporaries was abandoned during the Revolution in favour of slender white dresses with delicate borders of embroidered lilies of the valley and ferns. Woodland flowers were tentatively introduced as motifs in the second half of the eighteenth century. I. P. Jacobsen, in Niels Lyhne, mentions 'the periwinkle, blue as heaven never was, Rousseau's favourite flower.'

Everything has its time, and interest in garden flowers, including the tulip, reawakened. Though tulipomania came to an abrupt end in 1637, the tulip continued to be included in the bouquets – and especially wreaths – exemplifying the floral magnificence of the seasons and often symbolizing life. In the course of the nineteenth century, the tulip became appreciated in and of itself. It made its appearance, for example, in the tiny window-sill gardens, one of the most charming features of the Biedermeier period, beloved and never relinquished (fig. 18). Hyacinths were grown in glass jars and tulips in pots. Hans Christian Andersen gave potted tulips as presents, and received them at Christmas and on his birthday (2 April). A beech or cherry branch – set in water to help it blossom – might also be placed on the window sill. Hans Christian Andersen presented close lady friends with flowering branches that had been forced

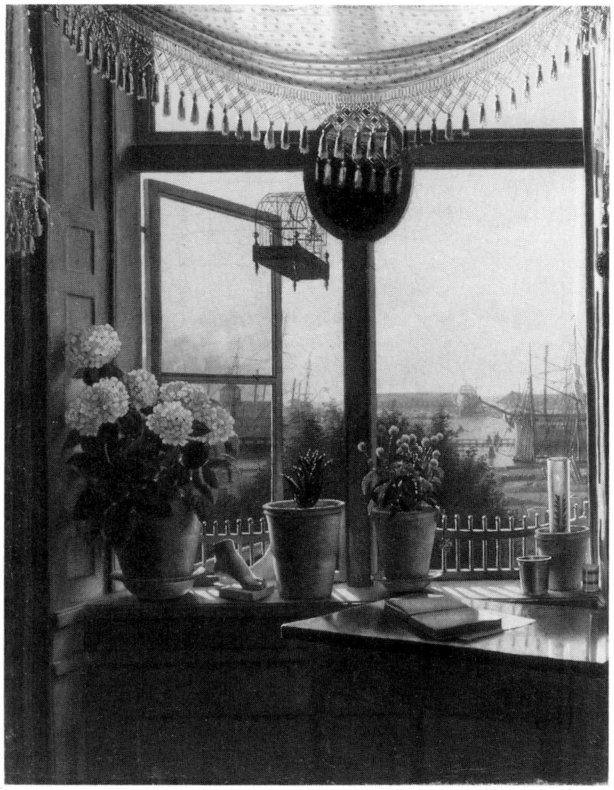

18 Martinus Rørbye, *View from the artist's window*. Oil on canvas. Denmark ca. 1825
Statens Museum for Kunst, Copenhagen (*cat. 24*)

in this way, a courtesy that was highly regarded. Other plants belonging in the setting included fragrant heliotropes, wallflowers and stocks and, in addition, there were often one or more cuttings protected by a glass cylinder to create a hothouse effect. Geraniums could be bought in Denmark from about 1830. Somehow, they thrived better in small homes out in the country than anywhere else. Well-to-do citizens could transform a window into a proper little hothouse – plants were widely available. However, in the spacious houses of princes and noblemen, flower-tables and étagères were filled with plants from their own greenhouses. It often seemed to be a question of cramming as many plants as possible into the rooms; not only in the winter gardens large and small – which any self-respecting minor German prince possessed, but also in the living rooms, where they rose from pedestals beside the sofas or were placed on the floor next to a lady's bureau.

The flower as a motif was more dearly loved in the nineteenth century than at any other time. Thus it was entirely in the spirit of the century's delight in Shakespeare and flowers that in 1835 Mrs. Clara Maria Pope painted the poet's bust surrounded by all the flowers referred to in his plays and sonnets, attaching a list of their names and where they are mentioned (fig. 19). Shakespeare's flowers belong both to the natural world and in the well-trimmed garden; together with Rousseau, he may have been responsible for the fact that from the middle of the 1830s on the hawthorn, marguerite, cornflower and poppy gained increasing popularity in flower pictures, as can be seen in exhibition catalogues.

However, credit is not due to them alone. Patriotic feelings were running high in Europe at this time, bringing with them the realization that a modern, democratic state must have an identity based not only on its language, but on its geography, flora and fauna as well. For instance, Denmark's history was gently manipulated to conform to the desired image. Hans Christian Andersen saw to it in his fairy tales and stories that the Danish language, as spoken, reached a wide audience. Responsibility for Danish flora lay in the hands of the politically influential Joachim Frederik Schouw (1789-1852). As professor at the botanical garden in Copenhagen he laid out a special section as a national garden. At one time Andersen had a view of this garden from his home, and described it in his fairy tale *The Gardener and the Squire* (1872). Young Danish artists who supported the ideologies of the period, i.e., N.F.S. Grundtvig's influential religious ideas, were sensitive to the beauty of nature and wild flowers. The landscape painter P.C. Skovgaard became engaged to Schouw's daughter and, for their wedding in 1851, he designed her bridal veil, the lower edge of which was embroidered with a border of wild Danish plants (cat. 311).

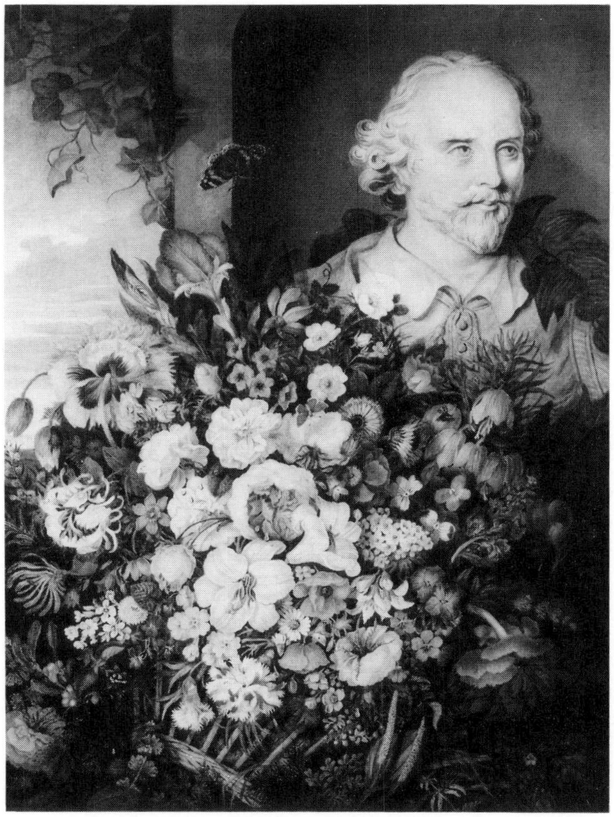

19 Clara Maria Pope, *Shakespeare's flowers*. Oil on canvas. 1835
Sir John Soane's Museum, London

Despite the interest in flowers, flower painting proper though profitable – was not fully recognized as a specialty. It had a wide public, but a public that wanted something nice to look at and by all means something modern. The subject of the painting, whether a bouquet of meadow flowers or costly flowers and fruits from royal hothouses, was up to the person who commissioned the painting. There was no lack of buyers and many women helped to meet the demand. They were often dismissed somewhat derogatorily as 'female flower painters,' due to the uneven quality of their work which ranged from the purely amateur to highly skilled. Nevertheless, it was acceptable for women who had to earn their own living to paint flowers as well as give instruction. However, they were not admitted to the Royal Academy and therefore did not receive the same thorough training as their male colleagues. Another reason for the uneven quality is the fact that demand was high enough so that even mediocre painters could continue working. During the nineteenth century Denmark had two flower painters who achieved international recognition in their lifetime. One of them, Johan Laurentz Jensen, the son of a schoolteacher in Gentofte – now a suburb of Copenhagen but a village at the time – always spent his summers there because he loved being in the country. The Crown Prince, later King Christian VIII – who wanted to support the Royal Copenhagen Porcelain Manufactory in Copenhagen – arranged for Jensen, whose talent he recognized, to learn the technique of multicoloured overglaze painting at the porcelain factory in Sèvres. In 1825 Jensen was appointed senior painter at the Copenhagen factory, a post which gave him financial security, though the work did not appeal to him. As an easel painter he could judge with each brushstroke whether he had achieved the desired colour. When painting porcelain, however, he could never be certain how it would turn out after firing (fig. 21). For his rich patrons he painted pictures of rare flowers, often arranged in fine antique vases (fig. 22). Yet he was equally happy to paint small, modest pictures for he felt that everyone should be able to own something pretty to hang on the wall.

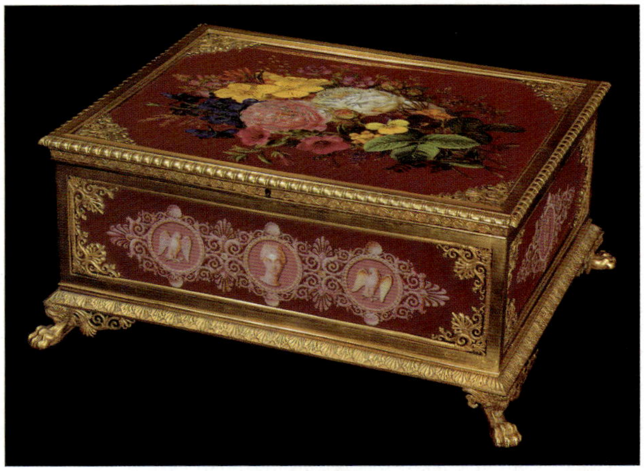

21 I. L. Jensen. *Jewel box*, with flower painting. Porcelain and bronze. The Royal Copenhagen Porcelain Manufactory, Copenhagen 1836
The Royal Collections, Rosenborg Palace, Copenhagen (*cat. 127*)

22 ▸ I. L. Jensen, *Vase with flowers*. Oil on canvas. Denmark 1834
Statens Museum for Kunst, Copenhagen (*cat. 25*)

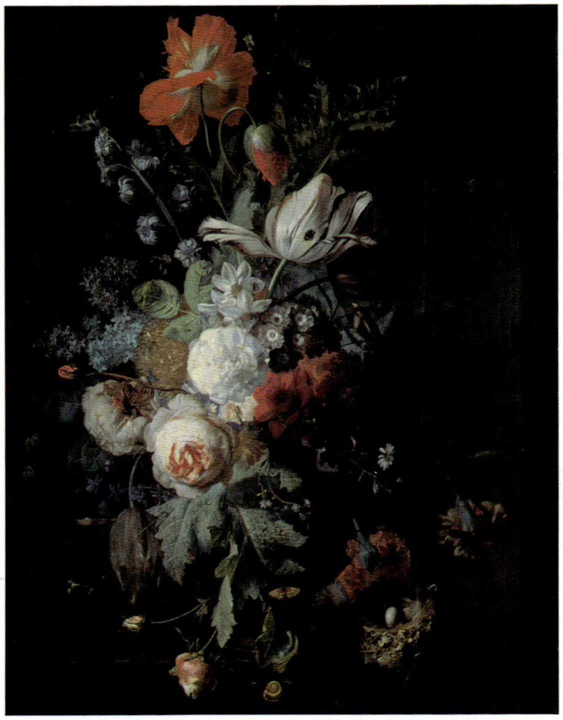

20 Jan van Huijsum, *Flower piece*. Oil on panel
Statens Museum for Kunst, Copenhagen (*see cat. 38*)

Otto Ditlev Ottesen, the second of these artists, came from Schleswig on the Danish mainland. He was born into a family of simple farmers and at the age of eight had to work as a shepherd. His desire to paint was so strong that, for want of paper and other requisites, he would split a willow branch and paint with the shredded end of a twig on the white surface exposed by the cut, using juice from the berries of the

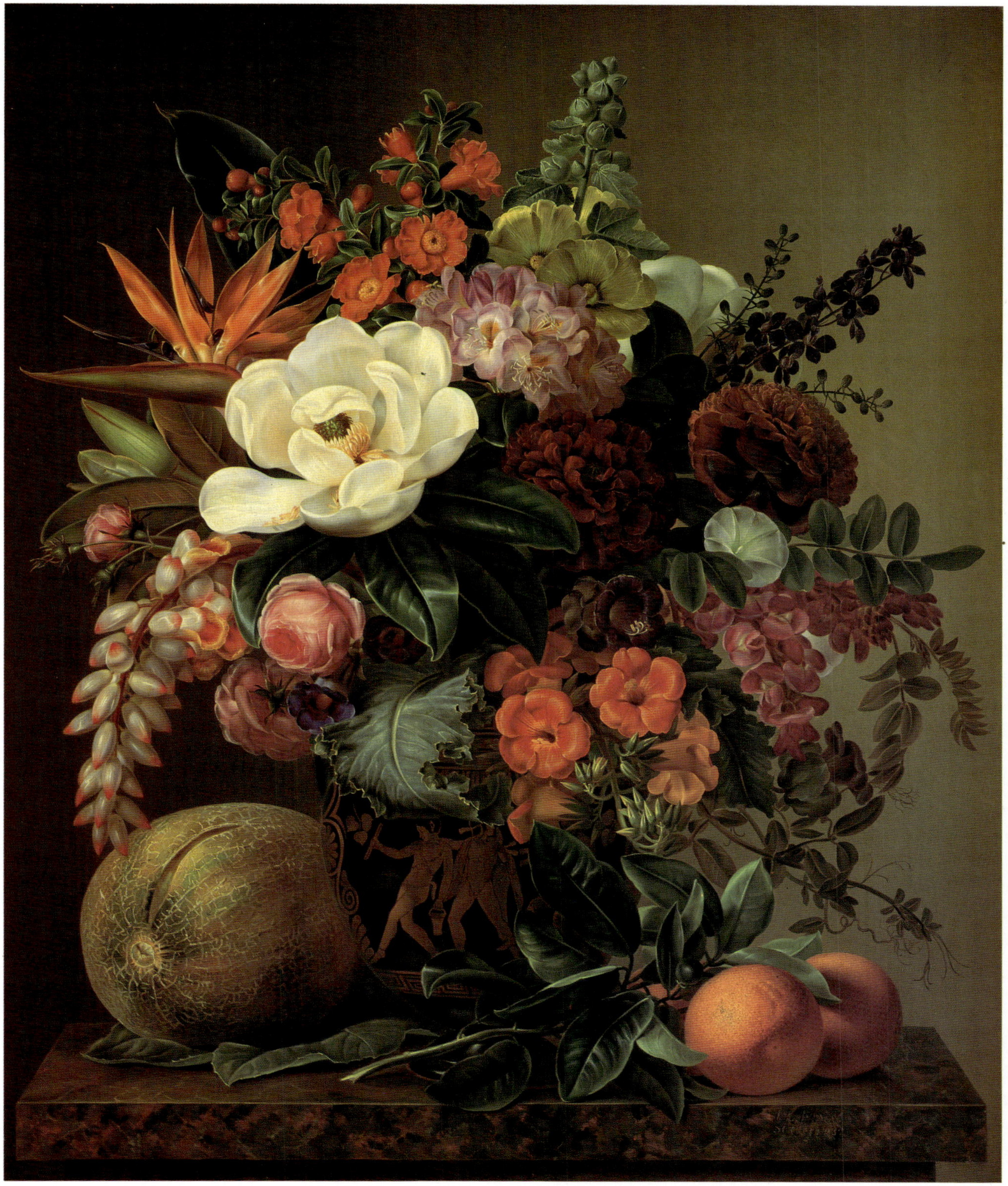

moor as pigments. He came to Copenhagen when he was about nineteen and found employment as a painter's apprentice. He also attended classes at the schools of the Royal Academy, where he made contacts that were to help him later in life. His model as a flower painter was Jan van Huijsum (1682-1749) whose confident use of light Ottesen admired. He further appreciated Van Huijsum's way of lovingly painting each individual flower so that even a botanist could recognize them. Visits to Paris and Lyon failed to convince him that anyone could paint flowers better than Van Huijsum. He was therefore delighted – and so was I.L.Jensen – when Jan van Huijsum's *Flower piece* was acquired by the Royal Collections (now Statens Museum for Kunst) in 1843 (fig. 20). The painting had been in Norway for some years previously, where it inspired the poet Henrik Wergeland to write a poem (1840) describing the picture, flower by flower, in such a way that the whole idea of it reflects the wars in Flanders. Thus, he turned an innocent flower painting into a historical painting with political overtones.

Both Jensen and Ottesen copied Van Huijsum's picture. Ottesen moreover painted his own (reversed) paraphrase of it, perhaps with hints at the Dano-Prussian war of 1863-64. After all, he grew up in the bordering country. Ottesen concluded his biography with the words: 'But we still, always, find the best subjects in nature' – a point on which he and Jensen agreed. But while Jensen represented ideal flowers, without a dead leaf or a worm spoiling the rose and looking as perfect as if they were in the Garden of Eden, Ottesen saw the Creator's will everywhere, even in the worm. His reaction to nature was intense, and his representation of it a concentrated interpretation of deeply-rooted childhood memories (fig. 23).

Ottesen also introduced a new approach to flower painting in Denmark by breaking away from the confines of the window sill and going out into the open air to paint growing plants. Eugène Delacroix had already done the same in the 1840s, when he painted a clump of peonies in a garden (Ny Carlsberg Glyptotek, Copenhagen). He moved close to the white and pink flowers amongst the green foliage, completely omitting foreground and background and focussing only on the peonies, whose narrow, fine, silky petals amongst the green leaves are shattered by an inner storm.

In the first half of the nineteenthe century, Europe was marked by a certain cultural and political uniformity. In the aftermath of the Napoleonic Wars, the bourgeoisie licked its wounds while trying to build up new and more democratic forms of government. The second half of the century, however, experienced an explosion of overlapping and often conflicting trends. It was the era of imperialism, magnificently symbolized in Leopold II's greenhouse in Laeken. The blue flower as a symbol of Romantic yearning was long since dead, replaced by other flowers. The distant colonies provided exotic plants that could be cultivated under glass and that were commercially successful. Orchids in particular were popular as place decorations at elegant dinner parties and remained in vogue until the 1940s as corsages. In Marcel Proust's *A la recherche du temps perdu,* Swann's beloved, Odette, uses the cattleya as her signature. The orchid competed with the gardenia and carnation for a place in the dandy's buttonhole. The orchid also gained ground in the literature of the 1890s as a symbol of passion, and is found in the decorative art of the period, especially in exquisite jewellery. On the other hand, it failed to arouse any particular interest among painters. It was too strange and a little menacing. The dangerous, downright poisonous flowers are mostly to be found in literature. Baudelaire's *Les fleurs du mal* (1857) is about women whom the poet enjoyed and analyzed as if they were flowers touching on their shape, their colour, their fragrance. I.P.Jacobsen wrote about woman as a lethal flower in his first great arabesque ('En Arabesque', 1860s), because he was afraid of women. In the writings of August Strindberg flowers also have symbolic value. Briefly summarized, his theme is that earthly love may be regarded as a flower that grows out of the mire and into the light, there to bloom and die. Eros/Amor is the cruder emotion, the lust of the flesh, standing in the way of 'Caritas,' the mental, all-embracing and noble emotion. Strindberg was revolted by the human body and its functions.

The old familiar flowers also took an exotic turn under Japanese influence. The tulip, for example, was transformed from the faithful harbinger of spring in the window sills into a flower with an aesthetic message. In *The Picture of Dorian Gray* (1891) Oscar Wilde (fig. 24) describes the fashionable home of a

23 O.D. Ottesen, *Flowers in a vase*. Oil on panel. Denmark 1869
Statens Museum for Kunst, Copenhagen (*cat. 34*)

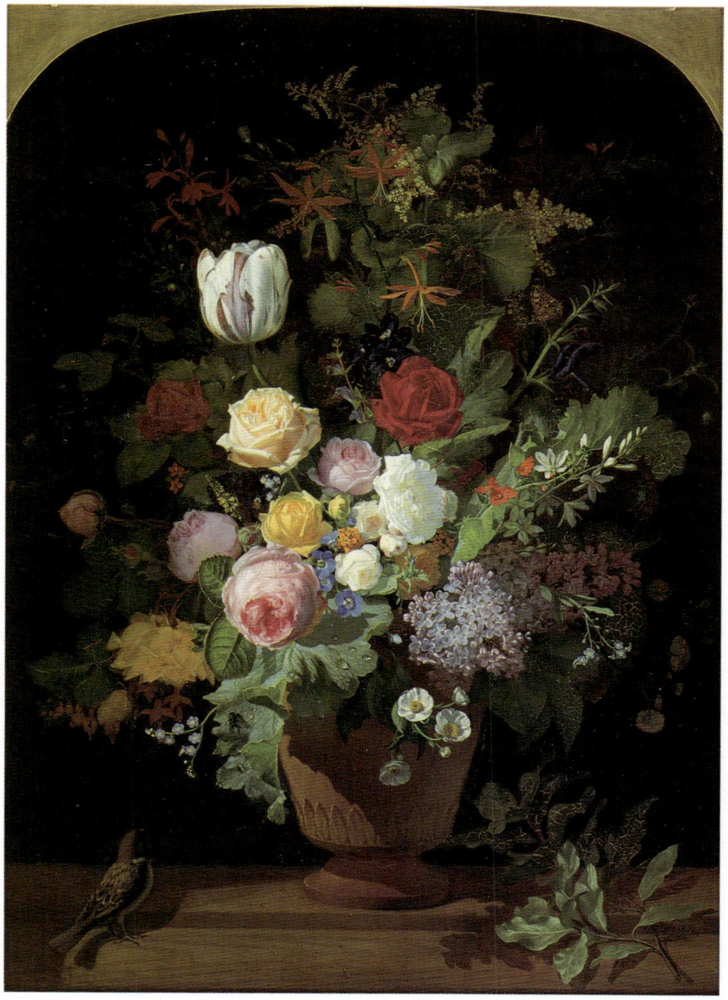

real aesthete: 'Some large blue china jars and parrot-tulips were arranged on the mantel-shelf.' The blue jars have associations with the Orient, as do the flowers. The parrot tulips were not meant as an expression of some kind of neo-tulipomania but were supposed to be Japanese, resembling chrysanthemums: double, curled, strange. It is unclear whether they are at their zenith or just beginning to die. However, with dry petals and wilted stalks, they take on new beauty at their death. The tulip's decorative qualities lent themselves admirably to applied art, and the flower's ambiguity representative of life and death simultaneously – coincided very well with the mood of the 1890s. It is a dualism that corresponds to Yin and Yang.

In his famous poem 'The Old Vicarage, Grantchester,' written on a sultry day in Berlin in 1912, Rupert Brooke recalled the cool, informal loveliness of the English garden by observing the flower beds in German parks: 'Here tulips bloom as they are told.' We all know parks where bulbs are planted to bloom in formations, erect, uniform and exact, with leaves as stiff and pointed as bayonets. As early as the 1830s Hans Christian Andersen had been aware of the tulip's somewhat masculine appearance, comparing it with the tightly corsetted aunts who ensure decorous behaviour at balls. This is only a short step away from the German grenadier tulips.

Turning to female painters we discover a completely different conception of tulips. Anna Ancher painted a bowl full of them at about the same time as Rupert Brooke wrote his poem. Hers are genuine gar-

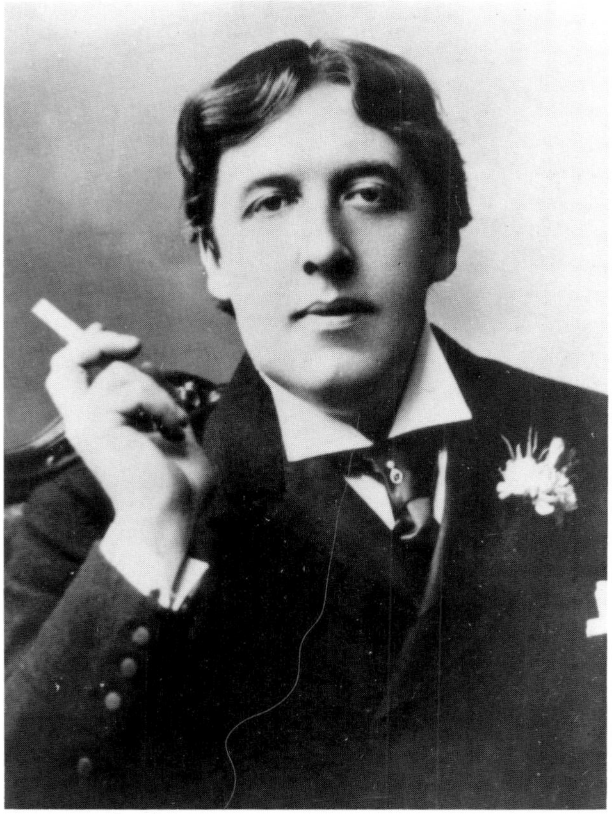

24 Oscar Wilde (1856-1900). Photograph
Det kongelige Biblioteks billedsamling, Copenhagen

den tulips in pale pastel colours; from the green bowl right down to the surface of the table, they humbly bow their heads in full bloom resting on their long, curving stems (Skagens Museum). Karen Blixen often did justice to the feminity of the full-blown tulip in her famous and much-praised flower arrangements. But not always. In the more modern English fashion – perhaps also the old Dutch – she would sometimes strip the green leaves from the flower. Technically, this practice extends the life of the cut flower, because it no longer needs the water for the leaves. Aesthetically, it allows the calyx to grow large on a stalk that remains stiff longer. Blixen alternated between tulips that were to remain straight and those that would look best when the stalks had become pliant, depending on what she wanted from her 'flower paintings' – which is how she thought of them – and selected the flowers according to the role she wished them to play. This is also a woman's way of looking at matters. While both women and men need flowers to express themselves, a woman would hardly have said what a Danish castigator of the social system, Poul Henningsen, claimed in an article written around 1933: 'You can tell whether a tulip has been painted for or against Hitler.'

In the works of Henri Matisse, where everything expresses delight in colours and light and in life itself, there are always flowers and vegetable matter: flowers as a subject in themselves, leaves – or seaweed – because they are so beautiful; flowers and women. He annexed a refrain from one of Baudelaire's poems, 'Luxe, Calme, Volupté,' endowing it with new meaning. In the 1970s, the Anglo-American artist David Hockney painted a series of portraits including flowers (cat. 59) that are supernaturalistic and reminiscent of still lifes. It may be a white lily or a blue iris thrusting aggressively into the picture though, as a rule, Hockney prefers tulips which he uses in a very individualistic manner: completely fresh and crushed together in a vase, exuding an almost indecently abundant vitality. Yet, in a watercolour entitled *Celia in a black dress with white flowers* (1972) two tulips bend gently towards the woman portrayed.

The tulip is thought provoking. So is the poppy, but in a completely different way; it leaves no doubt regarding what is life and what death. Its bloom, like that of the peony, is either present or not there at all, for when it withers all the petals fall off at once. What remains is the capsule containing sleep, death and the flower's eternity. The capsule of the poppy has been the symbol of death since ancient Greece. It was depicted much later by Thorvaldsen in a relief called *Night,* and in even later sepulchral monuments. The flower itself can be an early summer garden plant, beautiful, decorative and devoid of all symbolism, or it can be seen as one of the national flowers of the nineteenth century in the form of the simple field poppy, or horn poppy. As such it was later (1872) recalled, in I. P. Jacobsen's short story *Mogens*, by the man in love who wanted to see it as a wreath round the head of his dark-haired young bride. Given that he was a farmer, this was quite appropriate, yet it also reveals a new sensibility and significance beyond his sense of the decorative. It also stands for fertility and was thus a symbol of death's youngest brother, pas-

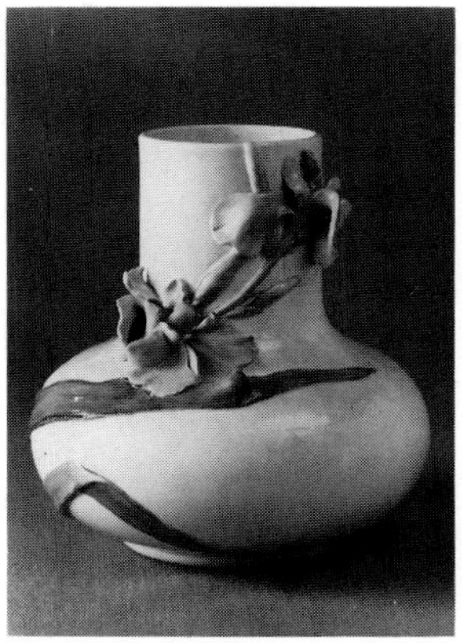

25 *Vase*. Faience. Around the neck a freely modelled yellow iris. Gustavsberg, Sweden 1897
Nationalmuseum, Dept. of Decorative Arts, Stockholm (*cat. 206*)

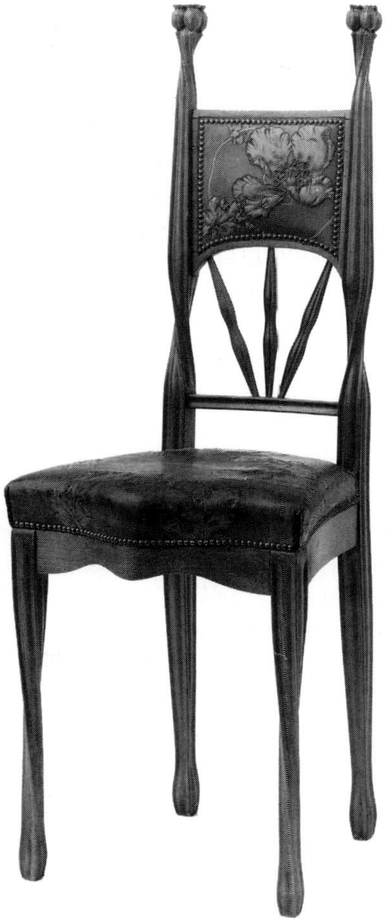

26 ▸ Louis Majorelle. *Chair*. Beechwood and walnut. Upholstered in leather with large poppy pattern. Nancy, France ca. 1900
Kunstindustrimuseet, Copenhagen (*cat. 255*)

sion. Under the influence of Japonism the poppy naturally also became accepted as a decorative flower in fashions for women. When Marcel Proust wrote *A la recherche du temps perdu* he asked his female acquaintances for permission to look at the dresses they had worn twenty years earlier to see if he had remembered the fashions correctly. In *Guermantes* he writes: 'Majestic, tall and imposing, she glided in wearing her long yellow atlas dress adorned with tremendous black poppies; it was the duchess.' A few pages later we read: '[Charlus] had painted yellow and black irises on the large fan, which at this moment the duchess unfolded.'

In this context another old European favourite must be mentioned, rediscovered during these years via Japan, namely the iris. In his novelette *Sommerglæder* (1902) Herman Bang describes a young woman holding 'five irises in her hand; their stems were so long the mauve capsules rose right above her head.' And in a nostalgic moment, Marcel Proust recalls what the world was like in his youth, comparing it with the world around 1910: 'But how should these people, who regard these terrible creatures with hats like veritable bird-cages or kitchen gardens, have the slightest idea how enchanting it was to see Madame Swann with... a little beret, decorated with a single iris.'

Both the iris and the poppy were taken over by the decorative arts (fig. 25). For instance, the iris found its way onto bookbindings and the poppy appears on a chair with flowers on the upholstery and seed capsules on the back posts (fig. 26). The liberation of the poppy as a decorative motif and the fantasy used in its application is owed to Japan rather than to antiquity. However, antiquity's association of the poppy as one of death's plants was not forgotten and the little red flower became the symbol of the blood shed by the countless young men who died on the field of Flanders in the first World War (1914-18).

A new era viewed the poppy quite differently. The Expressionist artist, Emil Nolde, imbued not only poppies with their clashing reds – but also sunflowers with individual character (fig. 63). Furthermore, Georgia O'Keeffe painted poppies and irises the way she painted all other flowers: large and from very close up – as if visually embracing everything about them. She said of flowers: 'Still – in a way – nobody sees a flower – really – it is so small – we haven't time – and to see takes time, like having a friend takes time'. The same applies to flowers as to art: seeing and giving yourself time. It is the only way to become friends.

While Japonism coloured European culture to its farthest corners, like a drop of wine in a glass of water, during the complicated second half of the nineteenth century another element made its presence felt. The sunflower's arrival as a much-loved motif for painters can be connected with the prosaic fact that the plant was being cultivated for its oil. It was 'rediscovered' and moved from the fields into gardens, both as a decorative plant and one useful for bees. Painters soon noticed it and depicted it as never before; Van Gogh's sunflowers have become the most famous example. His ideas about them and their yellow colour may have encouraged others to see their colouristic possibilities. In Denmark, Michael Ancher painted his version of the theme in *Girl with sunflowers.* He even painted it twice but, despite minor differences, both pictures more or less depict a bunch of sunflowers just being brought in by a girl (fig. 27).

In the 1890s the sunflower appears again and again, for example in Edvard Munch's pictures.

However, Munch painted the whole flower, not in a vase but growing, often from a grave, as described by Strindberg, Munch's close acquaintance at the turn of the century. He too allowed his flowers to grow up out of the mire, bloom and then quickly die. The sunflower also symbolized the sun, and thus life itself. Henrik Ibsen anticipated this in 1881 with the closing line of *The Ghosts*: 'Mother, give me the sun.' The sunflower, whose Danish name corresponds to the French name, *tournesol*, that is, a flower that turns with the sun, has twisted and turned many times since its emblematic use in the days of Van Dyck.

Strictly speaking, all plants begin their lives in the darkness and emerge to bloom in the light. What matters in the visual and decorative arts is what artists

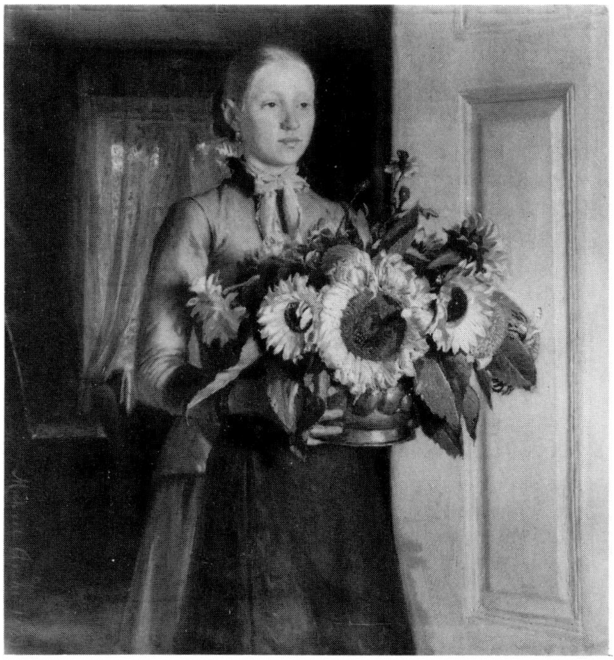

27 Michael Ancher, *Girl with sunflowers.* Oil on canvas. Skagen 1889
Statens Museum for Kunst, Copenhagen (*cat. 39*)

read into this general state of affairs. The water lily, for example, grows in a darker and more obscure depth than any other plant. It sends up its flower, reaching for the light, through the water – yet another element – where it and its leaves unfold and lie quietly on the surface (fig. 28). In Romanticism, a movement concerned with good versus evil and light versus darkness, the lily was an obvious motif. It is moreover a Nordic flower. Hans Christian Andersen's *Thumbelina* can be read as a children's story with a happy ending, or interpreted as a Christian parable. Thumbelina (read mankind in all its suffering), is carried away by the powers of darkness (the toad), thereafter to dwell in the mire for all time. But the small fish (the fish is always a Christian symbol), bite through the stalk of the lily on which she has been placed, and the butterfly (immortality) carries her away from evil, to repose, so to speak, in the hand of God. The evil nature of the water lily is given form in J. W. Waterhouse's painting Hylas and the nymphs (1896)(fig. 29). Waterhouse was a follower of the English Pre-Raphaelites and all they stood for in the way of Christian and ethical ideas. Hylas was the favourite

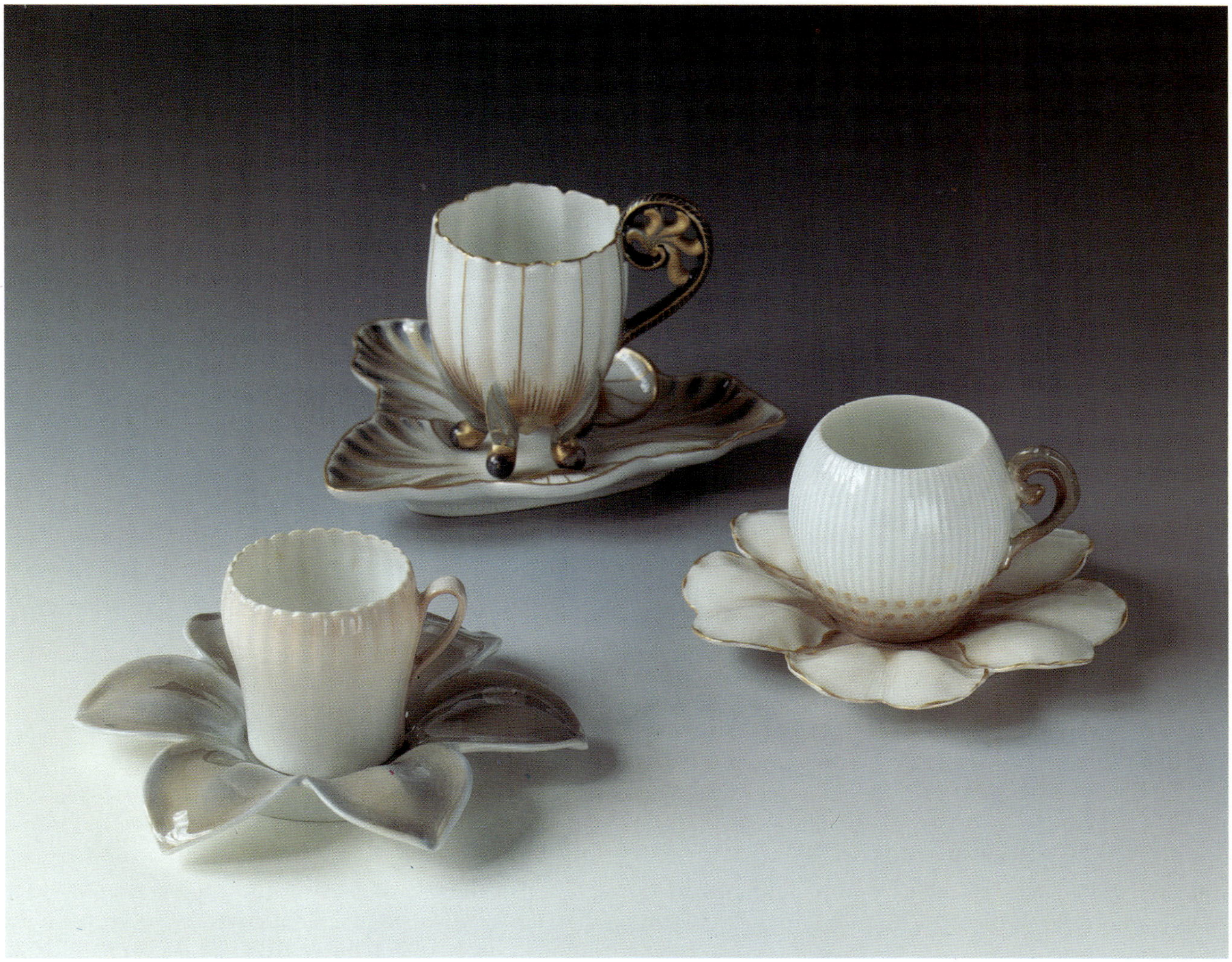

28 Pietro Krohn, *Three cups and saucers, Cinquefoil, Water lily*, and *Narcissus*. Bing & Grøndahl's Porcelain Manufactory, Copenhagen 1888-91
Kunstindustrimuseet, Copenhagen (*cat. 133*)

of Heracles, who had fought tirelessly against wild animals, monsters and other kinds of evil. One day he was to fetch water from a spring inhabited by eternally youthful nymphs. In Waterhouse's painting the nymphs appear among the Nordic water lilies on a grey Nordic day and reach out to grasp Hylas. Their arms, above water, are similar to the stalks of the water lily below; they entwine themselves around him and drag him down into the depths. Though the literary exploitation of the water lily as a theme came to an end, its strange beauty persisted. The long, twisting, elastic stalks lent themselves admirably to the decorative idiom of Art Nouveau as did its flowers, with their slightly sentimental associations (cat. 136). However, a great writer like Marcel Proust during his walk in *The Road to Swann* could still be puzzled by the mystery of the leaf on the surface that moves with the stream and yet always returns to its starting point and continues to do so, as if in accordance with an eternal law.

The second half of the nineteenth century was inclined to opulence and the preferred perfumes were pure but heavy flower scents: rose, heliotrope, violet and lilac. A taste for simpler things emerged towards the end of nineteenth century and was expressed in

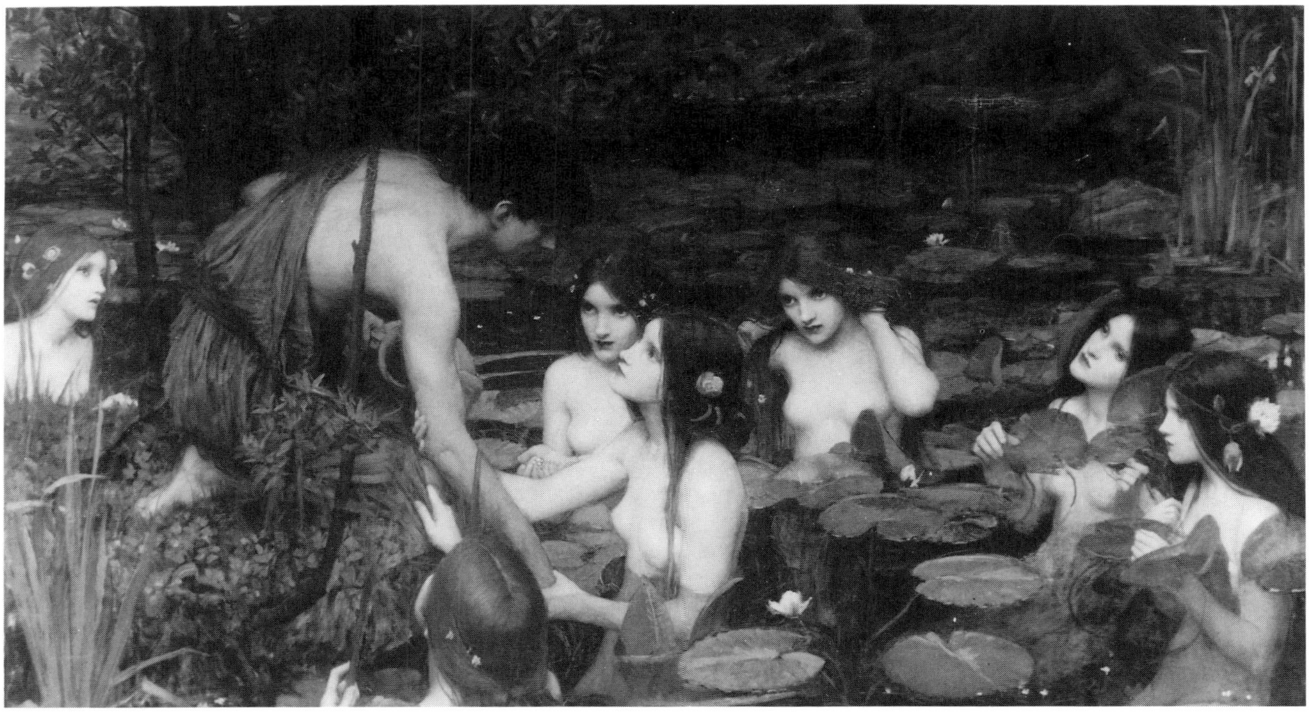

29 J. W. Waterhouse, *Hylas and the nymphs*. England 1896
Manchester City Art Galleries, Manchester

the summer homes which the upper middle classes began to acquire. They developed a liking for pinewood furniture painted in watercolour and earthenware pots filled with wild flowers. In their town homes as well the feeling ruled that flowers should be placed in vases, in harmony with their nature, and not according to the tastes of florists. It was a new kind of 'back to nature,' although a fondness for refinement had not yet vanished. During the Edwardian age's brittle and slightly anaemic classicism, the humble lily of the valley with its decorative little bells was restored to favour. Marcel Proust captured the prevailing taste around 1910 in the words 'white Louis XVI drawing-rooms with blue hydrangeas.'

The elegance of simplicity has characterized the twentieth century's taste in flowers, despite extravagance with roses, lyme grass and black berries, or sentimental bridal bouquets of wild flowers. Our century is the first to cultivate the single flower in a vase. This may stem from a desire to preserve the purity of the architecture and assign the flower a role as an unchanging element in interior decoration. For this purpose artificial flowers are perfect. Our surroundings are supposed to be a work of art, and thus immutable.

Nonetheless, a single flower is above all – and always romantic. Just think of the silver rose in Richard Strauss' and Hugo von Hoffmannthal's opera *Der Rosenkavalier* (1911), in which there is a drop of Persian rose oil (cat. 350), or the rose in Anthony Hope's novel *The Prisoner of Zenda* (1894) wrapped in a piece of paper with the words 'Rudolf – Flavia -Always' written on it, exchanged every year between the lovers who had renounced their love out of devotion to duty.

Eternity, the immortal, is expressed by the most ephemeral things in the world: flowers.

Bettina von Meyenburg

'Saying it with flowers'
The flower as an artistic motif from the late Middle Ages until the Baroque

Flowers have always fascinated man. Yet their healing power alone does not account for their symbolic value as an invigorating force in the cycle of nature. With the changing seasons, flowers, above all, show that winter is waning and spring is on its way. Their vegetative life cycle – to burgeon, bloom and bring joy, to droop, fade, wither and finally die – is similar to the course of human life. The life of flowers from darkness to light, from seed to bloom, elicits a chain of associations reflected in the visual arts: the dream of eternal life, an awareness of its evanescence, and praise to God as the creator of nature.

In antiquity as well as in Christian tradition, flowers represent not only the transitoriness of human life, but also life after death. The concept of 'the bouquet of life' already appears in the paintings of bound bouquets of flowers in Egyptian grave chambers. The combination of consecrated lotus and papyrus are an offering which promises life after death. On Christian epitaphs, flowers, and particularly ears of corn, symbolize the hope of resurrection, in the words of St. John: '[...] unless a grain of wheat falls into the earth and dies, it remains alone; but if it dies, it bears much fruit' (John 12:24).

Flowers also provide a framework for innumerable festive occasions. Flower festoons, bouquets and scattered flowers represent joy, abundance and sensuality (figs. 30, 31). The sight of flowers also evokes a longing for paradise lost, a golden era when man, animals and plants were in harmony with God and living in a state of innocence in an eternal spring in the Garden of Eden.

The history of flowers is linked closely to that of gardening. The convent garden of the Middle Ages was the earthly substitute for the garden of Paradise; its flowering plants were mostly medicinal herbs. In the visual arts, saints and martyrs are often shown surrounded by the medicinal plants used by a particular monastic order. For example, St. Anthony is shown on Grünewald's *Isenheim altar* in Colmar in a flowery meadow with the medicinal herbs used by the Anthonites to treat gangrene. In the monastery garden of the late Middle Ages, however, flowers were grown for their beauty and fragrance as well – to create a conception of heavenly paradise as a happy and carefree place. In the painting of the *Garden of Eden* (fig. 32), the selection of flowers reflects the monastery garden of the late Middle Ages. The ornamental plants sprout freely on the lawn, while the medicinal herbs and the kitchen garden are laid out in beds along the convent wall. The garden had the status of 'consecrated ground,' while the surrounding untilled natural area is in a state of 'original sin.'

Gardening in the late Middle Ages also included the *locus amoenus*, a pleasure garden with flowers, trees and clear spring water. Here the aesthetic concept of nature is more important than the interest in medicinal plants. During the age of chivalry, floral beauty was compared to the gracefulness of women. The pleasure garden was the poet's most intimate scene, where earthly needs could be satisfied. In 'The Song of Solomon,' too, there is a touch of the erotic in the verses: 'A garden enclosed is my sister, my spouse; a spring shut up, a fountain sealed.' The pleasure garden as an earthly paradise is the refuge of love, the secularized counterpart of the convent garden's mystical concept of paradise. The love garden reflects the way of life of the aristocracy. For several centuries after Guillaume de Lorris wrote his *Roman de la Rose* (1230), it served as a model for floral motifs for tapestries. The love garden was the site of idle pursuits and courting, and thousands of flowers – millefleur – cover the tapestries. Here, flowers do not refer to the

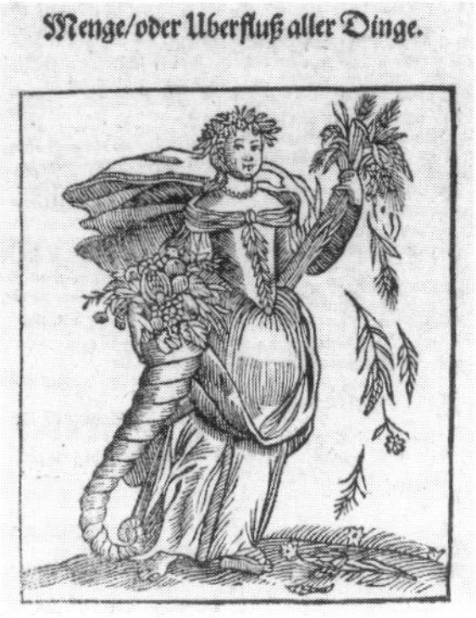

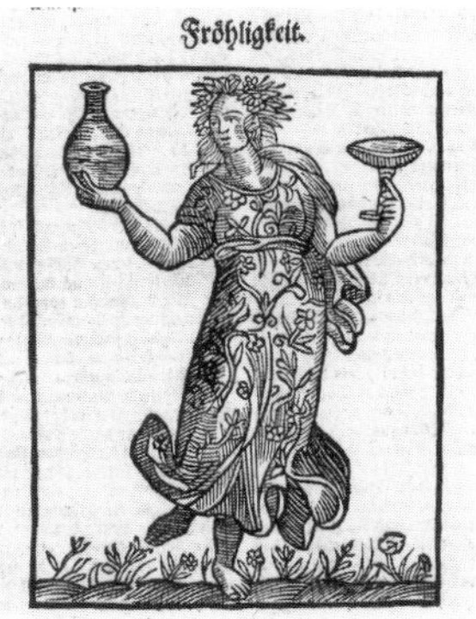

30-31 Cesare Ripa, *Iconologia*, Frankfurt 1669. Woodcut. *Abundance* and *Sensuality*
Kunstindustrimuseet, Copenhagen

Virgin Mary, as they do in the Garden of Paradise, but are symbols of love, sung by the poets. This 'courtesy garden' of the aristocracy corresponds to the Cockaigne of idleness of the lower social classes.

The origin of botanical gardens is likewise related to man's longing for paradise. The establishment of the first botanical gardens coincided with the great voyages of discovery. The lost paradise, it was believed, still existed on the other side of the globe. Even though a botanical garden was laid out as a *hortus medicus,* the result was an attempt to recreate paradise. Gardening was regarded as an innocent and redeeming activity allowing one to recreate nature as it was before the Fall. Artists did the same by rendering bouquets with flowers and plants from different seasons, gathered in a 'botanical encyclopaedia.' Such idealized flower paintings were often included in the *Kunst- und Wunderkammern*. When the botanist Carolus Clusius wrote his book *Rariorum Plantarum Historia* in 1601 (fig. 44), his motivation was not only scientific, but also embraced the idea of placing all the flowers of the world 'in one garden.'

During the late sixteenth century, botanical gardens attached to castles served as the outdoor parallels to the indoor *Kunst- und Wunderkammern*. In the garden, the individual plant was a museum piece. According to Francis Bacon, a garden containing both wild and cultivated plants was part of the 'museum' of the nobleman – a concept which included a library, a cabinet of curiosities and a room where the philosophers' stone and various instruments could be found. Such diverse collections and the heterogeneity of shapes and materials reflected the age's quest for universality. Collecting and growing flowers did not, however, remain the privilege of princes and the aristocracy for long. Wealthy citizens emulated the princely pursuit by adopting their customs and behaviour. The princely gardens became models for the gardens of the rich bourgeoisie whose aim was to manifest their mercantile hegemony. Scientific curiosity combined with factual knowledge was reflected by the learned man's garden, a private garden with botanical features.

Garden flowers as a source of artistic inspiration – The botanical gardens of persons of discernment have always been a source of artistic inspiration. While depictions of plants had previously consisted of copies from the canonical works of antiquity, such as Dioscorides' five-volume *De plantis* or the works of Theophrastus and Pliny, during the sixteenth century they became reproductions of reality. In the meticulous rendering of botanical details, the illustrations satisfied the patrons' interest in the exotic features of plants, as well as in the exact morphology of a given plant. One example was Otto Brunfels' *Herbarum vivae eicones* from 1530 with woodcuts after the herbal studies in watercolour by Dürer's student Hans Weiditz (fig. 1). The engraved illustrations of the florilegia were so precise and the selection of flowers so exquisite that they were used as patterns for the finest goldsmith works and, later, for decorations on porcelain and faience (fig. 33).

The French kings' gardens, in particular, became a source of inspiration for artisans. Late in the fourteenth century, Charles VI promoted the planting of roses, lilies and irises, a tradition continued by the Bourbons right up to the end of *l'ancien régime* in the greenhouses of Malmaison. The gardens of the Dukes of Burgundy in Hesdin, with their assortment of flowers, became models for the millefleur tapestries' rich flower grounds. Duke René d'Anjou was a passionate gardener and was responsible for acclimatizing the 'Rose de Provence' and the carnation in the Anjou region. In the 1630s, Gaston d'Orleans established the famous botanical garden at the castle in Blois that became the model for Louis XIII's Jardin des Plantes in Paris, and then for Louis XIV's botanical endeavours in the service of art.

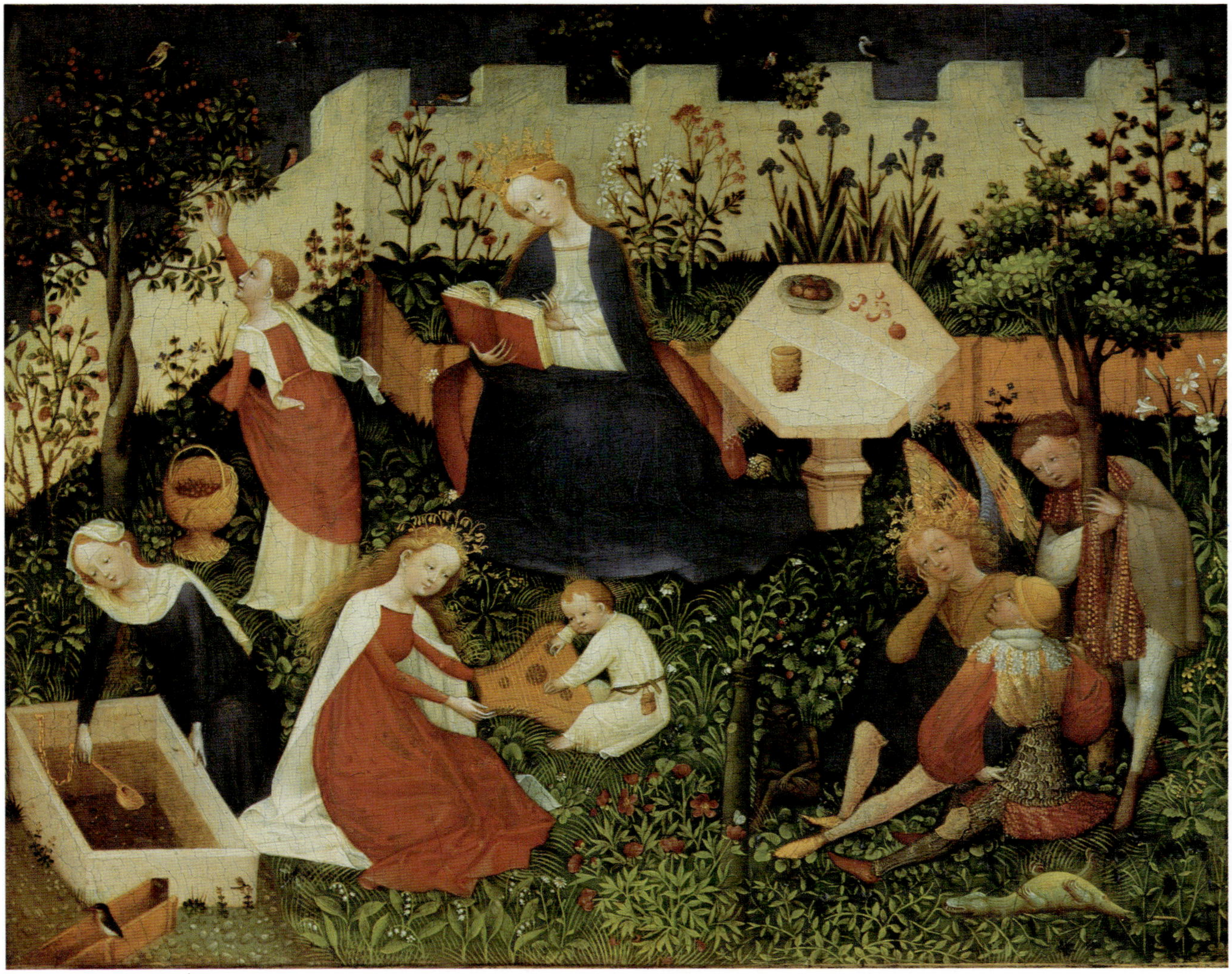

32 Anonymous south German master, *Garden of Eden*. Oil on panel. ca. 1410. The garden as hallowed ground is emphasized by the presence of the Holy Virgin reading in the flowering meadow

Städelsches Kunstinstitut, Frankfurt am Main

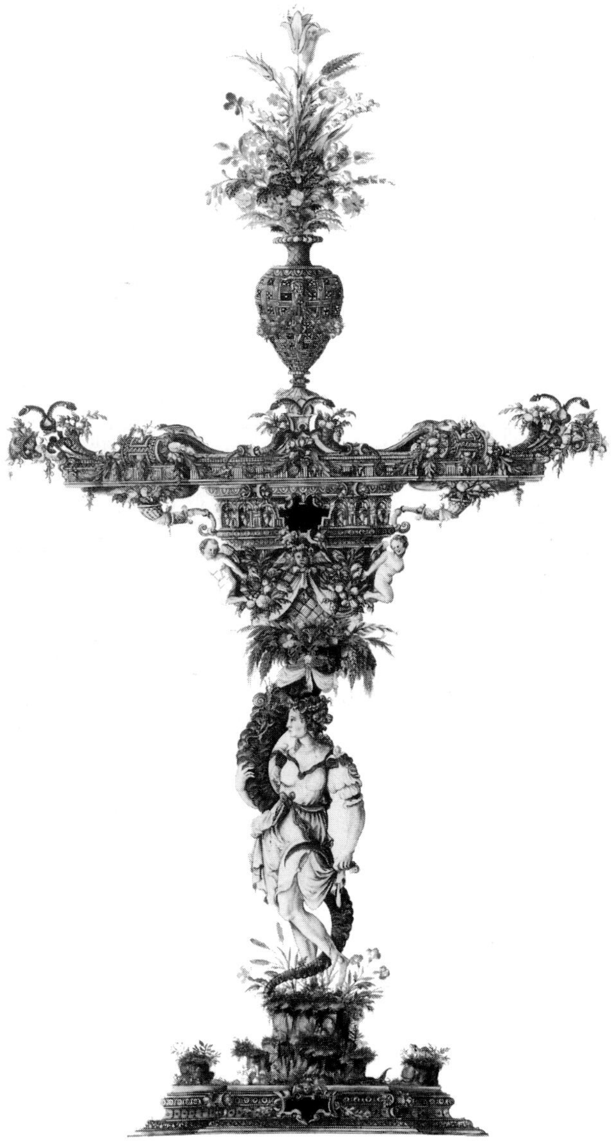

33 Wenzel Jamnitzer, *sketch for the 'Merkelsche' epergne*. Hand-coloured drawing. Nuremberg before 1549
Germanisches Nationalmuseum, Nuremberg

From the beginning of the seventeenth century, Florentine and Venetian artisans virtually spread the treasures of the botanical gardens over panels, tables and the drawers of cabinets in stone intarsia. This branch of exquisite handicraft, called *pietre dure*, might have inspired inlaid work with fine woods, ivory and shells depicting naturalistic flowers (fig. 48). Jan van Mecheren's furniture made in Amsterdam and The Hague were the prototypes for André Charles Boulle's inlaid flower motifs on furniture during the reign of Louis XIV – an example of how much the floral motif in French art owes to Dutch inspiration.

Cartesianism rejected stylized and fantastic forms and preferred realistic renderings, and the enthusiasm for flowers culminated in the eighteenth century. It was the great epoch of herbal and floral ornamentation in the field of decorative art, a time during which people of noble and bourgeois origin alike were fascinated by flowers. Their form, colour and fragrance satisfied the senses and their commercial value made them status symbols. An artist's career as a painter of flowers, for example that of Jan van Huijsum, often began in a tapestry or faience factory where flower motifs dominated.

The aesthetics of the floral still life – The concept of beauty held by the aristocracy in the high Middle Ages was extremely selective. Only gentle, graceful and 'humanized' forms of nature were accepted, and only the cultivated landscape was highly valued. This attitude left its mark on the development of the floral still life and its aesthetics.

Whereas at the end of the sixteenth century the open landscape as a pictorial motif was still almost exclusively imaginary and depicted as a section of wild and uninhabited nature, the floral still life reflects a different attitude. This is seen in the works of artists who concurrently painted landscapes and floral still lifes, for example in the paintings of Roelandt Savery (1576-1639). In his landscapes, he depicts wild and mostly imaginary mountains, emphasizing the fantastic elements, while in his flower still lifes, he seeks intimacy and realism (fig. 34). Flowers were considered attainable and relevant, while the landscape was alienating or at best a challenge.

The aesthetic goal in the depiction of a bouquet of flowers was to visualize 'real' nature, close up, in the way it was seen and enjoyed in the garden. The background in a floral still life is generally neutral and places attention on the stationary object in the foreground. No story unfolds: the only action possibly taking place is in the fauna surrounding the bouquet, where a lizard lies in wait for a butterfly.

In contrast to the miniaturists' floral depictions of the Middle Ages, the floral still life of the Renaissance appears to express a more conscious longing for nature, a more rational search, in which the point of departure was the botanically correct, documented plant. Last but not least, a painting of flowers had to have a sensuous as well as an instructive aspect, adapted to the divine order under Calvinist or Catholic rule.

The interest of the sixteenth century in natural science led to the questioning of dogmatic forms of antiquity, and the discovery of new values in the empirical characterization of plants. Emperor Rudolf II in Prague was a pioneer of this new view of nature. A contemporary chronicler, Emmanuel Sweerts, describes him as the greatest admirer of flowers and art. Botanists employed at the court were to seek truth in reality. Artists in the service of natural science were not content with just imitating nature, but wanted to attain the 'ideal' imitation where the microcosm of a plant corresponded to the world's macrocosm. It was crucial to represent every detail accurately and on the basis of careful observation, reflecting a scientific naturalism in which no part is subordinate to another and all elements are equally important.

At the same time, this form of scientific naturalism contains hermetic ideas. Joris Hoefnagel (1542-1600), employed in the service of Rudolf II, called himself 'Inventor hieroglyphicus et allegoricus.' His watercolours after nature and the prints from the series *Archetypa studiaque* (1592) by his son Jacob Hoefnagel (1575-1630, fig. 35) contain many veiled allusions to the philosophy of nature.

A common trait of both empirical and symbolic trends in conceptions of nature was, according to Rudolf II, the search for the philosophers' stone and the acceptance of the totality of existence as a homogeneous whole, in order to gain control of the world. In part, the new demands made of artists re-

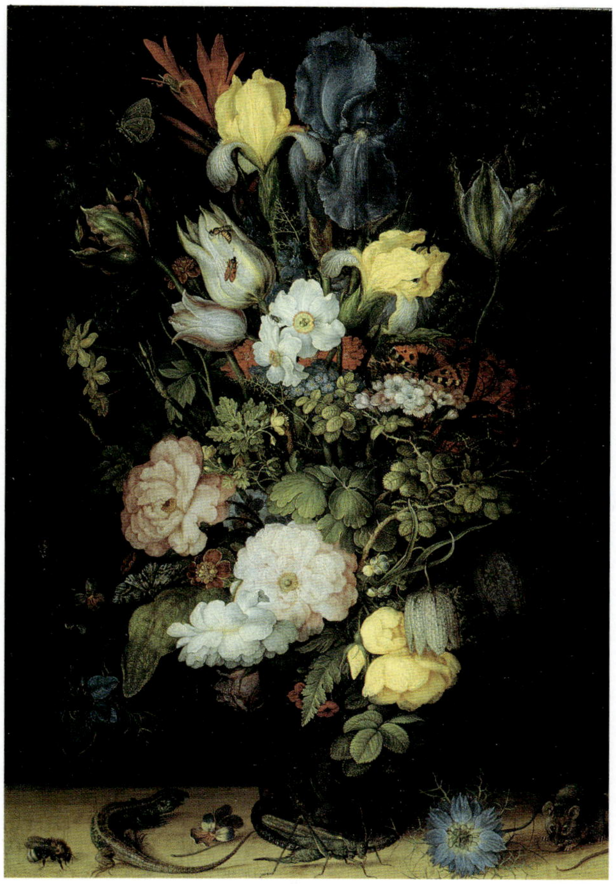

34 Roelandt Savery, *Flower still life*. Oil on panel
Collections of the Prince of Liechtenstein, Vaduz Castle, Liechtenstein

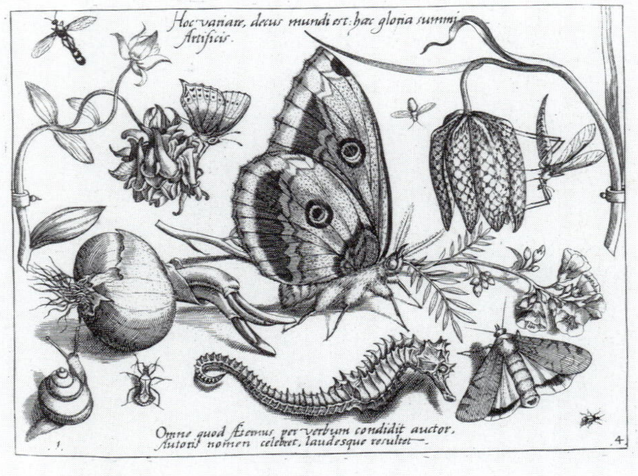

35 Jacob Hoefnagel, *Archetypa studiaque*. Engraving. Frankfurt 1592
Kunstindustrimuseet, Copenhagen

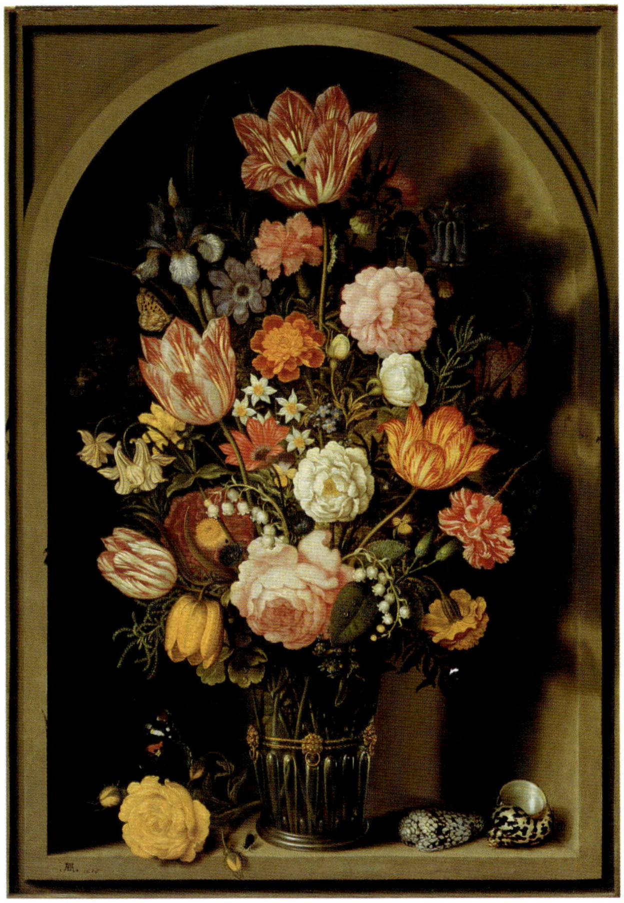

36▸ Ambrosius Boschaert, *Flower still life*. Oil on panel. 1618. The bouquet is composed of flowers from different seasons, based on accurate plant studies in watercolour or crayon
Statens Museum for Kunst, Copenhagen

sulted in the elevation of their status. In 1595, the art of painting was accepted as one of the seven liberal arts.

While the renowned botanist Carolus Clusius had plant rarities, including the tulip, sent to the imperial court in Vienna, Rudolf II established his own botanical garden at Hradcany in Prague, giving the emperor's flower painters direct access to their subject. In this intellectual climate, Roelandt Savery's wonderfully painted flower bouquets were created during his stay in Prague from 1604 to 1618. His floral still lifes are among the earliest and most beautiful in Dutch art. Botanically, they excel in their variety of flowers and green plants. Wild and cultivated flowers, such as the tulip and the rose, are found side by side in the same bouquet. In addition, the artist must have had an eye for the plants along the roads since he also depicted wild flowers. Savery made many landscape studies, yet his floral studies have not been preserved. The imperial *Kunstkammer* housed florilegia by, among others, Jacobo Ligozzi and Jacques de Gheyn and emblem books by Joris or Jacob Hoefnagel (fig. 35). Such editions can be seen as direct models for Savery's depictions of flowers and insects, thereby establishing a connection with the tradition of miniature painting.

Savery places bouquets either in a stone niche or in front of a velvety dark, impenetrable background. Due to its lack of space and perspective, the motif in the foreground stands out with maximal effect. An impression of transitoriness is created, not with shadow, but through a finely graded interaction of light and dark with transparent, delicate colouring. Some of the flowers are in full bloom and others already fading, with heavily bent heads. In contrast to Ambrosius Boschaert's flower still lifes, with their saturated colour (fig. 36) and botanical brilliance, Savery's flower pictures capture the atmosphere of

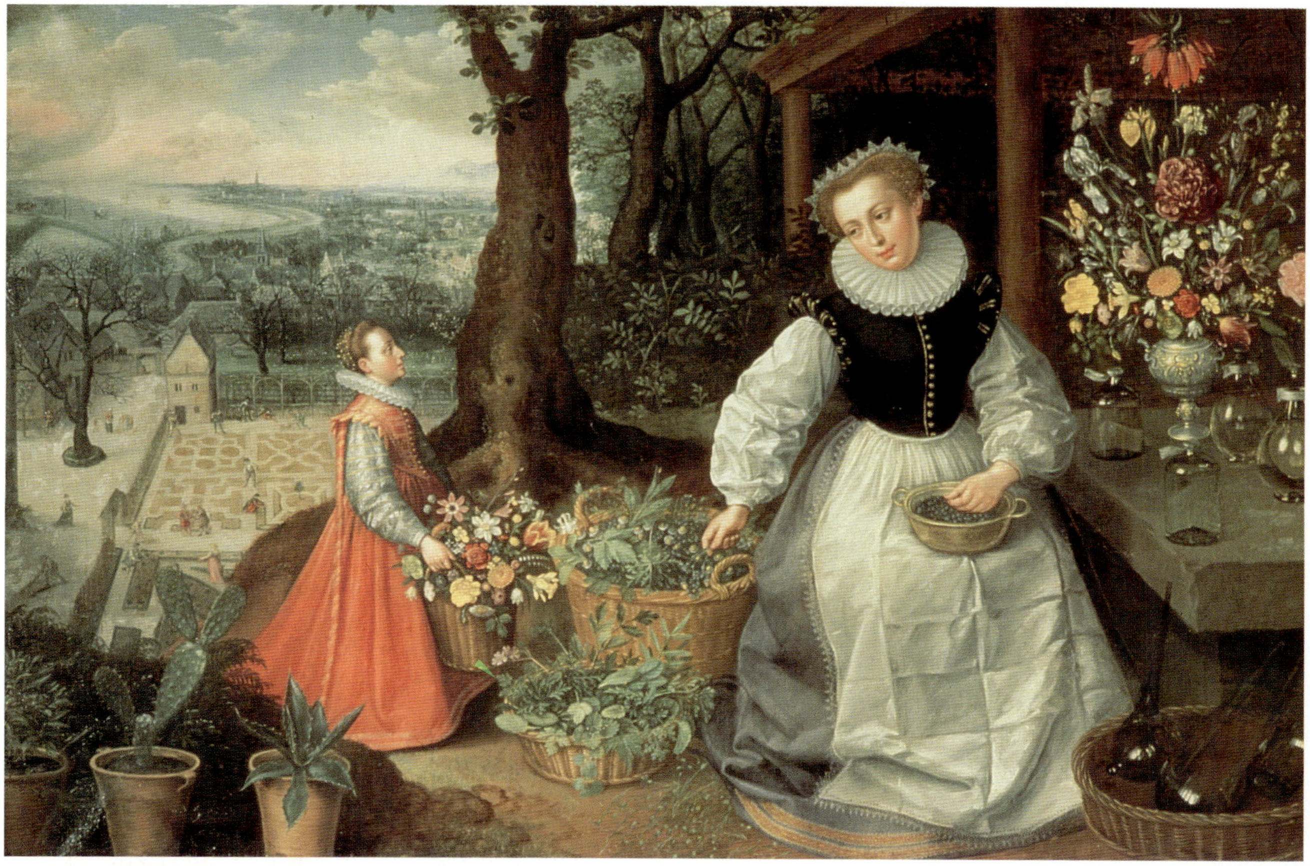

37 Lucas van Valckenborch and
Georg Flegel, *Spring*. Oil on canvas.
Frankfurt 1595
Private collection, Sweden (*cat. 1*)

the metamorphosis of nature seen by a person with a melancholy disposition; he registers the development of the plant as a whole in the cycle of nature.

Ambrosius Boschaert's (1565-1621) elaborately arranged and radially composed bouquets are an homage both to God as the creator of nature and the happy owner of the flowers (fig. 36). They are, in fact, a collection of expensive floral rarities. Even though the flowers in the image are mixed together, their individual characteristics are emphasized; an aesthetic visual norm which also takes heed of economic considerations.

Since flowers from various seasons are shown together in one bouquet, they must have been painted from careful individual studies made while each plant was in bloom. However, the sketch-like quality of the study has disappeared in favour of pictorial perfection. The flower picture is thus a substitute for an experience not possible in reality. Sensuousness is virtually reduced to abstraction and replaced by ideal beauty; it is not a picture of a real floral bouquet, but an idealization of it.

The mimetic naturalism of the flowers may well be related to a terminology which was not yet clearly developed. Until the second half of the seventeenth century, flowers were categorized according to smell, taste, colour and their healing effects. The principle of natural science was *curiositas* and not yet the elucidation of biological regularities and principles. Clarity of composition, visual 'legibility' and empirical views were more important than old dogmas. While interest in classification had yet to emerge, the naive desire to look at pictures, study the textural quality of the flowers and carefully observe light and colouring according to the stage of bloom had sharpened the artist's sensitivity to aesthetic effects.

In a painted bouquet of flowers from various seasons, the flora is available all year round, a condition which can never exist in nature. Illusionism takes on magical significance when the picture becomes a visual replacement for the transitory bloom, a trompe l'œil. The artist revises nature by conquering the flowers' fragility and placing it beyond the ravages of time. He preserves their transitoriness and takes them out of nature's blind cycle. The artist heightens the viewer's confrontation by placing the bouquet on a stage with a closed background.

During the seventeenth century, flower still lifes were very costly, yet the genre did not receive due art historical recognition until the nineteenth century. It was deemed lacking in direction and historical content, and few people recognized qualities such as the realistic rendering of nature as documentation, its cosmographic poetry and atmosphere. In a floral still life, the artist eliminates action in favour of an eternal moment.

The floral still life culminated as a genre during the Baroque, especially in Antwerp and Utrecht. In Catholic Flanders, the flora was richer, fuller and more flamboyant than in Calvinistic Holland. The list of flower painters is long and varied, and they were not all equally good; it would appear that the greater the zeal for imparting moral or symbolic messages to the spectator, the lower the quality of the art. Representative of the statically composed still life is Georg Flegel's (1566-1638) bouquet (fig. 37), primarily composed of large cultivated flowers in strong colours, and Ambrosius Boschaert's works (fig. 36). The minute details of the flowers clearly rest on individual studies made while the flowers were in bloom. From sketchbooks, flowers were selected and arranged in two symmetrically composed halves carefully balanced with regard to colour and spatial content. Though his paintings never achieved the sensuous and suggestive tension of Roelandt Savery's works, Boschaert was more aware of trends in contemporary floral taste and gave them lustre.

Another famous flower painter was Balthasar van der Ast (1593-1657), Ambrosius Boschaert's brother-in-law. He combined the symmetry and equivalence of colour of the latter's floral still lifes with a more sensitive element; his colours have a warmer glow.

Jan Brueghel the Elder (1568-1625), called 'Velvet Brueghel,' painted towering bouquets. A myriad of flowers hich may exceed a hundred species – are placed in small wooden bins. In a carefully balanced distribution of colour accents, he painted bouquets composed of a combination of wild flowers and botanical rarities. The flowers appear almost luminous in front of the dark background. Contrary to normal compositional practice, his bouquets are composed with the weight in the upper section, where the fullest flowers are placed.

The specialty of Jan van Kessel (1626-1679), the son-in-law of Jan Brueghel the Elder, are allegorical pictures for princely *Kunst- und Wunderkammern*. Some, including the one with 'Europe' as its theme, are now in the Alte Pinakotek in Munich. An enormous floral still life is depicted in the foreground as an homage to nature. Kessel's works draw further attention to the dominant place of the flower in a European collection intended for a humanistically oriented prince.

Another member of the circle around Jan van Kessel, Abraham Mignon, and Jacob Marell was Maria Sibylla Merian (1647-1717, figs. 10, 11). Her fame as a painter of nature reached far beyond the borders of the Netherlands. Joachim von Sandrart recounts in detail her interest in flowers, fruits and birds, her pictorial descriptions of the metamorphosis from larva to butterfly, as well as the plants on which it feeds. Sandrart praises Sibylla Merian's coloured drawings and etchings and wonders about the waterproof colour she used on silk and canvases, filled with flower motifs serving as models for embroideries.

Jan Davidsz de Heem (1606-1683) and Simon Verelst (1644-1721, fig. 38) belong to the next generation of flower painters who were masters of mimetic virtuosity, and atmospheres redolent with meaning and symbolic references, as well as a colour intensity achieved by vibrant light effects.

With Jan van Huijsum's (1682-1749) opulent cascades of flowers, Dutch painting experienced a final achievement within the genre (fig. 20). In the bouquet's apparently accidental arrangement, balance and harmony are sought in asymmetry. The dynamic of movement is only reluctantly restrained and alludes to free nature. The flowers were painted while in bloom. Thus, at the beginning of the eighteenth century, the notion of a botanical encyc-

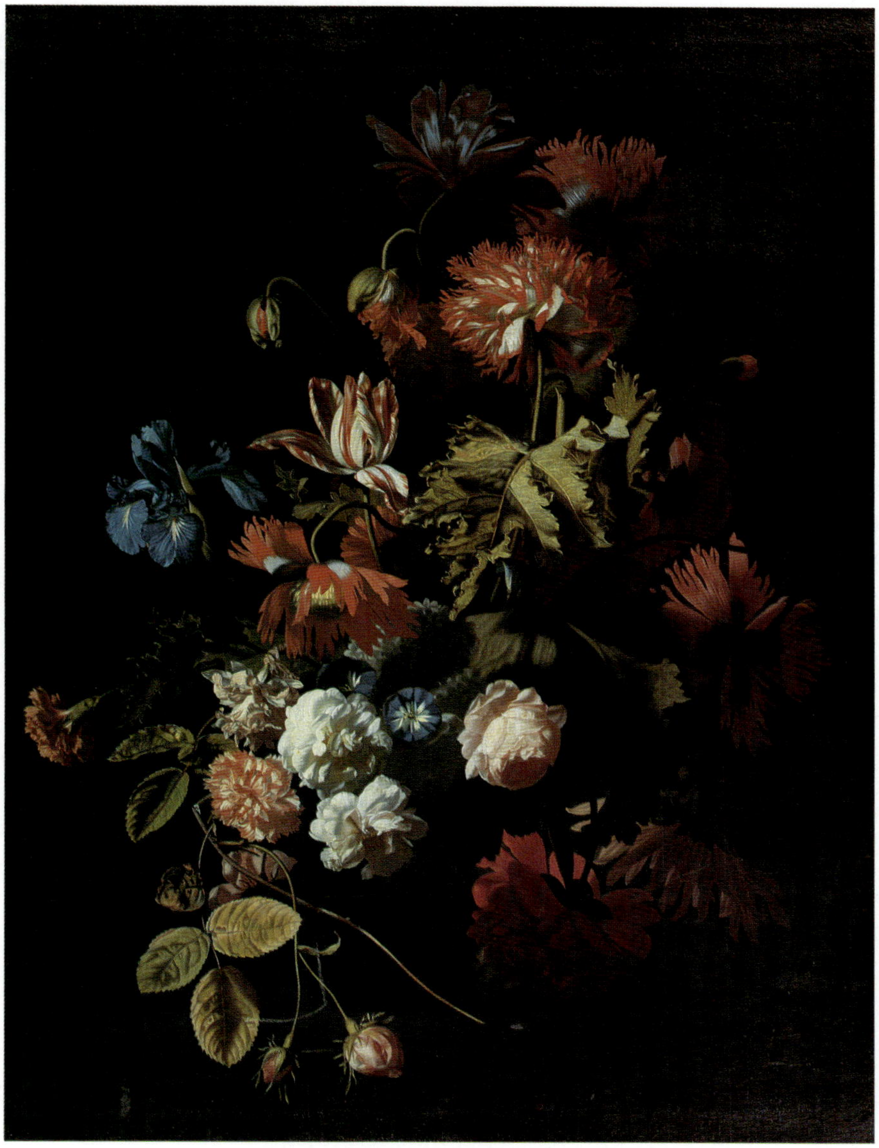

38 Simon Verelst, *Glass vase with flowers*. Oil on canvas. The Netherlands
Statens Museum for Kunst, Copenhagen (*cat. 8*)

lopaedia was abandoned in favour of greater floral spontaneity.

The development of flower painting in the Netherlands drew to a close with very professionally painted floral still lifes of great elegance. Despite all their colouristic splendour, the freshness of the flowers gradually faded. According to Gerard de Lairesse's (1640-1711) recommendations in his *Groot Schilderboek*, the artist would do better to use brilliantly made artificial flowers in paper and silk, even egg shell membrane, as models, than living flowers – a procedure employed in Jan van Os' (1744-1808) flower still lifes.

Flower symbolism in the seventeenth century – Flowers have always exercised a suggestive, seemingly irrational power in man's consciousness and conveyed numerous associations. In the Christian tradition, flowers are generally a symbol of love; in the intellectual world of the Reformation, they evoked the idea of fate and transience. In the botanical world, flowers were associated with scholarship and knowledge; in mythology, they represent metamorphosis, a vital natural force appealing to the emotions.

In seeking the symbolic meaning of flower motifs, differing answers will be found, depending on the viewer and the time in which he lives. There are many links between religious-Christian and pantheistic-philosophical ways of thinking. The frame of reference may include erotic as well as social and spiritual ideas. In the beginning, botanical science was completely in the service of the Christian faith. As of the mid-sixteenth century, Piero Valeriano's work *Hieroglyphica sive de sacris* (Basel 1556), including a whole volume on the symbolic meaning of flowers and plants, was probably part of every educated artist's library. In 1593, Joachim II Camerarius, botanist and son of a famous humanist and member of the Reformed church, published his first emblem book with floral symbolism as a moralizing textbook, *Symbolorum et emblematum ex re herbaria* (Nuremberg 1593). Catholic emblem books were published at the same time. The Jesuit Jacob Masen's *Speculum imaginum veritatis occultae* (Cologne 1650) and Abbé Picinelli's *Mondo symbolico* (Milan 1654) were used at the time as symbolic, mythological and biblical dictionaries. Numerous theses by Jesuits, whose emblem books on flowers were written in the spirit of Ignatius Loyola, deal with the world of the imagination and the senses.

The books of symbols and encyclopaedias of the day certainly do not have a common concept concerning the objects they describe; the authors often wanted to add something original to their predecessors' interpretations. Picinelli, in particular, drew up lists of interpretations with partly contrasting symbolic meanings in his *Mondo symbolico*. What mattered was reaching a comprehensive whole in the overall interpretation, even if it meant accepting differing symbolic meanings and ambiguity. The viewer can interpret the motif as good or evil, significant or not, as he wishes. Allegories of the five senses refer to the ambivalence of human nature. Flowers can seduce one person into shameful lust and provide another with certainty of God's presence in nature.

The interpretation of 'the Flower and the Woman,' for example, differs according to the concepts of the period. Where the flower, together with female beauty and love, was viewed benevolently up until the late Middle Ages, the motif was seen as a warning against depravity during the Reformation (fig. 39). With the spread of Christian moral norms during the sixteenth century, the love idealized in the age of

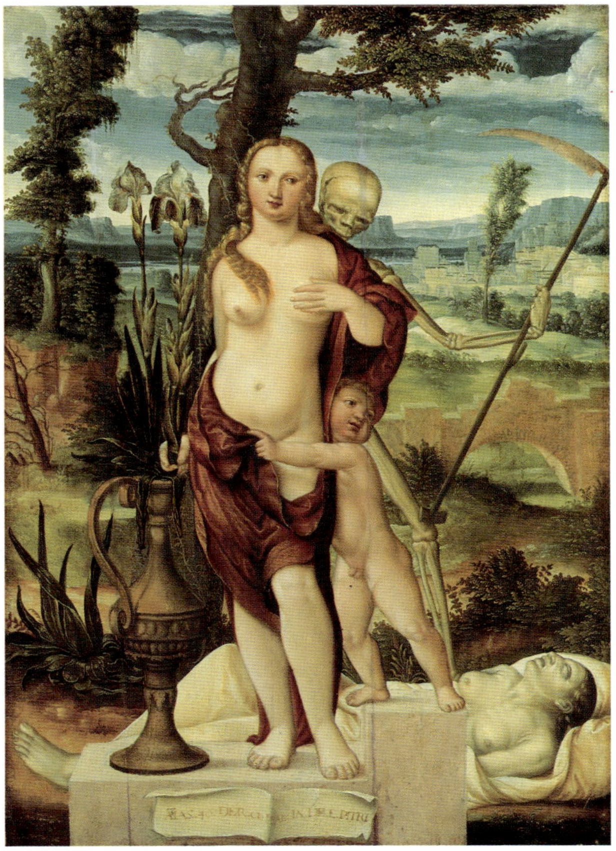

39 Bartel Beham, *Woman, flower and death*. Oil on canvas. 1540
Hamburger Kunsthalle, Hamburg

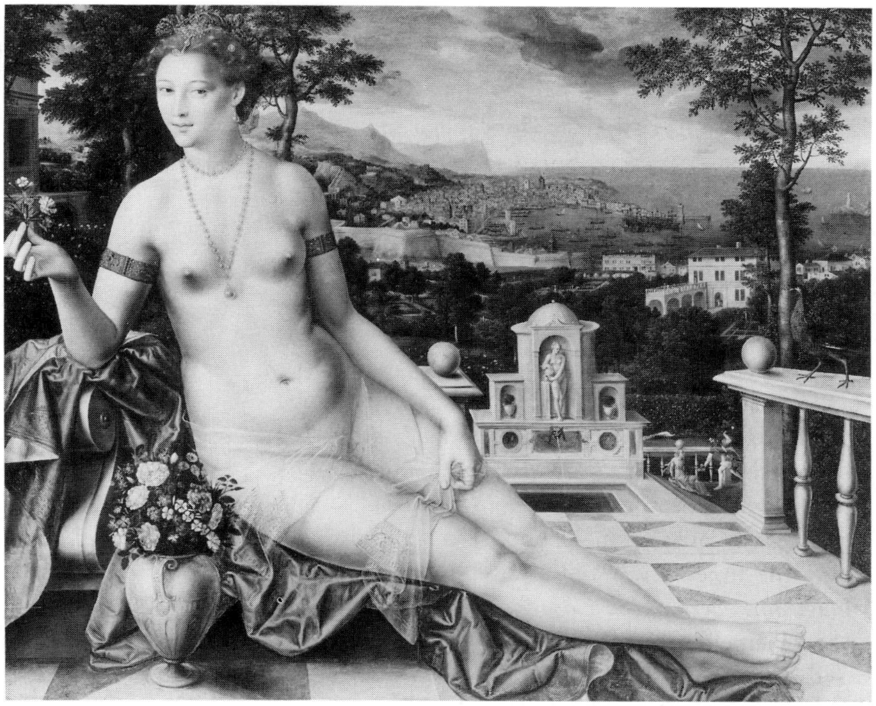

40 Jan Massys, *Flora*. Oil on panel. 1561. The city of Genoa is seen in the background. In a very similar painting in the Kunsthalle, Hamburg, the city is replaced with a Dutch landscape. Swedish war booty from Prague
Nationalmuseum, Stockholm

chivalry decayed, and the motif of flower and woman combined with death became a theme of seduction and vanity.

In contrast, the Virgin Mary was exalted and the symbols of earthly and celestial love merged. 'Mary and Her Garden' became the symbol of the living paradise. The flowering meadow around her indicates her predominant qualities: love, virginity, nobility and self-sacrifice. After the Reformation, the Virgin Mary's flowers became symbols of Christ as well.

The lily of the valley stands for the birth of Jesus and the joy to come. The lily's radiant whiteness signifies chastity, purity and virginity. In a bouquet of flowers, the lily can be seen not only as a symbol of Mary's Immaculate Conception, but also as a sign of God's grace and justice on the Day of Judgement. The columbine symbolizes the Holy Ghost; seven flowers of the same kind can be interpreted as the seven sorrows of the Virgin; the anemone for disease and death. Since the fifteenth century, marguerites have been equated with innocence. The hyacinth represents wisdom and a longing for heaven. The carnation's main meaning is salvation through Christ's suffering; violets designate humility.

The rose is Mary's most important floral symbol. During antiquity, the rose was the flower of Venus, dedicated to love and its magic. In Christian tradition, the rose was changed into a symbol of the Virgin Mary and her heavenly, unspoken love. Words spoken under the rose, sub rosa, must not be repeated. Thus, there is often a rose in the middle of the canopy of the confessional.

A flower's symbolic meaning may also vary according to fashion, i.e., public acceptance or rejection, depending on cultural, political and economic conditions. Jan Massys' *Flora* (fig. 40), from ca. 1560, evokes Ovid's story about the high-class Roman whore and the floralia's exuberant flower festivals of ancient Rome (*Fasti,* verses 200-206), and also wealth, luxury, feasts and fertility in Dutch aristocratic and high bourgeois circles. Massys' *Flora* resembles one of the nudes in Francis I's castle of Fontainebleau; the bouquet, with its cultivated floral rarities, alludes to the aristocracy's love of fragrant beauty and status symbols. The carnation – in religious pictures and portraits an indication of Christ's sacrificial death and resurrection and thus man's hope for salvation through Christ's suffering – is profaned into an aphrodisiac in the hand of Flora.

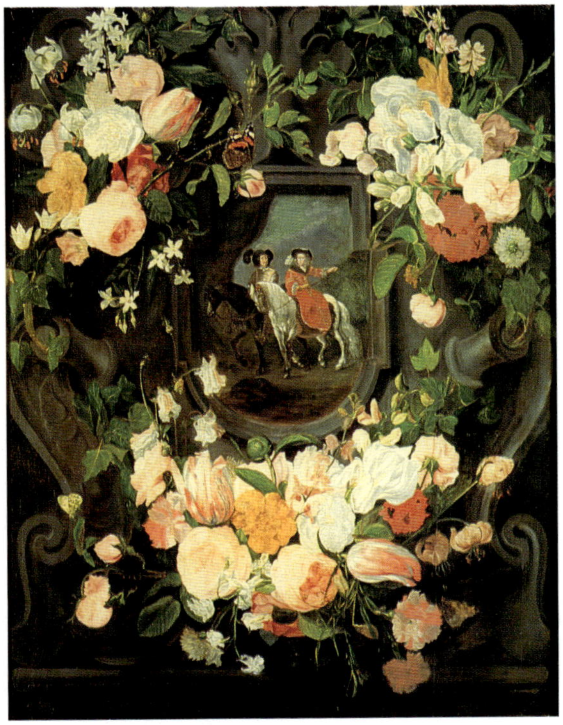

41 Ottmar Elliger the Elder, *Frederik* III *and Sophie Amalie on horseback* in a cartouche decorated with flowers. Oil on canvas. Denmark ca. 1654
The Royal Collections, Rosenborg Palace, Copenhagen (*cat. 4*)

The flower as an emblem of divine nature – A tricoloured floral bouquet or the placing of three flowers of the same colour in a conspicuous place in the picture's composition can be seen as a Christian symbol of the Holy Trinity.

Festoons and flower wreaths were originally antique decorative elements. However, they acquired their most realistic significance and religious symbolism with the pantheistic trends of Mannerist painting and as a motif among seventeenth-century flower painters in Antwerp. Radiant light and glowing colours characterize the flowers surrounding a religious scene when 'Velvet Brueghel' used a flower festoon as a compositional element. Flower wreaths emphasize the consecrated character of the motif and the dignity and virtues of the persons portrayed (fig. 41). The Virgin Mary surrounded by a wreath of flowers becomes a devotional motif, and the Virgin Mary herself a cult figure. The motif with the flower bouquet in a stone niche can also correspond to the enclosed garden as a sacred place.

The flower as an allegory of earthly nature – With the flower as an allegory of earthly nature, we reach the imagery of the five senses. The floral splendour of a garden is visually alluring, and erotic sensuality is evoked when a nude reposes in its midst. Since the late Middle Ages, this image has lent wings to poets' fantasies. 'Velvet Brueghel' and others painted this motif of a nude in the midst of an intoxicating abundance of flowers, yet its evocation of desire was condemned by Christian morality as depraved and an obstacle to the soul's salvation.

People attributed greater significance then to the flowers' fragrance than we do today. According to Francis Bacon, Queen Elizabeth I's Lord Chancellor, flowers for the gardens were selected by taking their scent into consideration: 'The fragrance of the flowers drifts like music through the air.' During the seventeenth century, the image of a woman with a vase of flowers is an allegory of the five senses, generally the sense of smell. In Wilhelm Altzenbach's series of engravings, allegorical scenes of the senses are represented in cartouches on vases filled with opulent bouquets (fig. 42).

In Vredeman de Vries' theoretical book on architectural styles, 'Odour' is juxtaposed with the Ionic style. A noblewoman sits on the stairs by a large peristyle and picks a flower from the vase in front of her. To see the human body in harmony with the styles of antique architecture was originally a Vitruvian concept. It was taken up again in Vredeman de Vries' theories, which excercized great influence on North European architecture, particularly garden architecture.

Even without such an architectural framework, the picture of a woman with a flower vase such as 'Odour' or *Odoratus sensorium* is the well-known symbol of the sense of smell (fig. 43). Maerten de Vos (1563-1603), a pupil of Frans Floris in Antwerp, also drew a series of the five senses, the favourite motif of the late-sixteenth and early-seventeenth centuries. The sense of smell was represented allegorically by a flower-bedecked woman with a large vase on her lap. With the biblical background scenes of Christ with

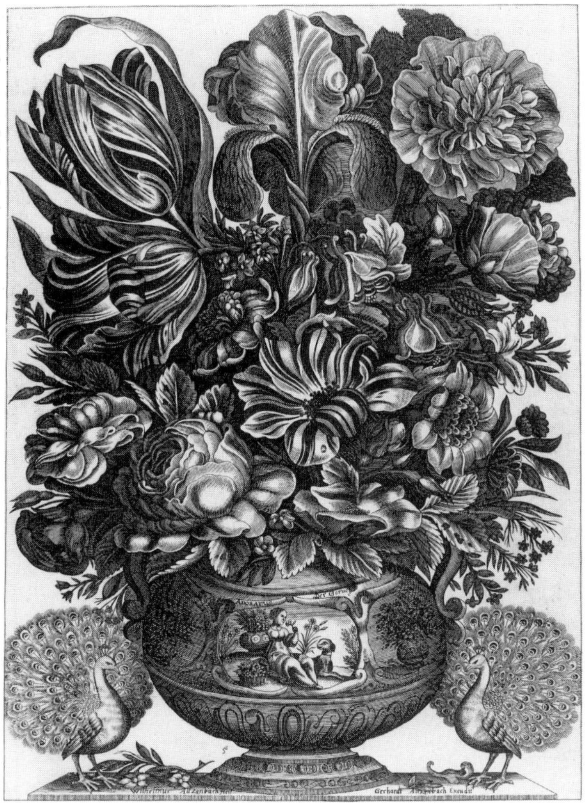

42 Wilhelm Altzenbach, *Flower vase*. Allegory of the sense of smell. Engraving after J. Toussyn. Seventeenth century
Kunstindustrimuseet, Copenhagen (*cat. 51*)

Adam and Simon, the image is a typical example of the contemporary taste for mingling biblical, mythological and allegorical scenes. According to Fr. Barberino's *Documenti d'Amore* (Rome 1640), the motif of a woman with a flower vase may also signify 'discretion,' i.e., an homage to women's tact, modesty and reserve. In a printed illustration by Lorenz Greuter, a woman is shown in the middle of the scene picking flowers from a vase. She discards the thorns and places the flowers in a basket held by a cupid.

The four seasons and the four elements (water, earth, air and fire) are often alluded to in floral pictures. The floral cycle reflects the changing seasons and thus with their references to the four seasons and the four elements, flowers unite natural phenomena into an understandable whole.

Fauna around a painted floral bouquet has a religious, moral, or physical symbolic meaning. The butterfly and the dragonfly, symbols of the spirit and the soul, may be placed in opposition to the lizard and the fly, representatives of death and decay. Birds and insects are taken to symbolize the *vita activa*, while flowers stand for the *vita complentativa*. The white butterfly signifies 'day,' the moth and beetle 'night.' The age's interest in the lives of insects and the metamorphosis of butterflies is apparent from Johannes Goedaert's *Metamorfosis naturalis* and Maria Sibylla Merian's work *Der Raupen wunderbare Verwandlung* (1679, 1685). The butterfly pollinates the flowers and thus serves to propagate the species. Metaphysically, the metamorphosis of the butterfly, the transformation from imago to flying insect, was seen as the beginning of life after death – resurrection.

The flower as a symbol of transitoriness – The flower's association with transience may best be described in the words of the Bible: 'For all flesh is as grass, and all the glory thereof as the flower of grass. The grass withereth, and the flower falleth. But the word of the Lord abideth for ever' (1 Peter 1:24-25). Thus the limited time flowers can be enjoyed before they wither and die leads one's thoughts to the transitory nature of human life on earth. The flower's melancholy aspect is expressed in our realization of its beauty; simultaneously we realize the futility of fighting our fate.

Since flowers were still considered a precious luxury during the seventeenth century, they became associated with *vanitas*. The motif of a skull and withered leaves recalls the necessity of ultimately parting from worldly possessions.

The *vanitas* aspect is emphasized when the flowers in a bouquet are depicted in minute detail, and with almost luminescent colour. Naturalism and illusionism in such paintings result in a sensual surface which we recognize, but which exists only seemingly. The symbolism of the flower bouquet and its aesthetics can also be found in the words of Job: 'He cometh forth like a flower, and is cut down. He fleeth also as a shadow, and continueth not' (Job 14:2).

Tulipomania – The tulip made its advent in Europe in the mid-sixteenth century. From Turkey via the court

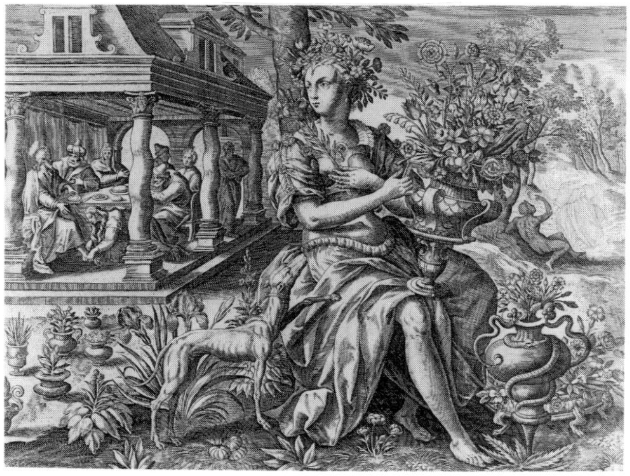

43 Adrian Collaert, *The sense of Smell*. Engraving. The Netherlands seventeenth century
Den kongelige Kobberstiksamling, Statens Museum for Kunst, Copenhagen (*cat. 45*)

in Vienna, it began its triumphal progress from princely to bourgeois and peasant gardens. As a wild tulip – and in any number of cultivated variants – it became the most popular garden flower of all time. Its regular, even shape lends itself just as much to realistic artistic representation as to stylization, which ensured it equally wide distribution in folk culture and in the visual arts.

It was a big step from the modest wild, rather small, tulip's blue-gray leaves and white-yellow flower to the cultivated tulip the size of a goose egg. The colour scale ranges from indeterminable colour combinations to dark, esoteric, deep tones – from variegated, pure colours to pastel shades. Its otherwise firm and clear floral structure is sometimes transformed into irregularly lacinated, creased, or curly shapes. It blooms early and quickly in spring and is as colourful as it is unpredictable. When tulipomania raged from about 1630 to 1637, certain bulb species were weighed against gold and diamonds. Passions ran high: tulipomania was soon confronted by tulipophobia.

The tulip was introduced into Europe together with other spring flowers from the East: the narcissus, the crocus, the anemone, the crown imperial and the hyacinth, all vernal, delicate, elegant flowers with remarkable colours and sweet scents. In Turkey, the tulip grew wild. This wild variety, called *lalé*, is smaller than cultivated types and is fragrant. Among the cultivated species, the acufoliate *Tulipa acuminata* was preferred. The first tulip vogue culminated in Turkey during the reign of Suleiman the Great (1520-1566). Every spring, lavish flower festivals were held with the tulip as first lady.

The tulip in Europe – In Europe, the tulip became known through contact with the Ottoman court in Constantinople. In spite of the Turkish wars, trade with the empire was never interrupted. Augier Ghislain de Busbecq (1522-1592), the Austrian Emperor Ferdinand I's Ambassador, described the sight of all the wonderful winter flowers in a letter from A-

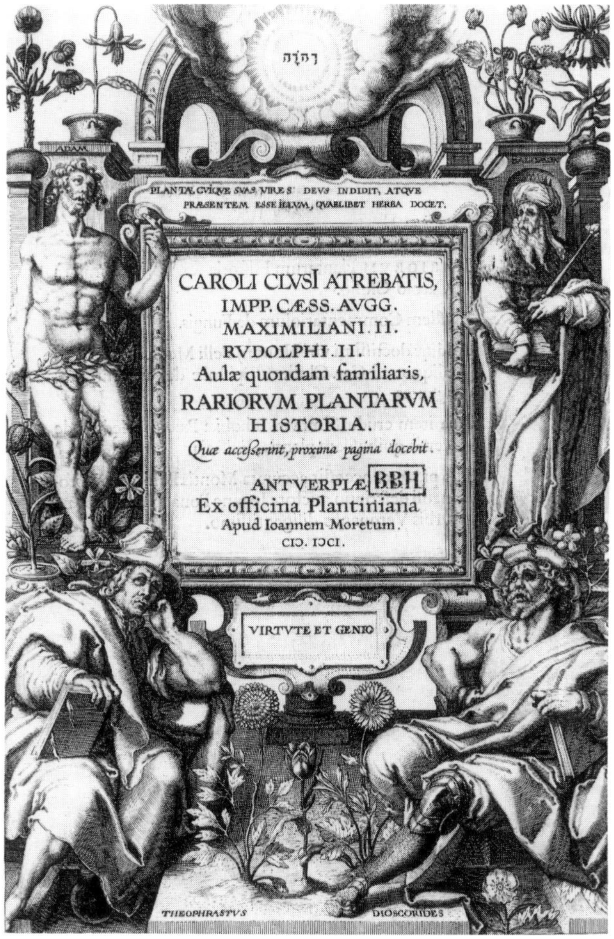

44 Carolus Clusius, *Rariorum Plantarum Historiae*, Antwerp 1601. Title page
Botanisk Centralbibliotek, Copenhagen

drianopel (Edirne) in 1555. He erroneously called the wild tulip 'Tulipam,' which in Turkish means turban, to which the form of the flower was compared. Gislain de Busbecq probably sent seeds and tulip bulbs to Vienna. From there they later found their way to the botanical gardens of the European nobility in Germany, France and the Netherlands, and especially to Europe's newly founded botanical gardens.

The natural scientist Conrad Gessner of Zürich saw the tulip in Augsburg and described it for the first time in his book *Hortus Germaniæ* (1561). The Dutch botanist Carolus Clusius played a key role in the dissemination of the tulip in Europe. After his appointment as head of the botanical garden in Leiden in 1592, he experimented with cloning tulip bulbs. He had noticed the tulip's capacity for variation and maintained scientific contacts with the leading botanists in Europe, exchanging plants and information. The painter Jacques de Gheyn portrayed the internationally renowned man. On the title page of Carolus Clusius' book, *Rariorum Plantarum Historiae* (Antwerp 1601, fig. 44), the tulip holds the place of honour, flanked by Theophrastus, the philosopher and father of botany, and Dioscorides, known for his books on medicinal plants.

Emmanuel Sweert's *Florilegium* (Frankfurt 1612, fig. 6), Crispin de Pas' *Hortus Floridus* (Arnhem 1614, fig. 7), and Johann Theodor de Bry's *Florilegium novum* (1611) definitively established the rage for tulips in Europe. The many fine engraved illustrations with sparse texts in the florilegia provided patterns for artists and craftsmen. First as the flower of the privileged and later also as a wealthy citizen's status symbol, the tulip's unparalleled fame reached Dutch and German cities and from the 1620s spread throughout the Netherlands, France and western Germany.

In England, the royal gardener dynasty, the Tradescants, cultivated the tulip under Charles I and Charles II (1600-1685). It might have been the contact with the Tradescants that inspired the pharmacist John Parkinson to publish his book *Paradisi in sole* (London 1629, fig. 45). In his sunny garden several exotic flower species sprouted, among which the tulip held a central place. On the title page's illustration, he promoted the flowers, spices and fruit trees suitable for growing in England, to recreate 'paradise on earth.'

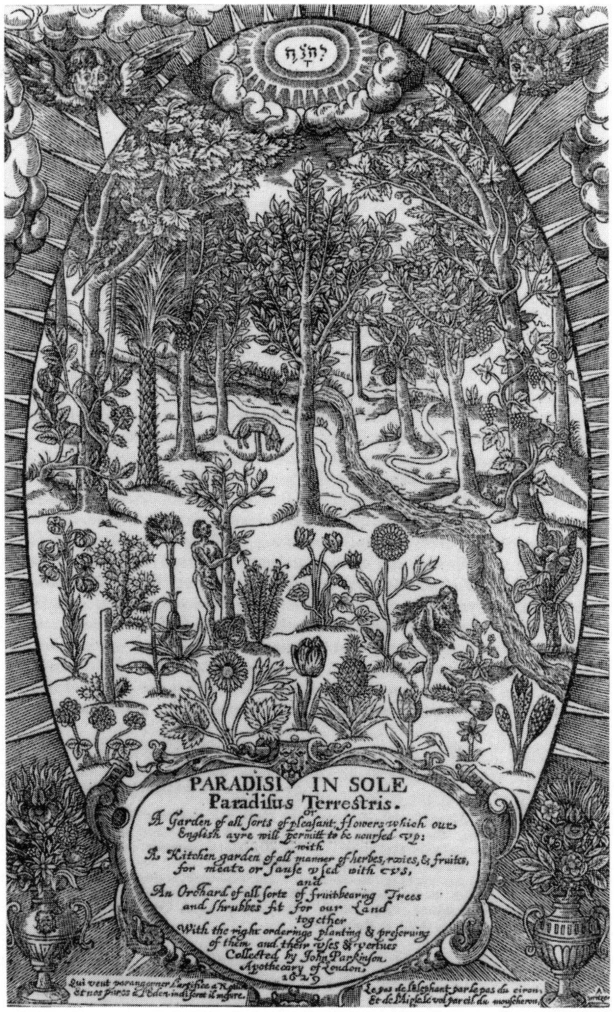

45 John Parkinson, *Paradisi in sole*, London 1629. Title page

Tulipomania, horticulture unbound – The variegated richness of the tulip is due to its spontaneous cross-fertilization via pollination in the garden. The result is the admixture of colours into more or less contrasting patterns. When a dark colour on light ground runs along the edge of a petal, it is the result of a rare and complicated process of hybridization. However, the variation can also be due to viral attack on the bulbs. In this case, one finds feathery traces of colour on fair leaves and at the same time the tulip behaves like a chameleon, varying its appearance unpredictably from sprouting to sprouting. The virus infection is transferred from mother to daughter plants.

In a hierarchical age, people soon became absorbed in establishing an order of precedence for tulips which led to fashions. Multicoloured tulips, already seen in Roelandt Savery's and 'Velvet Brueghel's' painted bouquets, were much in demand. Flamed or spotted patterns like those on feathers were highly valued. Among the monocoloured tulips, the order of precedence went from the bright to the black tulip. Most prized was the pale-blue tulip, although 'only few people had ever seen it' (*Zedlers Universal Lexikon,* Halle/Leipzig 1732-50).

The tulip connoisseurs' taste is clearly apparent in contemporary flower paintings (cat. 6). Clues to the dating and provenance of these pictures can also be found, since Flanders and Holland did not value the same tulip varieties. Among the most popular tulip painters were the Dutchmen Herman Hengstenburgh and Simon Verelst (fig. 38), the latter favoured by the Duke of Buckingham. His paintings of white-pied tulips were especially renowned for their wonderful brilliance.

As a result of the value placed on the tulip, it not only appeared in elaborately arranged bouquets, but was also depicted as a plant growing in a flower bed. This novel motif was taken up again by nineteenth century painters. Artists such as Van Gogh and Emil Nolde painted entire borders (cat. 41, 42), and flower beds in sunny colours appear in Monet's garden pictures.

The simple shape of the tulip is easy to stylize and its colourful variations made it suitable as a decorative motif in all branches of handicraft. From the middle of the seventeenth century, tulips have been found in tapestries and embroidery, on porcelain and faience. It was the favourite flower of the French kings Louis XIII and Louis XIV (figs. 46, 47, 49).

The tulip's erect, regular bell shape was subsequently incorporated into folk art. The popularity of the tulip culminated once again in the floral world of eighteenth century folk art. As a stylized motif, with little consideration for botanical details, the tulip was often combined with herbal ornaments.

The collapse of tulipomania – The rage for tulips ended dramatically. The botanist Carolus Clusius demanded high prices for his cultivated tulip bulbs. With the growing fame of rare species, prices increased so exorbitantly that wealthy citizens saw the

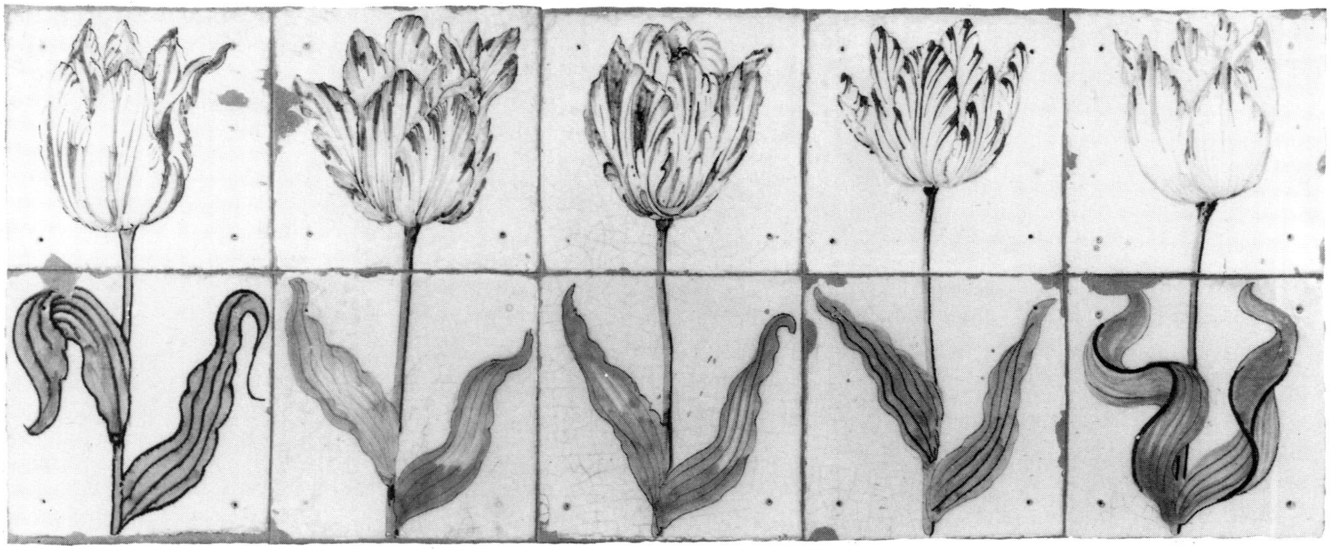

46 *Tile picture*. Tin-glazed earthenware. Ten tiles with multicoloured tulips. Hoorn, the Netherlands ca. 1640. Museum Boymans-van Beuningen, Rotterdam (*cat. 139*)

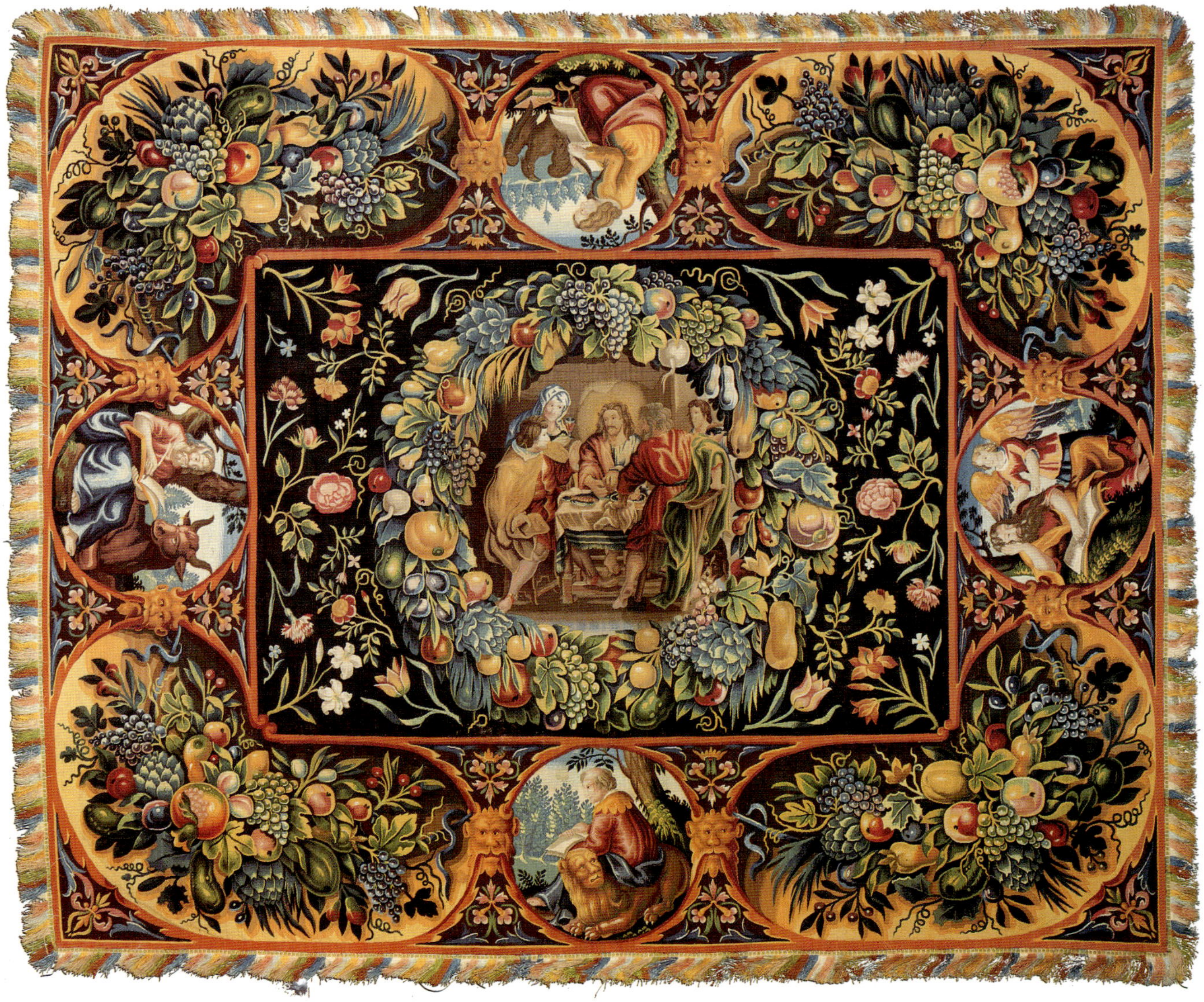

47 *Table cover*. Wool and silk tapestry. Central figure scene with Christ at Emmaus framed by fruit vine and scattered flowers. Border with the evangelists' symbols and fruit festoons. Delft or Gouda, the Netherlands mid-seventeenth century
Her Majesty Queen Margrethe of Denmark (*cat. 277*)

tulip as a means of investment. In the 1630s, a 'Viceroy' cost 10,000 guilders, the price of a large house. In the Netherlands, the same situation prevailed for shells. A few species had become similar objects of speculation, and the market could sustain itself only as long as their rarity could be guaranteed. Like shells, flowers were imported from Asia Minor, southern Europe, America and South Africa, reflecting European trade routes.

How precious tulips and shells were in the local economy becomes apparent when we see them as individual portraits in still lifes. As showpieces, they made great demands on the artist: they needed to be 'aesthetically readable.'

Shells are nature's works of art and cannot be cultivated. In contrast, tulips can be cultivated in many hundreds of variants. With nature's help, the tulip became a brilliant work of art under human guidance, proof of the ingenuity of botanists and gardeners. The cloning of tulip bulbs, the innumerable ways in which wild tulips and the most highly developed hybrid plants could be combined and cross-pollinated, were still in line with Mannerist art and the age's love of collections. Tulips thus became part of the sixteenth century's *Kunst- und Wunderkammer* tradition. Around 1630, the number of species grew to several hundred. They were initially named after famous generals, admirals and commanders; royal names had fallen into disfavour in the Netherlands at that time. After 1637, the nomenclature was restricted to a simple numbering of the species (fig. 48).

Tulips had to be bought and sold when the bulbs were not germinating, i.e., from May to October. To give the potential buyer a visual impression of the flower, artists were engaged to make garden catalogues with the tulips depicted in watercolour, gouache or etching from natural models. As time went on, the bulbs themselves were no longer on the table during business negotiations; certificates and a picture of the tulip concerned sufficed. At least seventeen tulip books have been preserved; particularly outstanding are the works by Judith Leyster (Frans Halsmuseum, Haarlem), Anthony Claesz (spread over several collections), and Jacob Marell (Rijksprentenkabinet, Amsterdam). Judith Leyster's tulip watercolours served, among others, as patterns for decorations on Delft faience.

Flower painters were an important factor in maintaining tulipomania and its commercial aspects. A depiction of the tulip prior to a purchase of the bulb was important for the seller's credibility. But in 1637, prices dropped drastically – especially due to the discovery of a simpler and faster way of reproducing the bulbs. In part, because of the hybridogene nature of the tulip and its vulnerability to viruses, tulips as objects of speculation were no longer attractive. The abundance of variations and their unpredictability had reached the stage at which pictorial description and reality no longer coincided. Even attempts by the States General to help prevent financial ruin were in vain; tulipomania ended in a collapse.

Symbol, emblem and satire – Symbolism in floral still lifes often reflects the contemporary political and economic situation; the tulip was associated – particularly while the epidemic vogue was still raging – with elegant extravagance and lavishness, i.e., with *vanitas.* As the tulip trade had elicited a welcome dynamism in the economic as well as the social structure, in the eyes of the speculators, the tulip motif became an emblem of luck, *Fortuna.*

In the golden age of Dutch culture, when drama and farce were never far apart, tulip fever frequently engendered pictorial parodies. As was the case during the Reformation with the German artist Sebastian Brant's satires of human folly and blindness, Dutch artists pilloried the rage for tulips.

Roemer Visscher was quick to find a motto: 'A fool and his money are soon parted' (*Sinnepoppen,* Amsterdam 1614). With the tulip as a warning, he satirized the Dutch citizens' hectic stock-exchange fraud. Jan Brueghel II ridiculed the tulip trade by letting the monkey in the satirical iconography serve as a symbol of human folly. In Crispin de Pas' allegory

48 ▸ *Tulip cabinet.* Ebony veneer, mother of pearl inlay, the inside drawers painted with multicoloured tulips. The Netherlands second half of the seventeenth century
Museum Boymans-van Beuningen, Rotterdam (*cat. 252*)

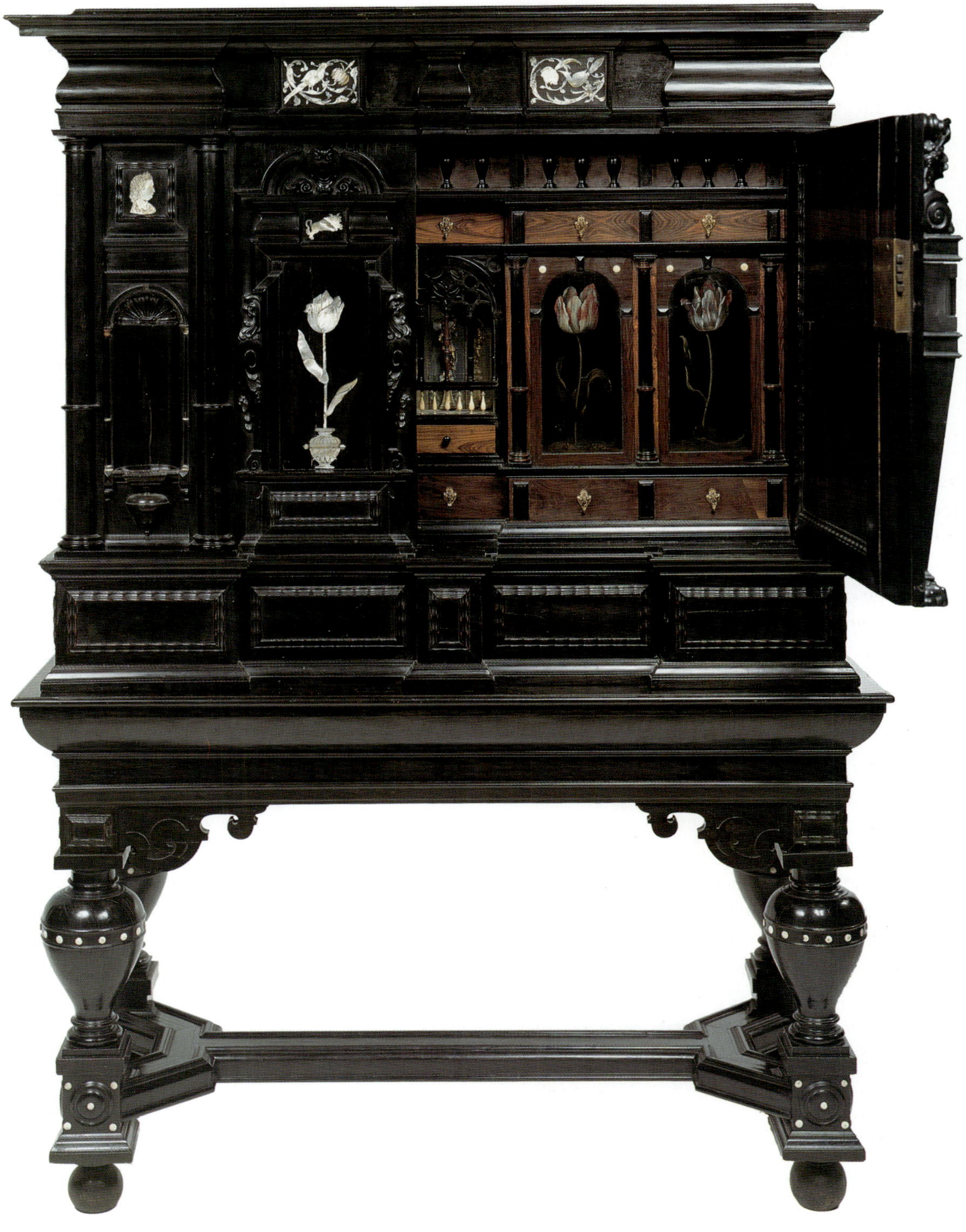

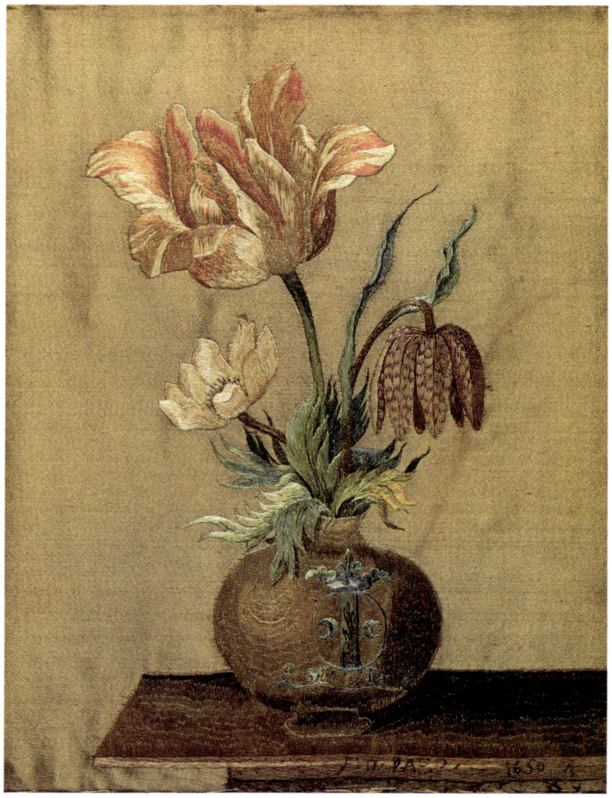

49 *Flower piece*. Coloured silk embroidered on brownish satin. F. v. Paep?. The Netherlands 1650
Kunstindustrimuseet, Copenhagen (*cat. 276*)

50 Hendrik Gerritszoon, *Floras Mallewagen*. Oil on canvas
Frans Halsmuseum, Haarlem

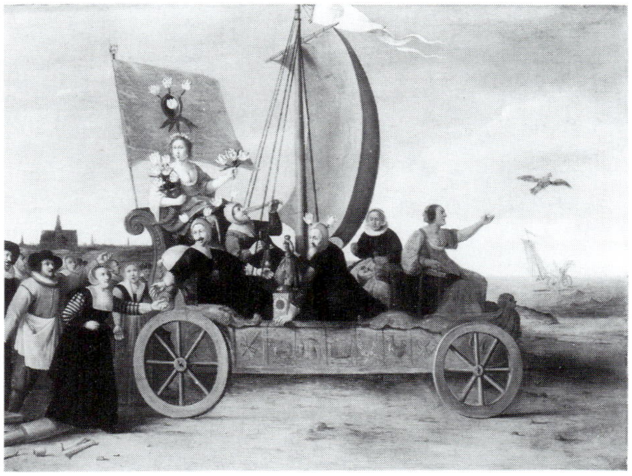

Floras Mallewagen (1637), Flora decorated with tulips, and well-dressed people with fools' caps sit in a triumphal chariot with sails set (fig. 50). In the background, the chariot is shown capsizing – the well-known symbol of *navigatio vitae* – steered by false hope.

Since the beginning of the seventeenth century, flowers have been part of our everyday life. Although tulipomania degenerated into gambling by stockbrokers, this enthusiasm originated from the high esteem accorded the flower itself. What a pleasure it must have been in the middle of the seventeenth century to wander in the Berliner pleasure garden, the famous Teatrum Tuliparum (1647-48).

Saskia de Bodt

An encyclopaedia of forms
Artists and their gardens in the second half of the nineteenth century

Anyone investigating flowers and plants as a source for ornament and decoration in the (applied) arts of the second half of the nineteenth century, inevitably ends up considering theorization about ornament in general.[1] According to Emile Gallé (1846-1904), modernity in the applied arts means that an object must be useful to modern man, that is, it must be logically and practically constructed and have no excessive decoration. For Gallé, beauty meant 'natural' form and decoration and – in his opinion – the most satisfactory of all decorative motifs was the floral motif.[2] Gallé, one of the most influential artists of the Art Nouveau movement, does not fundamentally differ in theory here from Henry Cole (1808-1882), one of Britain's most important reformers in the field of design. Cole, who organized the Great Exhibition of 1851 in London and who was the founder and first director of the South Kensington Museum, later to be known as the Victoria & Albert Museum, appealed to the Victorians for 'appropriate ornament,' by which he meant naturalistic rather than historicizing ornament. In Britain, this literally meant, at least initially, ears of corn as the handles of a breadbasket and bunches of grapes on a wine jug.

The radical innovators of the proto-Art Nouveau movement were the theoretician John Ruskin and designers such as William Morris (1834-1896) and, later on, Walter Crane, who assigned a more profound significance to decoration. Decoration has its purpose and meaning and is never there for nothing, argued William Morris in 1877 in a lecture entitled *The lesser Arts*. 'For [...] everything made by man's hands has a form, which must be either beautiful or ugly; beautiful if it is in accord with Nature, and helps her; ugly if it is discordant with Nature, and thwarts her; it cannot be indifferent. [...] Now it is one of the chief uses of decoration, the chief part of its alliance with nature, that it has to sharpen our dulled senses in this matter: for this end are those wonders of intricate patterns interwoven, those strange forms invented, which men have so long delighted in.'[3] Furthermore, Ruskin urged all artists, whether free or not, never to see themselves as mere decorators and 'artificers' but to proceed using their own perceptions and sensibilities and to study nature as closely as possible. For through nature it is possible to convey the essence of life itself.[4] This same idea is expressed in the above-mentioned theoretical article by Gallé, which deals specifically with the art of furniture design. By faithfully following the natural lines of appropriately chosen plants, the logic and essence of life itself will become one (fig. 51).[5]

To a certain extent, the pictorial and the applied arts were experiencing the same developments. For instance, studying nature – a practice followed by the Barbizon painters – was an important part of the artistic creed. The weakening of the dividing line between fine art and the applied arts is particularly evident in the work of the Pre-Raphaelites and their contemporaries, where a shift sometimes occurs and nature plays a more dominant role. As in the garden poetry of Tennyson and other Victorian writers, nature is given greater prominence. This is apparent, for example, in the work of Edward Burne-Jones (1833-1898) where the same attention is given to flowers and vegetation as to figures. *Flora* by Burne-Jones's follower Evelyn de Morgan (1855-1919) is an almost purely decorative work, as are Dante Gabriel Rossetti's (1828-1882) *La Ghirlandata* (1873, Guildhall Art Gallery, London) and *A Vision of Fiametta* (1878, private collection). At the same time, the ornamentation on the vases and plates of potter and writer William de Morgan (1839-1917) make them decorative works rather than utensils.

The period which saw major innovations in the field of design in Britain dating from the 1850s up to and including the flowering of the Art Nouveau movement in France, also witnessed the climax in the use of naturalistic decoration in general and floral and plant motifs in particular. It is my intention here to discuss the relationship of a number of important artists with nature – which they so diligently studied – the landscape around them and, in particular, with their own gardens. It is important, argued William Morris in *The lesser Arts of Life (1882)*, to transform the walls of our rooms into a green June forest or a summer garden.[6] 'The use of significant plants in your patterns and the reference to gardens and fields, trees, boughs and tendrils is essential.'[7]

What did William Morris's own gardens look like? And what were his ideas and those of his colleagues Dante Gabriel Rossetti, Ford Maddox Brown, Edward Burne-Jones, William and Evelyn de Morgan concerning gardens and nature? Furthermore, what significance did Emile Gallé attach to gardens? Which artists drew their main inspiration from their own gardens? The following discussion is the result of provisional research during which it became clear that information concerning artists' gardens is, on the whole, scarce and widely scattered. There are some notable exceptions, such as Claude Monet's famous garden at his home in Giverny and Emil Nolde's garden at his last studio in Seebüll (near Niebühl, Schleswig-Holstein), both of which have been restored and attract huge numbers of visitors. It is not within the scope of this brief discussion to provide analyses of gardens. It is, however, relevant in the context of an exhibition about the treasures of Flora, to consider the extent to which a number of artists – in whose development floral/natural motifs played a significant role – sought to bend nature to their will. How some of them actually carried this out in practice is another question, which cannot be discussed here, but possibly at a later date, after follow-up research.

The fact that Henri Fantin-Latour (1836-1904), who frequently moved house in Paris, used the garden of Buré (L'Orne) where he stayed during the summer solely for picking the flowers which he subsequently painted indoors,[8] is just as significant in this context as Dante Gabriel Rossetti joking that he intended to heat his garden with hot water pipes in

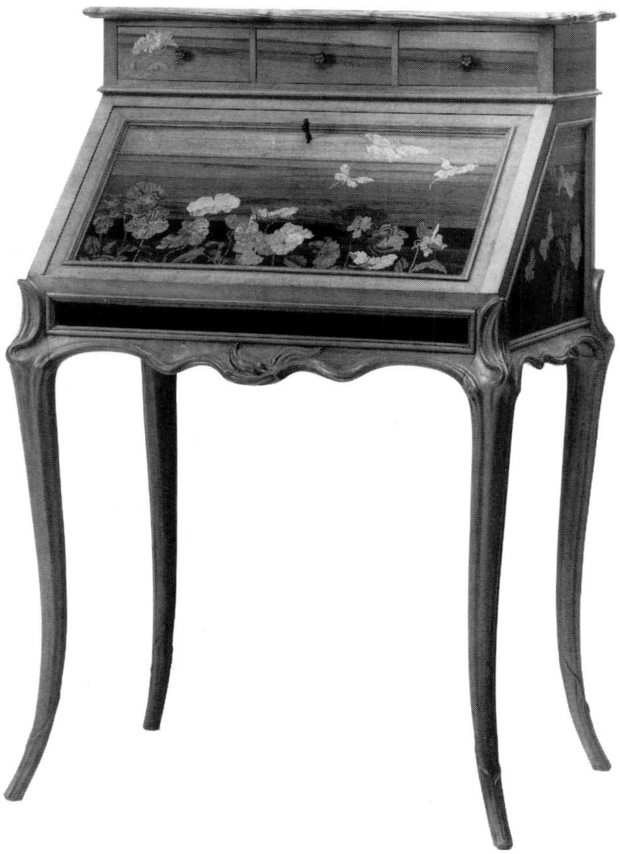

51 Émile Gallé, *Ladies writing desk, 'Bureau Pensée.'* Nancy, France 1900 Kunstindustrimuseet, Copenhagen (*cat. 254*)

order to keep a lion there.[9] As, indeed, is the fact that the De Morgans contributed significantly to the urbanization which they deplored – of rural Chelsea by digging up a large part of their garden at The Vale to build a huge studio for Evelyn, after which they promptly left for Italy to gain inspiration in the gardens of Florence.[10]

William Morris – 'Gardens are a reflection of their owner,' wrote Alfred Austin, a friend of William and Evelyn de Morgan, in *The Garden that I Love* (1896, p. 112): 'A garden that one makes oneself becomes associated with one's personal history and that of one's friends [...] and constitutes a sort of unwritten, but withal, manifest autobiography.' It is not surprising that William Morris's gardens were based on the idealized picture of the Middle Ages which prevailed at that time, for Morris had been fascinated by the medieval period ever since his student days. In 1858, two years before he moved into his own 'medieval' home, Red House, Morris described such a garden in his poem 'Golden Wings.'[11]

Midways of a walled garden,
In the happy poplar land,
Did an ancient castle stand,
With an old Knight for a warden.

Many scarlet bricks there were
In its walls, and old grey stone;
Over which red apples shone
At the right time of the year.

On the bricks the green moss grew,
Yellow lichen on the stone,
over which red apples shone;
Little war that castle knew.
[...]

In 1859, William Morris commissioned the architect Philip Webb to build him his own 'castle,' Red House. He had bought land for this purpose in Upton near Bexley Heath, Kent; 'a roadside orchard surrounded by meadows,' with so much space that the house could be built without having to chop down many trees.[12] Georgiana Burne-Jones, wife of the painter and one of the co-founders of Morris & Co., Edward Burne-Jones, gives a clear description of the gardens at Red House and the surrounding greenery: 'Many flowering creepers had been planted against the walls of the house from the earliest possible time, so that there was no look of raw newness about it; and the garden, beautified beforehand by the apple-trees, quickly took shape. In front of the house it was spaced formally into four little square gardens making a big square together; each of the smaller squares had a walled fence round it with an opening by which one entered, and all over the fence roses grew thickly.'[13] In one corner of the garden was a stable; further, there were two porches, one at the front and the other at the rear of the house. The latter porch was practically a small garden room, with a table and a bench where Georgiana often sat together with Morris's young wife and model, Jane: '[...] and talked and looked into the well-court, of which two sides were formed by the house and the other two by a tall rose-trellis. This little court with its beautiful high-roofed brick well in the centre summed up the feeling of the whole place' (fig. 52).

A writer, not mentioned by name, who is quoted by a friend of Morris', Aymer Vallance, in the biography published by the latter a year after Morris' death adds: 'The first sight of the Red House in 1863 gave me an astonished pleasure. [...] the surrounding garden divided into many squares, hedged by sweetbriar or wild rose, each enclosure with its own particular show of flowers; on this side a green alley with

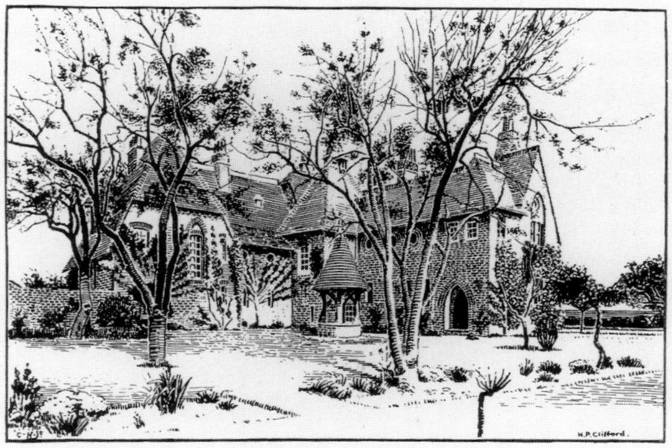

52 William Morris' *Red House*. Built by architect Philipp Webb 1860. Drawing by H. P. Clifford

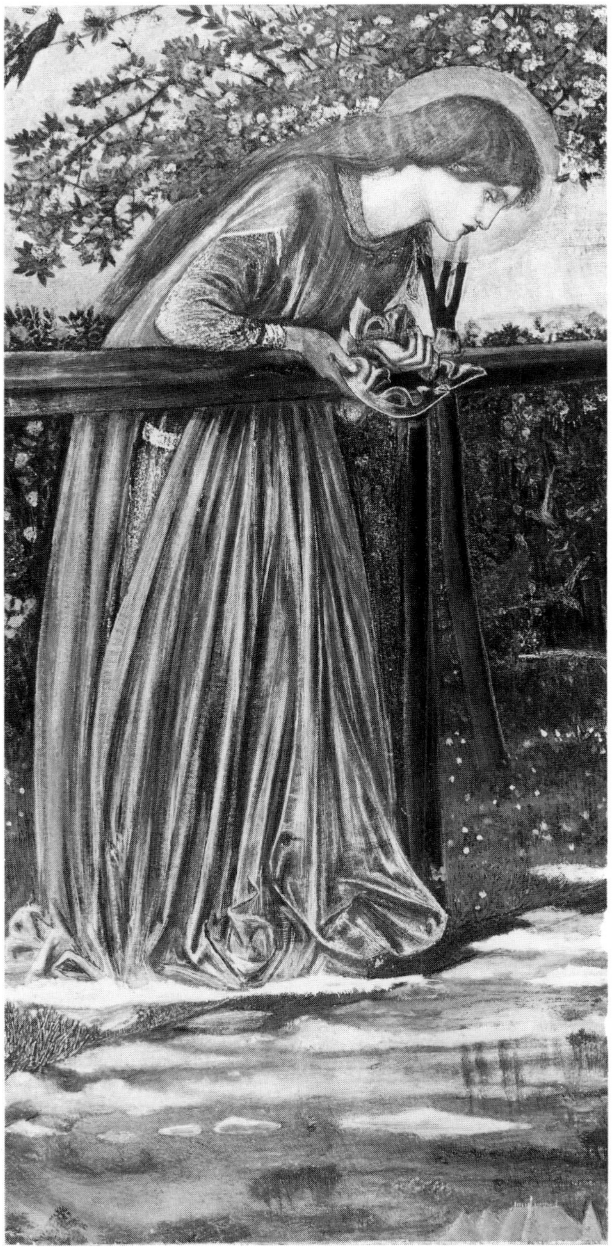

53 Edward Burne-Jones, *The Blessed Damozel.* Gouache. 1860
The Fogg Art Museum, Cambridge, Massachusetts

a bowling green, on that orchard walks amid gnarled old fruit-trees; – all struck me vividly picturesque and uniquely original.'[14]

A feature of the garden at Red House, which Morris had to sell in 1865 due to financial difficulties, is that it consisted of a number of sections. The most characteristic section was divided into four large squares surrounded by rose hedges and these were again divided into smaller squares, between which a variety of flowers bloomed. It was not a strictly formal garden, but it was 'orderly,' and it was a garden style which was to become extremely influential in Britain. Another section of the garden consisted of the old orchard which was highly praised, among others, by Burne-Jones.[15] Undoubtedly this was a place where the Pre-Raphaelites often painted, for blossoms frequently appear in their early work. According to his wife Georgiana, Edward Burne-Jones took two years to paint the blossoms in *The Blessed Damozel* (fig. 53). Each time he found a good example to paint from nature, bad weather struck and a storm would blow up.

Another characteristic of Morris' garden – the first he himself laid out – was the enclosed court with its 'old' well, considered a haven of peace. In 1865, *The Story of the Unknown Church* was published, in which Morris included a description written in his youth of a medieval court in an old abbey: '[...] and in the midst of a cloister was a lawn, and in the midst of that lawn, a fountain of marble, carved round about with flowers and strange beasts; and at the edge of this lawn, near the round arches, were a great many sun-flowers that were all in blossom on that autumn day; and up many of the pillars of the cloister crept passion-flowers and roses.'[16] The story continues with a lyrical description of a large garden close to the abbey. 'In the garden were trellises covered over with rose, and convulvulus, and the great-leaved fiery nasturtium; and specially all along by the poplar trees were there trellises, but on these grew nothing but deep crimson roses; the hollyhocks too were all out in blossom at that time, great spires of pink, and orange, and red, and white, with their soft, downy leaves. I said that nothing grew on the trellises by the poplars but crimson roses, but I was not quite right, for in many places the wild flowers had crept into the garden from without; lush green briony, with green-white blossoms, that grew so fast, one could almost think that we see it grow, and deadly nightshade, La bella donnna, O! so beautiful; red berry, and purple,

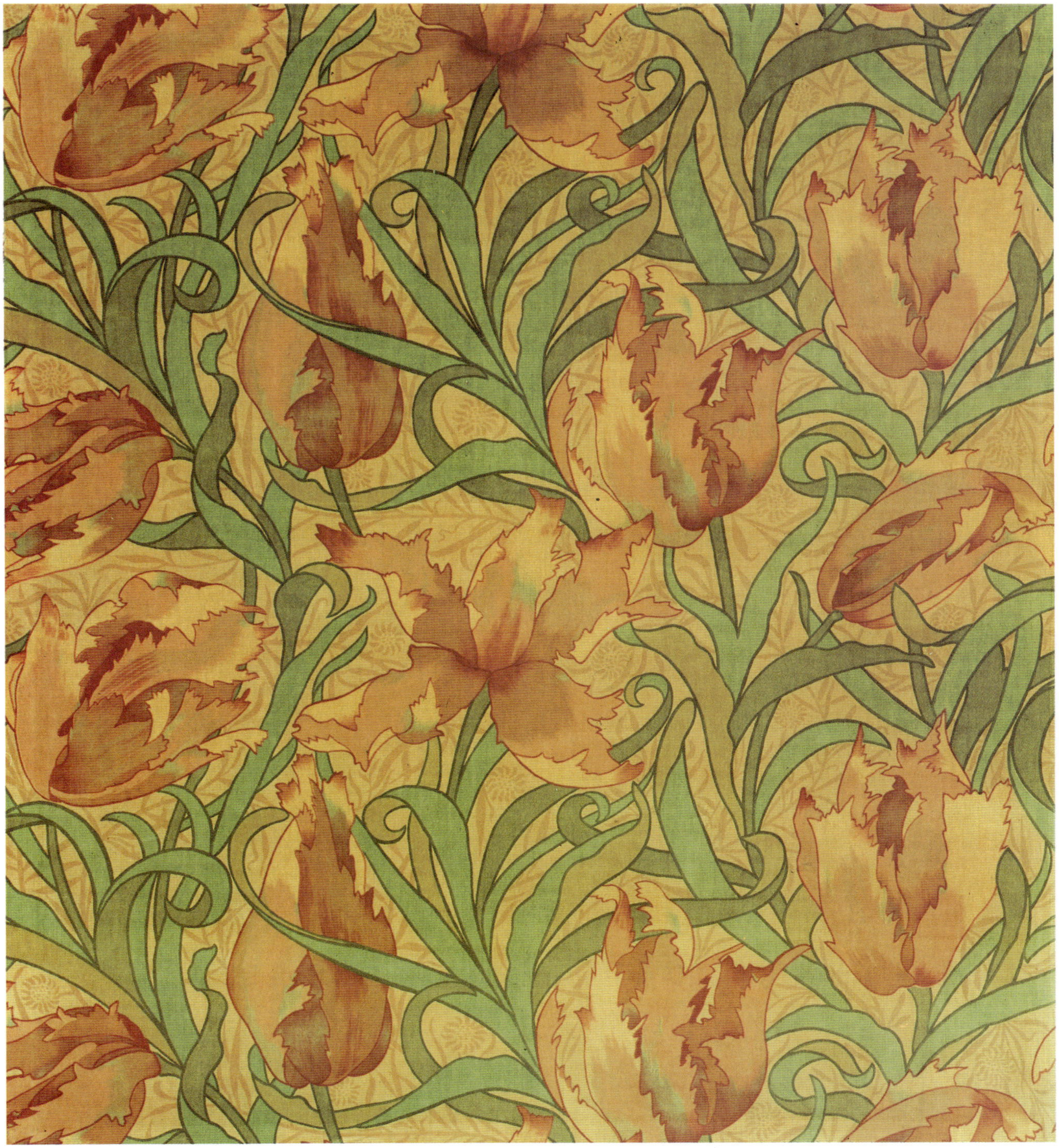

54 *Fabric*. Cotton velvet with printed decorations. England ca. 1895
Kunstindustrimuseet, Copenhagen
(*cat. 319*)

yellow-spiked flower, all growing together in the glorious days of early autumn.'

All of the flowers contained in this description are, even for the second half of the nineteenth century, 'old-fashioned,' and are typically English varieties: sunflowers, passion flowers, roses and hollyhocks, convulvulus, nasturtium.[17] Like Ruskin, Morris was a well-known and fervent opponent of artificially cultivated flowers. He considered it amoral – with the exception of botanical gardens – to wrench flowers away from their natural, ecological environment. According to Morris, exotic varieties belonged in warm countries, not in heated glasshouses. In a lecture given in 1882, *Hopes and Fears for Art,* Morris lashed out fiercely at the 'commercial florists' who brought about change for the sake of change without giving a thought to true beauty. He went still further in his criticism and called their attitude one 'which has played such a great part in the degradation of art in all times.'[18] Morris's viewpoint on this influenced an entire group of landscape architects and theoreticians, the most well-known of whom was Gertrud Jekyll.

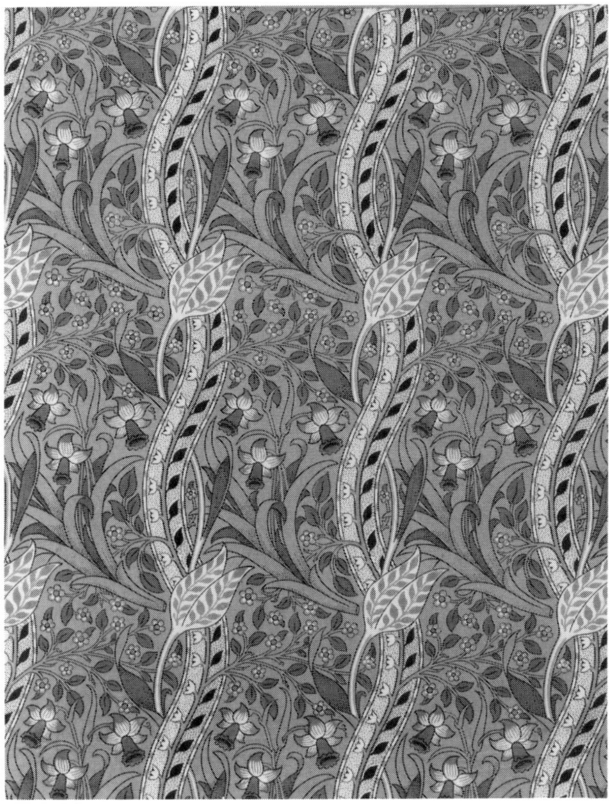

In addition, Morris had a kindred spirit in the then extremely popular publicist in the field of gardens, William Robinson (*The Wild Garden,* London 1870 and *The English Flower Garden,* London 1883).[19]

William Morris's designs for decorative embroideries, tapestries, wallpapers, fabrics and printed materials were also based on old-fashioned, and sometimes wild, flowers. Morris had begun designing while furnishing Red House.

His first three commercial 'repeating' designs, made in about 1862 for wallpaper, were *Daisy, Fruit* and *Trellis* (a design which also appeared as a fabric in 1868, with the name *Jasmine Trellis*). His first printed cottons were produced in the late 1860s and, again, only old-fashioned flowers were used in the designs, which were either drawn by Morris himself or under his immediate supervision. Favourites in the 1870s were: rose, jasmine, tulip, marigold, delphinium, carnation, anemone, acanthus, iris, harebell, lady's smock, African marigold, honeysuckle, fritillary, willow, peony, grape, sunflower (fig. 54).[20] By now, Morris had become an expert in the field of old textiles and was adviser to the South Kensington Museum, which had been established in 1852 as a museum where students and designers could draw from life. On his advice, in 1893 the Museum purchased the famous Ardabil carpet, a high point in Persian carpets. It was covered completely with a floral design and dated 1539/40.[21] Morris's own designs gradually developed from the naturalistic to the more formal under the influence of old Persian, Turkish and Italian textiles which he saw in those countries and which he collected himself. He was also influenced by his assistant John Dearle who worked with him in the 1880s (fig. 55).[22]

Morris also applied his (often quoted) ideas about 'invention.' For Morris was not concerned with the faithful rendering of the motif: 'Beauty mingled with invention, founded on the observation of nature, is the mainspring of decorative design. If it is not beau-

55 William Morris, *Fabric* (daffodil design). Cotton with printed decorations in Persian-Rhodian style with tulips, daffodils, lillies of the valley etc. Morris & Co., ca. 1894
Kunstindustrimuseet, Copenhagen

56 Felix Aubert, *Fabric*. Cotton with printed decoration. White irises in water with ripples. Pilon & Cie., Paris 1897
Kunstindustrimuseet, Copenhagen (*cat. 318*)

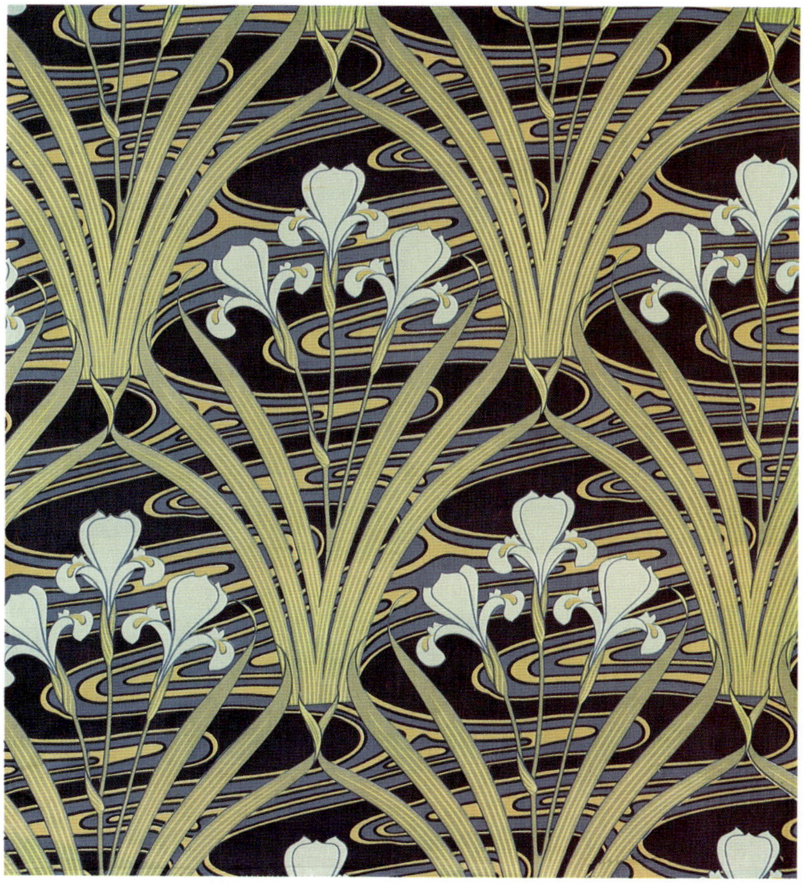

tiful it has no right to exist; if it is not invention it becomes wearisome.'[23]

The colours of his textiles were of particular concern to Morris and he shared John Ruskin's ideas on this subject. The latter argued that nature itself produced indescribably beautiful colours: 'There are no colours, either in the nacre of shells, or the plumes of birds and insects, which are so pure as those of clouds, opal, or flowers, [...] in some birds, also, as in our kingfisher, the colour nearly reaches a floral preciousness.'[24] Morris hated synthetic colours and experimented extensively with natural dyes. Describing her visit in 1886 to Merton Abbey, where Morris & Co. had established their textile dye works in 1881, an American woman writes: 'Scrupulous neatness and order reigned everywhere in the establishment; pleasant smells of dried herbs exhaled from clean vegetable dyes, blent with the wholesome odors of grass and flowers and sunny summer warmth that freely circulated through open doors and windows.'[25] Morris himself considered the area surrounding the workshops at Merton Abbey, with its orchard, vegetable garden and meadows, as a small paradise and he wrote regularly to his family telling them how wonderful it was there and which wild flowers were in blossom. 'I've been at Merton today [...] on the whole things are going on fairly: the marsh marigolds are all out and are splendid; one clump by the tail-side is a picture...'[26]

Morris's general ideas concerning gardens changed radically when he became an active socialist. His second real garden, that at Kelmscott Manor, the country house he rented from 1871, differed from that at Red House in that it was less historicizing. Morris saw the house – which dated from the sixteenth century but had many later additions – and the surrounding area as the realization of his ideal: a place which had evolved slowly over the centuries due to the work of men's hands (fig. 57).[27] As far as is known, Morris did not devise a rigid medieval layout

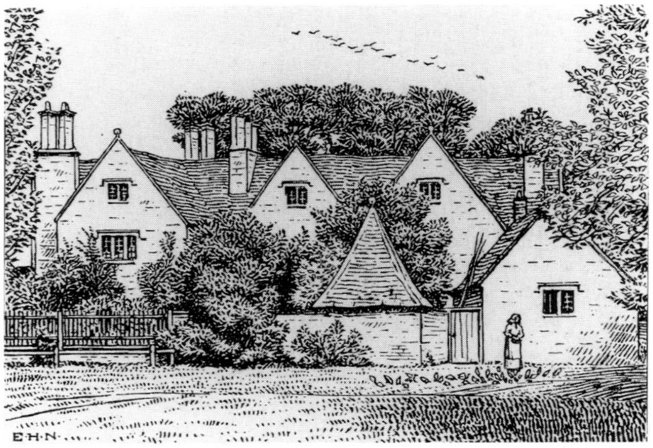

57 The entrance to Kelmscott Manor. Title page from William Morris' *News from Nowhere*, Kelmscott Press, London 1892. Woodcut by C. M. Gere

for his garden here, something he was in fact to do in his rectangular town garden at Kelmscott House (Hammersmith) in 1878.[28] Dante Gabriel Rossetti, who spent the first summers at the Manor together with his mistress and model Jane Morris, described it as paradise on earth. Rossetti wrote many poems and made preliminary studies for a number of important paintings there. Ford Maddox Brown also worked at Kelmscott and painted, for example, a large part of his *Cromwell on his farm* in the open air near the Manor.[29]

The house was situated in the midst of the river landscape at the edge of the village, on a road which soon turned into a cart track. It was reached by first passing through a gateway in a large, ivy-covered wall and then crossing the garden. In *News from Nowhere* (1890) – Morris's socialist utopia in which he sketches an ideal world, far removed from nineteenth-century Britain, ruined by industry and capitalism – the characters are described arriving at Kelmscott Manor. 'My companion gave a sigh of pleased surprise and enjoyment; nor did I wonder, for the garden between the wall and the house was redolent of June flowers, and the roses were rolling over one another with that delicious superabundance of small well-tended gardens which at first sight takes away all thought from the beholder save that of beauty' (fig. 58).[30]

58 William Morris' *Kelmscott Manor*. The back of the house seen from the meadow. Drawing by E. H. New

During the period in which he wrote *News from Nowhere*, William Morris was convinced that nature was of paramount importance for society as a whole. As early as 1880, he described the ideal living space as containing – in addition to a bookcase, a pleasing design on the walls and a stove – one or two vases in which to place flowers; the latter being especially essential for city dwellers.[31] In *News from Nowhere,* Morris opened the way for the English Garden Cities. He described, for example, the entire country, including London, as having the appearance of a single

59▸Edward Burne-Jones, *Flora*. Tapestry, wool. The flowers designed by William Morris 1886. *Executed for Morris & Co*
Whitworth Art Gallery, Manchester

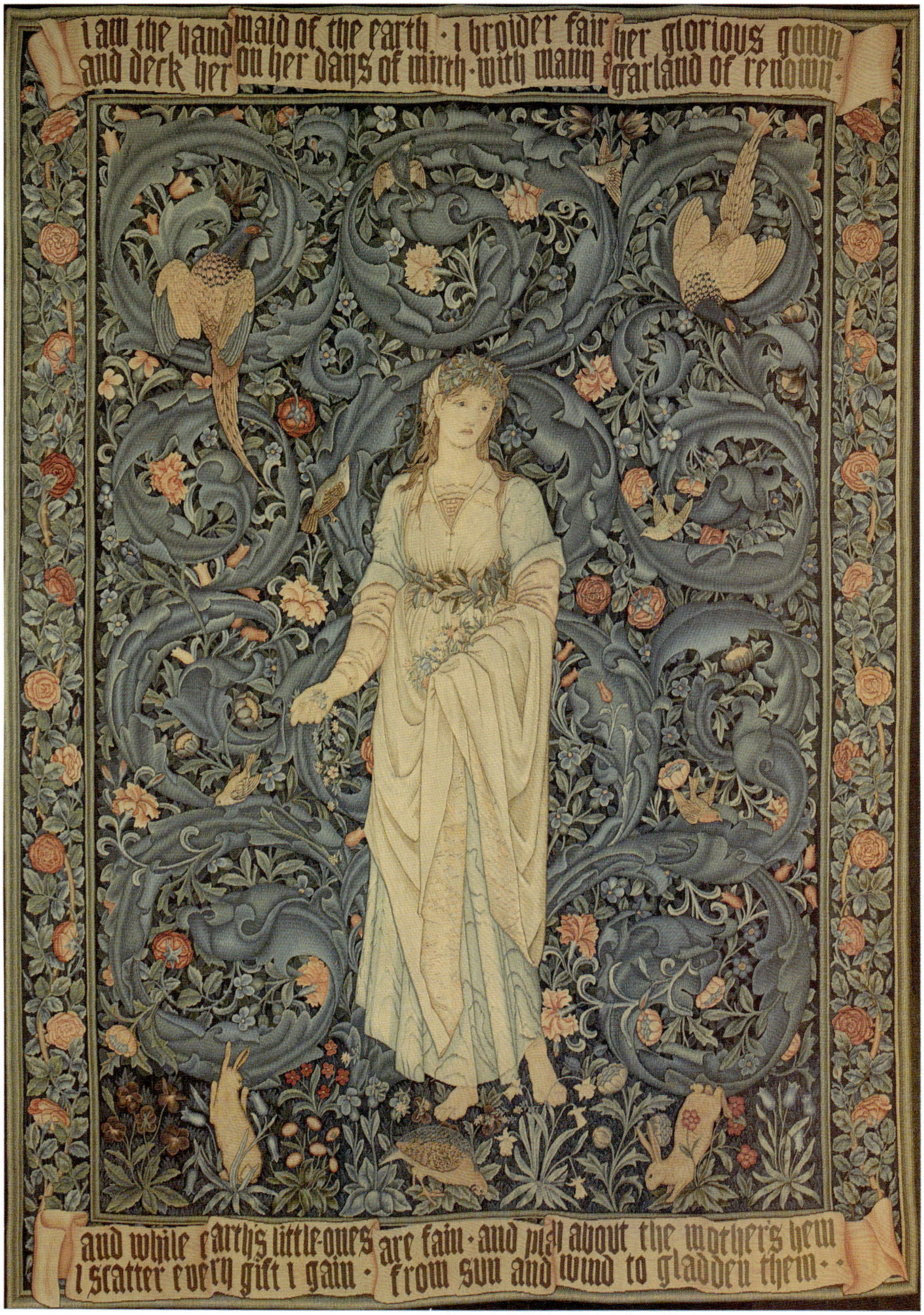
i am the handmaid of the earth · i broider fair her glorious gown
and deck her on her days of mirth · with many a garland of renown ·
and while earth's little-ones are fain · and play about the mother's hem
i scatter every gift i gain · from sun and wind to gladden them · ·

large garden containing houses. In Morris's view, a garden is no longer simply an idyllic spot, but forms an inseparable part of everyday life, in which the distinction between work and pleasure no longer exists.

Flowers also play an important role in the unworldly, romantic paintings of Edward Burne-Jones. In the early designs for Morris & Co., such as the tapestry *Flora*, the flowers were sometimes drawn by William Morris (fig. 59), but Burne-Jones too made extremely careful flower studies in which he rendered his 'models' with great accuracy. As already mentioned, Burne-Jones made numerous preliminary drawings of blossoms for *The Blessed Damozel*: initially, in orchards in Warwickshire and Worcestershire – where they were blown away by the wind – and later in 1858, he continued his canvas in the garden of a friend in Maidstone.[32] In 1863 he made studies in woodland for the background of *The Merciful Knight*, 'but the towngarden of Russell Square (Burne-Jones's own house) furnished the marigolds that fill in the space in the foreground.'[33] One of Burne-Jones's favourite flowers was the sunflower, which had returned to fashion in the 1860s and, indeed, later became part of an entire cult and the symbol of the Aesthetic Movement (Oscar Wilde).

Burne-Jones was a forerunner. 'Did you ever draw a sunflower?' he wrote in 1861, '... it is a whole school of drawing and an education in itself. [...] Do you know what faces they have – how they peep and peer, and look arch and winning, or bold and a little insolent sometimes? Have you ever noticed their back-hair, how beautifully curled it is?'[34] When, in the early 1890s, he was asked by a young artist for advice because his work had come to a standstill, Burne-Jones wrote telling him that, when finding himself in a similar situation in his youth, he had gone, day after day, into the gardens of Oxford to draw trees, flowers and grass.[35]

Unlike those of William Morris, the gardens of Edward and Georgiana Burne-Jones do not appear to have been designed according to specific ideas. Edward knew nothing about gardens and wrote in 1865 of their new house in Kensington: 'We have a garden, ever so long – how shall our garden grow? I am the veriest cockney and know no times or seasons of planting.' According to Georgiana, it was a small but, especially in the spring, beautiful garden with an abundance of fruit blossom, of which Edward Poynter once made a watercolour. Edward Burne-Jones himself made studies there of lilies, a flower which frequently appears in his work. After two years, the Burne-Jones family moved to the house where they were to remain, The Grange, Fulham, with its old mulberry tree, peaches growing against the wall and enough apple trees for it to be called an orchard. When they moved into the house, they found late-flowering roses and a fragrant lavender bush. It was only in the following season that they discovered plums and apricots, a walnut tree and a large bed of lilies of the valley.

In later years, Burne-Jones's attitude towards nature became somewhat mystical, even sentimental. From his house in Rottingdean, he noted in the summer of 1887 how tears sprang to his eyes when he saw the hills covered with sheaves of corn. Shortly afterwards, he wrote from The Grange to his daughter Margareth: 'The garden looks lovely still – a little sad, except in the first morning hours when the autumn sun shines upon it and makes it look divine, but in the afternoon it is given over to sadness and at twilight is haunted, by spirits, not ghosts – wraith and spectre never entered in this dear garden, not ever a ghost I think, but a soft Spirit there is I am sure.'[36] The garden had by then acquired a totally different significance for him and he had, for some time, no longer used it as a source of reference. Flowers, for Burne-Jones, had taken on a metaphorical meaning. In 1882 he began a so-called *Flower Book*, which he was to work on intermittently for sixteen years. It was full of drawings with flower titles such as Love-in-a-Mist, Black Archangel, Key of Spring, Love in a Tangle, Grave of the Sea, Golden Greeting. However, the entire album contained not a single 'real' flower, although Burne-Jones himself called it his 'Book of advanced Botany.'[37]

Emile Gallé – In England where, for example, Tennyson's 'garden poetry' had had a great influence – not only on the well-read Pre-Raphaelites and the subsequent generation of artists, but also on the middle classes in general – a contributor to *Blackwood's Magazine* wrote in 1854: 'The poets, blessings on them! have done more to awake a love of nature and of flowers; and to cherish a taste for horticulture, than all the professional horticulturists.'[38] In France, flowers played an equally important and particularly symbolic role in poetry. Either directly inspired by nature or using natural imagery, writers and poets such as Victor Hugo, Stephane Mallarmé, Robert de Montesquiou, Marcel Proust and Charles Baudelaire, had an enormous influence on the fine and applied arts and these in turn influenced the public at large. The 'flower language' used in French Symbolism was much more loaded and erotic than the more matter-of-fact Victorian flower symbolism, exemplified in the extremely popular book by Kate Greenaway, *The Language of Flowers* (1884).

The glassblower and decorative artist Emile Gallé is an excellent example of an artist who not only crossed the dividing line between fine art and the applied arts, but also had literary interests and, moreover, held strong views about botanical and flower gardens. His father, Charles Gallé, had settled in 1844 in Nancy where he married the daughter of a mirror manufacturer. Charles Gallé expanded the business and began producing glassware, the designs of which were based on flowers: jugs with petals as spouts and glasses with plant stems.[39] Around 1900 Emile Gallé wrote: 'Heureusement, l'amour de la fleur régnait dans ma famille; c'était une passion héréditaire.'[40]

While at school, Gallé had been instructed in 'herborisation' by D.A.Godron, author of *La Flore Française* and *La Flore Lorraine*, and became a renowned botanist. Gallé's first publication was an account (1 August 1877) of a regional flower exhibition in Nancy in the *Bulletin de la Société d'horticulture de Nancy*, a journal to which Gallé continued to contribute throughout his life. In 1908 Henriëtte Grimm, Emile Gallé's wife, published a number of these scientific articles about 'floriculture' in addition to her husband's most important writings on the applied arts. She argued that if Emile Gallé had revived the decorative arts, it was due to his having studied flowers and plants both as a scientist and as an artist (fig. 60).[41]

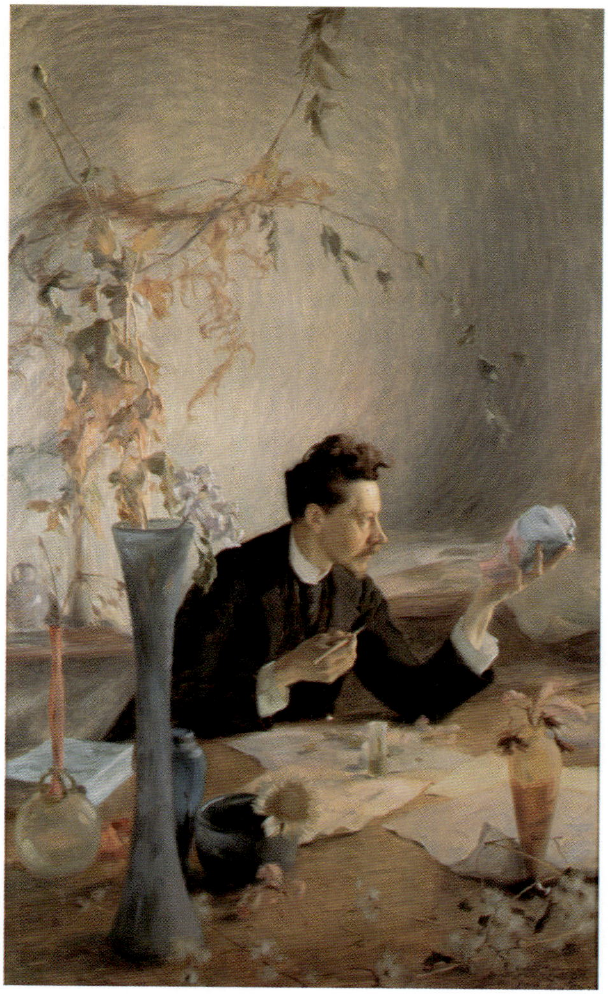

60 Victor Prouvé, *Portrait of Émile Gallé*. Oil on canvas. 1892
Musée de l'École de Nancy, Nancy

Unlike Morris and Ruskin, Gallé had no objections to exotic plants, although in his work he used primarily varieties which grew in the Alsace. He was extremely interested in unusual species. In 1877, he described the flowers and gardens he encountered during a journey through the Alps, from Switzerland to Italy.[42] He wrote lyrically, for example, about the exotic flowers and plants Prince Pierre Troubetzkoï showed him in his famous garden in Intra on the Lago Maggiore: from the six metre tall and blooming *Agave Salmiana* – the subject of much discussion in the scientific journals at that time – to unusual species from India, China, Japan and Australia. Later in Italy, during the same journey, he compared – again in a lyrical description – the gardens at the Villa Prina with art and Italian opera scenery. The landscaped gardens on the Isola Madre evoked for him images from Virgil, Claude Lorrain and Poussin. In his article of 1877, Gallé gave particular emphasis to the fact that many of the exotic plants were growing out-of-doors: 'le serre c'est le ciel bleu de l'Italie.' In his own garden in Nancy, Gallé tried continually to grow as many different species as possible next to each other. He sought to achieve a 'poetic and evocative microcosm of vegetation, taken from the widest possible range of climates.'[43]

Although extremely passionate about exotic species of plant, Gallé had strong views concerning the role of French flower growers and was highly critical of what he considered to be the over-cultivation of species for commercial reasons. The important thing, according to Gallé in 'Le Mieux est l'ennemi du Bien,' was to emphasize the decorative, elegant qualities of certain flowers and to exalt their beauty as far as possible. Their natural qualities must not be distorted: 'une rose verte n'est plus une rose, c'est un choux de Bruxelles' and a *fuchsia erecta* looks as if it is made of iron, he argued.[44] Gallé viewed flowers through the eyes of an artist, or rather, of an art critic, and he applauded species which, in his opinion, were successful as works of art. One of Gallé's favourite flowers, the gladiolus, which Victor Lemoine had grown in subtle shades of blue and red, was repeatedly described in highly evocative language in his articles. Gallé frequently spoke of flowers as if they were women and he compared Lemoine's 'glaïeul' with the dancer Loïe Fuller, 'cette magicienne aux reflets mouvants': 'Lemoine immortalizes this pursuit of yellows and reds, these transient blues and reds on a single solitary flower petal.'[45]

Gardens were extremely important to Gallé; the gardens of others, as we have seen above, were nurseries eliciting his wonder and delight. His own garden where, escapist as he was, he could retreat in order to work were particularly significant for him. Gallé's studio in his house, La Garenne in Nancy, was surrounded by a large garden, laid out from 1873 onwards by his father and intended to be used as a living source of reference when designing.[46] In 1878, Emile Gallé built new ovens and workshops near La Garenne. These were light and spacious rooms with numerous windows and a view of the landscape and the garden. The design studios had their own flowerbeds, serving as a model and source of inspiration. Gallé regarded botanical observation, as he himself repeatedly said, as a point of departure for the artist as 'grand visionaire.' He writes about this in his description of the vase presented to Louis Pasteur in 1893 on the occasion of his seventieth birthday. Just as Pasteur had succeeded in penetrating 'nature's mysterious depths,' Gallé sought in his own work to penetrate the mysterious depths of life and the soul ('traduire la vie et l'ame latentes sous l'enveloppe', fig. 61).[47]

Claude Monet – Gallé's contemporary, the Impressionist Claude Monet (1840-1926), had an entirely different point of departure for his work and this is directly reflected in the layout of his garden. Monet's chief reason for moving to Giverny, a village on the Epte between Paris and Rouen, in 1883 was to be able to paint in the open air. Monet was also beginning to develop his conviction that a single painting hardly did justice to a motif and thus created a series of paintings of the same subject in which he sought to capture changes in light and atmosphere. In 1892/93, he painted a series of canvases showing the cathedral of Rouen at different times of day and in different weather conditions. Following his precepts, in 1903 he painted the Houses of Parliament in London and, finally, created his famous series of water lily paintings, which he began to show in 1909.

Monet's garden at Giverny was, from the outset, a source of inspiration for him. He began laying out the garden in the spring of 1883 with the aim – as he wrote to the art dealer Durand-Ruel – of having 'flowers at hand to paint' when the weather was too poor to be able to work along the Seine.[48] The garden soon became a subject in itself and served as an open-air studio in which Monet and his numerous painter visitors spent many a day. Monet concerned himself with every detail of the layout and maintenance of the

61 ▸ Émile Gallé, *Vase*. Opalescent glass in various colours. Decorated with carved narcissi in relief and engraved: 'Une âme qui revient... Ch. Baudelaire'. Nancy, France 1891
Kunstindustrimuseet, Copenhagen (*cat. 95*)

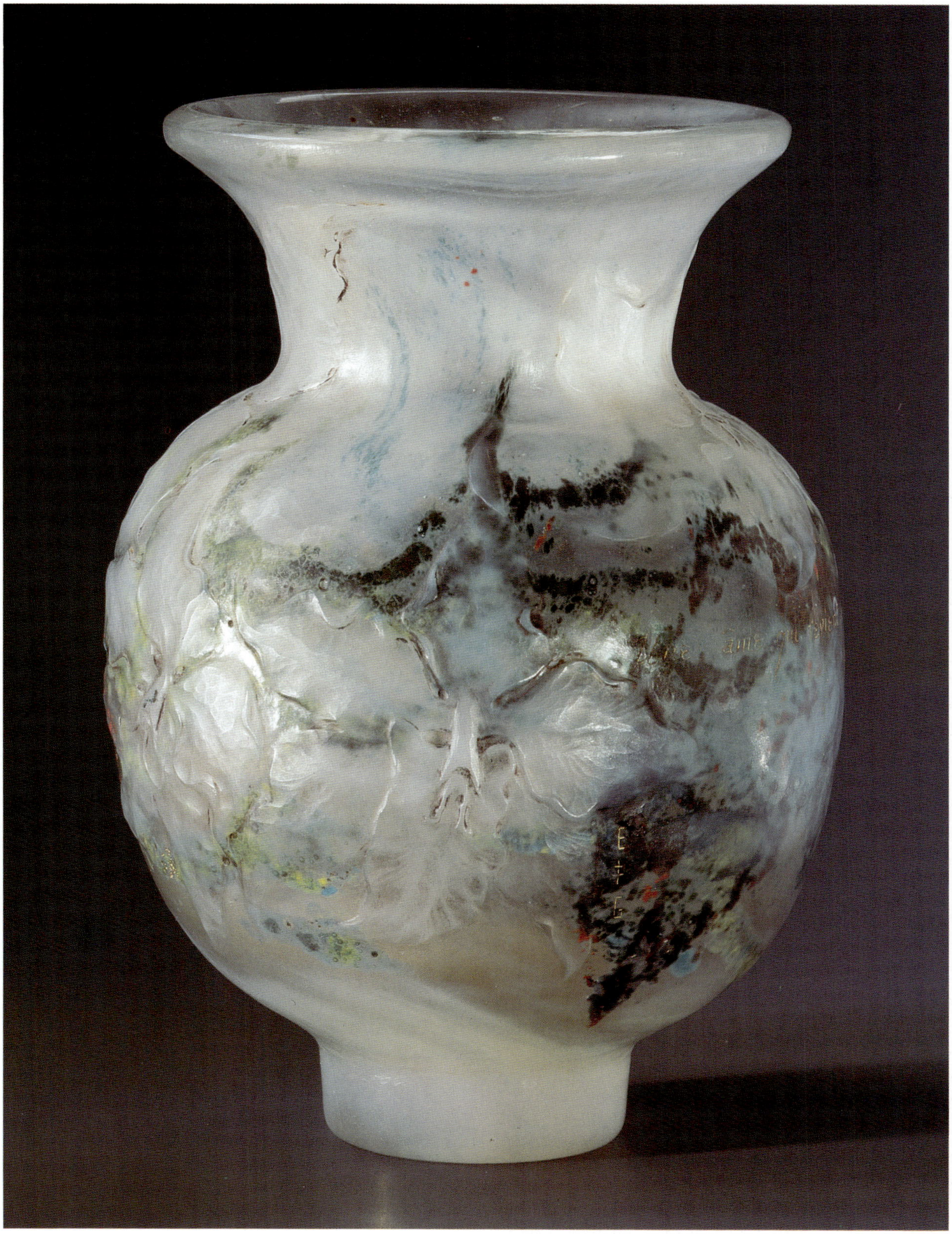

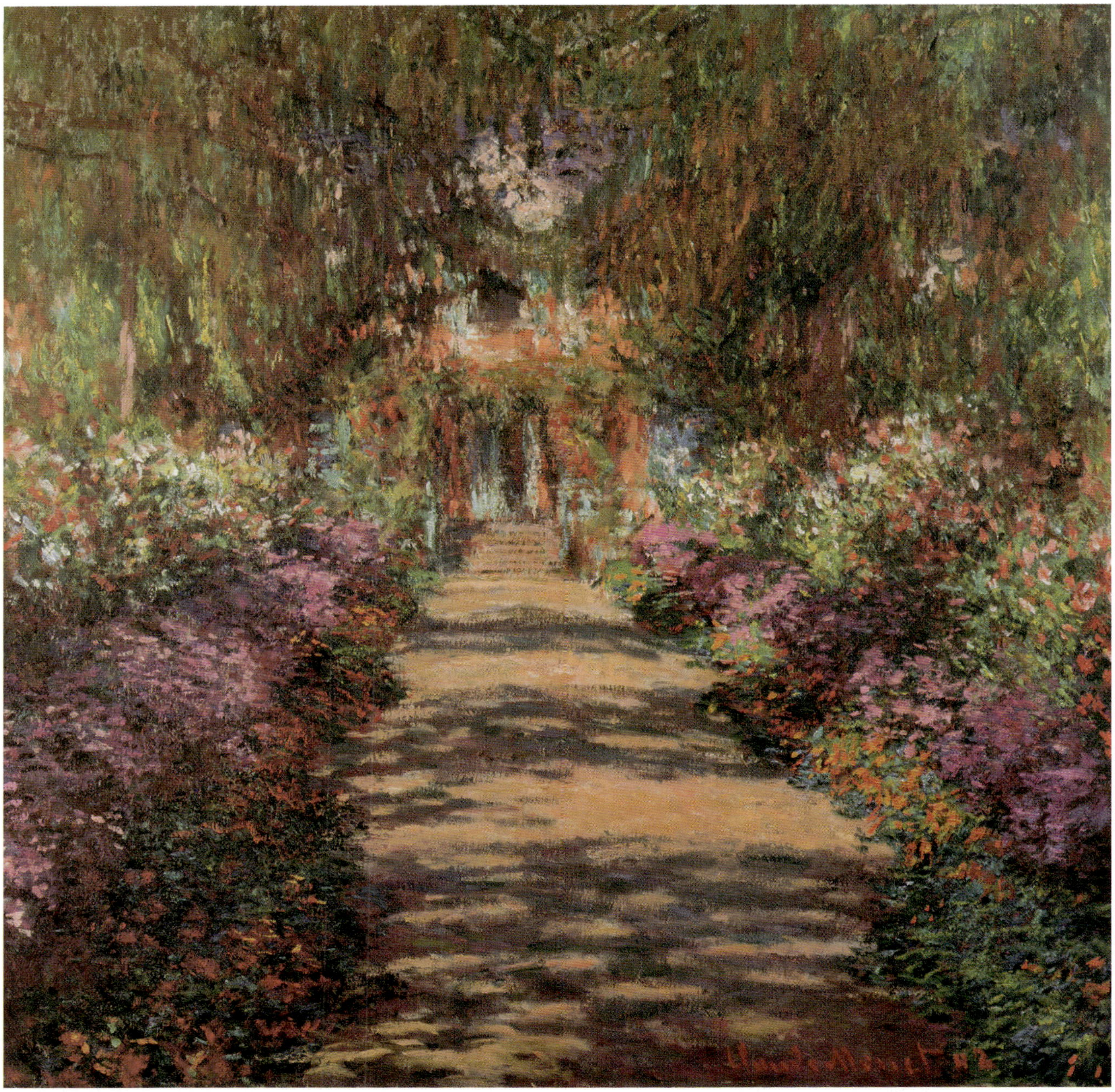

62 Claude Monet, *The central lane in the garden at Giverny*. Oil on canvas. 1902. Monet laid out the wide central lane as a tunnel of colours which culminated in the autumn
Österreichische Galerie, Vienna

garden, and was thus able to deliberately stage manage the motifs for his paintings. His chief aim was to create as large a sea of colour as possible, over which the light could freely play. This was especially the case in the rectangularly designed section of the garden closest to the house, with its immense central path. Here Monet created a tunnel of colour, to the left and right of which were swathes of different hues. In the autumn, the garden looked as follows: orange/yellow nasturtiums creeping along the ground; immediately above, deep purple asters beyond which were dahlias, roses and a variety of other flowers in shades of red/white and yellow (fig. 62).[49] A letter written to one of his gardeners gives a clear idea of the quantities of flowers Monet sowed and planted in the spring: three hundred pots of poppies, sixty pots of sweet pea, sixty pots of white and sixty pots of yellow agrimony. The list goes on; dahlias, irises, lilies, roses, gloxinias, sunflowers, clematis, Japanese peonies and in the glasshouses, orchids and blue water lilies.[50] Monet maintained good relations with the Hortus Botanicus in Rouen, where he could view and order special colours and rare species.

In the section of the garden farthest from the house was the famous water lily pond which Monet widened and deepened. This part of the garden was (and is) very different in character from that close to the house. It is more landscaped and contains Japanese elements: a high bridge with wisteria (see the prints of Hokusai, for example) and small, isolated trees each with its own particular blossom interspersed with precious, botanical flower species. In this dreamlike atmosphere, Monet painted his famous *Nymphéas,* or rather, made the sketches which he later worked out in his studio.

The motifs Monet created for himself in his carefully devised garden are an expression of his consistent ideas about colours and the tension they are capable of creating. The stage managing of the garden is matched by that of the house, whose occupants were continually subjected to sudden colour contrasts when they passed, for example, from the completely yellow dining room to the adjoining bright blue kitchen. Moreover, when the windows were open, the brilliant green of the exterior of the window frames added to the sharp colour contrasts. The manipulation of these sorts of pronounced colour effects together with the vibrations created by non-manipulatable exterior influences, such as the constantly changing light, are characteristic of Monet's life style, and made themselves felt in his house and garden as well as in his paintings. Indeed, one was the direct result of the other.

Emil Nolde – The various gardens of the painter Emil Nolde (1867-1956) had quite a different effect on their owner. His flower paintings, which he made from 1906 onwards, show a clear development away from an impressionistic towards a strongly pronounced expressionistic style. In addition to his house in Berlin, from 1902 on, Nolde always owned a house in the country which he surrounded with a brightly coloured ring of flowers. Initially, this was on rather a modest scale at his fisherman's house at Alsen. In connection with his early, relatively lighthearted flower paintings, Nolde – in a letter to his biographer Max Sauerlandt in 1908 – declared that he loved to see the small painted flower gardens with their vivid, serenely radiant colours. He was concerned with conveying the peaceful mood of a tranquil garden: 'Es sind stille, schöne Stunden, wenn man am friedlichen Sommertage zwischen den duftenden und blühenden Blumen geht oder dasitzt. Von dieser Schönheit möchte ich zo gern, das meine Bilder etwas geben. Ich selbst habe ja vor den Bildern diese Empfindung. Das erste schöne Glück – ein starkes Mitempfinden wird wohl nicht ausbleiben können.'[51]

In his biographical sketches, Nolde tells how the luxuriantly flowering garden at his second country house, Utenwarf near Tøndern, which, together with his wife, he had created out of nothing in 1921 had become a place of interest for the inhabitants of the flat, bare region: 'Die leuchtendroten rosen lagen in Wellen den Südhang hinunter, und oberhalb um den schmalen Teich, der ganz voller Fische war, blühten alle schönsten Stauden. [...] die Einbildung, dass in der Marsch keine Blumen wachsen können, war widerlegt. Die Menschen von Mögeltndern und sonstwoher pilgerten hinunter und gingen still auf dem Sommerdeich am Garten vorbei, stehend, schauend.'[52] He writes further of how he would become enraptured when the evening mist descended upon the 'dreary' surrounding landscape and how only the outlines of the cows, horses, roofs and a solitary tree remained visible.

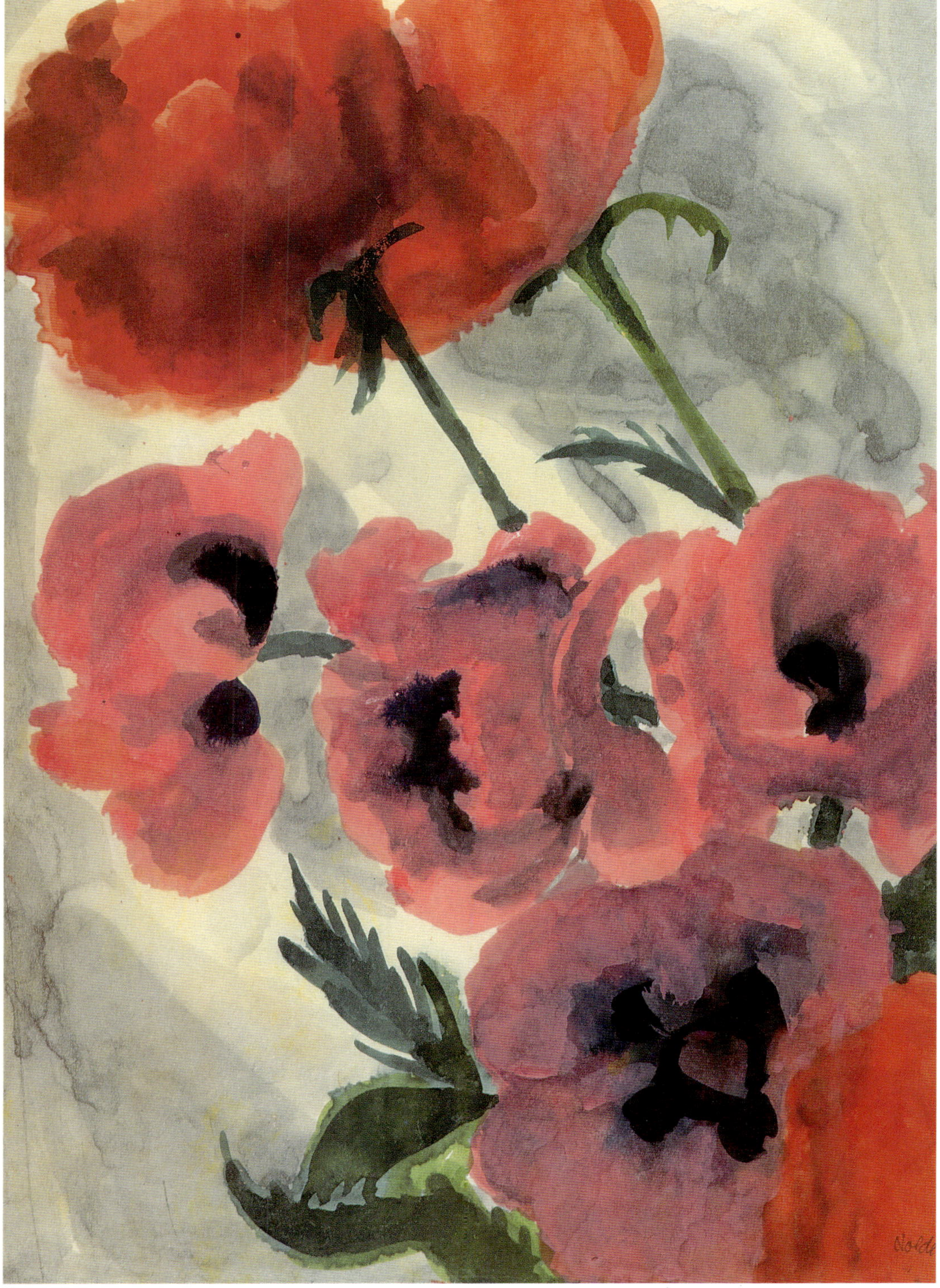

Without these two elements, his flower garden and the landscape, Nolde's best, expressionist work – including his paintings without flowers as their subject – would never have come into being. He not only needed his surroundings as a source of inspiration in order to convey a congenial mood, but also as an initial impetus for a state of mind which caused him to create his most mystical work. In 1921, Nolde wrote of this: 'Wenn, aus der Grossstadt kommend, wir auf Utenwarf angelangt waren, dann bald überkam mich das unwiderstehliche Verlangen nach künstlerischem Schaffen. Die Blumen im Garten leuchteten rein und schön mir jubelend entgegen, und die herrliche Landschaft um uns beschaftigte mich, bis es dann an figürliche Darstellungen ging, oder, dem Fluge zum freiesten Schaffen folgend, in faustische Mystik und Tiefen.'[53] Nolde needed to feel a close bond with nature in order to create as freely as possible.

In 1926, Nolde and his wife Ada felt compelled to move due to an irrigation project which completely changed the appearance of the landscape around Utenwarf. In 1926, Nolde bought an old farm, Seebüll, where he built first a new studio and then a house. Together with his wife, he laid out a large garden and incorporated an A and an E next to each other in the ground plan – which, according to Nolde, even the gardener never discovered. Nolde went through a difficult period at Seebüll; he was considered *entartet,* he was banned from painting, and moreover, his entire studio in Berlin was destroyed by fire during the war. The garden at Seebüll with its intensely coloured country flowers – a profusion of anemones and poppies – served as a source of inspiration for Nolde's increasingly ecstatic work (fig. 63). Owing to circumstances, this consisted of large numbers of small watercolours.

Having arrived at the twentieth century by way of such diverse artists as Morris and Burne-Jones, Gallé, Monet and Nolde, we can conclude that the Art Nouveau theoretician Tschudi Madsen was right when he argued that in art nature is always conveyed 'à travers d'un tempérament d'artiste.' It is an interesting fact that the guiding principles artists adopt when laying out their gardens are virtually the same as those they bring to bear in their work. Morris and Burne-Jones both focussed on detail and had historical leanings, but, at the same time, incorporated flowers and plants as an artistic motif into a larger whole. Gallé too, in effect, only saw individual flowers, being susceptible to exoticism; his observation enabled him to lay bare the depths of his soul. Monet and Nolde did the same, but for them the garden itself was central; they saw the garden in its entirety and incorporated it as such into their work. Morris made an enumeration of separate elements: Nolde used the separate elements in order to give expression to his ecstatic vision, in which each individual flower communicates a powerful intensity.

63 ‹Emil Nolde, *Poppies*. Watercolour. Germany ca. 1934
Statens Museum for Kunst, Den Kongelige Kobberstiksamling, Copenhagen

Maria Fabricius Hansen

Flowering welfare

With its economic boom and the attendant changes in world views and attitudes to life, the period from around 1960 to the early 1970s now appears as a time of rupture between old and new; a time of solidarity and carefreeness; a myth of youth and freedom. The flower has become part of this myth on many levels, entering the imagery of social concerns.

Balenciaga and the flower as feminine exclusivity – A dress for evening wear – or, to be more precise, a profusion of appliqué pink and white flowers with green leaves in the thinnest silk – was Balenciaga's bid for haute couture in the summer of 1964 (fig. 64 and cat. 335). Balenciaga was one of the greatest names in the post-war fashion world. He was called the architect of haute couture because of his severe, perfectly tailored suits. The cut of his clothes was simple, bordering on the abstract, and the result was like a precious wrapping for a woman whose function was primarily to look good – in this context, freedom of movement was of lesser importance. The decoration (for example, pearl embroidery, lace or, as in this case, extraordinarily luxuriant silk appliqué) could emphasize the gala nature of a costume. The motifs were often picked from the world of flowers; the flower became the poetic element amid Balenciaga's simplicity, a symbol of the delicate and feminine.

Balenciaga created clothes for an elite. The basic premise of haute couture was exclusivity, the individual creation for the individual woman. Aristocratic singularity was the ideal, and the fashion designer the highest authority on good taste.

During the 1960s, this authority was gradually undermined by the emergence of different concepts of fashion, as well as of the ideal woman. The individual was replaced by the type; in the world of fashion, the mature, sophisticated woman was replaced by the anonymous, classless, teenage model. Self-confidence and independence replaced the conception of women as delicate flowers. Pop art, op art and science fiction inspired clothes without reference to the abundance of nature, illustrating belief in the future and progress in technology and industrialization.

In 1968, the year that saw the culmination of the youth revolution, Balenciaga decided to close his Paris fashion house. Like many others, he could not or would not lower the standards of traditional haute couture. This could be seen as evidence of the youth movement's success in its endeavour to break down conformity and convention. Among the norms current in the 1960s were the traditional role assigned to women and the class consciousness reflected in haute couture.

Wilhelm Freddie took the traditional association of the flower with the feminine to its ultimate conclusion in a 1966 exhibition. He transformed a well-known model into a flower and a work of art: her legs became the stem, the torso the flower itself and the white lily in her hand a symbol of innocence as contrast to and accentuation of the erotic undertones of the tableau (fig. 65).

Warhol, pop art and the banal flower – Freddie let the model personify the flower by transforming it into a woman. Andy Warhol drew away from concrete, material existence in his imagery. The flower as a popular, but abused and exhausted motif forms the point of departure for Warhol's flower series, the earliest of which date from 1964 (fig. 66). A few years earlier, Warhol had rejected traditional means of painting in favour of creating his pictures mechanically. Thus, he not only used the imagery of the commercial world, which he knew and understood thoroughly because of his background as a graphic

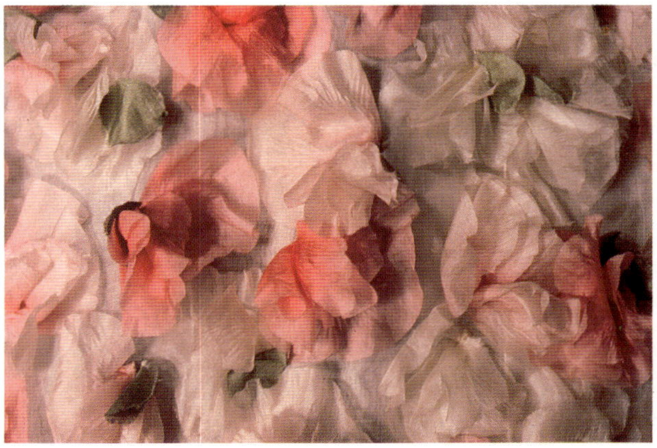

64 Balenciaga, detail of *Evening dress*. White organza with appliqué silk flowers. Paris 1964
Hubert de Givenchy, Paris (*cat. 335, ill.*)

designer, but also expressed the spirit of industrialization and mass production.

At a time when modern art seemed increasingly isolated and inaccessible to ordinary people, Warhol sought his motifs in the everyday flood of images: movies, newspapers, magazines, advertisements, etc. The actual model for the flower series was selected randomly from a photo magazine. The recognizable and easily understood motif has been taken out of its original context, blown up and printed in new, strong colours. The subject has been repeated in a seemingly endless series, all in the same square format. In this way, Warhol neutralized the meaning of the motif. By turning the process and the serialization into themes, Warhol made the banalization of the motif, as well as its transformation from a given content at a specific moment into a decorative pattern in a timeless series, the main content of the picture.

Youth culture, fashion, and the flower as pop – The simplified, stereotyped pop-art flower, with its non-naturalistic stretches of colour, recurs in the style or cultural manifestation which is designated 'pop.' The style culminated in the mid-1960s and was decidedly urban, with London as a focal point. It was closely related to the euphoric expectation of a growth of social prosperity based on the development of technology and industrialization.

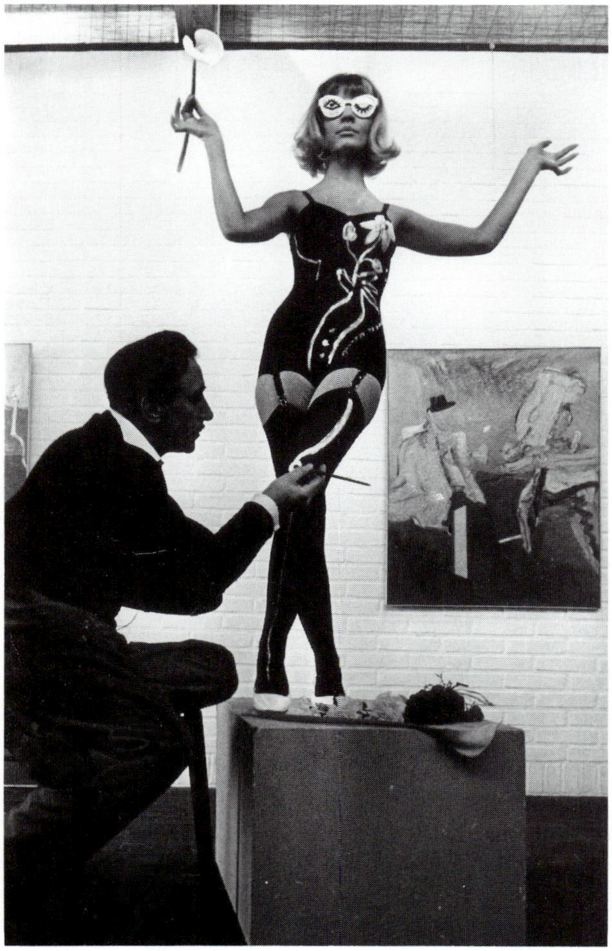

65 Wilhelm Freddie painting a flower on the model Lise Bodin. Louisiana, Denmark 1966. Photo: Jørgen Sperling, 1966

Nature itself is difficult to discern in this context, both with regard to motif and materials, and to the actual processing and colours, for industrial design dominated the mid-1960s. In her textile piece *Unikko* from around 1965, the Finnish artist Maija Isola's use of the pop flower resulted in a lively and informal large-patterned effect (fig. 67). Informal and unconventional are key words during the early 1960s. In London, Mary Quant, who chose a simple flower in the style of that period as her logo, became in many ways an exponent of everything new which was, to a great extent, an expression of a changed understanding of the world, rather than just a chance fashion.

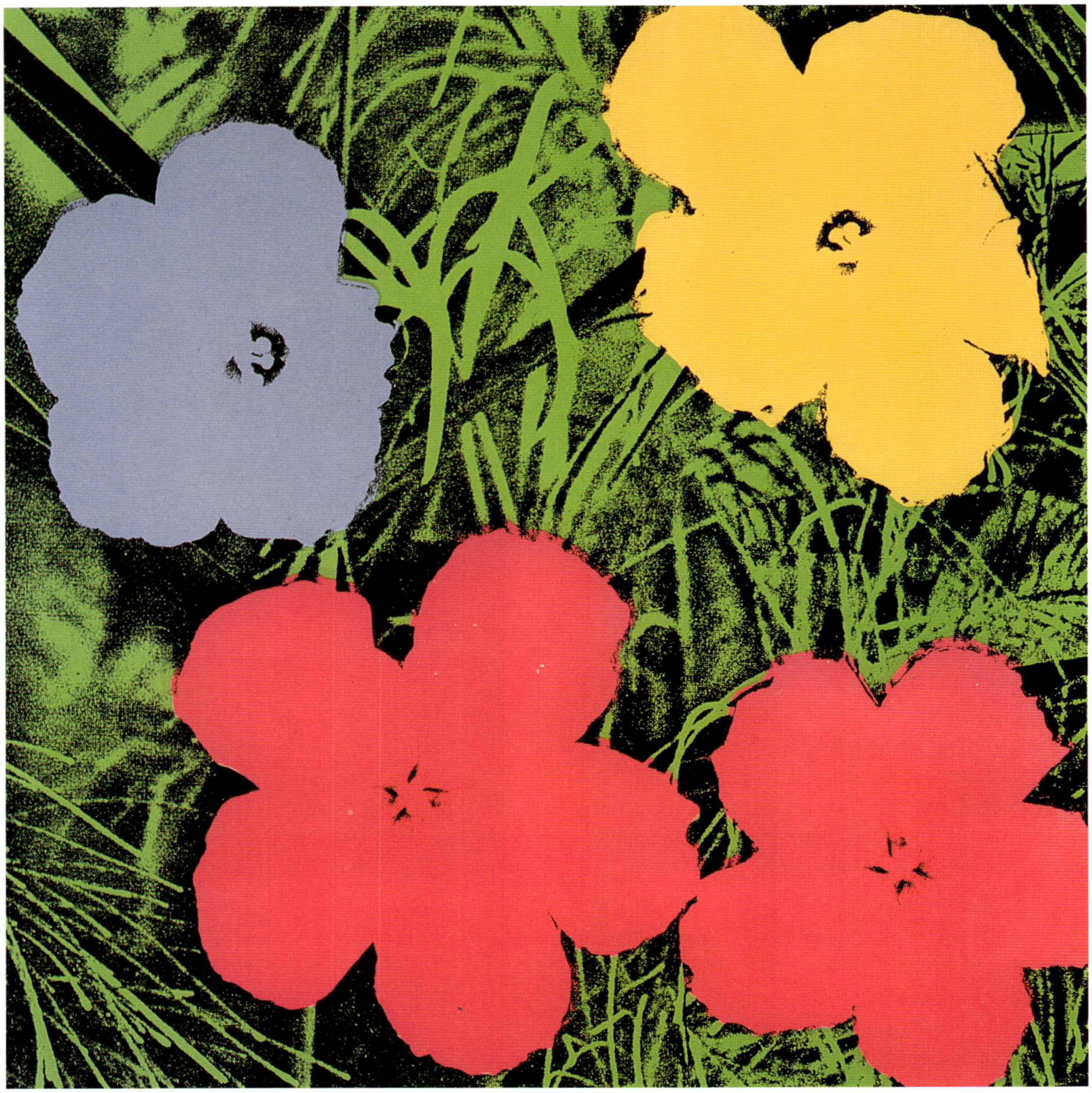

66 Andy Warhol, *Flowers*. Colour serigraph with flowers on grass background. New York 1970
Kunstbiblioteket, Lyngby (*cat. 58*)

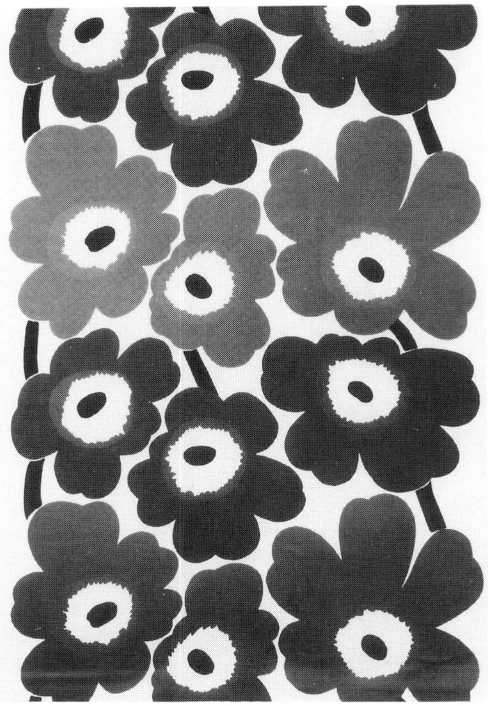

67 Maija Isola, *Unikko*. Length of fabric. Cotton. Printed pattern of stylized poppies. Designed for Maritextil, Finland 1965 (?)
Kunstindustrimuseet, Copenhagen (*cat. 336*)

The youth culture was dictating style. Youthfulness had become the ideal, and the flower motif was employed as its metaphor.

The youth culture was partly a product of increased prosperity which – initially in the USA – made it economically possible for parents to allow adolescents time to be teenagers. This newly defined age group became a new consumer group with its own taste in fashion, music, etc. Mary Quant sold fashion created specifically for the young in an environment which in itself was part of the youth culture, including an informal atmosphere enhanced by pop music. Where fashion had previously been dictated by haute couture, it was now being created in direct interaction between designer and consumer. The demand for renewal turned traditional values like quality and durability into anachronisms, and the prefabricated, mass-produced garments reflected the ideology of social equality.

In 1966, the seventeen-year-old Twiggy was elected 'Face of the Year' and 'Woman of the Year.' The success of her sad look, emphasized by heavy eye make-up and false eyelashes, painted freckles and the thin, androgynous body, marks the breakthrough of the infantile ideal in the established fashion world. The miniskirt – launched by Mary Quant – belonged to the youth. It signaled freedom of movement, as well as freedom from the standards of the older generation. The fact that the fashions of the young became popular with all ages proves its quality as an ideal for the entire society.

The hippie culture and the flower as symbol of peace and love – Despite the generational clash, the pop version of the youth culture was conformist in its entire economic and market-oriented foundation. Concurrently, however, another youth movement emerged that questioned the legitimacy of the consumer society and the quality of the welfare boons. In more conscious circles, this movement eventually became a youth revolution, as increasingly radical opinions and the resulting opposition to established society began to manifest itself.

Around 1960, anti-nuclear marches testified to the influence of popular demonstrations on political opinion. In the mid-1960s, protests against the Vietnam War were voiced throughout the world, resulting in demonstrations and clashes with the police. The student revolts leading to the occupation of universities in the spring of 1968 strengthened the new generation's opposition to social authority.

Some young people tried alternative life-styles in quest of a new and better society. The hippie culture with its message of 'flower power,' reached Europe from the United States and bloomed around 1967. Love and mutual responsibility were to replace individualism and exploitation of others. The flower-power movement resulted in 'love-in' gatherings such as on Langelinie in Copenhagen, 1967 (fig. 68). Hair was allowed to grow as a sign of equality between the sexes, and an image of a happy, unspoiled, natural state. The simple, abstract style of the pop clothes, predominantly white, gave way to a multicoloured, patterned design inspired by the third world, particularly India, a country which came to stand as an ideal, in part because of its pre-industrialized state. The

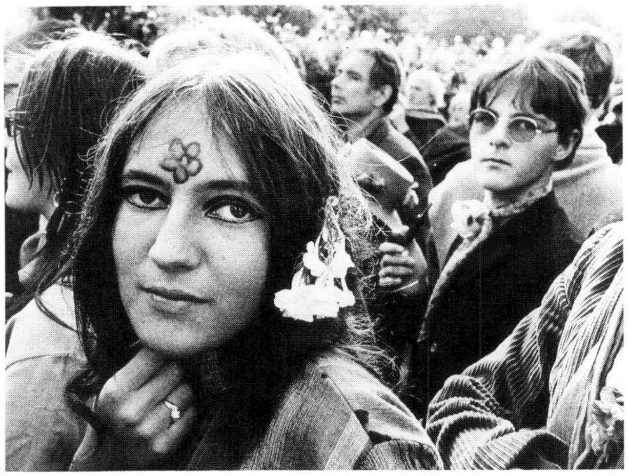

68 *Love-in*. Flower children on Langelinie, Copenhagen 1967. Photo: Jørgen Schytte

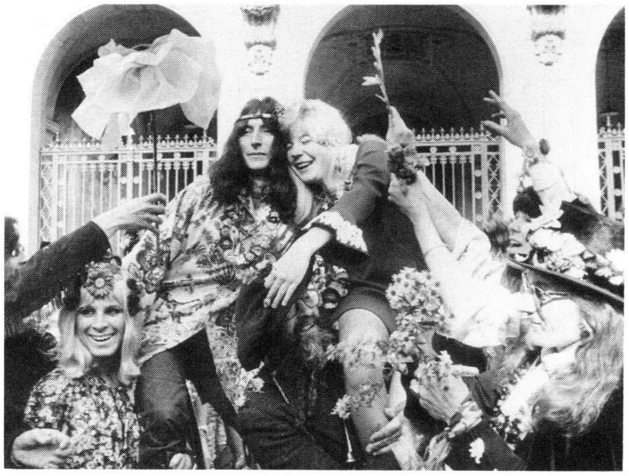

69 Photograph of *hippie wedding*. France 1969

flower stood for imagination and fertility, creativity, naturalness, happiness, sensitivity, peace and love (fig. 69).

The flower as symbol of the flower-power movement was immediately taken over by conventional fashion media and made fashionable and harmless as seen on the cover of American *Vogue* from July 1967. Twiggy poses with a flower painted on her face, dressed in an exclusive fur coat with flower motifs (fig. 70).

As social consciousness grew, it led to protest against established society's lack of interest in its weaker members. Simultaneously, concern for the state of the environment was expressed. Some of the first actions drawing attention to the excessive exploitation of nature occurred in the late 1960s. The pop culture's obsession with synthetic materials and colours was replaced by the desire to live in harmony with nature.

An element of nostalgia, a longing for the pre-industrial world, made the handcrafted and the unique attractive again. In the early 1970s, blue jeans, the all-dominating symbol of equality and rebellion and the epitome of the youth movement itself, were covered with appliqués, sewn in contrasting colours, embroideries, etc.

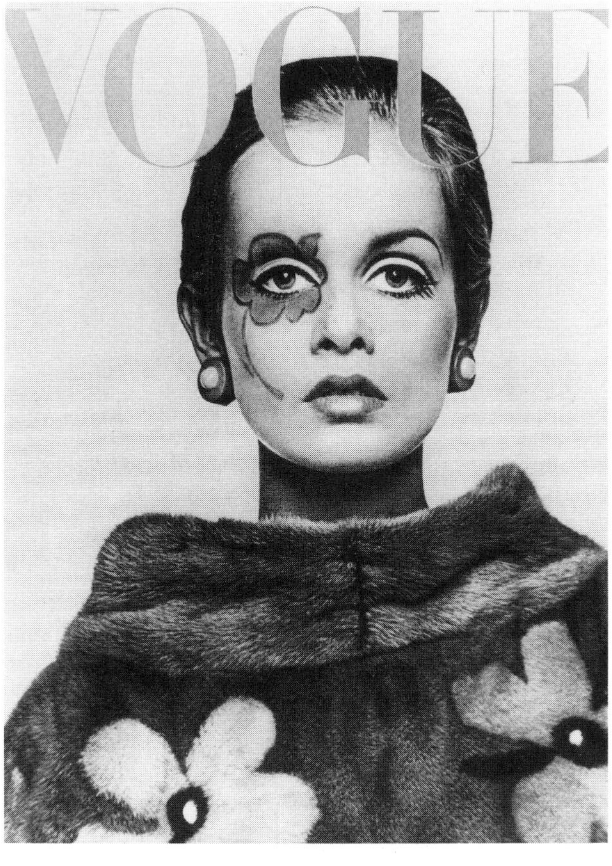

70 ▸ Cover photograph of Twiggy on the American *Vogue* 1967. Photo: Richard Avedon

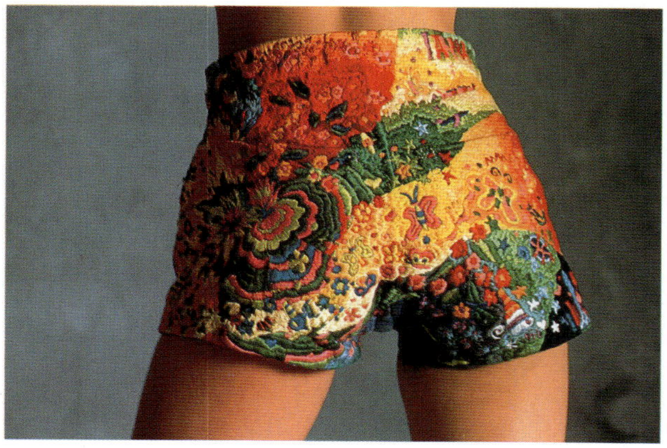

71 Anna Polesny, *International Levi's*. Blue jean shorts with flower embroidery in bright colours. USA 1973
Julie Schafler Dale, New York (*cat. 337*)

International Levi's, a pair of shorts which had led a varied and changeable life since their origin as long blue jeans in the early 1960s were, over the course of a few years, completely covered with embroidery by their owner, the American Anna Polesny. The designs included a butterfly, flowers and patterns embroidered in bright colours (fig. 71). Each motif carried a particular memory, and in this way, *International Levi's* was gradually transformed into an icon of personal imagination and creativity.

Music and the flower as imagination – Music became one of the most marked cultural manifestations of the youth movement: it was a common focal point defying social boundaries. Special music magazines and posters were sold in shops decorated in a brightly coloured, ornamental neo-Jugendstil.

The Beatle's 1967 LP, *Sergeant Pepper's Lonely Hearts Club Band* was revolutionary not only because of the music, but also because of its visual appeal, and the cover's connection with the album (fig. 72). The four Beatles are dressed in old-fashioned uniforms in vibrant pop colours. The background collage shows photos of people from the world of popular entertainment, celebrities, movie stars and the like, including the group itself as it looked some years earlier. In the foreground the name of the group is spelled out by a bed of flowers. This visually and musically complex record illustrated the multiplicity, eclecticism and the burgeoning nostalgia of the passage from pop to hippie culture.

A new element in the imagery of the period was the attempt to depict phenomena experienced under the influence of drugs, primarily LSD. The brilliant colours and chaotic images can be seen as a visualization of a dream-like state. A hookah on the cover of *Sergeant Pepper* is a more direct allusion. In the song 'Lucy in the Sky with Diamonds,' where the initials of the title form the acronym LSD, John Lennon sings about just such a surreal, dream-like state: 'Cellophane flowers of yellow and green, towering over your head...' is part of his vision. The flower in flower-power culture thus becomes not only a symbol of freedom to use one's imagination in one's relation to conventional society, but also an image of the exploration of consciousness and imagination.

The psychedelic imagery which developed concurrently with the flower-power culture typically was used for record covers. As a result, they acquired a new function as the visual expression of a consciousness-exploring and total musical experience. An example is the English group Cream's 1967 LP, *Disraeli Gears* (fig. 73). The cover is dominantly red, pink, yellow, pale blue and pale green, a choice of colours similar to that of the Beatles for *Sergeant Pepper*. The imagery is a collage of photographic elements and cartoon motifs, such as lightning, speed stripes and bubbles, which signal dynamism and outbursts of energy. In the use of strong colours and the completely over-decorated surface, the flowers once more become a symbol of the fertility of the imagination. At the same time, the images of watches and old postcards with flower motifs indicate a nostalgic dimension to this pictorial universe.

Several Danish groups simply let the flower be part of their English names, and in this context, the flower was both wild and young: The Savage Rose, formed in 1967, and The Young Flowers, whose first LP, *The Flower Pistol,* was released in 1968.

In 1970, after the Beatles' break-up, John Lennon proclaimed in a song, 'The dream is over...' It was not only the mythologizing of the Beatles that he referred to, but the whole dream of being able to change the world and become happier through flowers and love.

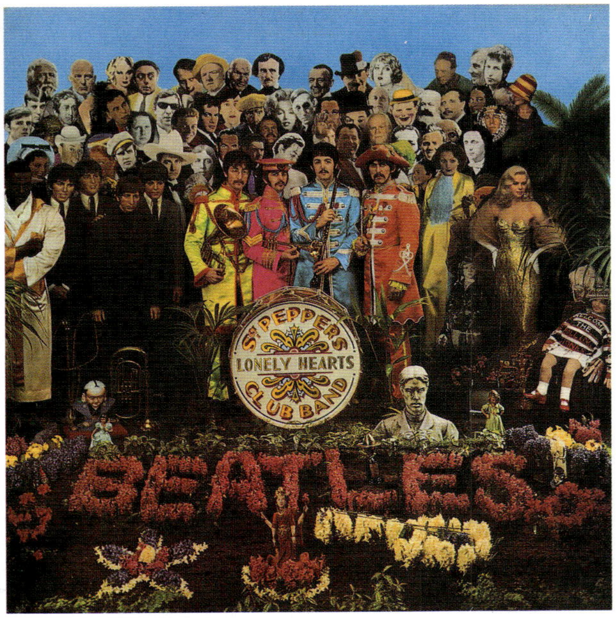

72 Peter Blake and Jann Haworth; Beatles, *Sgt. Peppers Lonely Hearts Club Band*. Record cover. EMI Records, England 1967
Private collection (*cat. 55*)

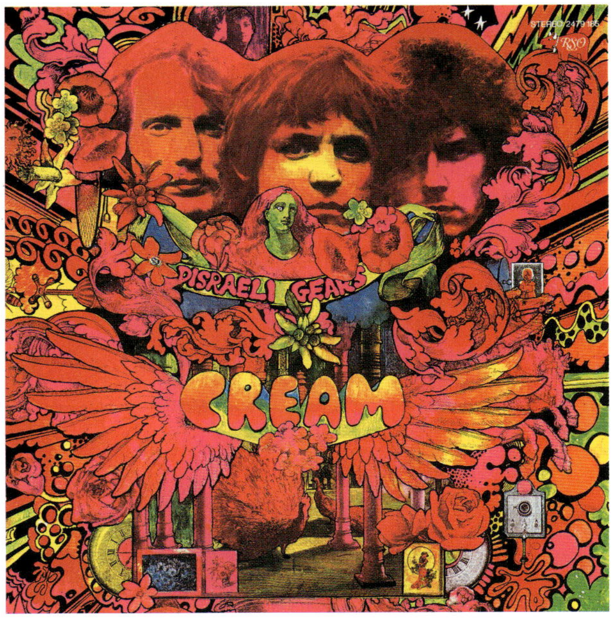

73 Martin Sharp; Cream, *Disraeli Gears*. Record cover. Polydor Records, England 1967
Private collection (*cat. 56*)

Irving Penn – Beauty in decay: the flower photo as memento-mori – Irving Penn's 1970 photograph *Blue Moon Rose* could be an illustration of Lennon's message (fig. 74). The photograph is a study of a dream about ideal beauty – and its decay.

The flower has been taken out of its natural context. Its stalk is cut by the edge of the picture, and the flower is placed on an anonymous background. The rose is perfect in its symmetry and circular shape. The seeming perfection is broken, however, by the incipient curling up of the leaves. A delicate but intense backlight makes the brown parts of the withering leaves appear as golden contrasts to the pink colour of the blossom. It is the back of the rose one sees: the flower is turned away from the spectator. By eliminating any reference to the environment and avoiding any anecdotal content in the composition, Penn succeeds in making the flower itself, its shape, its averted heart, its decay, the actual content of the picture.

The use of close up and the composition of the flower's stalk and head associates the image with the genre of portraiture. Just as Penn's portraits are without reference to the sitter's environment or social context, the flowers are solely studies in formal effects.

The innovative quality of Penn's fashion photos for *Vogue* during the 1950s was the result of his intense concentration on the model, on costume and pose without reference to environment. It is the imminent individuality of the moment which is being cultivated. The radical changes in fashion and in the role of women during the 1960s led to new demands in photography. In Penn's 'portraits' of flowers, the earliest from 1968, the aesthetics of his earlier fashion photography are applied to a new subject.

Of course, Penn's choice of the flower as motif is not accidental. In the tension between traditional values, between nature's perfection and the fascination of decay, Penn's flower photos reach beyond the trivial and attain a universal validity.

The *Blue Moon Rose* has bloomed and is now withering. Through the insistence on an irrevocable moment in the process of decay, the course of time itself is made the theme. The photographic depiction of transitoriness adds a new dimension to the memento mori motif so often encountered in the history of art.

The flower motif reflects the changing ideas and attitudes of the period. The flower was used both as an image of conventional values and as the symbol of revolt. The naturalistic flower was trivialized in the process of cultivating the possibilities of technology, and in its triviality became an artistic expression of modernism. The flower thus came to express the altered consciousness of the 1960s, and the breaking down of the boundaries of authority and normalcy have also been demonstrated. Everything from the creativity of the individual to the sense of powerlessness when confronting the withering of the dream and the intrusion of reality has been visually expressed by the flower.

The extraordinary versatility and symbolic power of the flower motif is illustrated by the many uses and interpretations it has been given throughout history, and by the immediate and universal significance that has resulted from this.

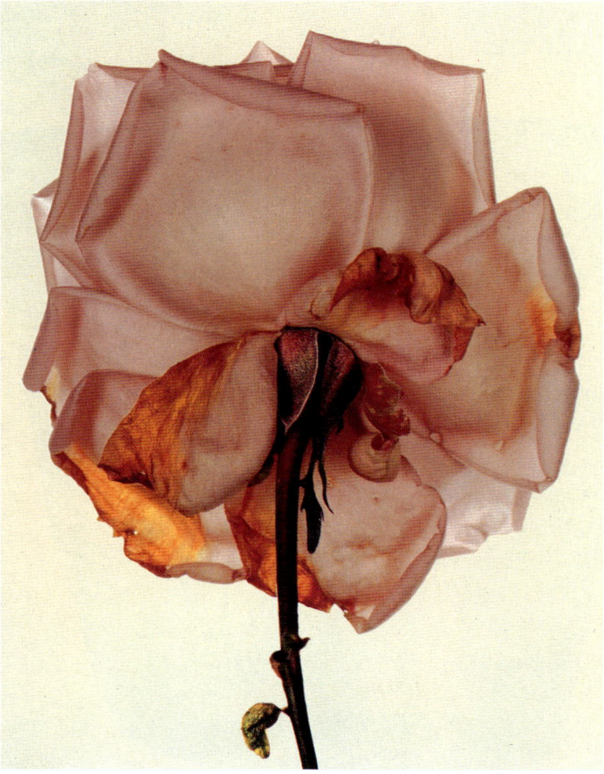

74 Irving Penn, *Blue Moon Rose.* Photograph, USA 1970

Winfried Baer

Botanical décors on porcelain

Of the wide range of décors used by European porcelain manufactories – which are and always have been strongly influenced by the fashion, philosophical ideas and history of the day – by far the most constant element has been that of flower painting. Naturally this, too, has experienced many variations in the course of time.

In the field of flower painting on porcelain, however, the exclusively botanical décors represent the smallest group. They are primarily one-time orders, often produced for botanists or royalty who either had a special interest in the subject or who had been patrons of research projects. Such documentary plant drawings, seen through the eye of the botanist, differ greatly from ordinary flower painting whose purposes are solely aesthetic and decorative.

Like much of the other porcelain decoration, the botanical décors were mainly based on graphic sources, primarily the colour illustrations in the fine scientific botanical works that, especially since the late eighteenth century – the heyday of the scientific encyclopaedia – were in vogue.[1] Thus, these purely botanical décors in porcelain painting reflect the age's enthusiasm for nature, including the animal world, particularly birds and butterflies.

The botanical depictions strive for comprehensive description as well as illustrating a scientific perception of the plant's character. Such images of plants were not intended to delight the flower lover's eye, although they certainly may have. They were meant instead as a realistic, faithful portrayal of nature which is why – in this context – people tend to speak of 'plant portraits.' Goethe, a great admirer of botanical illustrations, spoke of the two contradictory motivations driving the plant illustrator: the first, an instinctive response to the very beauty of the plant; the second, a more detached desire to reveal the plant's true nature.[2]

This conflict must have been experienced more strongly by the porcelain painters, whose task was basically decorative, than by the plant illustrators of the botanical profession. Thus, on occasion porcelain painters gave preference to the more decorative aspects. Tentative efforts at botanical plant depiction were already evident relatively early on at the two oldest European porcelain factories, where initially the focus was on imitations of the Japanese Kakiemon and Imari flowers and, to a limited extent, on the Chinese *famille verte* and *famille rose* which were called 'Indian flowers.'[3] The mid-1720s saw the emergence of this new and very naturalistic style, and the stylized 'Indian flowers' were abandoned in favour of the more realistic, so-called 'German flowers,' mainly composed of European plants.

As is evidenced by a silver-mounted tankard in the Österreichisches Museum für Angewandte Kunst in Vienna, this 'German flower' trend can be traced back to 1725 in Du Paquier's factory in Vienna. Rainer Rückert has shown that the service, produced in about 1735 for Prince-bishop Von Ermland, as well as a platter from the service for the Doge Carlo Ruzzini (1732-35), are the earliest examples from the Meissen factory. As the terms for some variants of this new décor indicate – *Holzschnittblumen* (woodcut flowers), *ombrierte Teutsche Blumen* or *Saxe ombré* (depictions of plants with shading) – these flowers were obviously copied from other botanical sources.

Tobias Frankenberg's *Newes Blumen Büchlein* (Strasbourg 1662) probably inspired these depictions of plants and insects with shaded outline. One also had recourse to Wenzel Hollar's *Insektenbüchlein Muscarum Scarabeorum Vermiumque Variae Figurae et Formae ex Collectione Arundeliana* (Antwerp 1646) for the many insects.

The first reliable source for this kind of plant depiction is the *Weinmannische botanische grosse Werk,* the famous work by the Regensburg pharmacist Johannes Wilhelm Weinmann, *Phytanthozaiconographia,* which appeared in four volumes in 1735-45 and was referred to in a Meissen factory report in 1745. Today, the Meissen factory only possesses the first volume which was printed by Hieronymus Lentz in Regensburg in 1735 with the title *Eigentliche Darstellung einiger Tausend in allen vier Welt-Theilen gewachsener Bäume, Stauden, Kräuter, Blumen, Früchte und Schwämme,* illustrated by the famous Augsburg artists Bartholomäus Seuter and Johann Elias Ridinger.

A leading painter of *botanische Blumen* (botanical flowers) was the artist Johann Gottfried Klinger who worked in Meissen from 1726-46 and continued this décor when he moved to the Imperial Porcelain Manufactory in Vienna in 1746.[4]

The 'German flower' décor was not confined to these two early factories, however, but also played a role for many porcelain manufactories such as Vincennes, Chelsea, Bow and others, all of which in their early days were inspired by the Meissen style. Even though these factories were obviously aware of the scientific source material, the level of botanical accuracy and quality of execution had yet to meet high standards. Botanical illustrations and decorative engravings were only one of many sources of inspiration for the porcelain painter at this time. Therefore, these early naturalistic plant depictions should only be regarded as budding attempts at botanical decoration without intending to provide actual scientific information.

The series of porcelain services with botanical illustrations begins with a tea service made in China for the great Swedish natural scientist Carolus Linnaeus (1707-1778), in which each piece is decorated with the *Linnaea borealis* L., a small, pink flowering plant which grows along the ground.[5] Linnaeus collected the plant on his travels in Lapland in 1732 and later gave it his name. The plant is also found on many of Linnaeus' personal possessions and in his coat of arms (fig. 75).

The idea for this service came from Linnaeus' pupil, Pehr Osbeck, who had it made during his trip to China in 1750-52. The service was to have been a surprise, but this failed because a large part of the porcelain was damaged during transportation. Shortly afterwards, the Swedish East India Company was asked to commission a new service. For this purpose, Osbeck sent a page showing a drawing of the *Linnaea borealis* L. taken from Linnaeus' *Flora Svecica* published in 1745. This first classic botanical service also highlights the significant role of the trading companies in the field of botany for, since the mid-sixteenth century, when Europe began to expand toward America, Africa and the Far East, they carried artists and natural scientists on board who not only made major improvements in cartography, but provided firsthand information on the foreign flora.

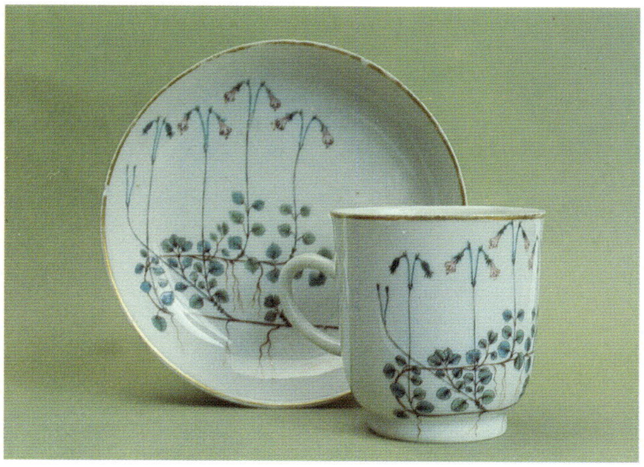

75 *Cup and saucer.* Porcelain.
Decorated with *Linnea borealis L.*
China, Ch'ien-Lung ca. 1754
Linnémuseet, Uppsala (*cat. 170*)

Linnaeus, too, had good contacts with the Swedish East India Company and had it bring back plants for him from distant lands. Apart from this hitherto earliest-known example of an accurate plant portrait on porcelain, a few plates are known from eighteenth-century China bearing plants and insects in *famille rose* colours.[6] Although no direct link has been established so far, there seems to be a connection between these plant illustrations and Maria Sibylla Merian's (1646-1717) *Metamorphosis insectorum Surinamensium,* the description of the scientific findings of her travel to the Dutch West Indies in 1698. Furthermore, one occasionally still finds Chinese imitations of plates featuring 'Hans Sloane's plants' made by the Chelsea porcelain factory. But none of these porce-

76 *Plate*. Porcelain. Decorated with *Acanthus Spinosus*. Chelsea, England ca. 1755-58
The Board of Trustees of the Victoria & Albert Museum, London (*cat. 184*)

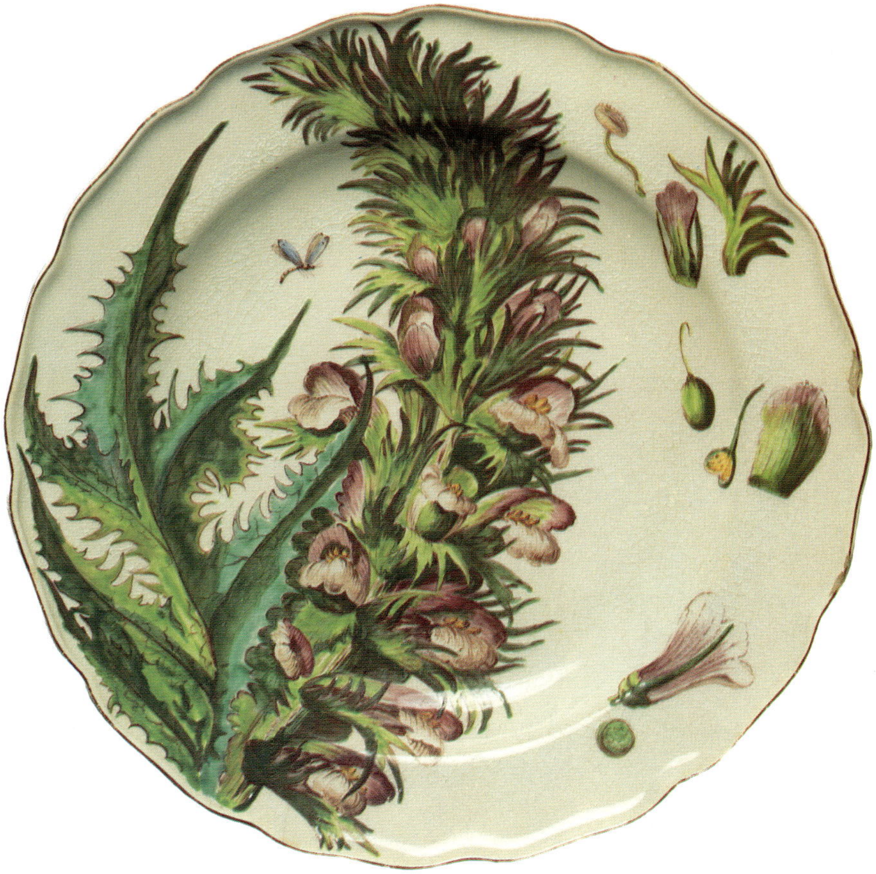

lains, produced for export to Europe, achieves the degree of scientific botanical accuracy found in both versions of the Linnaeus service.

England's oldest porcelain manufactory, Chelsea – founded in 1745 – was the first porcelain factory in Europe to apply particularly large, purely botanical motifs to porcelain doing so during the red anchor period (1753-56) which is considered the most important in the factory's history.[7] An important prerequisite for this was the strong preference for naturalistic shapes, vessels in relief imitating blossoms and leaves, and tureens and pie-molds in the shape of fowl. In this regard, Chelsea went further than its Meissen model. This naturalist style was an expression of English taste, and is found in most English porcelain manufactories. This naturalism played an important role particularly in the nineteenth century, and resulted in English porcelain being decorated with botanical motifs to a much greater extent than that of the competitors on the Continent. A second and more important prerequisite for Chelsea's botanical décor were the so-called 'Sir Hans Sloane's plants,' a reference to the natural scientist, Sir Hans Sloane (1660-1753), whose influence on the creation of Chelsea's 'Physic Garden' was great. However, the inspiration for the botanical decoration on parts of the service has been found to stem not from Sloane, but from illustrations from Philip Miller's *Gardener's Dictionary,* Christoph J. Trew's *Plantae selectae* and Georg Dionysius Ehret's (1708-1770) *Plantae et Papiliones rariores.* It was Ehret, the leading scientific plant painter of his time and with botanical ambitions of his own, who drew on this source material. These botanical décors on Chelsea porcelain are clearly based on very fruitful contacts between Chelsea's 'Physic Garden' – London's only botanical garden at that time – and the porcelain factory. Ehret might even have been directly involved. As no botanical reference works have as yet been found for the majority of the plants it is conceivable that the porcelain painters worked from living models – the plants in the 'Physic Garden' (figs. 12, 76).

Not only did the Chelsea Factory continue this décor in the subsequent golden anchor period (1758-70); the Chelsea style of botanical decoration was also imitated by the Bow manufactory. Furthermore, as mentioned above, David Howard and John Ayers, have found evidence of it on Chinese export porcelain of the same period.

A further step was taken by the Fürstenberg factory in the first purely botanical decoration on the Continent with its multicoloured plant depictions on tiles with strikingly large inscriptions.[8] These rectangular tiles 'von Porcellain von Kräutern nach dam Leben' were produced around 1759-60 for the Herzogliches Kunst- und Naturalienkabinett founded in Brunswick by Duke Carl I of Brunswick (1735-1780) and belonging to the 'Collegium Carolinum,' the predecessor of the oldest technical college in the Holy Roman Empire. This Ducal Cabinet was intended as a public collection of teaching aids for students. Only six tiles from this wall covering, which also included animal depictions, have survived in the Herzog Anton Ulrich-Museum, Brunswick.

This early evidence of deliberate renderings of naturalist illustrations an porcelain at the same time highlights the difficulties facing the painter lacking experience in this specifically botanical genre. Even if we know of no source material, we must assume that botanical reference works rather than living plants were used. However, these were not the earliest beginnings of an instructive naturalist décor by this young factory which was only founded in 1747. The factory director, Von Langen, reports as early as 30 July 1754, that they had begun to 'make life-like models of all known and in some cases foreign animals, birds, and fish, something which will also later be done with plants in the hope that those who wish to apply themselves to natural science will find them useful.'

What these early Fürstenberg tiles lack is botanical accuracy of execution, something that we do not find until some twenty years later in parts of a service with plant depictions from the Manufacture impériale et royale in Tournai (in the then Austrian Netherlands).[9] This porcelain service, stylistically dating back to approximately 1780 and decorated à la *fleur d'herbier* or *aux fleurs naturelles,* is noteworthy in that – for the first time in the history of European porcelain – motifs are rendered with utmost botanical accuracy, and correct botanical inscriptions are found on the back of the porcelain.

In 1972, Mireille Jottrand was able to trace seventeen pieces of porcelain from this service, based on the graphic illustrations used by Chelsea – Trew's *Plantae selectae.* In contrast to Chelsea, however, the very decorative insect depictions were sacrificed in favour of botanical objectivity.

Curiously, there exist pieces of the same service in which a more decorative perception of the plant predominates and, in addition, there are considerable misspellings of the plant names. This part of the service is not drawn from Trew's *Plantae selectae,* and one has not yet been able to find any other deluxe botanical works which could have served as a model.

The 1,802-piece *Flora Danica* service produced between 1790 and 1802 by the Royal Porcelain Manufactory in Copenhagen marks the climax not only of the botanically decorated services, but of all table services in the history of European porcelain. The service drew on source material taken from *Icones plantarum,* published by the director of the Copenhagen botanical garden, G. C. Oeder (1728-1791) from 1761 onwards and not completed until 1883 (fig. 77).

This unique idea of using the flora of a country, to the extent to which it had been published, as a porcelain décor goes back in all probability to Theodor Holmskjold, pupil of Linnaeus, natural scientist and physician who at the time was also a member of the board of directors of the Royal Porcelain Manufactory, Copenhagen.[10] The *Flora Danica* service was originally intended as a present for the Empress Catherine the Great (1762-1796). However, as it was unfinished when she died, it came into the possession of the Danish royal family upon completion. The first and best of the illustrators of this great, deluxe, botanical reference work, Johann Christoph Bayer, was engaged to repeat the plant drawings on porcelain, and he is responsible for most of the works (fig. 78). For the first time, all the plant drawings already published were applied systematically – without regard for their botanical significance or aesthetic appearance – to porcelain. Thus, we find not only fruits but even fungi and algae.

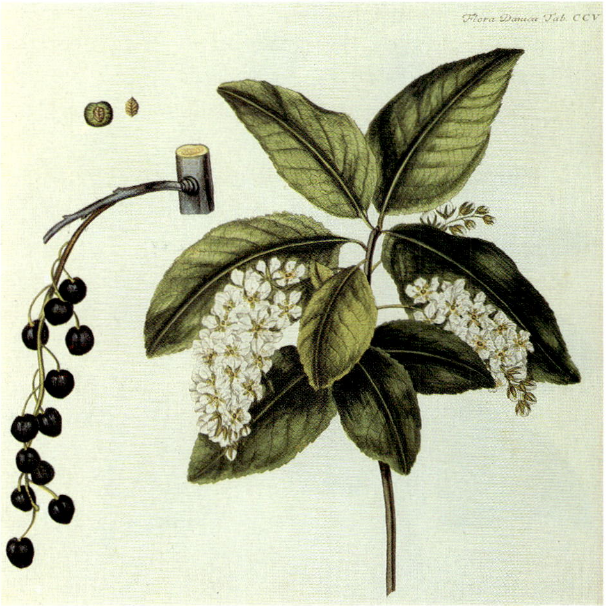

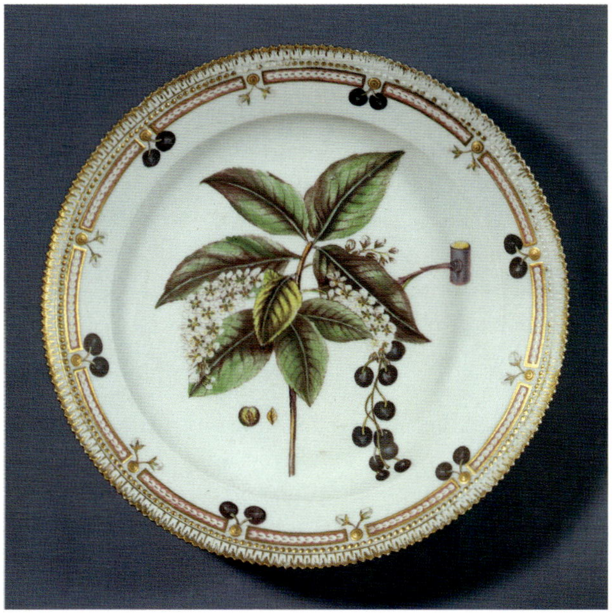

77 *Illustration* CCV from the *Flora Danica work. Prunus padus.* Hand-coloured. Model for the plate in fig. 78
The Royal Collections, Rosenborg Palace, Copenhagen (*cat. 76*)

78 ▸ *Plate* from the *Flora Danica service,* Porcelain. The Royal Porcelain Manufactory, Copenhagen 1790-1803. Decorated with *Prunus padus* after plate CCV in the *Flora Danica work* (fig. 77)
The Royal Collections, Rosenborg Palace, Copenhagen (*cat. 118*)

The close link with the source material becomes especially clear from the inscriptions on the porcelain which give not only the Latin names, but also the fascicle and plate numbers of *Icones plantarum*. This 'botany on porcelain' was so comprehensive that the Flora Danica work, which also constantly grew in size, could not always keep pace with the service. Therefore, many plant pictures are repeated two or three times on different pieces of porcelain.

In addition to Copenhagen, the English porcelain factory Derby, which was in contact with Tournai, produced various exclusive services with classic form and colour toward the end of the eighteenth century.[11] The botanical decorations are in the style of William Curtis' plant depictions in his *Botanical Magazine,* which began publication in 1787 in London. All the pieces bear English and in some cases Latin inscriptions on the back. The enthusiasm for realistic and naturalist motifs persisted in English porcelain factories during the first half of the nineteenth century, and Derby in particular succeeded during that period in making a considerable botanical contribution (fig. 79). Of the scientific plant drawings, the work of William Pegg (1775-1851) who, because of his religious convictions was generally known as 'Quaker' Pegg, stands out especially.[12] Pegg is rightly counted amongst the most prominent plant painters on porcelain of all time and his famous drawing of a thistle on a bowl (Derby museum) is considered one of the most lifelike portraits of plants ever to have been executed on porcelain (cf., F. Barret and A. Thorpe). His plant depictions, often close to natural size and in very subtle colours are – particularly during his second period at Derby (1813-20) – scenic, almost impressionistic in character, effortlessly capturing the essence of the plant. The Quakers in particular have, due to their religiously motivated, very positive attitude to nature as well as natural science, produced outstanding scientists and have been exceedingly active in publishing deluxe botanical reference works. They placed particular em-

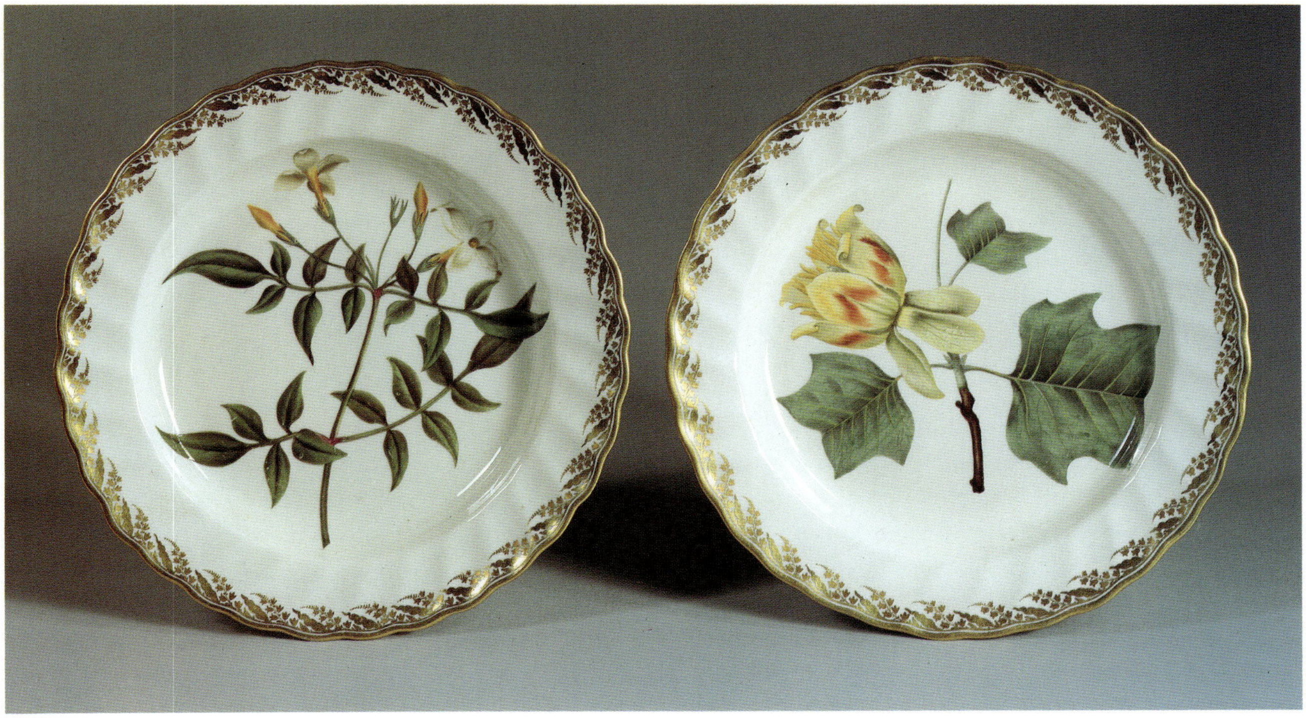

79 *Two plates.* Porcelain. Decorated with jasmine and tulip tree. Derby, England after 1794
Private Collection, Germany (*cat. 189*)

phasis on the personal care and cultivation of the plants in their own gardens.

'Quaker' Pegg, too, must have had access to such a garden because his unique, very personal plant interpretations are, as far as we know, exclusively based on studies of living plants. However, in all plant depictions, decoratively attractive though they may be, the botanically informative element was always stressed by providing the plant's correct name in English on the back of the piece of porcelain.

Outstanding plant depictions, which around 1800 were by no means the sole preserve of Derby as an excellent dessert service from Coalport shows,[13] were also produced by William Billingsley (1758-1828), Moses Webster (1792-1870) and Joseph Bancroft (1796-1857) who are known to have worked at various English porcelain factories.[14]

One of the most fascinating personalities to devote herself with great personal commitment and enormous sums of money to the advancement of botany from the turn of the century onwards was Joséphine Bonaparte (1763-1814), from 1804 Empress of France. In memory of her youth amongst the fertile, tropical vegetation of the West Indies, she transformed her favourite residence, Malmaison, into a unique botanical garden where between 1804 and 1814 some one hundred plants hitherto unknown to botany were cultivated. The fantastic and romantic court of Malmaison was not without parallels in the later court life at Neuschwanstein, the castle of King Ludwig II of Bavaria. The magnificent botanical works of reference which the Empress Joséphine's patronage made possible were not without influence on the development of the botanical décors of the various European porcelain manufacturers.

Special mention should be made here of the Manufacture impériale de Sèvres which produced a 'Service de dessert de Liliacée, plantes grasses et plantes du jardin de la Malmaison d'après Redouté,' which was delivered to the Empress at Malmaison in 1805.[15] Of this service, a few pieces have only recently been identified again, it having been given as a wedding present to her adoptive daughter, Stéphanie, on her marriage to the Heir Apparent, Prince Karl von Baden, in 1806 (fig. 80). The quality of these plant depictions from the Sèvres factory matched the fantastic source material by the most celebrated flower painter of France, Pierre-Joseph Redouté (1759-1840). It seems understandable, therefore, that the Empress had to be provided with a replacement for the service given as a present. This honourable task fell to the Königliche Porzellan-Manufaktur (KPM) in Berlin after the Napoleonic occupation in October 1806 (fig. 81).[16] Why the Berlin manufactory was entrusted with the production of such a precious service decorated with exotic plants, we do not know as yet. It seems all the more surprising as the person most likely responsible for the commission, Napoleon's Commissary General, Pierre-Antoine-Bruno Count Daru, had been appointed director of both the Vienna and Sèvres factories in 1805, after Napoleon's capture of Vienna. Financial considerations probably played a role when placing this order, as the debts of the Empress who lived a life of utmost extravagance often gave rise to ill-feeling with Napoleon. Moreover the bill for this Berlin service which came to 18,000 Taler was not paid in Paris.

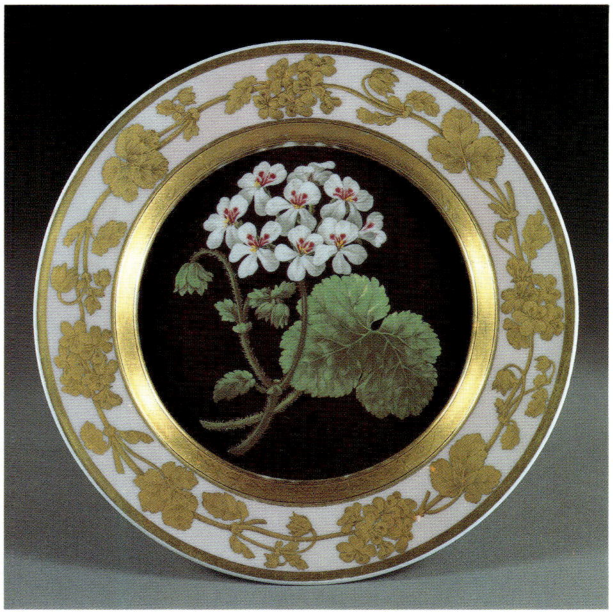

81 *Dessert plate.* Porcelain. Decorated with *Pelargonium echinatum.* Königliche Porzellan-Manufaktur, Berlin (KPM) 1806/07
Berlin-Porzellansammlung Belvedere, Schloß Charlottenburg, Berlin (*cat. 194*)

80 *Wine cooler.* Porcelain. Decorated with *Talinum anacampseros* MOENCH and *Mesembryanthemum calamiforme* L. Sèvres, France 1805
Private Collection, Germany

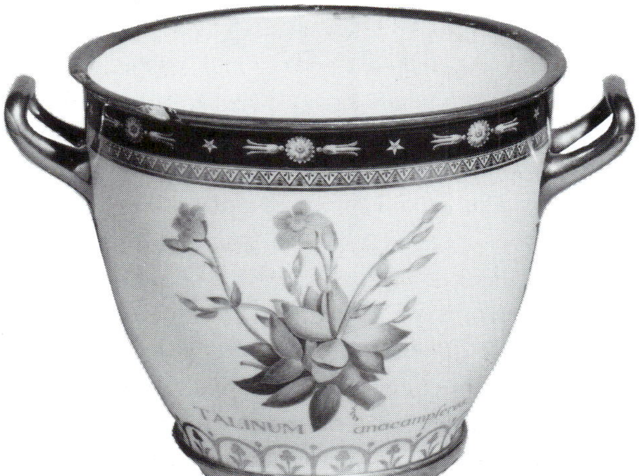

In 1804, Alexander von Humboldt received from the Empress Joséphine in Paris 'a very beautiful copperplate work on her plants' and remained in Berlin during the production of the service. Von Humboldt was possibly involved in obtaining the very expensive source material for the KPM, some of it only recently published, such as E. P. Ventenat's *Jardin de la Malmaison* (Paris 1803-05) and P.-J. Redouté's *Les liliacées* (Paris 1802-05).

None of the lavish reference works mentioned above is amongst the small amount of the KPM's historical collection of source material to have survived. However, the existing illustrated botanical books such as the first volume of N. J. von Jacquin's *Hortus botanicus Vindobonensis* (Vienna 1770), the first volume of Ch. J. Trew's *Plantae selectae* (1750), and fascicles of A.-P. de Candolle's *Plantarum historia succulentarum* (Paris 1799-1800) are eloquent proof that the Berlin factory afforded itself the luxury of such expensive specialized works. Of the twenty-two plates which have reappeared so far, the majority of the coloured engravings are found in E. P. Ventenat's

Jardin de la Malmaison, for whose illustrations Redouté was responsible.

In contrast to the Sèvres service, the KPM plants appear against differently coloured grounds, a characteristic of the Empire taste for covering the white biscuit in its entirety. Compared to Sèvres, one is struck by the greater austerity of the imagery, the pictorial element receding before the drawing, the almost pedantic effort to capture the character of the source material. There is consensus between the two services where the inscriptions are concerned. In addition to the plant's Latin name, its country of origin is given in French.

The catalogues of the Berlin Academy exhibitions show clearly that this big French order did not find the KPM unprepared for in 1804 samples of this special décor with correct botanical inscriptions had already been exhibited.[17] The Berlin factory created an unusual botanical décor with a strong English influence on a tea service (1817-23, fig. 82).[18]

The service exhibited in the Berlin-Porzellansammlung Belvedere, Charlottenburg Palace, of which four place settings having octagonal plates still exist, was painted after engravings from *Curtis's Botanical Magazine* and *Andrews's Botanist's Repository.* Most of the plants depicted stem from the British Empire and were grown in Kew Gardens (Royal Botanic Gardens). As the generic names of the plants are reminiscent of British botanists who belonged to either the Horticultural Society of London or the Linnean Society of London, this service was probably intended for a famous English botanist or one of Kew Gardens' prominent benefactors.

Redouté's botanical source material was drawn upon not only at the Sèvres and Berlin porcelain factories, but in Russia too. Around 1821, the Imperial Porcelain factory near St. Petersburg made a dessert service for the Rose Pavilion at the Emperor's palace of Pavlovsk.[19] Its décor was drawn from Redouté's most famous deluxe work *Les roses* which had been published in thirty fascicles between 1817 and 1824, The 'Pavillon des Roses,' a wooden dacha built to plans by the architect Andrey Voronikhin between 1807 and 1812, was famous for the numerous rare rose cultures in its immediate vicinity. Emperor-Alexander I, who was a frequent guest in this idyllic house, probably remembered his meeting with the Empress Joséphine at Malmaison in 1814. It was the unique rose garden there that had inspired Redouté's later rose publication. The St. Petersburg service was only partly inscribed, whereas on a series of plates consisting of many pieces produced in Arkhangelse near Moscow for Prince Nicolai Borissovitch Jussupov, the names of the varieties of roses depicted are supplied in French under the plant itself (cat. 203).[20]

This private enterprise, which could more properly be termed a 'porcelain studio' having no commercial purpose and serving only the personal pleasure of its owner, confined itself to painting on white porcelain which was purchased from various factories. Judging by the way Jussupov's porcelain tended to be dated, the series of rose plates with their largely uniform decoration of the rim was made between 1822 and 1827.

The illustrations from Redouté's *Les roses,* which were more attractive and decorative compared with those of older deluxe botanical works and which were also drawn upon in Arkhangelskoy, were not the only source material in Russian factories. Compared with the many plant series, fruit motifs which curiously appear extremely rarely as purely botanical décors, were also considered very attractive and decorative on porcelain.

The factory near St. Petersburg appropriately decorated the dessert plates in the coat-of-arms service of 1827 for Pavlovsk Palace with dessert fruits on a white ground.[21] The pieces of the service, which have mainly French and in some cases English inscriptions on the underside, are stylistically modelled on Sèvres. They are certain to have been copied from different botanical sources as the different language in the inscriptions suggests, and they reveal a subtle feel for the subject matter. Judging by the style of these fruit depictions, they must have been executed after contemporary botanical publications which have not yet come to light however.

Another porcelain service bearing a botanical décor and Latin plant names was made in about 1820, in all probability for the Württemberg royal house, by the Ludwigsburg Porcelain Manufactory (1758-1824), which in its final years was beset by technical and financial difficulties.[22] We can gain a very clear impression of this service, of which only a few items still exist, from a large collection of watercolours in the

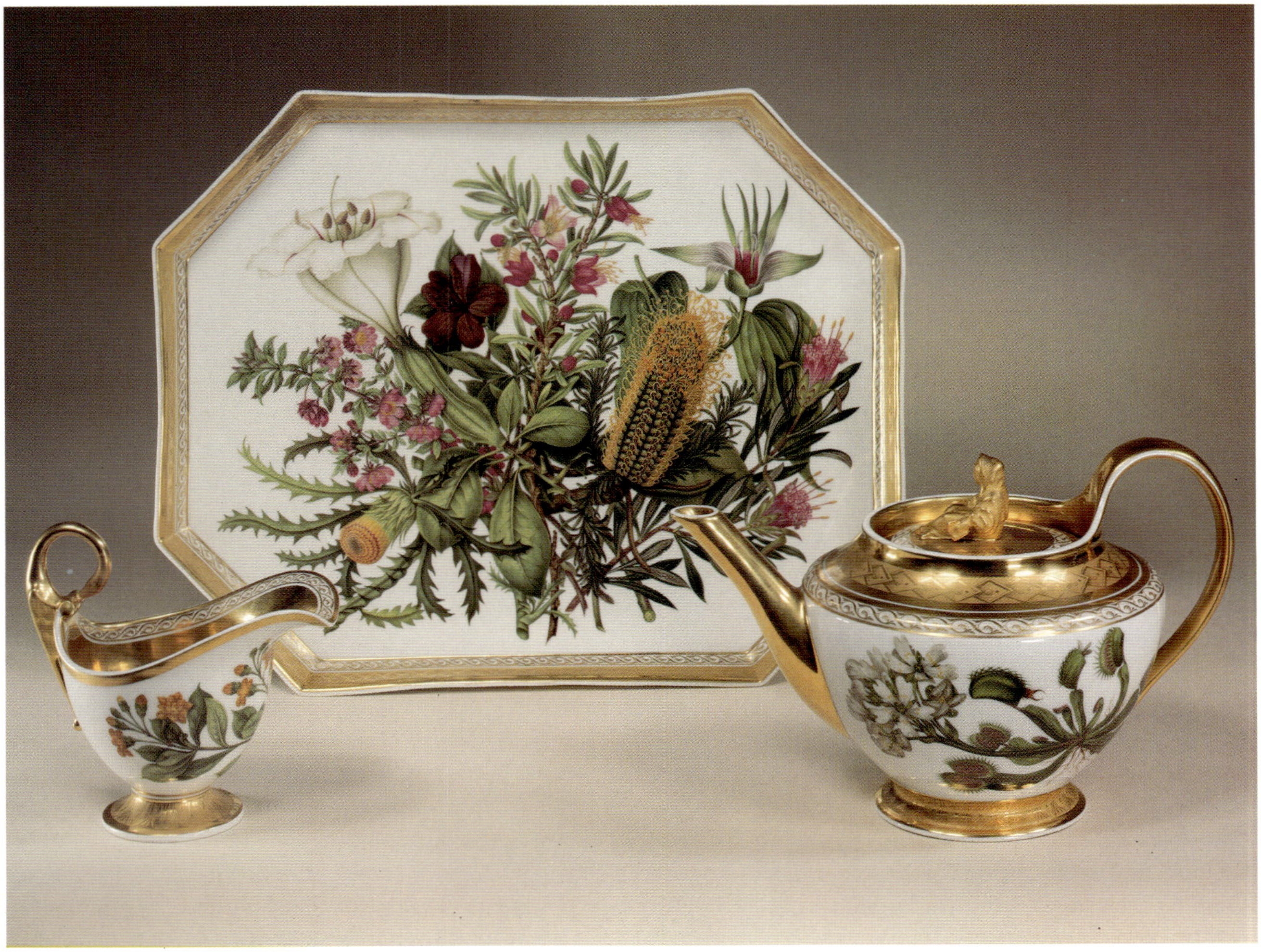

82 *Parts of a tea service*. Porcelain. Decorated with botanically accurate plants in natural colours. Königliche Porzellan-Manufaktur, Berlin (KPM) 1817-23. Most of the source material is from Curtis' *Botanical Magazine* and from Andrews's *Botanist's Repository*
Berlin-Porzellansammlung Belvedere, Schloß Charlottenburg, Berlin (*cat. 195*)

Württembergisches Landesmuseum in Stuttgart which served as direct models for the porcelain. H. W. Lack has established that the botanical source for large parts of this service, which has a white ground decorated only with polished gilding on the rim and is already suggestive of Biedermeier, was the *Hortus sempervirens* by the botanist and plant illustrator Johann Simon Kerner (1755-1830) who, as supervisor of the Royal Plant Cabinet and the botanical gardens, also had a close relationship with the Württemberg royal house.

This gigantic deluxe reference work totalling seventy-seven volumes was issued from 1795 to 1830 in ever new fascicles. As there is a close correspondence between the sketches and the source material from the reference work, and having made handwriting comparisons, Lack has suggested that both works might stem from Kerner. The often fairly dry, very simple, and somewhat flat style of painting of the sketches formerly held by the factory is doubtless due in part to the fact that Kerner's *Hortus sempervirens* was largely based on the source material of others as opposed to living plants. When making individual sketches, Kerner would sometimes change the original source material considerably, selecting individual blossoms and leaves and composing completely 'new' plants from them. In that way identification of the source material quickly becomes something of a jigsaw puzzle.

By contrast, examples of botanical décors produced by the Royal and Imperial Viennese Porcelain Manufactory during the first third of the nineteenth century are extremely naturalistic and vivid. The largest collection of such pieces of Viennese porcelain is found in the former Hoftafel- und Silberkammer in the Wiener Hofburg where today more than two hundred plates painted with mostly scientific botanical motifs and inscriptions on the underside are preserved (fig. 83).[23]

After 1800, flower painting in particular came into its own in Vienna as nowhere else. The *Alt-Wiener Blumenstück* is noted for its exceedingly high degree of naturalism, the culmination of which is the *Huldigungsbild* paying homage to Austria's Linnaeus, the natural scientist Joseph N. von Jacquin (1727-1817) and painted by the natural history painter, Johann Knapp (1778-1833).[24] The great economic and

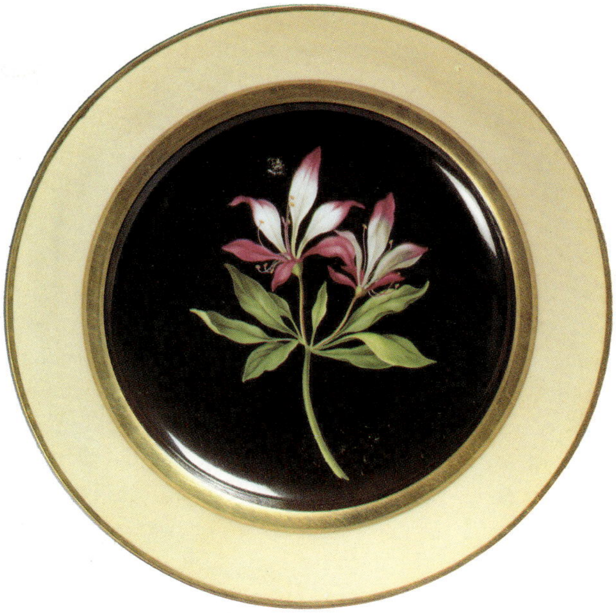

83 *Plate*. Porcelain. Decorated with *Alstroemeria pulchella*. K. K. Wiener Porzellanmanufaktur, after 1803
Private Collection, Germany (*cat. 201*)

cultural upturn following the Congress of Vienna (1814/15), had also given a strong boost to the porcelain factory, and so people speak of the period immediately afterwards as the 'golden age.'

These series of botanical plates, which originally might have been intended as a wall decoration – something not uncommon at this time – were, with few exceptions, painted after living plants.

When the porcelain factory closed down, the Österreichisches Museum für Angewandte Kunst in Vienna took over large portfolios of watercolours containing a host of first-class studies from living plants. Originally, the majority probably bore not only the signatures of the painters, but also – as can sometimes still be seen today the names of the plants depicted. If one surveys these preliminary studies and their execution on porcelain, one comes to understand certain maxims regarding botanical painting, enunciated by the Viennese Johann Baptist Ruprecht when he paid tribute to the above-mentioned *Huldigungsbild*. There he spoke of 'earnest, comprehensive, ceaseless studies,' of 'pursuing nature with tireless energy' and of 'faithfully rendering the endless variety of the most wilful of nature's creations, of capturing the most transitory of phenomena in pictorial form and making them universally intelligible.'

Here indeed a large proportion of the plant motifs have been made to appear so deceptively lifelike by the dense application of colour that one is almost inclined to speak of a photographic likeness. This attests to the enormously high technical and artistic standard of the factory a few years before the gradual decline that led to its closure. Some of the later examples of these watercolours which cover a wide time span already show signs of a trend toward a more stereotyped, superficial technique of painting. A small number of these plates, which were formerly the property of the imperial family, bear plant motifs of genres with names reminiscent of members of the Habsburg-Lothringen family.[25] The décors were executed after colour lithographs. The generic names – Trattinick describes them as 'vegetal monuments' – were published in J.P. Pohl's *Plantarum Brasiliae icones et descriptiones* in Vienna from 1826-33.

The botanical genre has held sway longest in England where it also spread to the many smaller factories, even penetrating the field of ceramics. Here, services with botanical décors are repeatedly found throughout the nineteenth century, even if the decorative aspect was again in the ascendant during the latter part of the century, and the didactic nature of the informative inscriptions was no longer of the essence.

In addition to Derby which in the twenties and thirties made botanical services that were Biedermeier in style,[26] we know of botanical services dating from about 1835 from the factories in Rockingham[27] and Swansea[28] and a dessert service with a dark blue rim from Worcester's Chamberlain period (approximately 1820)[29] as well as a botanical service from the Ridgeway factory from about 1850.[30] A Wedgwood dinner service with very graphic plant motifs and dating from approximately 1882 is probably amongst the latest botanical porcelain services of the nineteenth century.[31]

Peter Wagner

Icones Florae Danicae

The 'plant illustrators' of Flora Danica and the 'School of Illumination for Women'

During the reign of Christian VI (1730-46) an attempt was made to support industry, crafts, commerce and agriculture, a policy which was intensified under Frederik V (1746-66). The agricultural crisis that followed in the wake of the Great Nordic War (1700-20) necessitated finding new crops and thus new trade possibilities. This circumstance, together with the rapid development in the field of botany caused by the reform of the botanical system introduced by Carolus Linnaeus (1707-77), generated a desire to provide instruction in practical botany in Denmark. With this in mind, in 1751 J.H.E. Bernstorff summoned the German-born physician and botanist Georg Christian Oeder (1729-91). Attempts to secure Oeder a post at the University of Copenhagen failed, whereupon in 1752 the king granted him a salary from the Privy Purse and instructed him to draw up plans for a royal botanical garden. Oeder submitted various proposals in 1752 and 1753 which were examined and recommended by a commission before the plans were finally approved by the king in 1754.[1] They involved the laying out of a botanical garden and the provision of an adjoining library (the latter had already been established in 1752).[2] In the course of journeys through His Majesty's kingdoms and territories, Oeder was to gather information about existing plants and their uses, and experiments were to be carried out on the use of domestic plants, not only commercially but also for medical purposes in cooperation with the newly appointed senior medical physician at the Frederik's Hospital. The results were to be reported to users, i.e., farmers, priests, doctors, chemists and civil servants. They in turn were to submit reports of their experiences to the Royal Botanical Institute. Furthermore, experiments with imported plants were to be initiated in the Royal Gardens and foresters and gardeners were to receive better training. In order to help users become familiar with the plants and their uses a botanical work was to be published consisting of a textbook on botany, a list of the known plants in the twin kingdoms of Denmark-Norway and their duchies and counties and several volumes devoted to their uses. Finally, all the plants were to be illustrated with copperplate engravings so that everyone could become familiar with them. Today, all that remains of these plans is the work entitled *Flora Danica.* The volumes of illustrations, *Icones Florae Danicae* – the publication of which extended over 122 years – is the best known.

Some of the activities proposed were begun before the Royal Ordinance of 1754. Work on compiling the library had begun as early as October 1752 and plans for the botanical garden were presented in November of that same year. Material was also collected for inclusion in the botanical work *Flora Danica.* The illustrated volumes are the most interesting in the present context and only aspects of the work it involved will be touched on here.

The first problem to be solved was finding a suitable illustrator and engraver. In 1753 Oeder recommended three candidates to A. G. Moltke, Lord High Steward, as head of the Privy Purse responsible for the project. Oeder requested the applicants to fill in a questionnaire (fig. 84) providing information about their salary requirements and skills as well as submitting examples of their work for evaluation.

Christian Eberhardt, whom Oeder no doubt knew from Göttingen, where he had worked for Oeder's teacher, Albrecht von Haller, submitted several drawings including one of a thistle. He requested a salary of 200 rix-dollars per annum, and 2 rix-dollars for each drawing supplied. He estimated that he would be able to complete about eight drawings a month, however he could not engrave the actual copperplates.

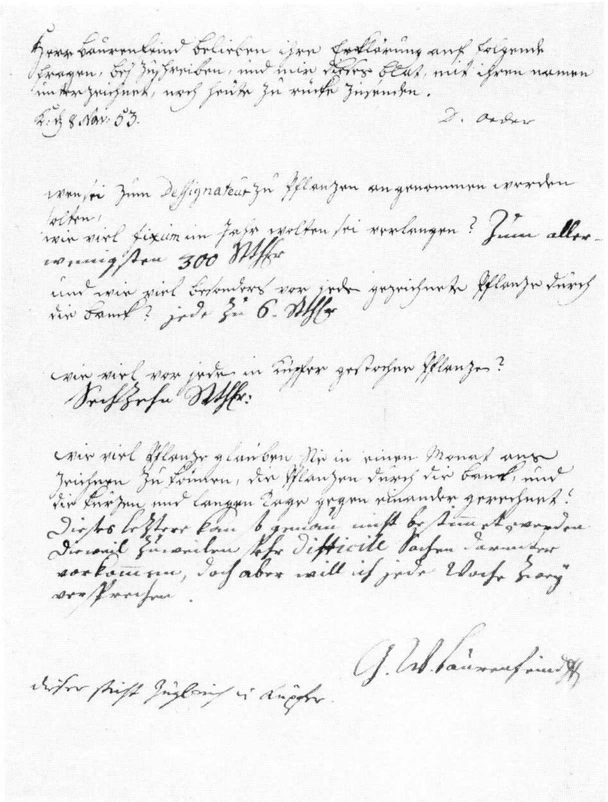

Herr Baurenfeind belieben ihre Erklärung auf folgende fragen, bei zu schreiben, und mir dieses Blat, mit ihrem namen unterzeichnen, noch heute zu rücke zusenden.

K. D. 8 Nov 53 D. Oeder

Wenn sie zum Dessignateur zu Pflanzen angenommen werden solten, wie viel fixum im Jahr wolten sie verlangen?

Zum allerwenigsten 300 Rther

und wie viel besonders vor jede gezeichnete Pflanze durch die Bank?

jede zu 6 Rther

wie viel vor jede in Kupfer gestochne Pflanze

Sechzehn Rther

Wie viele Pflanze glauben Sie in einen Monat auszeichnen zu können, die Pflanzen durch die Bank, und die kurzen und langen Tage gegen einander gerechnet?

Dieses leztere kan so genau nicht bestimmet werden, disweil zu vielen sehr difficile Sachen darunter vorkommen, doch aber will ich jede Woche zwey versprechen.

G. W. Baurenfeind

Dieser sticht zugleich in Kupfer.

84 *Questionnaire* filled in by G. W. Baurenfeind
Bregentved Archive.

Georg Wilhelm Baurenfeind (1728-1763), born in Nuremberg and summoned to Denmark as a copperplate engraver, also submitted a drawing of a thistle among others (fig. 85). He demanded a salary of 300 rix-dollars a year, 6 rix-dollars for each drawing supplied, and 16 rix-dollars for each copperplate engraving; he too felt he could complete about eight drawings a month. Baurenfeind was an experienced flower draughtsman having been one of the many who supplied drawings for Trew's *Hortus...amoenissimorum Florum* (1750-86).

Kaltenhofer (d. 1777), who was engraver to the university in Göttingen and known for his illustrations for Haller's works on anatomy, was Oeder's favourite; Oeder submitted three of Kaltenhofer's scientific illustrations for Haller. Kaltenhofer requested 200 rix-dollars a year, 5 rix-dollars for each drawing and 15 rix-dollars for each engraving. He estimated that he would be able to complete six drawings a month and would need three times as long to make engravings.

Moltke was unwilling to pay such a high amount. He was prepared to give him a fixed salary of 150 rix-dollars and 3 or 4 rix-dollars for each drawing and 10 or 12 rix-dollars at most for each copperplate. However, Moltke was prepared to guarantee him a total of 400 rix-dollars a year, which was what Oeder himself received. Furthermore, he would have to agree not to accept other work without permission and be prepared to accompany Oeder on his travels – in particular on an excursion Oeder wished to make to Norway – and to execute such drawings as he might be asked to make on the way.

Moltke sent the candidates' drawings to the professors at the Royal Sculpture & Painting Academy for appraisal asking them to indicate which candidate 'executed the best, most meticulous and accurate work with regard to lifelike drawing as well as copperplate engraving.'[3]

The professors were also asked to recommend one of their own pupils for employment if there was one

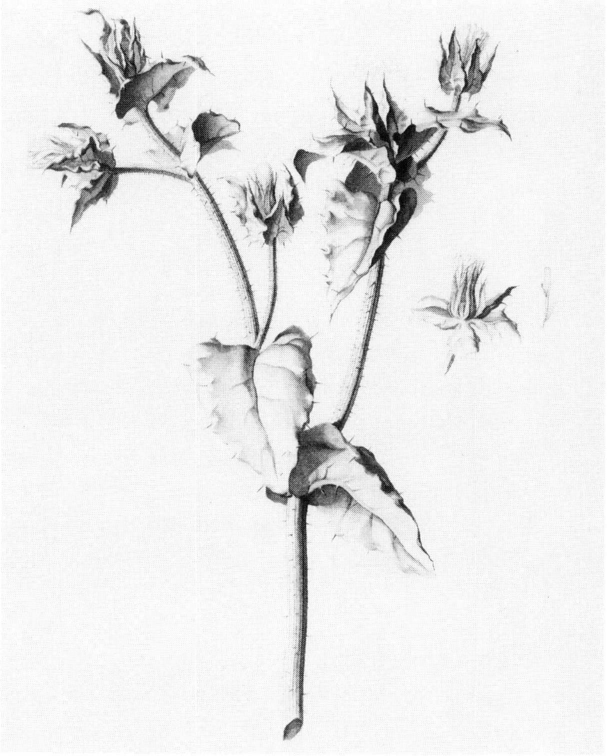

85 G. W. Baurenfeind, *Carthamus tinctorius*. Pen and watercolour. 1753
Bregentved Archive

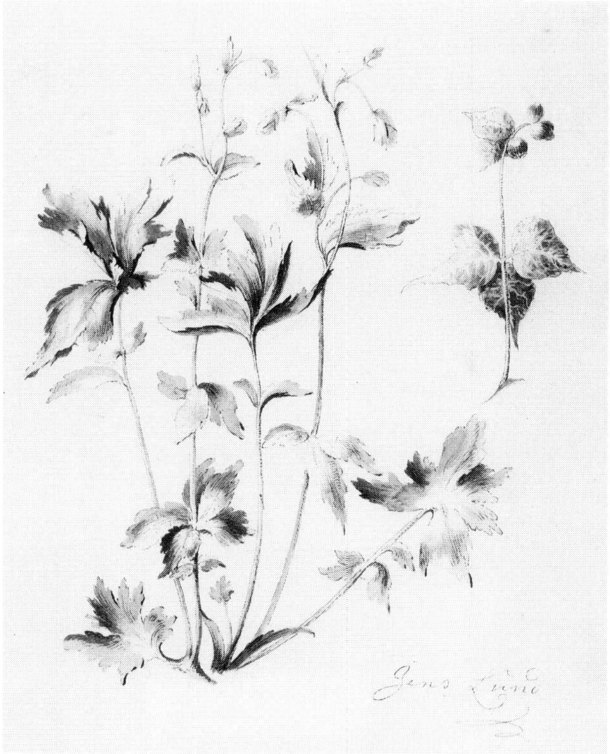

86 Jens Lund, *Avens* (Geum). Pen and watercolour. 1753
Bregentved Archive

good enough who would accept the same terms Moltke was prepared to offer Kaltenhofer. If a pupil as skilful as Kaltenhofer could be found, he would be preferred. However, samples of his work had to be seen.

The answers given by the professors demonstrated their complete ignorance of the requirements necessary for a skilful flower illustrator. In fact they felt Oeder's demands were unreasonable; the Academy would easily be able to supply a suitable person if given a little time to train him, for 'what Oeder demands is precisely the lowest level of proficiency in drawing, where all pupils commence.'

Kaltenhofer was considered the best of the three candidates. The professors also felt he should be content with the salary offered, 'particularly in consideration of the circumstance, as here in before stated, that this kind of drawing is one of the most inferior and calls more for diligence than perception, for which reason we humbly submit that it would be tantamount to abusing His Majesty's favour should any person be remunerated for this work alone with an annual salary of 50, let alone 100 rix-dollars, especially as such a plant illustrator will, in the future, when he does not know what else to do, be of no further use...'

Since His Majesty desired that one of the Academy's students be preferred, the professors proposed Jens Lund, 'whose drawing, which he has executed in the greatest haste and almost without any assistance,' they enclosed (fig. 86).[4] On the back of one of Lund's drawings, Carl Gustav Pilo (1711-1793) has written, in an odd mixture of Swedish and Danish, that the drawing though not as meticulous as Kaltenhofer's, was made by Lund in the greatest haste at the request of the professors, and that it is the first drawing of the kind he had made. Lund promised that after a fortnight's work in the genre he would be able to supply what Oeder required. The professors stressed that Lund would be satisfied with 4 rix-dollars per drawing and no fixed salary, and that one of their own number, I.M. Preisler (1715-1794), as copperplate engraver to the court, was already under obligation to engrave to His Majesty's orders. Lund was not an engraver.[5] The professors' recommendation was supported by a letter from the director of the Royal Academy, Nicolai Eigtved (1701-1754).[6]

Moltke sent the drawings and their evaluations to the royal physician, J.J. von Berger (1723-1791) and the royal surgeon, H.F. Wohlert (1703-1779), who constituted a small commission for the botanical institutions, requesting their opinion. They replied that they agreed with the Academy professors' preference for Kaltenhofer. Regarding the proposal to employ Jens Lund, they deemed themselves incompetent to judge, but felt they should stress that even were he to develop the necessary proficiency, the success of *Flora Danica* depended on the illustrator, and it would surely be difficult for Oeder to set a person to work who would first have to be trained. Furthermore, the time remaining before Oeder's excursion to Norway was too short for Lund to learn to draw flowers from life the way Kaltenhofer, as had been documented, was capable of doing. Moreover, it was known that Kaltenhofer could draw other subjects – this they added as a comment to the observation made by the professors that a flower illustrator could not be used for any other purpose than drawing flowers.[7]

Unfortunately Kaltenhofer refused to come; he had exploited the Danish negotiations to have his salary in Göttingen increased by 100 rix-dollars, since he was regarded as indispensable by the university.[8] Hence, the king decided that Oeder should look for a skilful illustrator during a tour through England, the Netherlands, France and Germany.[9] Oeder aimed high. In England he offered the post to the renowned Georg Dionysius Ehret (1708-1770) who, however, declined. Among the possible reasons for his decision were the fact that he not only was satisfied where he was,[10] but a few years previously he had resigned his post as illustrator to the botanical garden at Oxford University because he was dissatisfied. Besides, he had been offered the same salary as Kaltenhofer, who had not been tempted either.[11]

Later on his journey Oeder made an agreement instead with the copperplate engraver Michael Roessler (1705-1777) in Nuremberg; he had engraved some plates for Haller's works. From the contract, signed on 11 February 1755 and confirmed by the king on 8 March that same year, it appears that Roessler was to receive a fixed salary of 150 rix-dollars a year, 4 rix-dollars for every drawing, and 12 rix-dollars for every engraved plate. If Roessler did not receive enough work to earn 250 rix-dollars over and above his fixed salary and his annual income – thus not reaching the sum of 400 rix-dollars – the difference was to be made up. He was to obey Oeder's instructions and was not allowed to accept other work without permission. He was to accompany Oeder on the latter's travels.[12] The king granted him 100 rix-dollars for travel expenses and a fixed salary beginning 1 January of that year, since he had been unable to undertake work in Nuremberg while negotiations were in progress.

While Michael Roessler was employed as illustrator and engraver to the botanical institutions, it was his son Martin (1727-1782) who executed the drawings and accompanied Oeder on his travels, first in Norway and later to the island of Bornholm and the duchies of Schleswig and Holstein (fig. 87).

Due to Oeder's protracted sojourn in Norway (1755-60) publication of *Flora Danica* did not commence until 1761. The arrangement was that the king paid Oeder's and the illustrator's salaries, travel expenses and the cost of the individual drawings and engravings, while Oeder was responsible for the actual publication. The work was published in one 'black' (i.e., uncoloured) edition and one 'illuminated' (i.e., coloured) edition in sets, or fascicles, of sixty plates each. Oeder and the Roesslers had carefully worked out how the engravings had to be executed to ensure that both the 'black' and the 'illuminated' plates would be beautiful (figs. 88, 89).[13] The work was an immediate success – in fact so great that Oeder ran into difficulties. Far too many people wanted the hand-coloured edition, and Oeder's staff of illuminators was not sufficient to colour so many copies. Oeder was obliged to ask the king, through Moltke, for help, and by means of a grant from the royal fund for rent and fuel assistance he managed to secure the services of Mrs. J.A. Seizberg (ca. 1732-1772) to illuminate the copies of *Flora Danica* ordered by the king.[14] Mrs. Seizberg had come to Denmark with the copperplate engraver Frantz Michael Regen-

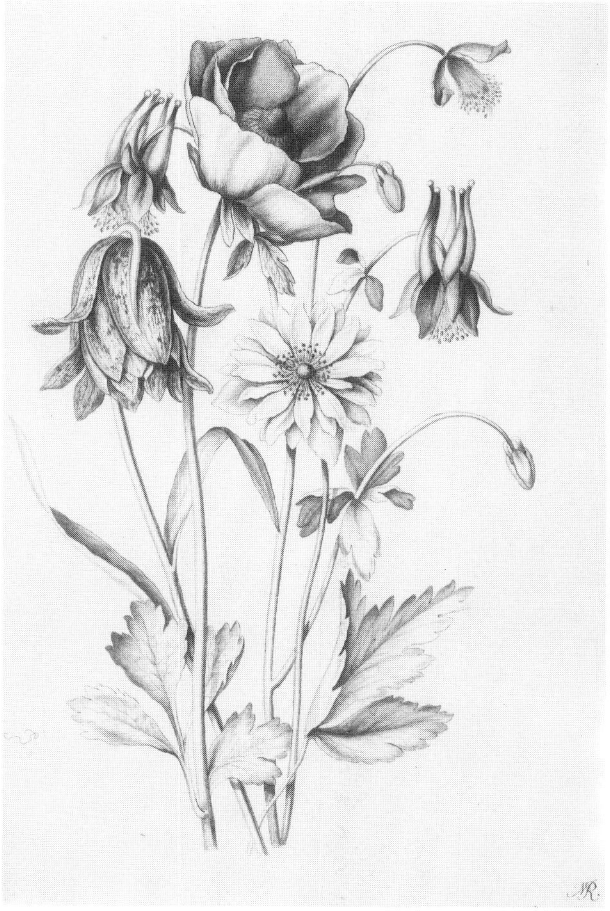

87 Martin Roessler, *Aquilegia sp., Anemone sp., Fritillaria sp.* With fully double bloom, *Ranunculacé*. Pen and watercolour. 1753
Bregentved Archive

fuss (1713-1780) to illuminate a conchological work he had published.[15]

Nevertheless, the problems were not solved, and at the end of November 1761 Oeder turned once more to Moltke. A skilful illuminator, he wrote, could colour twenty to twenty-two copies of a fascicle of sixty plates within a year. He already had orders for 185 copies, not counting those from abroad he had yet to receive.[16]

He was dissatisfied with the illuminators he was using, apart from Mrs. Seizberg, because they were 'slow and to a certain extent negligent.' They for their part were unhappy with their wages: 8 farthings per hour, or 5 rix-dollars per fascicle (the difference between the coloured and the uncoloured edition). Oeder had therefore sent forty-five copies to Brunswick, where there were plenty of illuminators and where the work could be done under the supervision of his brother, who was director of the collections of specimens of flowers, animals, etc. The actual illumination would also be cheaper there, only 4 rix-dollars per fascicle. Oeder also suggested to some of the Norwegian subscribers that they have only one illuminated copy sent to Norway and arrange for the illumination of the remainder themselves; it would be cheaper, and they would not have to wait so long for their copies due to 'difficulties in finding enough il-

88 G. C. Oeder, *Icones Florae Danicae*, Copenhagen 1761-1883. Uncoloured copy
Botanisk Centralbibliotek, Copenhagen (see *cat. 76*)

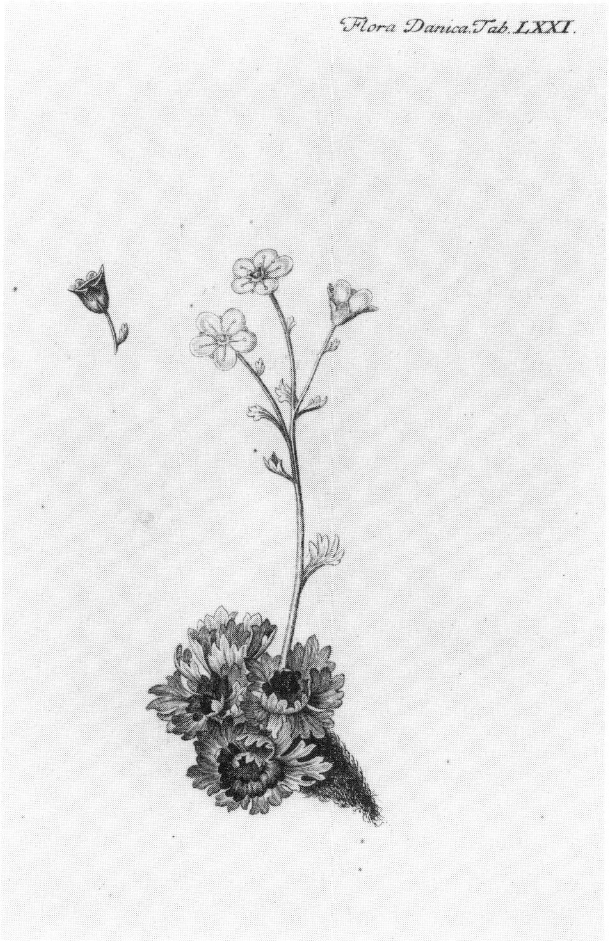

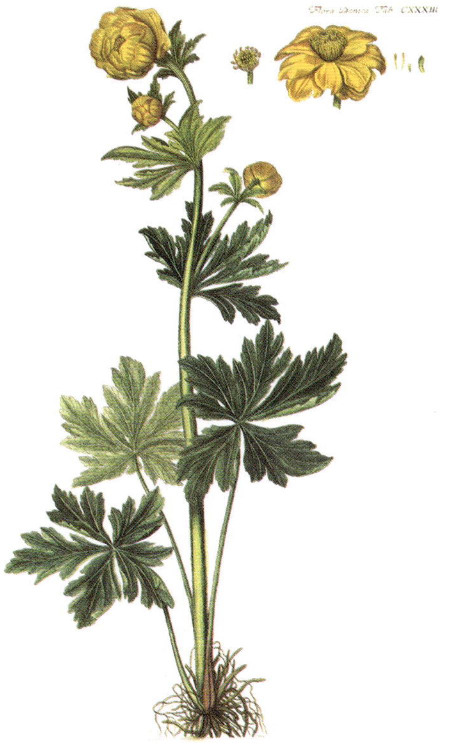

89 G.C.Oeder, *Icones Florae Danicae*, Copenhagen 1761-1883. Pl. CXXXIII, globe-flower, *Trollius sp.* Hand-coloured
Kunstindustrimuseet, Copenhagen (*cat. 76*)

luminators.'[17] But he knew he was only evading the issue and to avoid any further work being undertaken abroad he finally suggested that the Royal Academy be instructed to carry out the illumination of a number of the copies ordered by the king. Moreover, Mrs. Seizberg should be paid a salary by the king to teach 'some suitable young people to perform this work... these illuminations are in reality woman's work, through which such a person might easily earn 100 rix-dollars per annum and manage on this, which most men would find too little.'

Oeder probably formed the idea of training needy young women from his visit to the botanist Bernard de Jussieu in Paris. Jussieu, who was *demonstrateur* at the Jardin du Roi, worked together with Madeleine Basseporte (1701-1780), who was *Peintre du Roy, de son Cabinet et du Jardin du Roy.* She gave free tuition to destitute young girls in order that they might earn a living as flower painters.[18]

Fortunately, a sculptor named Starck from Nuremberg arrived in Copenhagen at this time. His wife was an illuminator, and had coloured the illustrations in Rösel's work on insects (on which Michael Roessler had also worked).[19] Oeder added in the letter that if a 'gratification' could be obtained from the king to enable the family to settle in Copenhagen it would be possible to engage her for the colouring of the royal copies (fig. 90).

Moltke gave Oeder orders to negotiate with the professors at the Academy as to how 'the illumination service for... flora could be established on the most useful footing for the kingdoms and territories, especially for women,' for the work was never to be sent out of the country again.[20] The professors were instructed to negotiate with Oeder 'as to how this illumination service could and should best be arranged as an ornament for the kingdoms and a most advantageous goal for the nation.'

The two ladies, Mrs. Seizberg and Mrs. Starck, were available. The king wished the plates to be executed 'with the greatest accuracy' and believed that this could best be achieved if the Academy supervised the work; the Academy was therefore obliged to help. Moltke was convinced that 'the Academy would be reluctant to appoint members of the male sex, or see them appointed, to the illumination service,' a threat which roused the professors to action, for they were not going to have their (male) pupils forced into women's work!

In Moltke's presence a meeting between the professors and Oeder was held at the Academy at the beginning of February 1762. It was agreed that an 'Illumination School' for 'Womenfolk' be established by appointing two 'mistresses' – whose number could be increased to three – with a salary of 50 rix-dollars a year; an additional 50 rix-dollars a year was to be provided for materials. The school was placed under the supervision of Pilo on behalf of the Academy and Oeder on behalf of *Flora Danica.* In addition to their salary the teachers were to receive payment for the actual illuminated sheets supplied, and when their pupils became sufficiently skilled they were to have a share of the earnings. Through the intervention of the priest at the Orphanage in Christianshavn Oeder had received the principal's permission to allow each of the teachers to have three or four orphan girls as

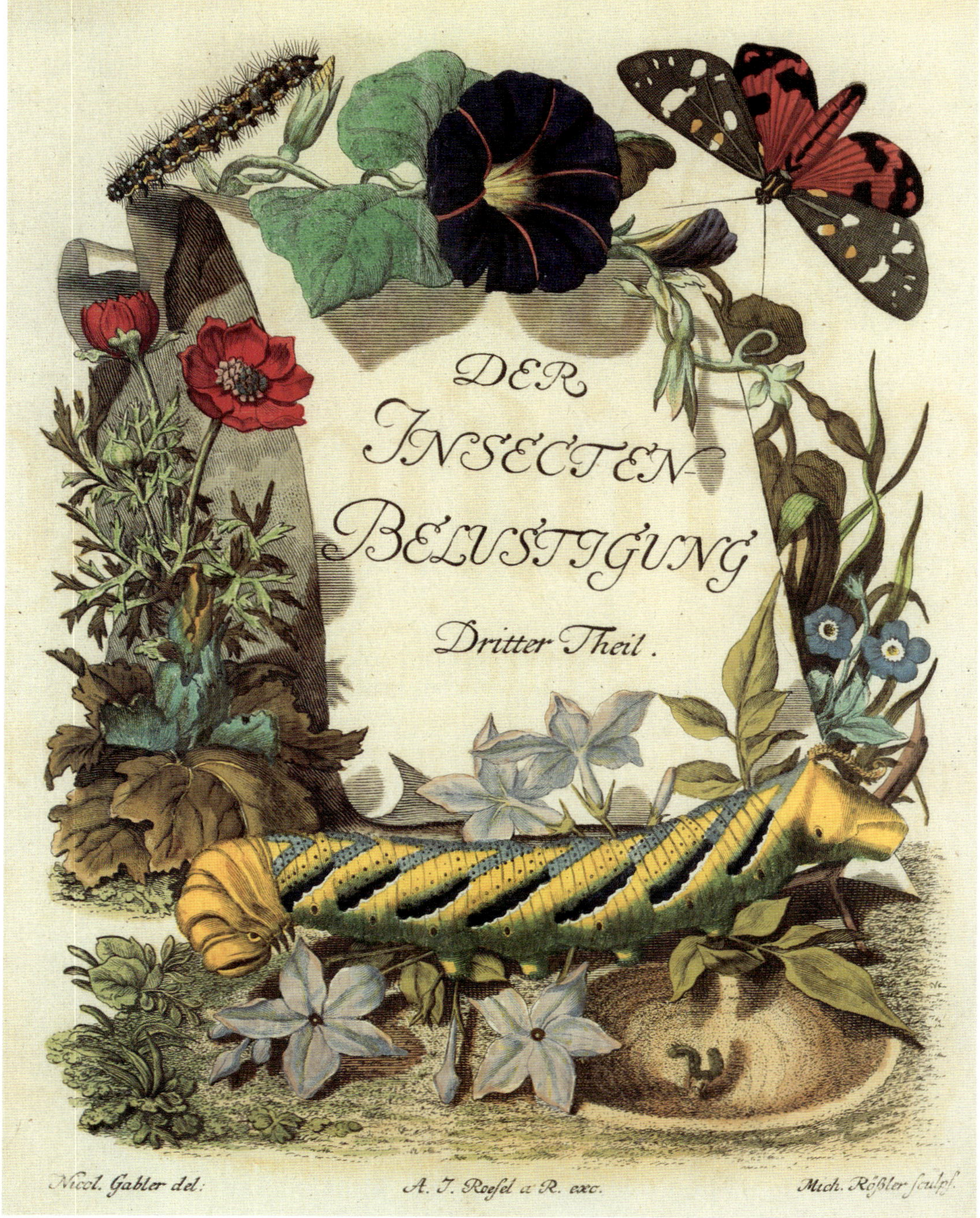

90 August Johan Rösel von Rosenhof, *Der monatlich herausgegebenen Insekten-Belustigung*, Nuremberg 1746-61. Zoologisk Museums bibliotek, Copenhagen

pupils. The teachers were now able to look for suitable premises in Christianshavn. Mrs. Seizberg and Mrs. Starck were appointed as from 1 April 1762 and the school was to continue 'until a sufficient number of illuminators has been trained so that the work of illumination can be completed in this country alone.'[21]

As far as can be deduced from available sources, the school functioned admirably. However, Oeder's problems were far from over. When publication began in 1761 a total of 183 illustrations and 131 engraved plates was available. Oeder was supposed to issue one fascicle per year, thus he had enough material for the first three years. However, since the engraver could not produce more than about thirty engravings a year it was obvious that problems would arise during the 1760s, especially when Oeder began issuing two fascicles a year as of 1768. Oeder therefore commissioned Kaltenhofer in Göttingen to execute drawings for fascicle No. 8 under the supervision of the university's professor of botany, I. A. Murray. These drawings were of plants 'common to the district around Göttingen and Copenhagen,' as Oeder wrote. The sixteen plates were thus drawn from plants found in Germany and not in the twin kingdoms.[22] Kaltenhofer engraved several of the plates, as well as a few after drawings sent from Copenhagen. For help with the copperplate engravings Oeder turned to the brothers Meno and Johannes Haas who, like the Roesslers, had been called in from Nuremberg.[23] It was not acceptable that the drawing of plants for *Flora Danica* should be made abroad, therefore, in 1768 Oeder summoned Johann Christoph Bayer (1738-1812) to help Martin Roessler, who was having difficulty producing the drawings quickly enough.[24] Two more illustrators, Søren Johannes Helt and Otto Christian Trolle (1736-1798) also worked on drawings for the Flora Danica in Oeder's time.[25]

Due to financial difficulties the royal botanical institutions were closed in 1770, but Oeder continued as publisher of *Flora Danica* until 1772, when, in connection with the Struensee affair, he was banished from Copenhagen and appointed 'Landvoigt' in Oldenburg. The publication of *Flora Danica* ceased for a while; the 'School of Illumination' was closed down and the illustrators were unemployed. While the engraver Michael Roessler was paid his salary, his son, who had been paid a sum for each drawing, was impoverished to such an extent that upon resumption of work on the flora in 1774 he had to be given a grant from the Privy Purse to buy clothes.[26]

The fame of the work, due in large part to the high quality of the engravings, ensured its continued publication. A successor proposed by Oeder himself, Otto Friedrich Müller (1730-1784), became publisher. The last fascicle was published in 1883.

Through its efforts the government achieved far more than the publication of a botanical work. With the illustrators and engravers who had been engaged, as well as the illuminators who had been trained, Denmark now possessed the necessary expertise to undertake the publication of works with coloured copperplate engravings.

Several of these were indeed published during the following years, including *Flora Aegyptiaco-Arabica*, the result of a Danish expedition to Arabia Felix. This included a number of drawings by Baurenfeind, who had been one of the original candidates for the post of illustrator to *Flora Danica*. Other works are a zoological counterpart to *Flora Danica* entitled *Zoologia Danica*, with drawings by Søren Helt and C. F. Müller; and Theodor Holmskiold's *Beata ruris otia fungis Danicis impensa*, probably the most beautiful work on mushrooms ever published. The illustrator of the latter work, I. C. Bayer, joined the Royal Copenhagen Porcelain Manufactory in 1776, where his chief contribution was the decoration of the Flora Danica dinner service.

Jørgen Hein

Fashions in floral enamels

Expeditions to the New World returned to Renaissance Europe with hitherto unknown riches, giving nature a new and central importance in the European conception of the world. Exotic plants and flowers quickly became coveted collector's items at court and were cultivated and improved in the new scientific workshops of the botanical garden. The results were described and reproduced in botanical works, the so-called florilegia, which in turn generated interest at all levels of society.

This new interest naturally carried over to the crafts, where the representation of flowers and plants was gradually liberated from Renaissance stylization, to unfold in a naturalism culminating in 1650-75. Borrowed from the silverware of the middle classes, the style is called 'floral baroque.' However, while the swelling blossoms and foliage of the silversmith were usually sculpted and executed by chasing or casting, the goldsmiths preferred another medium: the costly and brilliant gold enamel, consisting of glazes that, when fired, are bonded to the gold ground and acquire the hardness and lustre of metal. Enamel provided goldsmiths with the colours of the painter's palette and in combination with precious stones and pearls, became one of the high points of the goldsmith's art. This essay traces and illustrates the development of this technique with examples from Danish collections, particularly those from Rosenborg Palace. These floral enamels can be located to the period of conflict between the crown and the aristocracy around 1650, and the struggle for power between the children of Christian IV's first and second marriages, especially between Frederik III and his consort Sophie Amalie and her rival Leonora Christina, daughter of Kirsten Munk and wife of the Lord Steward Corfitz Ulfeldt.[1]

Mannerism favoured the pendant as jewellery, preferably decorated with the gods of antiquity or with the virtues posing on a stage with architectural scenery or in front of openwork scrolls, strapwork and grotesques, the so-called *Schweifwerk*. A popular variant included the use of 'baroque' pearls (large irregular pearls) for the 'body' or central portion of the pendant, as an expression of the Lord's creation. Here the goldsmith's challenge was to honour the pearl's divine form by displaying human ingenuity. An example of this is the pendant in the form of a crane (figs. 91, 92). The crane was considered an emblem of vigilance, for were the bird to fall asleep it would drop the stones clutched in its claws and awaken.

Like the pearl used for the body, the rubies in the wings reveal Mannerism's taste for vivid colour, especially red, green and blue. However, on the reverse is a new ornament which dates the jewel to around 1610: foliage and dots spread across the surface in spirals and branches surrounding a cluster of fruit with an insect. The tips of the pointed leaves are trilobed and like the leaf surface, which is usually pierced, curved and bulging to one side. The dots also form a curved line, like peas in a pod, leading to the identification of the style as the 'peapod style,' a stylized, plant-like ornament possibly derived from Islamic ceramic ware.[2]

Also typical of the time is a paler range of colour omitting the dominant red. Peapod ornament was frequently executed in the special *baisse-taille* technique of applying translucent enamel to a ground modelled in low relief by chasing or engraving. The reflexion of light causes the colours to change in hue and intensity depending on the thickness of the enamel and the underlying surface's hachure, as exemplified in the yellow and green of the central fruit motif.

The earliest peapod works appear to have been exe-

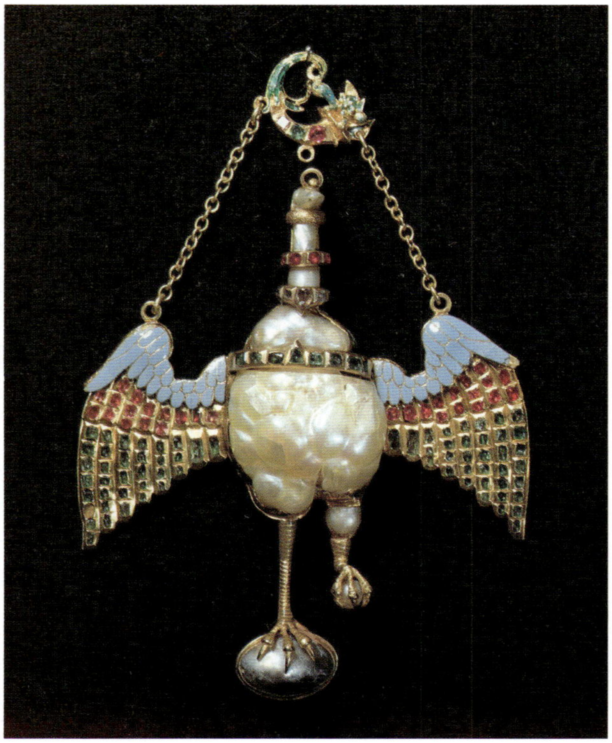

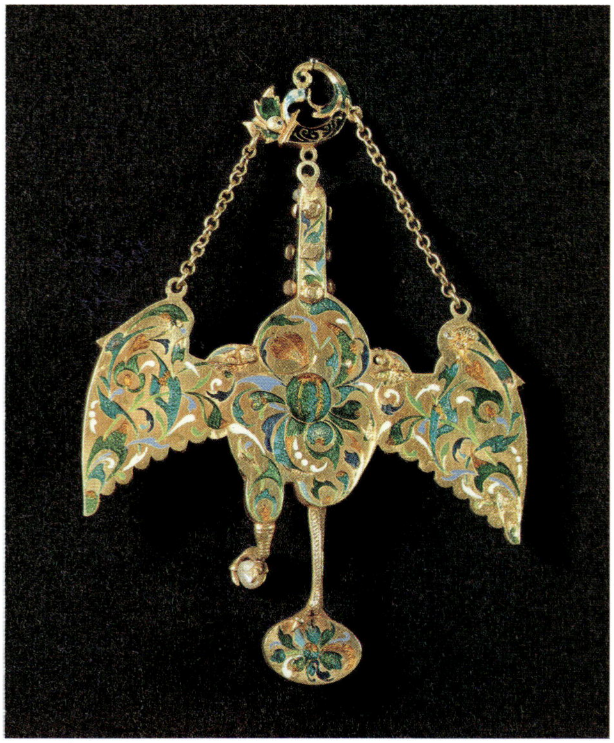

91-92 *Pendant* representing a crane, front and reverse. Pearls, gold, rubies, emeralds, diamonds. Northern Europe ca. 1610
The Royal Collections, Rosenborg Palace, Copenhagen

cuted in France, but this ornament quickly spread north. Danish examples include a parade rapier worn by the heir presumptive, the prince elect in a portrait from around 1620, as well as in jewellery decorating the riding trappings made for his wedding in 1634. In contrast to the peapod ornament on the reverse of the crane pendant, that on the trappings is generally on a ground of white enamel.[3]

The white ground recurs on the ceremonial anointing rapier of the absolute monarchy (fig. 93), but here the ornament displays a mixture of naturalism and stylization. It is seen most clearly on the inside of the hilt's scallop-shaped shell guard, where stems grow up from the bottom, bearing flowers and leaves which fill the surface. While the diverse, single blossoms have their counterparts in nature, they are shown here as belonging to one plant bearing several different flowers and the bulges and dots of the peapod ornamentation continue in the foliage of the stems.

These semi-naturalistic motifs are known from engravings for goldsmiths published by François Lefebure in 1635. On the anointing rapier's shell guard, the ornament is executed in enamel painting, a technique perfected in France in the 1630s and traditionally associated with the brothers Toutin. Here only opaque colours are used and applied by brush onto a ground, usually of white enamel, fired in advance.

The rapier's lavish diamond embellishment anticipates future styles and is a clear indication that enamel as ornamentation of jewellery was on the wane. Several reasons for this shift can be pinpointed. In part it was due to the increased availability of diamonds and the new rose cutting technique which created many facets thus enhancing the diamond's brilliance. Changing taste in costume and hair styles also played a role, as did new modes in interior decoration. The many mirrors and increased use of wax candles helped create an atmosphere which stressed contrast and coordination of details calculated to have an effect at a distance. For this, sparkling diamonds and gleaming pearls, combined in closed and simple forms, had a stronger visual effect than variegated, enamelled, figure jewellery like the crane pendant. Thus the abundance of individual jewellery gave way to sets of brooches and earrings, while necklaces and bracelets were replaced by pearls. Naturally, this development benefitted the jeweller and the enameller at the expense of the goldsmith, but the specialisation led to collaboration and at the same time the growing affluence created a market for what today we would call accessories or status symbols: watchcases, costume furnishings, jewel boxes and the like.

These precious objects, including the anointing rapier, rarely bear a maker's mark. However, newly discovered accounts show that the rapier was a gift from Christian IV to his second son, later Frederik III, on the occasion of his marriage to Sophie Amalie in 1643. The master responsible for it was Lucas Schaller of Hamburg, possibly an immigrant from Augsburg – Southern Germany's renowned city of goldsmiths – and presumably selected by the connoisseur Frederik himself.[4]

The bridegroom was not the only fashion-conscious member of the royal family, for the semi-naturalistic decoration on the rapier is found on a number of objects (fig. 94), for example on the reel case containing an almanac printed in Paris in 1647, the same year that Leonora Christina accompanied her husband Corfitz Ulfeldt, the king's Lord Steward, on an embassy to France. Although the almanac is not identified in the Ulfeldt's estate, it could well be a souvenir Leonora Christina acquired while shopping in Paris. From her mother, Kirsten Munk, she inherited a pendant (fig. 94) whose reverse shows a crowned K in a wreath of naturalistic flowers and peapod style leaves, executed in plane ground champlevé. The front is adorned with an older Renaissance cameo of onyx showing the animals boarding Noah's Ark. A section of the sky was broken off and the cameo, therefore, had to be remounted. The subject of the gem indicates that it was a token of the older Christian IV's love for the very young Kirsten in the years following their morganatic marriage in 1615: their children would populate a new and better world.

The monogram of their daughter's rival, Frederik III's consort Sophie Amalie, is on the scabbard of a hunting sword (fig. 94), a weapon used to put a wounded stag to death. Naturalistic flowers are combined with acanthus leaves, masks and game executed in polychrome enamel in low relief on a ground of horizontally hatched gold. The grips of the sword and matching hunting knives are of rhinoceros horn and decorated with lions, fantastic animals and acanthus leaves in a different sort of enamel. These might actually not have been a matched pair: Sophie Amalie may have had the scabbard made for the hunting sword which the prince elect's widow, Magdalene Sibylla, was obliged to relinquish after her husband's death. Also his, presumably, was the pair of spurs decorated with lions and flowers in higher relief and unfolding in full naturalism, delineated by bands, which retain the character of the peapod ornament on the rowels (fig. 94).

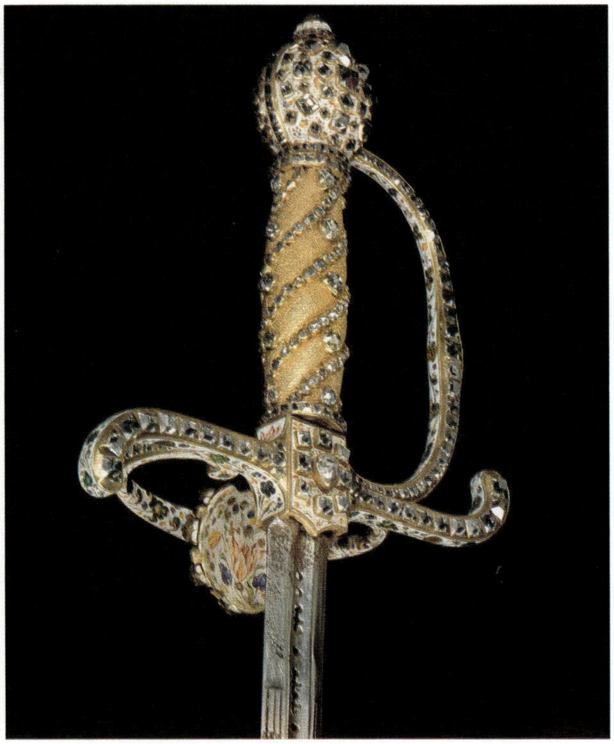

93 *The absolute monarchy's anointing rapier*. Originally a wedding present to Frederik III, 1643. Executed by Lucas Schaller in Hamburg. Gold, enamel, diamonds
The Royal Collections, Rosenborg Palace, Copenhagen

Magdalene Sibylla's monogram and the year 1650 adorn a gold pitcher in the Kunstindustrimuseet (fig. 95), whose sides are decorated with exquisitely en-

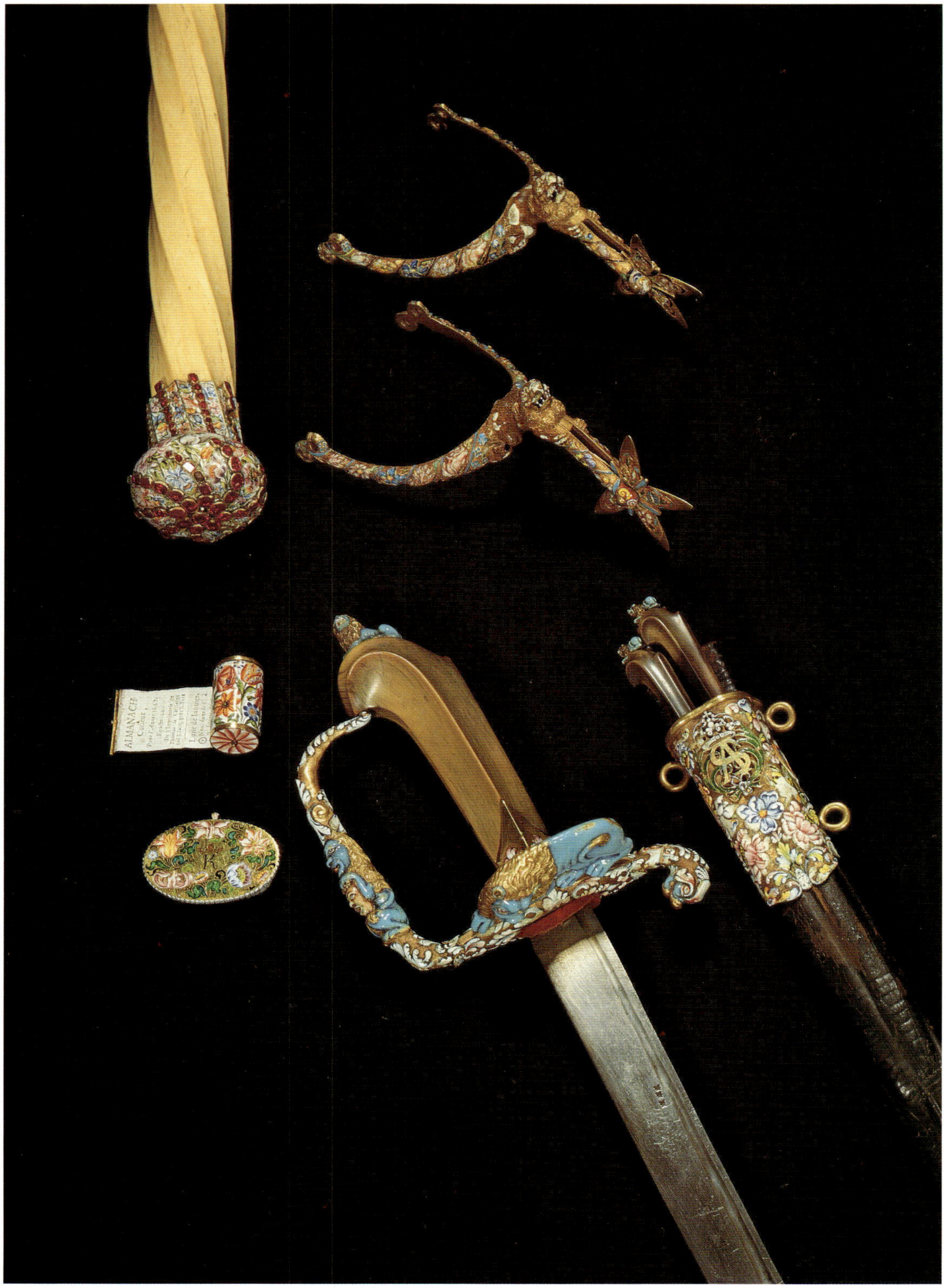
ALMANACH
Curieux

graved semi-naturalistic motifs. In the words of Erik Lassen, this pitcher is without parallel in Denmark. Whether intended for ecclesiastical use at the baptismal font or as a pouring pitcher for the hand basin during meals is uncertain and the goldsmith responsible for making it has not been identified. The master may have been the princely couple's court goldsmith Henrik Langemack, who also executed 'ein gülden Tulipan' and mounted the great sapphire, now on the front of the absolute monarch's crown, in a flower-shaped brooch for Magdalene Sibylla.[5]

Besides published engravings for professional use such as those of François Lefebure, goldsmiths could seek inspiration in the florilegia, the botanical works with copperplate engravings which were being published in most European countries. The binding of the prayer book (fig. 96) is an example of this. It must have been executed prior to Christian IV's death in 1648, since the prayers inscribed in it are written in the hand of his favourite daughter Anna Cathrine who died in 1633, one year after her betrothed, Frantz Rantzau, drowned in Rosenborg's moat after a drinking bout in the palace.

The naturalistic flowers, similar to those on the spurs but executed in translucent as well as opaque enamel, cover the binding in openwork relief and are arranged around *vanitas* motifs with scriptures; on the clasps are Anna Cathrine's monogram and on the spine her coat of arms as Countess of Schleswig-Holstein. In his book on Danish regalia, Gudmund Boesen demonstrated that the turban lily (Martagon), columbine and tulip were taken from the florilegia, though the colours are the invention of the enamellist. The same source inspired the anointment ampulla and sceptre executed for Frederik III's coronation in 1648. On the stem of the sceptre, naturalistic openwork like that on the bookbinding alternates with semi-naturalistic decoration, while the top unfolds in a full-blossomed lily (emblematically a fleur-de-lis, but actually an iris) encircling the crown (fig. 97) – a unique design in European regalia. Recently discovered accounts of payments, presumably made by one of the masters of the goldsmiths' guild, establish that the sceptre is of Copenhagen manufacture and serves as further evidence of the rapid dissemination of technique and fashion in Europe.[6]

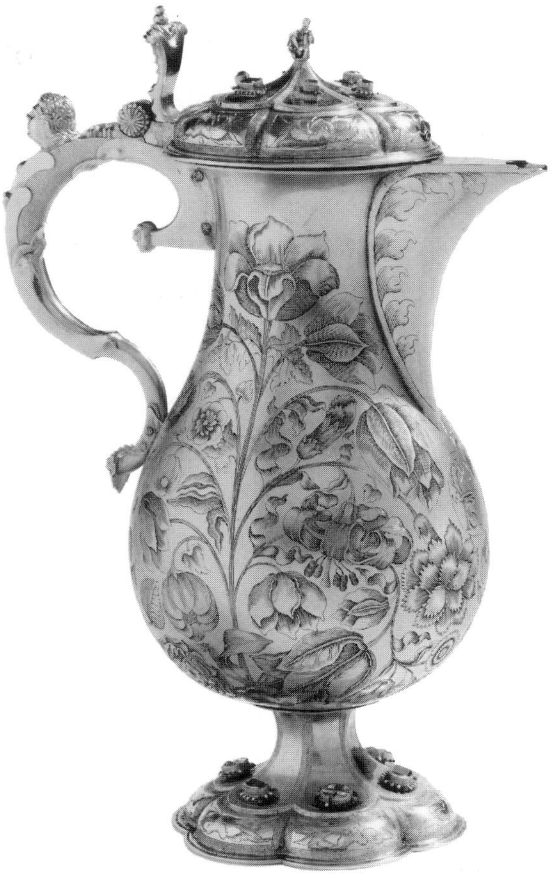

95 *Princess Magdalene Sibylla's gold pitcher*. Rubies and diamonds on lid and foot. Denmark ca. 1650
Kunstindustrimuseet, Copenhagen (*cat. 224*)

94 ◂ *Various enamel works*. Seventeenth century: Kirsten Munk's onyx cameo (*cat. 256*). Leonora Christina's Parisian almanac from 1647 (*cat. 223*). Sophie Amalie's hunting sword (*cat. 225*). A pair of spurs (*cat. 222*). Frederik III's unicorn cane with ruby studded pomander attributed to Paul Prieur of 1663 (*cat. 227*)
The Royal Collections, Rosenborg Palace, Copenhagen

In the period following the coronation, datable floral enamels are rarer. While the Danish-Swedish Wars spelled economic ruin they also paved the way for the absolute monarchy, which was initiated with hitherto unknown pomp and splendour and epitomized in the throne of precious narwhal tusk

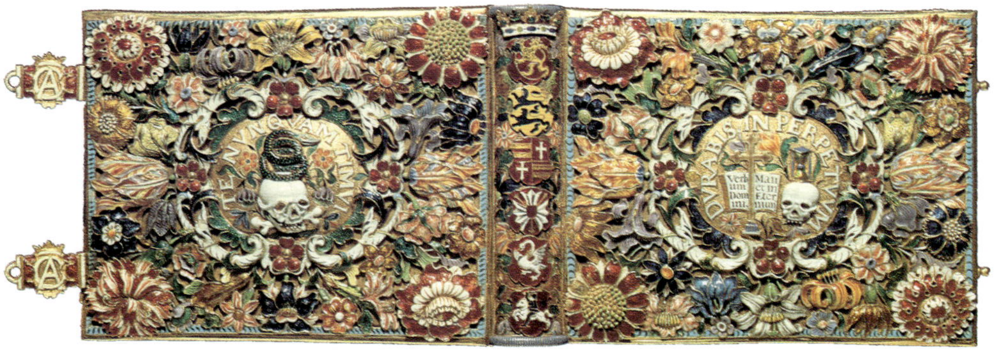

96 *Anna Cathrine's prayer book.* Paper, gold and enamel. Denmark 1640's (?)
The Royal Collections, Rosenborg Palace, Copenhagen

97 *Frederik III's sceptre.* Gold, enamel and diamonds. Denmark 1648
The Royal Collections, Rosenborg Palace, Copenhagen

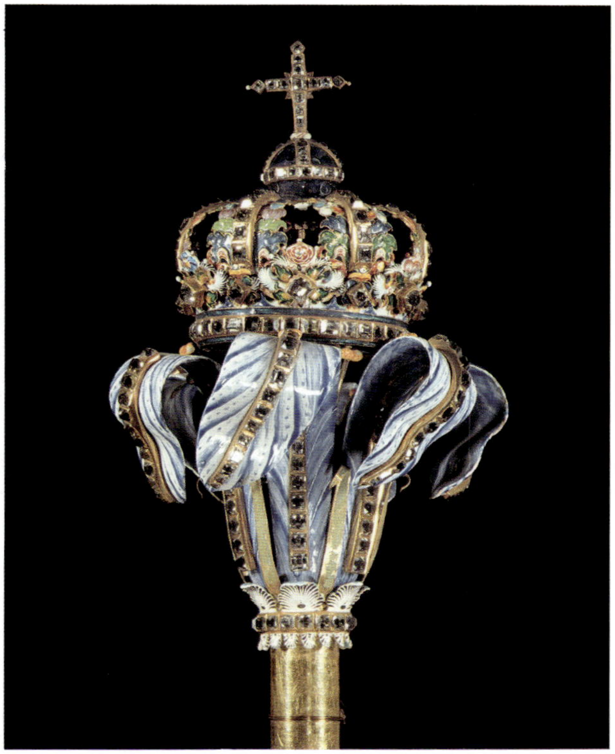

and life-size silver lions executed in the 1660s and consciously modelled on the account of King Solomon's throne in the Old Testament. Narwhal tusk, practically a monopoly of the Danish-Norwegian kingdom, including Greenland, was used for Frederik III's cane (fig. 94), in which the knob and ferrule are decorated with floral enamel embellished with rubies. The knob unscrews to disclose a perforated lid covering four small compartments meant to hold aromatic balsam – or perhaps snuff. These leisures served as pleasant refreshment should the audience turn tiresome. Moreover, the entire object possessed curative powers and afforded protection against poisoning in the form of the narwhal tusk, regarded as the horn of the unicorn. This type of floral enamelling was widespread and is familiar, for example, in Prague work of the 1650s (cat. 226). However, the flowers and foliage on the cane have a distinctive fullness which is repeated on a covered unicorn's cup with Frederik III's monogram and the year 1663. The date tempts one to identify the enameller as the newly arrived French miniaturist Paul Prieur, who in that very year executed the first of a series of portrait miniatures of the king. Prieur was trained in the Toutin tradition in France and Switzerland, where watchcases shaped like the knob of the cane were a speciality.[7]

The series of floral enamels discussed in this essay ends with the cane. A *nécessaire* from the 1670s has pierced and engraved flowers but these are combined with acanthus foliage and bordered by laurels. Taste and fashion had moved away from floral naturalism and were about to rediscover elements of Renaissance stylization, soon to be incorporated into French Baroque Classicism and into the *Laub- und Bandelwerk,* the succeeding styles in European ornament.

Charlotte Christensen

The flowers' metamorphoses

The lilies of the field neither toil, nor do they spin – yet even Solomon in all his glory could not compare with them. In reality, flowers are beautiful and inactive, rooted in the ground. In art, however, flowers have been accorded movement, speech and a soul. The sensitive plant occurs in the poetry of antiquity as it does in the picture books of the nursery – just as floral metaphor is the constant wellspring of love poetry: 'I am the rose of Sharon, and the lilies of the valley. As a lily among thorns, so is my love among the daughters.'

In comparison with our cultural inclination to annihilate other species, so-called 'primitive' religions held a view of nature that involved a more peaceful balance between human beings and the rest of the planet's flora and fauna. If we had a little more reverence for the whales of the deep and the plants of the rain forest we would cease to exterminate them with such abandon. Man's arrogance has led him to place himself above all other living things, with the right to destroy God's labour of the first five days of creation. On the third day the grass, herbs and trees were created, and on the sixth man was given the catastrophic instruction that he was to subdue the entire earth. Long interpreted as carte blanche to annihilate other life, in fact, God's instruction was that the plants were to serve man for his food (Genesis 1:29). In the following chapter in the Bible various amendments are enumerated, where it is even stated that in the Garden of Eden there were trees that were pleasant to the sight; implying that aesthetic enjoyment was also an aspect of their usefulness to man. The only tree that was forbidden was the tree of the knowledge – regardless, man ate of its fruit. Man has extinguished the wild violet in France and *Hibiscadelphus bombycinas* in Hawaii, the elephant bird and Grey's Wallaby, the great auk and the quagga. Man continues to reduce the number of species of both plants and animals. If flowers could speak they would surely decline the pretty metaphors in favour of survival.

Ancient cultures venerated animals and plants more than did Christianity, and some of their ritual observances are the basis for the stories told in Ovid's *Metamorphoses* and *Fasti*, epic poems concerning gods and festivals. In many religions anthropomorphic creatures – a blend of animal and human – as well as animals and plants are endowed with human souls. For instance, the Egyptian *Book of the Dead* contains a 'Formula for transforming oneself into a lotus flower,' and in Ovid's *Metamorphoses* can be found an abundance of beings which alternate between different natures: from God to animal, from statue to woman, from youth to flower.

The *Metamorphoses* were composed – and were nearly complete – when Emperor Augustus sent Ovid into exile near the Black Sea. According to the poet, he was banished because of 'a poem and an error' in 8 AD. For European pictorial art, the *Metamorphoses* became as inexhaustible a source of inspiration as the Bible, and its many odd couples exerted a powerful fascination on early Renaissance painters and sculptors. For them – as for the schoolmaster Holofernes in Shakespeare's *Love's Labour's Lost* – Ovid was a worthy ideal: 'Ovidius Naso was the man. And why, indeed 'Naso' / but for smelling out the odoriferous flowers of fancy, / the jerks of invention?' (IV, II)

Ovid described numerous transformations into vegetable matter, but they are not all equally amenable to plausible visual representation. Lotis and Cyparissus, Myrrha and Dryope are changed into trees, but for artists Apollo and Daphne were the lovers of choice – the culmination of which is Bernini's unforgettable rendering of the transformation from woman into tree. For the stories in which the characters are changed into flowers it is very rare to find pictures which reproduce the actual transition from the animal to the vegetable kingdom, of man into flower. Nearly all illustrations depict the state prior to the transformation. The subject is treated in five narratives: Narcissus, Clytië, Hyacinthus, Adonis and Ajax, and in one line Ovid mentions 'Crocus and Smilax, changed into tiny flowers.'

Smilax was a nymph who was changed into a bindweed, and the youth Crocus became the flower which bears his name. With regard to Hyacinthus, Adonis and Ajax it is their blood which is transformed into flowers. Apollo inadvertently fells his beloved, the youth Hyacinthus, with a discus, and is unable to keep him alive even though he: '... dried the hideous wound, and tried to call / The life-warmth back, and with a dressing, made / Of healing herbs, the escaping life delayed. / His arts were in vain: the wound all cure defied; / And as in gardens, by the waterside, / Struck down by some change blow, may violets fall, / Or lilies tawny tongued, or poppies tall, / Which on a sudden wilt,with head depressed, / And droop, with downward gaze, their sinking crest – / So dropped his dying face; so, weak and spent, / The neck, self-burdened, on the shoulder leant.'[1]

Apollo inscribes his plaint: 'AI AI' in the petals of the flower which sprouts from the blood. Somewhat confusingly, the same flower sprouts from the blood of the slain Ajax. In other sources the rose springs forth from the blood of Adonis, but in Ovid it is the anemone (windflower). Adonis is killed by a wild boar, and Venus wants to memorialize for eternity her lament for her beloved: 'His blood shall change to blossom. 'Twas no blame / For Ceres' child to change a woman's frame / To aromatic mint: then why in me / To change Adonis should it scandal be? / And, speaking thus, with nectar's fragrant dew / She dashed the clotted blood, which swelled and grew, / Fermenting with the contact, like a stream, / When midst the mud the rising bubbles gleam; / And after one full hour, a blossom grew, / Born from the blood, itself of sanguine hue, / Much like the flower pomegranates bear, which bind / So close their seeds beneath the stubborn rind. /But short its lease: it clings as best it may; / Then falls, by winds (that name it) swept away.'

In the tale of Narcissus it is the divinely beautiful and self-infatuated youth who is transformed into a flower after his death, and Clythië is so enamoured of Phoebus that she finally changes into a flower which perpetually turns its head toward the sun.

Ovid's works were read eagerly and assiduously even by the theologians of the Middle Ages, and stories from the *Metamorphoses* were frequently depicted in illuminated manuscripts, although not the theme 'half flower – half man.' Nor do even the lavishly illustrated printed editions from the Renaissance – which, as secular 'picture Bibles,' became models for artists all over Europe – contain anthropomorphic flowers.

In the Middle Ages, a comprehensive Christian flower language developed. The allegorical *Roman de la Rose* by Guillaume de Lorris and Jean de Meun relates the anti-hero Amant's sinful progress through a world of emblems, in which he spurns reason and arrives at a blameworthy and most fleshly union with the Rose. Like the *Metamorphoses* the *Roman de la Rose* was enormously popular in the Middle Ages, and became the most frequently illustrated work of poetry. The French king, Philip the Bold (1270-85), commissioned tapestries showing scenes from the allegory. The red rose symbolized carnal, impure love – and Amant's conquest of the Rose/woman was a sin. Ovid's poems were reinterpreted in the same spirit, and at various times were 'moralized' to fit a Christian point of view. The Renaissance revivified them, and in the sixteenth and seventeenth centuries the *Metamorphoses* were given substance in numerous paintings and sculptures. Nicolas Poussin illustrated the *Metamorphoses* under the influence of his Italian friend, the poet Cavaliere Marino, and was particularly fascinated by the plant transformations. He painted Pan and Syrinx, Echo and Narcissus, Venus and Adonis, Apollo and Daphne, and two great apotheoses of the world of flowers: *The Realm of Flora* (Dresden) and *The Triumph of Flora* (Louvre). In *The Realm of Flora* of 1631, Poussin assembles all of the flower myths told in the *Metamorphoses* and *Fasti* in a garden where spring reigns (fig. 98).[2]

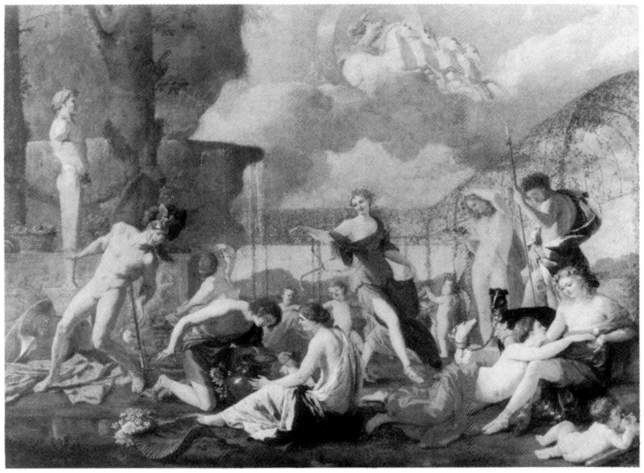

98 Nicolas Poussin, *The Realm of Flora.* Oil on canvas. Paris 1631
Gemäldegalerie, Dresden

In the same year that Poussin painted *The Realm of Flora* a masque titled *Chloridia*, with extravagant and sumptuous decorations and costumes, was performed at the court of Charles I in England. Its theme was Flora's garden and Ovid's description in *Fasti* serves as its remote source. Zephyr, the balmy western breeze, loves the nymph Chloris who is transformed into Flora (fig. 99). He presents her with a garden filled with flowers, quite a few of which are described in the *Metamorphoses.* Italian and English poetry of the Elizabethan era contains a wealth of enchanted gardens, which in turn provided themes for the great court festivals and their *ballets de cour.* The idea of gardens on the stage, or in the halls of the palaces, was tremendously attractive to the organizers of the festivities. In 1581 the French court saw Circe's enchanted garden in the *Balet Comique de la Reine,* and in 1617 the spectacle was Rinaldo in Alcina's enchanted garden (after Tasso's *Gerusalemme liberata*) in *Le Ballet de la Déliverance de Renau.* Queen Elizabeth I of England *was* a rose, the Tudor rose (the Eglantine), and duly celebrated as such by poets and artists. Their inventiveness did not surpass that of the Italian painter Arcimboldo, who composed Emperor Rudolph II's countenance out of nothing but vegetables, and in paintings of *La Primavera* created human heads consisting only of flowers. The expression of the times is drastic (Thomas Campion, 1567-1620):

There is a garden in her face
Where roses and white lillies grow,
a heavenly paradise is that place,
Wherein all pleasant fruits do flow.
Where cherries grow, which none may buy,
Till 'cherry ripe' themselves do cry.

However, it was not until the early nineteenth century that flowers and human beings began exchanging body and soul in earnest, blending osmotically so that flowers received faces and the ability to reason, to move and even dance. Poets like Keats and Shelley were still familiar with the poets of antiquity and Ovid was an important influence on their imagery; when he was a schoolboy Keats translated the *Aeneid*

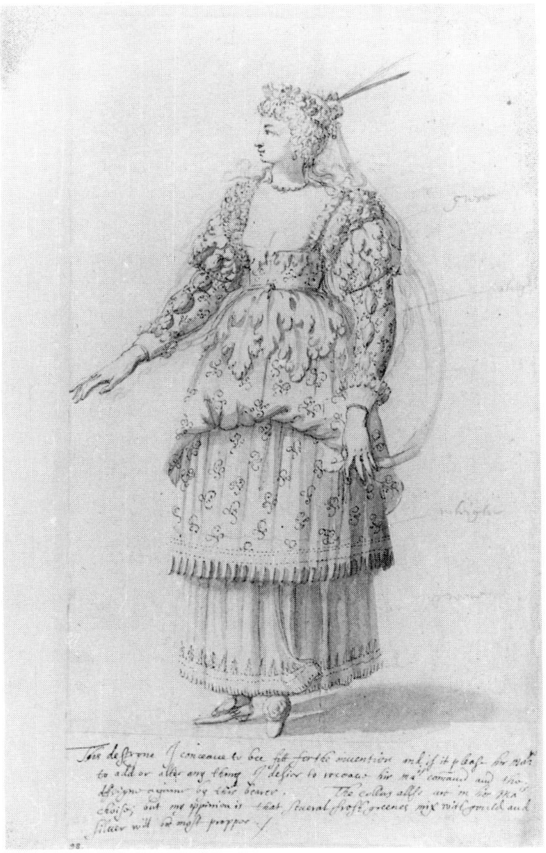

99 Inigo Jones, *Costume design for Henrietta Maria in 'Chloridia'.* 1631
The Trustees of the Chatsworth Settlement, England

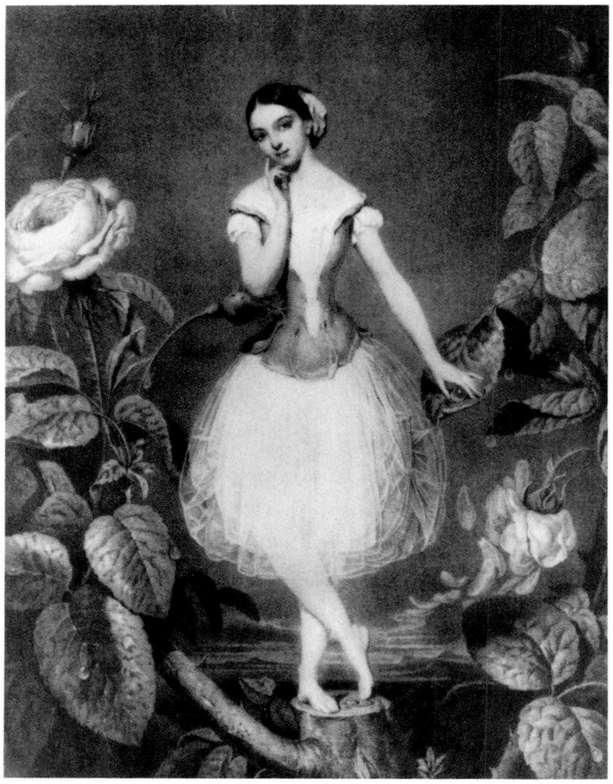

100 The ballerina Marie-Paul Taglioni in the title role of Auguste Bournonville's *Thea, or the Flower Fairy*, 1847
Österreichische Nationalbibliothek, Vienna

into English prose. Keat's floral metaphor is nearly as mannered as Campion in *La belle Dame sans merci*:

I see a lily on thy brow
With anguish moist and fever dew,
And on thy cheeks a fading rose
Fast withereth too.

Shelley, who translated Pliny's *Natural History* in school and was clever at composing Latin verse, uses more flowers than Ovid in his enchanted garden in *The sensitive Plant*. Among Shelley's flowers the narcissi are the most touching: '... The fairest of them all, / Who gaze on their eyes in the stream's recess / Till they die of their own dear loveliness.' In this poem the brief-lived flowers are not used to tell human beings that beauty is only fleeting ('Gather ye rosebuds while ye may'), instead Shelley comforts: 'For love, and beauty, and delight, / There is no death nor change...' (fig. 100).

Pictures of sentient flowers were created by the strange French artist Grandville, a pseudonym for Jean-Ignace-Isidore Gérard, who was born in Nancy in 1803. He began working as a caricaturist for several of the satirical journals in Paris, and caused a sensation with his animal figures dressed in contemporary clothes. Grandville found it easy to see an animal in his fellow man, and lifeless objects also were animated by his imagination. His most personal and imaginative work is *Un autre monde* of 1844, which attracted the attention of Baudelaire and later inspired both the Surrealists and Walt Disney. In the story *Une révolution végétale*, Grandville breathes life into the flowers for the first time. The flowers no longer want to be exploited; human beings use their petals for perfume, and the vegetables' small offspring are snatched away from them in tenderest childhood to be eaten as *primeurs*. The demagogue among the plants is a thistle by the name of Catilina who has made himself the leader of the conspiracy; but the revolution never takes place because dissent arises in the vegetable kingdom. Another story in *Un autre monde* relates the death of the *eternelle*. Long ago, the 'everlasting' asked for eternal life without receiving eternal youth in the bargain, so that she lost her freshness and became an old maid. A young lily, to whom she declares her love, turns away in disgust and calls her a flower of the grave. When her only companion, the water lily, leaves the 'everlasting' to go to a party she commits suicide by pulling herself up by the roots.

Grandville also made drawings for several books about the human, only too human animals, entitled *Scènes de la Vie privée et publique des animaux* (1842-44), which included stories by Balzac and Georges Sand. Shortly before his death in 1847 he had completed the illustrations for the great book of flowers, *Les fleurs animées*, published posthumously in 1847 with fifty hand-coloured steel engravings after Grandville's original drawings (fig. 101).

Les fleurs animées also begins with a rebellion. The flowers bring their complaint to the Flower Fairy: for thousands of years they have provided human beings with metaphors – without them poetry would not

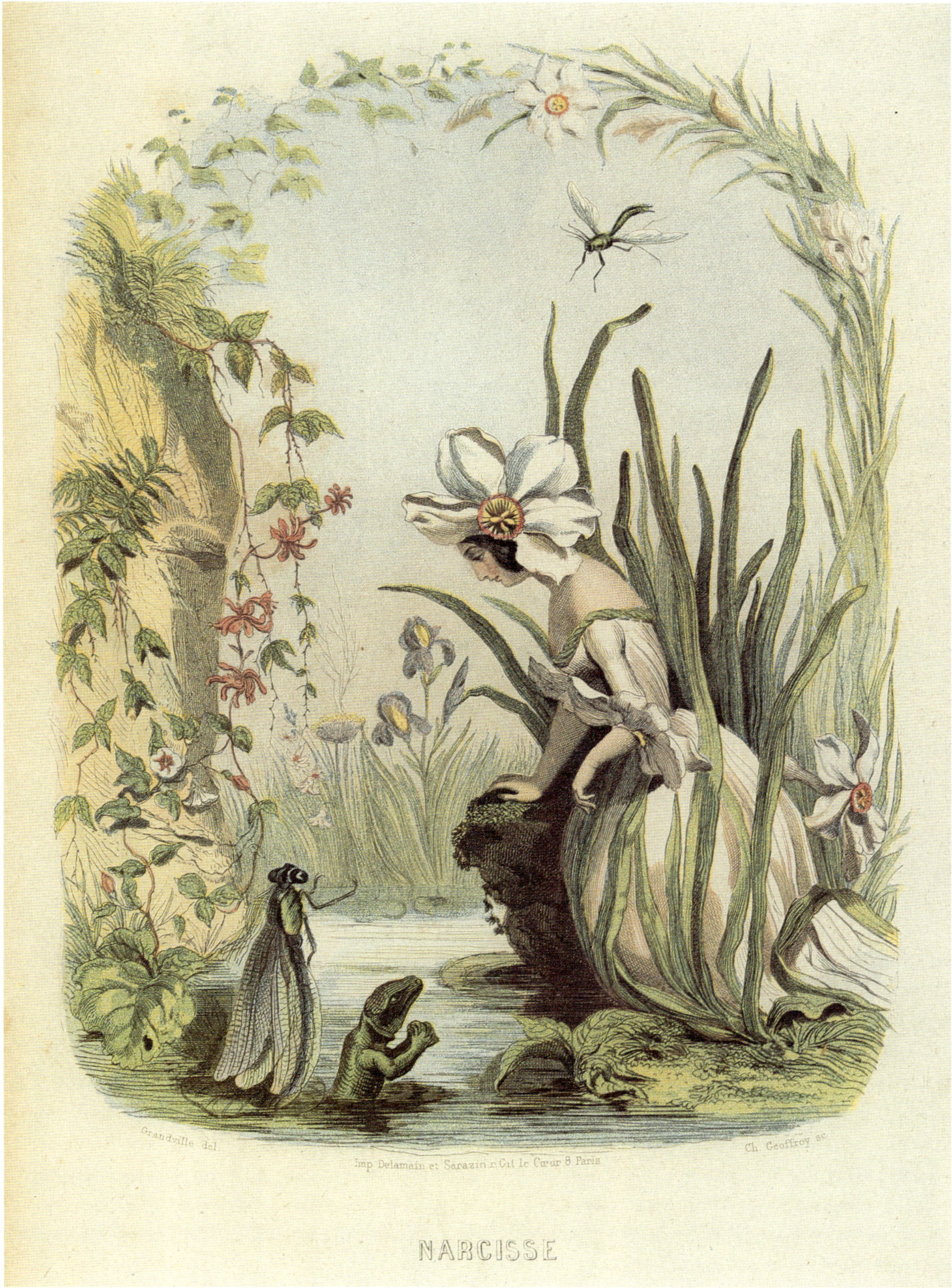

101 J.-J. Grandville, *Les fleurs animées*. Text by Taxile Delord. *The Narcissus*. Published posthumously in 1847 with steel engravings after Grandville's original drawings. Several later editions
Private collection, Copenhagen (*cat. 89*)

exist. Now they want to become human and learn whether what is reported about the flowers' characters agrees with reality. Their wish is granted by the Flower Fairy and a long series of stories about the individual flowers follows. They are very diverse, some are small love stories, others satires on womanhood and emancipation, still others contain long essays on the cultural history of the flowers. One brilliant little piece is the ironic tale of a rose's life as a political turncoat. She emigrates during the Revolution, returns during *Le Directoire,* wins fame for her salon during *l'Empire,* and finally ends up as a radical. However, she must suffer the humiliation of going out of fashion during the Romantic era, when the *Belle du jour* is supposed to be pale and consumptive. The camellia is a scentless beauty without a heart, and the woodbine a sweet little thing from the country who gets the prince only to discover that he is a dolt. She flees, and finds a shepherd to live with happily ever after. In a very instructive tale, 'La mode des fleurs,' we learn about the vagaries of taste and which flowers were preferred in different ages. A poisoner also lurks among the flowers, and another character is the dancer Grenadilla who is adored by the people of her native Mexico. Grandville's portrayal of her is based on Fanny Elssler's costume and appearance in the Andalusian dance *la cachucha.* Finally, all the flowers ask the Fairy for permission to give up their wretched human lives and return to their previous lives as flowers.[3]

Hans Christian Andersen knew Grandville's work – though how well is unclear. Andersen recalls a soirée he arranged in 1853 for a distinguished gathering: 'Christmas here at home was amiable and went well, [I] spent it as always with the Collinses, and also part of the evening at the Landgrave's where there were pretty tableaux for which I had written the verses. Princess Anna of Prussia was very sweet as one of the angels in Thorvaldsen's «Christmas Joy,»' and afterwards «a forget-me-not» in a bouquet of flowers arranged from Grandville, in the same Miss Tutein was an especially delightful pansy.'[4] The landgrave was Wilhelm of Hessen-Kassel, father of the later Queen Louise of Denmark, and Anna, born Princess of Prussia, was his daughter-in-law (fig. 102).

However, when Andersen wrote 'Little Ida's

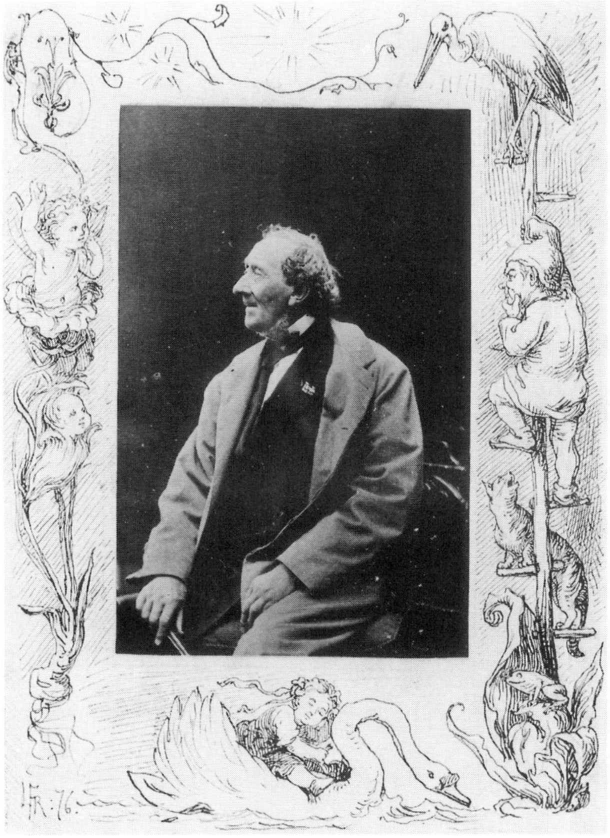

102 Lorenz Frølich, *Drawing framing a photograph of Hans Christian Andersen.* Pen, sepia ink. Denmark 1876
Statens Museum for Kunst, Den Kongelige Kobberstiksamling, Copenhagen *(cat. 37)*

Flowers', published in 1835 in the first collection of *Fairy-tales told for Children,* neither *Un autre monde* nor *Les fleurs animées* had been published in France. His flower tale was a little roman à clef about life at Charlottenborg Palace in Copenhagen where the secretary of the Royal Academy J. M. Thiele had his home overlooking the botanical gardens. The fairy tale was written for little Ida Thiele. Whereas Grandville's animations were thoroughly French and topical, the flowers in Hans Christian Andersen's fairy tale were Danish in sensibility and language, and represented the poet himself and disguised members of his circle of acquaintances. When Vilhelm Pedersen was to illustrate 'Little Ida's Flowers,' Andersen drew the artist's attention to Grandville, and the parade of the flowers is a replica of the funeral procession in 'The death of the everlasting' from *Un autre monde.*[5] Whether Andersen had encountered Grandville in the French original editions or perhaps was familiar with the German translations still remains uncertain. An example of Grandville's flowers on Danish soil is the publication of a plagiarism in 1851: *De talende Blomster. Efter det franske (The talking Flowers. From the French).*

Ovid's erotic adventures had now reached the nursery. In England, Grandville provided inspiration for the Reverend Charles Dodgson and his illustrator, Sir John Tenniel. In *Alice in Wonderland* it is the animals who have human character, but in the sequel, *Through the Looking-Glass* from 1871, talking flowers make their appearance. The illustrated children's book was raised to an altogether unique level of art toward the end of the nineteenth century, especially due to the efforts of the English graphic artist Walter Crane who strove to create beautiful books even for the very young. He too was familiar with Grandville, and created a series of small flower story books, the first in 1879, for his own children in which the daffodil, the violet, the poppy and the bluebell appear as girls' figures. Walter Crane's drawings are not drawn from nature but seek to create a modern version of the woodcuts in the early herbariums. In 1896 he wrote: 'As, until recently, I suppose I was scarcely known out of the nursery, it is meet that I should offer some remarks upon children's books. Here, undoubtedly, there has been a remarkable development and great activity of late years. We all remember the little cuts that adorned the books of our childhood. The ineffaceable quality of these early pictorial and literary impressions afford the strongest plea for good art in the nursery and the schoolroom. Every child, one might say every human being, takes in more through his eyes than his ears, and I think much more advantage might be taken of this fact.'[6]

Walter Crane's greatest exploit within the field of the illustrated book, both for children and adults, is *Flora's Feast,* with forty full-page colour lithographs of Flora as she calls the flowers forth from their winter sleep, summoning them on stage in the sequence of their flowering season. The book was published in 1889 and became a European hit (fig. 103). 'There is something, I suppose, in university of appeal – and everybody loves flowers,' is Walter Crane's own explanation for the book's popularity.[7] It was followed up by *Queen Summer or the Tournay of the Lily and the Rose* in 1891, in which the flowers hold a tournament to see who wins the beautiful Queen Summer, and subsequently by even more works by Crane with flowers in the principal roles.

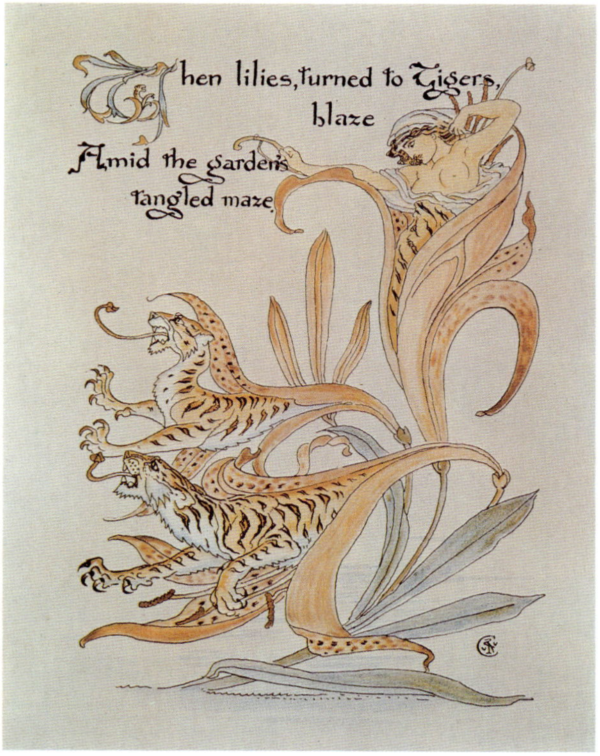

103 Walter Crane, *Flora's Feast,* London 1889. *Tiger Lily.* Colour lithograph

In 1896, after a protracted tour of the Continent, a large Walter Crane exhibition came to Scandinavia. It created an effect like rings spreading on water. While in London, the Swedish artist Ottilia Adelborg had become enamoured of the work of William Morris and Walter Crane, and she published two children's books in Sweden strongly influenced by Crane: *Prinsernas blomsteralfabet (The princes' flower alphabet)* (1892), *and Blomstersiffror med rim (Flower numbers with rhymes)* (1894, fig. 104).

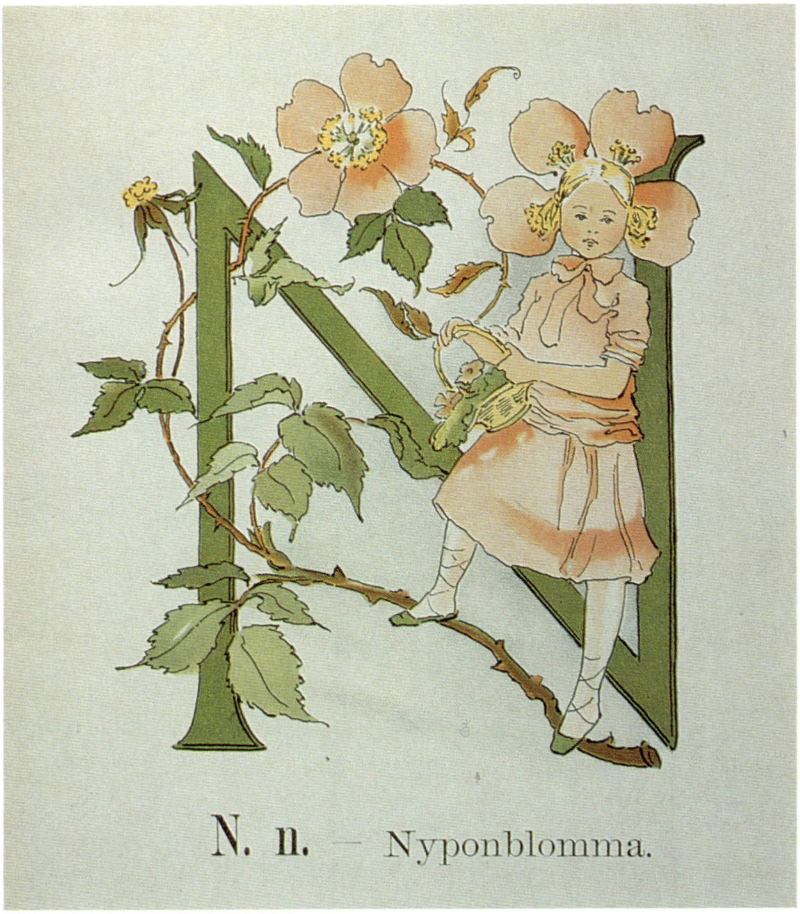

104 Ottilia Adelborg, *Prinsernas blomsteralfabet*, Stockholm 1892. Dog-rose. *Nyponros*

When the Walter Crane exhibition came to Stockholm it was a revelation for artist Elsa Beskow, who decided that her vocation would be to create children's books. The first time Elsa Beskow depicts flowers in human shape is in the illustration to a poem, 'Blommornas bröllop' ('The flowers' wedding'), in *Jultomten* 1900, and in 1903 a little bluebell girl accompanies the sheet music of a song by Alice Tegnér. *Blommornas bok (The flowers' book)* followed in 1905 – the same year Louis Moe published *Blomsternes Bog* in Denmark which in turn was followed by *Blomsterfesten i Täppan (The Flower festival in Täppan)* in 1914.[8] Elsa Beskow's personifications are very Swedish – these are not Grandville's modish Parisiennes who could appear in the Copenhagen residence of a landgrave at Christmas, nor are they Walter Crane's 'aesthetic' beauties reviewed by Oscar Wilde in *Woman's World.* They are related to the native wholesomeness which Zorn and Carl Larsson had promulgated for adults. Elsa Beskow's flower people are the most endearing of them all in the European bouquet. They were the artless flowers of the Swedish countryside, buttercups and bluebells – not heartless gardenias and demonic tiger lilies (figs. 105, 106).

Elsewhere in Europe, another Swede cultivated a very different diabolic communion with the flowers. August Strindberg's second wife, Frida Uhl, recollected: 'We both love flowers passionately, he and I. We can stand bent over them for hours. He lulls them to sleep with morphine, like people. He is able to give them tetanus. He knows all the places where they are especially sensitive, and he also knows all the places where he can kill them... We do not yet have many nor the right experimental subjects at hand. But after the child is born (their daughter Kerstin was born in

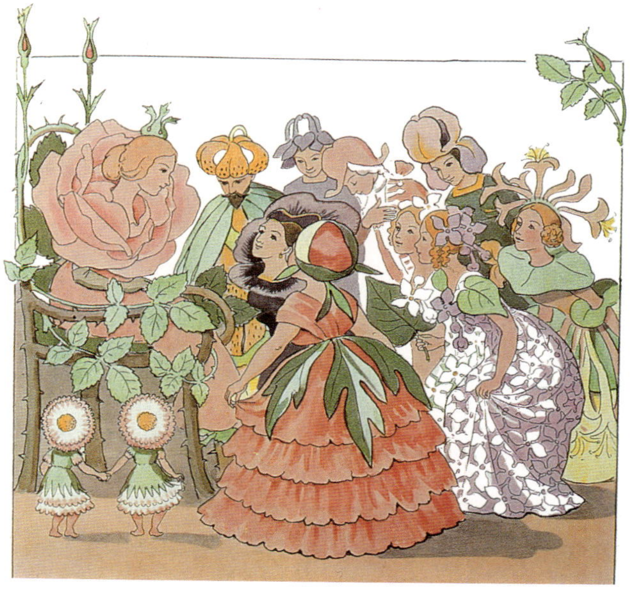

105 Elsa Beskow, *Blomsterfesten i Täppan*, Stockholm 1914
Danmarks Pædogogiske Bibliotek, Copenhagen

May, 1899) we will be thoroughly absorbed in the spiritual life of plants... Just recently, however, he displayed truly refined cruelty towards a hyacinth. He wanted to study its nerves; for that purpose they had to be dyed with osmium first... But how was one able to induce a nervous irritation in flowers? Strindberg knew only too well how nervous irritations in general arise: The owner of the nerves needs to be properly annoyed! And so he set about cold-bloodedly annoying the hyacinths' (cat. 52).[9]

When Frida Uhl fled from Strindberg and the flower experiments, eleven lovely Viennese (*Impatiens Holstii*) were chloroformed. Strindberg, however, worked on in the summer of 1894: 'Had he really succeeded in demonstrating that the plants have nerves and nerve centres, that the sharp dividing line between plant and animal does not exist in nature in the way the experts assume, he would have shown vital misconceptions in the botany of his time and cleared the path for a new direction in research.'[10]

As an antidote we must conclude with the Egyptian *Book of the Dead's* formula for turning oneself into a lotus-flower: 'I am the purest lotus which came forth from the sunshine, and which is at Ra's nostrils and at Hathor's nostrils ... I am the pure lotus which came up from the fields of Ra.'[11]

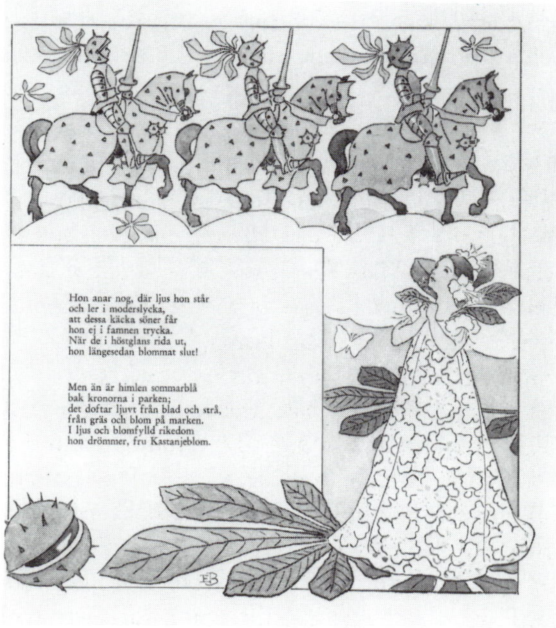

106 Elsa Beskow, *Blomsterfesten i Täppan*, Stockholm 1914
Danmarks Pædagogiske Bibliotek, Copenhagen

Charlotte Paludan

A beguiling similarity
A contribution to the history of artificial flowers

'The prettiest and most simulating flowers are made in Paris.' Thus wrote the knowledgeable compiler of an encyclopaedia of merchandise in 1831.[1] In the nineteenth century artificial flowers were enormously sought after and manufactured in most countries, both industrially and as amateur labour. A few years previously the Danish physician H. C. Lund had published a booklet containing directions for the manufacture of these imitations of nature, for, as he says, 'Flora's gift, the natural flowers so hastily wither,' but 'Fashion would that such artificial flowers be worn by elegant ladies' (cat. 87).[2]

As a matter of fact, such artificial flowers had been fashionable for a long time, and their antecedents can be traced back to the distant past. Flowers made of dyed linen have been found in ancient tombs in Thebes, the capital of the kings of Egypt throughout several dynasties.[3] Imitation flowers were also used by the ancient Greeks and Romans. Among the latter, floral victory wreaths played an important ceremonial role, and for part of the year they had to be replaced by imitations. In advanced cultures, the imitation was accorded the same symbolic value as the product of nature, and revered just as highly.

Flowers have always adorned the dead as a symbol of love. In the North one thinks immediately of the full-blown yarrow flower which was found in the Egtved maiden's coffin, a memento of a Bronze Age summer. Subsequently, artificial flowers acquired the same acceptance in northern as in southern civilizations. An interesting example can be dated to 1578. When the casket said to contain the Earl of Bothwell's remains – located in the crypt of Faarevejle church, North Zealand, Denmark – was opened in 1862, several small rosette-like flowers cut from black paper were found on the white linen shroud. During a new examination conducted in 1978, enough remained to prove that they were three-dimensional imitations of flowers, composed from a number of concentrically arranged perianths (fig. 107).[4]

Renaissance artists made extensive use of the rosette which is the stylized version of the rose. In religious usage the rose is associated with Marian symbolism, and it is representative of purity and innocence. In secular art, on the other hand, it exemplifies immediate sensuous beauty, which the rose embodies in its form, colour and scent. Both as a flat ornament and in three-dimensional configuration, the rosette was used frequently in Renaissance costume. It appears commonly as shoe roses, which adorned the leather vamps of men's – and at times women's – shoes like huge pompons. In women's costume, rosettes occurred as various types of adornment, sprinkled over the gown or placed in the hair. As a rule they were made of silk and frequently enhanced with gems. An example can be seen in the portrait of an English noblewoman, Anne Russell (Badminton, England), from the end of the sixteenth century. Her bodice is sprayed with such cloth roses, each one with a gem in the centre.[5] Similar roses are worn as hair adornment by Kirsten Munk and her three daughters in Jacob van Doordt's portrait of 1623. They appear to be made from red and white silk ribbon wound around a centre of small pearls, as worn by the daughters, or with a large precious stone in the middle, as worn by Kirsten Munk.

Artificial roses made of silk ribbon (*cordelle de seta*) are mentioned as early as 1590 by the Venetian Cesare Vecellio. Such roses were most likely made by court tailors. Although these products never created the illusion of genuine flowers, they could be made to smell like them with the use of perfume. Goldsmiths and jewellers, however, came much closer to nature with their art. The skill of producing lifelike artificial

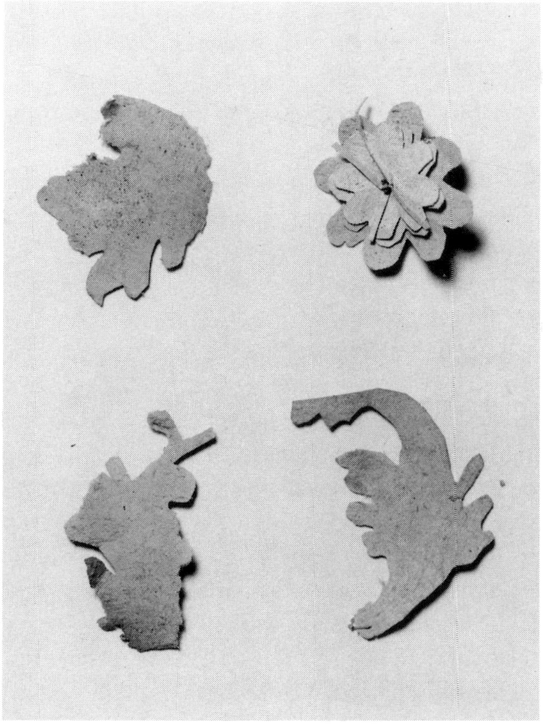

107 *Flowers*. Made of black paper. From the Earl of Bothwell's casket in Faarevejle church. Denmark 1578

flowers was almost unknown outside Italy where, since the Middle Ages, nuns had developed a more or less professional skill in making adornments for altars and pictures of the Madonna.

By the fifteenth century this floral art had developed from a modest craft into a flourishing industry. Small objects made of silk, paper, parchment or thin metal foil were in great demand as fashionable accoutrements.[6] In his 1590 book on costumes, Cesare Vecellio mentions that the women of Padua, Genoa and Vicenza wear coiffures adorned with flowers of silk. In Vicenza thus 'They set their hair in very pretty coiffures, and arrange their plaits with many flowers of silk or gold.'[7] These flowers look modest in the accompanying engraving; while modesty hardly applies to the floral headgear worn by the allegorical figure of *Luxury* drawn by Pisanello in the 1430s (fig. 108).

The manufacture of flowers was principally the domain of convents, and in 1655 the Dominican father Domenico published instructions for making flowers from fish glue. However, flowermaking was also a favourite occupation among Italian noblewomen.[8]

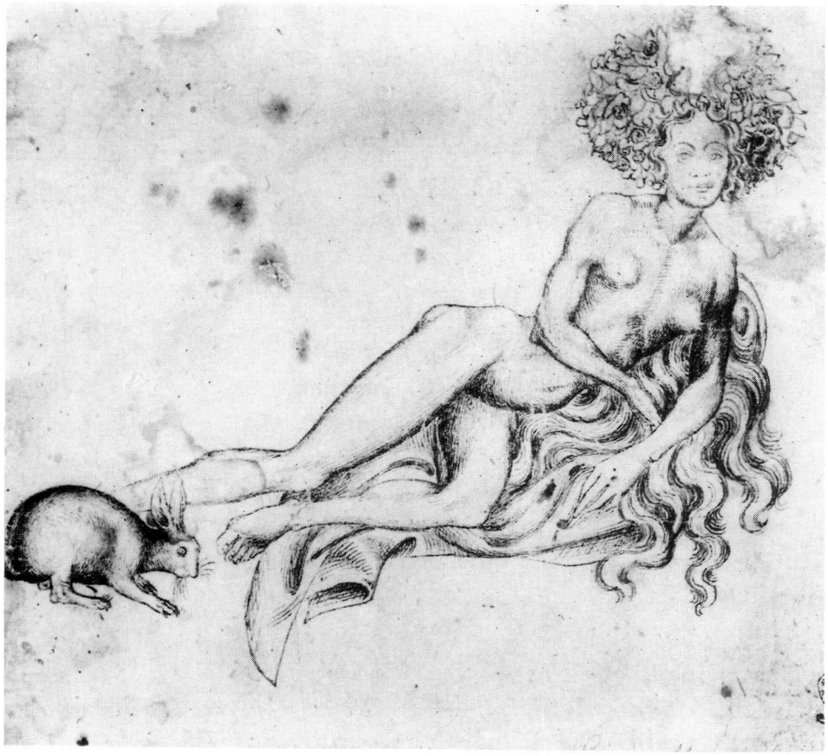

108 Pisanello, *Allegory of Luxury*. Pen on paper. Italy 1430s
Graphische Sammlung Albertina, Vienna

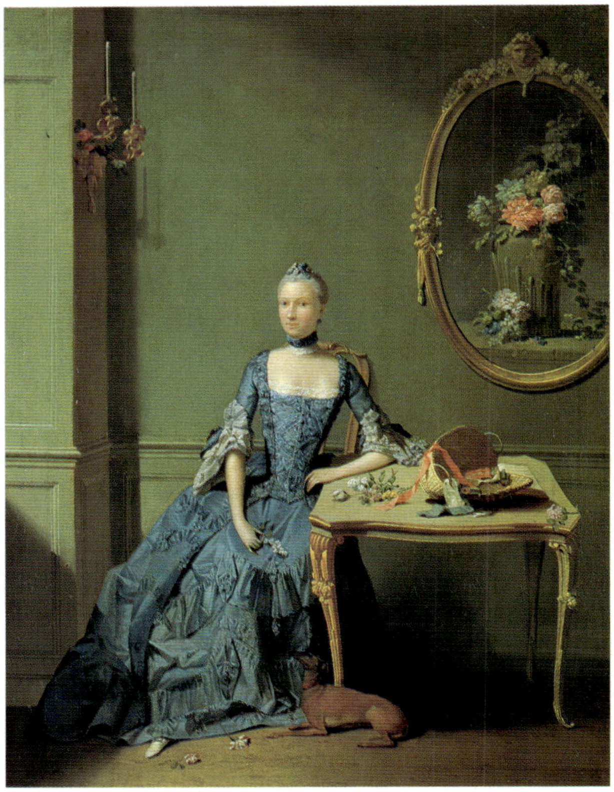

109 Peter Cramer, *Anna Marie Køster*. Oil on canvas. Denmark 1762
Det Nationalhistoriske Museum på Frederiksborg, Hillerød (*cat. 12*)

In France, flowermakers – *plumassiers* – had been granted statutes under Henri IV (1589-1610), giving them the right to dye feather bouquets for church altars, table decorations and decorations surmounting the corner posts of canopy beds.[9]

Gradually, the use of imitation flowers for secular purposes became widespread. Kings and men of wealth had their halls and closets decorated with artificial flowers. The French royal inventory (*Inventaire des Meubles de la Couronne*) from 1673 mentions no less than 3,039 floral bouquets of pleated silk gauze in diverse colours, and in addition 171 other sorts of floral bouquets from China, executed in rolled-up silk ribbon.[10]

Artificial bouquets as room decorations are known at Rosenborg in Copenhagen where, since the beginning of the eighteenth century, and probably even earlier, two magnificent bouquets in vases had their place on the mantelpiece in Christian IV's writing room. The tall, balloon shaped bouquets, of which one is still in its vase on the mantelpiece, consist of leaves and flowers of silk with fruits of coloured wax, while the stalks are made of iron wire wound with silk. The cut-out silk leaves are pressed in shape with painted or embossed veins and stiffened with size, presumably gum arabic (fig. 110).[11]

It was as table adornments, and especially as an important component in dessert settings, that true-to-nature flower imitations found their most imaginative use. The dessert – regarded as the dinner's poetic conclusion – was supposed to be recuperative, not only for the stomach but, by means of surprise and delight, for the senses as well. Therefore it was served in grand houses as a *surtout de table* filling the entire table, in which sweetmeat in various figures and forms and real fruit were arranged and garnished with artificial flowers and leaves.[12]

Floral art was highly developed in China, with antecedents as old as in the West. Naturalistic floral imitations had been developed early on, executed in silk or fine linen, with remarkably transparent flower petals. They could also be lightly dusted with powder to create the illusion of the soft glow of real flowers. Chinese flowers were an important article of millinery, competing with the Italian and later the French flowers. In Denmark, the Asiatic Company imported Chinese flowers: an advertisement from 1760, for various Chinese and East Indian goods mentions 'Chinese Flowers, 3 for 4 schillings and 100 for 9 marks, and ditto bigger.'[13]

In the course of the eighteenth century, the flower industry in France flourished and *les plumassiers* and *les bouquetiers* competed with the couturiers in decorating women's costumes with a profusion of flowers (fig. 112). Lavish floral ornamentation is characteristic of the Rococo, when the stiff, ritual social conventions of the Baroque had been replaced by a more relaxed and spontaneous lifestyle (fig. 111). The arcadian pastoral life was now the ideal of fashion in

110 ▸ *Vase with flowers and fruits.* Porcelain, silk and wax. Vase made in Japan 1660-70s
The Royal Collections, Rosenborg Palace, Copenhagen (*cat. 341*)

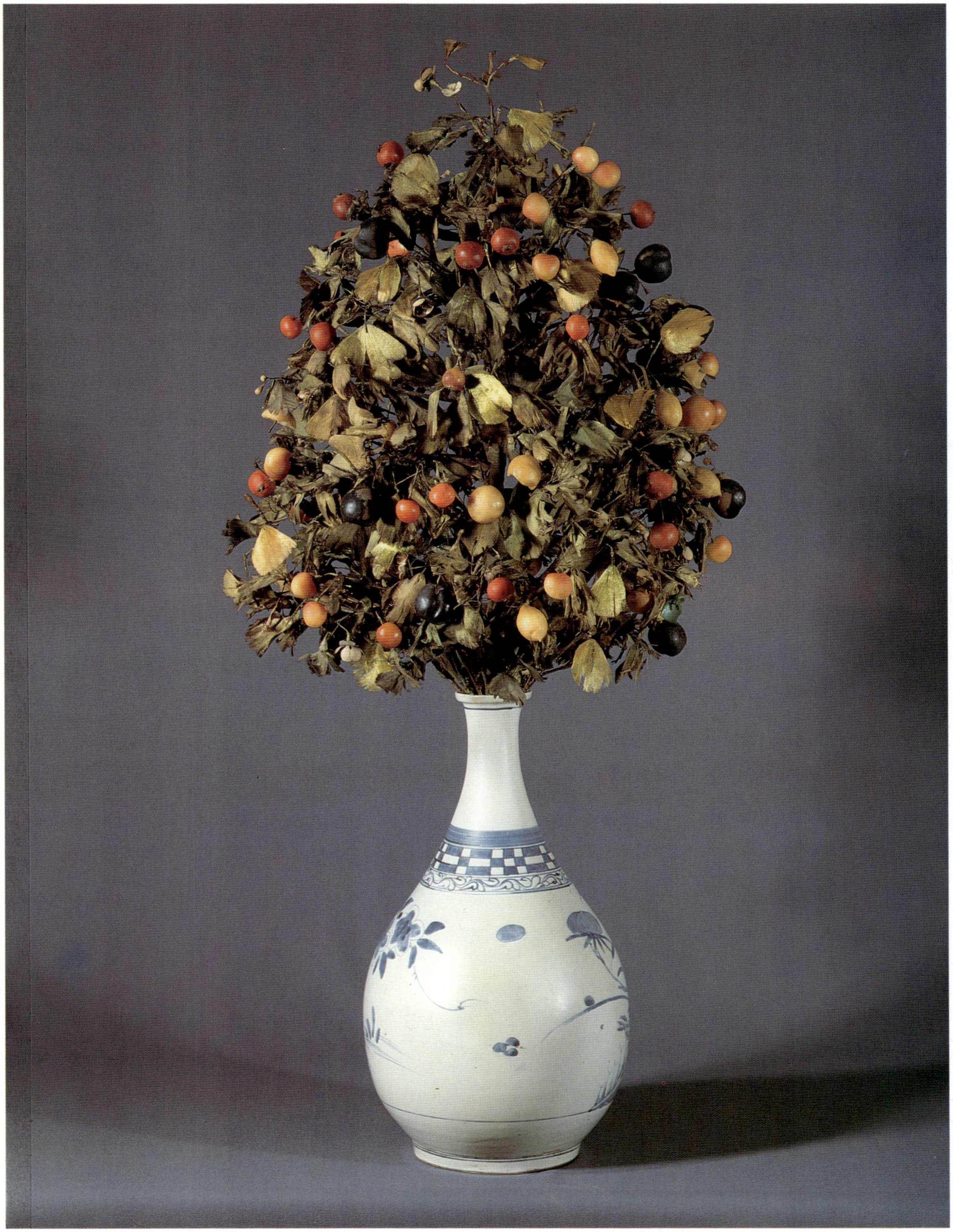

both convention and dress. Flowers had an important place as symbols of Venus, or Aphrodite, the goddess of beauty and idyllic love, protectress of gardens and summoner of spring's exuberant profusion of flowers. Myrtle, the rose and the anemone are sacred to her, as is the apple which signified her victory in the gods' beauty contest. She is worshipped on her island Cythera, carried there by the foaming sea responsible for her creation, where she is attended by the Graces who bathe, anoint and dress her in seductive garments permeated by the scent of spring flowers.

The whims of fashion are as changeable as the winds of Cythera, and women ignored none of the unlimited possibilities for drawing flattering attention to themselves: 'Besides precious stones and gold embroidery, ribbons, laces, agréments and scallops in profusion are placed on all their clothing; flowers, feathers and everything nature produces have either been used or imitated on numerous articles of their adornment,' reports *Fruentimmerets Ven (The Woman's Friend)* in 1761.[14] He continues: '... now she fastens a bracelet in order to expose a pretty arm, now she adjusts a necklace or a posy that a white throat be seen... Now she laughs again to show her pretty teeth... or moves a beauty spot...' Imitations of flowers and other products of nature are useful – the author states – in the service of coquetry, which is probably the essence of the tremendous consumption of flowers during that century.

The French realistic floral imitation – comparable to the feats of the Italians – is said to have originated with a flower manufacturer named Séguin from Mende in Languedoc, who settled in Paris in 1738. While studying chemistry and botany, he began producing flowers in accordance with scientific principles.

He soon attracted pupils as well as numerous imitators, though only a few were his equal. Nonetheless their works were far superior to the usual 'bizarre bunches of feathers with poor colours.' Séguin himself became famous for his inventiveness and ability to imitate not only flowers but also whole sections of gardens (parterres), trees with great trunks and flowering branches, architectonic objects in pasteboard covered with delicate foliage and flowers, and much more, intended for table decorations.

Séguin invented all of his own tools, such as hammers, chisels, pressing and crimping irons, etc., just as he researched and perfected a special colouring technique. Further improvements were effected by a Swiss who devised a means of cutting out several identical components simultaneously with a metal punch. Later, a shaped die constructed like a waffle iron was developed that corresponded precisely to the contours of the punching tool and that created an embossed network of veins on the little leaves. By the end of the century, Paris had taken the lead in the manufacture of flowers. One of the eleven important flower manufacturers was the renowned Joseph Wengel, originally from Bohemia, who became purveyor to the court at Versailles with Marie Antoinette as his first customer. He also taught the art to the ladies of the court, however his plan for starting a factory employing 4,000 women workers was, along with the rest of his enterprise, destroyed by the Revolution. It was not until the end of the Directory (1795-99) that flowers again became a sought-after item of fashion.[15] In 1807, Bruun Juul's Danish encyclopeadia of merchandise stated that the most beautiful flowers were made in Paris, and that at first sight they were nearly indistinguishable from natural flowers.[16]

In Denmark in the seventeenth and eighteenth centuries the floral fashion was supplied chiefly through imports. Fancy goods of all kinds were in demand and throughout the period French products were particularly esteemed, even though 'Italian flowers' had long been the designation for the lifelike and eventually predominant artificial flowers.

By this time the cocoons of silkworms were widely used, a waste product of the large-scale silk production in Italy. After the floss husk was removed, the cocoon was cleaned, cut open and separated into its individual layers which, after drying and punching, could be used as lifelike petals for the so-called 'cocoon flowers.'[17]

In the meantime, much floral finery was being produced on an amateur basis by the consumers them-

111 ▸ Alexander Roslin, *La Baronesse de Neubourg-Cromière*. Oil on canvas. Paris 1756
Statens Konstmuseer, Nationalmuseum, Stockholm (*cat. 11*)

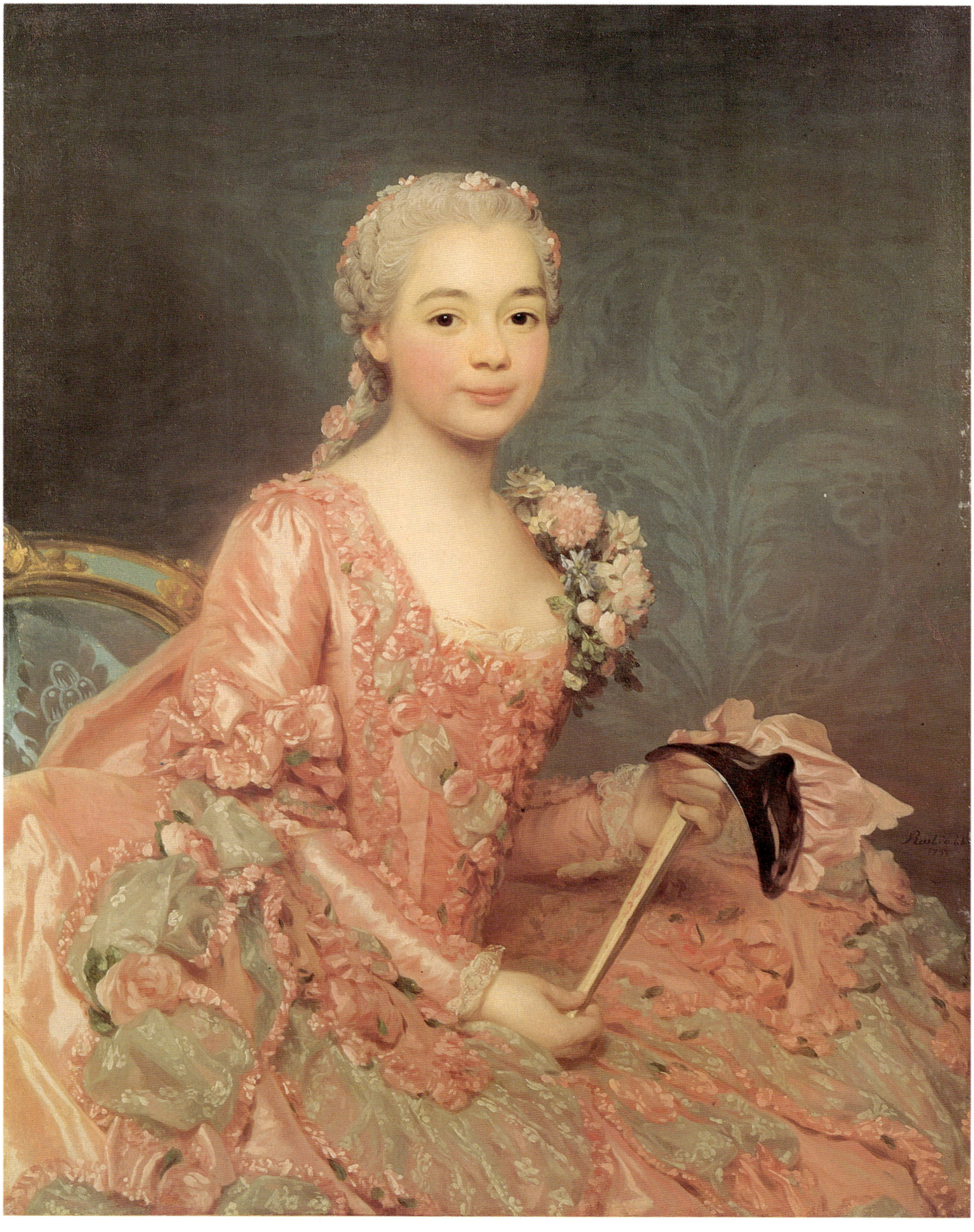

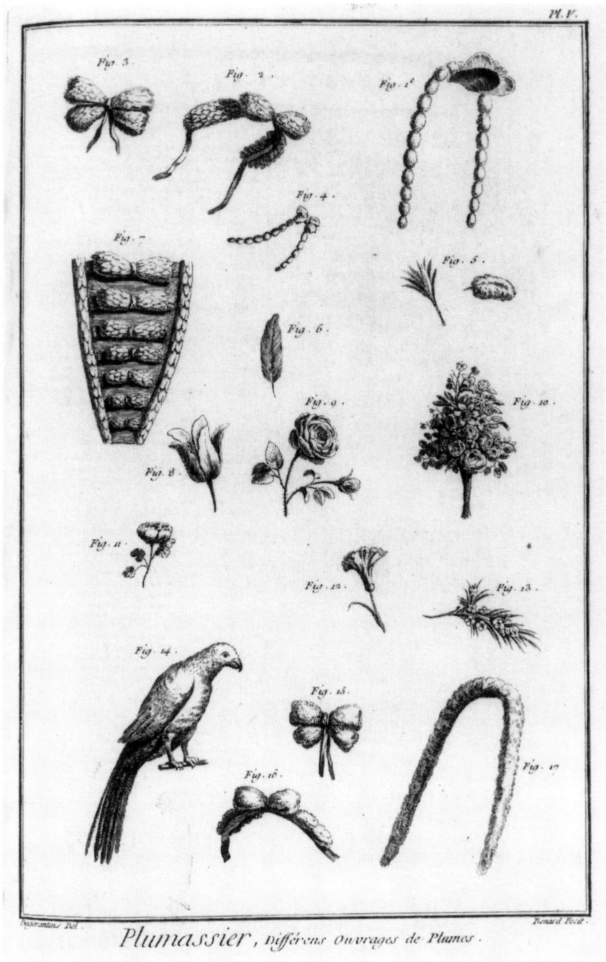

112 *Feather work*, including flowers. Fig. 5 is a so-called *sultan*, Plate VIII, *Plumassier-panachier*, from Diderot & d'Alembert (eds.), *Encyclopédie*, Paris 1770

selves, and local advertising journals such as *Københavns Adresseavis* contained numerous offers of instruction in which: 'Honest folk's children can be informed in the making of all sorts of flowers, including binding nosegays and embellishing headgear...' or young girls instructed 'in sewing as well as the preparation of all kinds of fancy articles and flowers...'[18]

Anna Maria Køster, whose portrait was painted by Peter Cramer in 1762, was obviously one of these amateurs from the middle classes (fig. 109). In the painting she is seen sitting at her worktable with different examples of flowers including roses, several of which have fallen on the floor, while in her hand she holds a wreath of white flowers. Her workbasket lies overturned on the table, spilling out the silk ribbons and thread used for making ribbon flowers. The astonishing flower arrangement in a carved frame on the wall may possibly be her work as well.

The demand for artificial flowers was so great, however, that professional flower manufacturing also flourished in this country. Ribbon manufacturer Johannes Pullich, who came from Basel in 1756 and set up a factory in Copenhagen, advertised his 'exceedingly beautiful flowers and bouquets with matching headgear and much else suitable for garnishings – all flower-work made of ribbon...' or 'diverse sorts of floral tiaras, Sultans [an erect adornment over the forehead, originally made of heron feathers] bosom-nosegays, diverse loose flowers, shepherd's hats...'[19] The pastoral fashion was cultivated in Denmark, too, and the broad-brimmed hats – usually of straw – with floral adornments continued to reappear in fashion at various intervals (cat. 314 and 326). Nor does the wording of an advertisement in 1762 leave any doubt that replicas of nature were intended: 'Magnifique bosom-bouquets, made after natural flowers, and head-flowers are for sale in Gothersgaden...in the ribbon manufacturer's house.'[20] It is interesting to note that the ribbon manufacturers made and marketed these artificial flowers. There is good reason to believe that the French technique using punched or cut-out flowers of silk cloth was still unknown in domestic use. The flowers were probably made by itinerant Germans from Saxony, whose arrival in 1761 was reported in the following manner: 'The Saxon people who have arrived in the city are known for their workmanship in all kinds of flowers and nosegays, as well as other women's fancy goods, which are now to be had in Borgergade, and likewise in Ribbon-Manufacturer Pullich's boutique in Østergade just as cheaply as amongst themselves.'[21] Besides flowers and nosegays they also sold headgear, garnishings, bags, and so forth, so it would appear the market was flourishing.

In the same period there was at least one professional woman flower manufacturer in Copenhagen, and even some kind of factory for ladies' adornments. In 1750 Anna Dorethea Kuhn was granted a royal

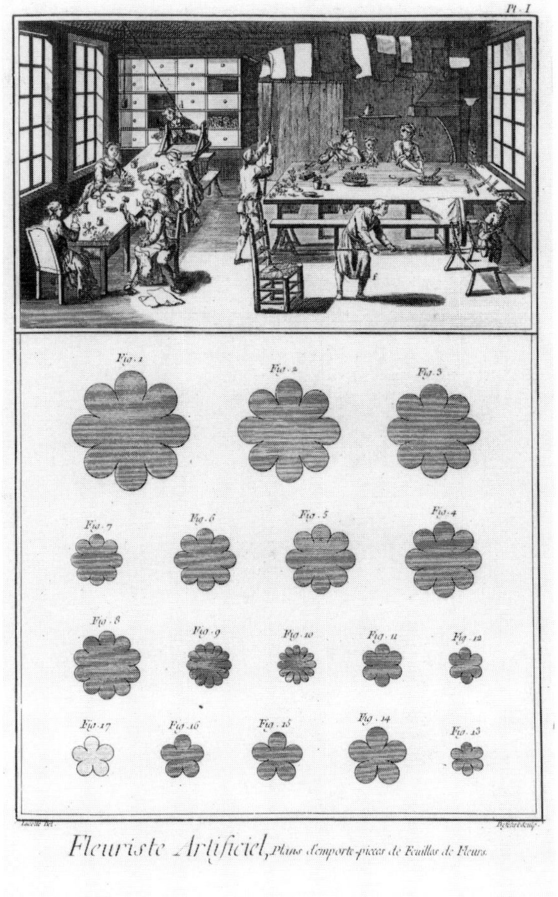

113 *French workshop for manufacturing artificial flowers*, ca. 1765. Below templates for flower petals. Plate IV, *Fleuriste artificiel*, from Diderot & d'Alembert (eds.), *Encyclopédie*, Paris 1765

license to turn out 'diverse kinds of women's adornments, such as agréments, trimmings, flowers etc.,' which she herself had thought of making. In her application she mentioned that her husband, who had been a sergeant for thirteen years, had been discharged from the king's service because of illness, and that she was obliged to provide for their income. The license was granted in disregard of the passementerie makers' guild, which hitherto had sought to put an end to her activities through police obstruction.[22] Following her death in 1764, Drude Povelsdatter was ready with an application to take over Kuhn's license in order to prevent the factory from shutting down, and the many pauper children who had earned their daily bread there from losing their incomes. Her license, issued with identical wording in 1765, included the manufacture of flowers.[23]

In Haderslev in North Schleswig, a sizeable production of *gemachte Blumen* took place, probably without any form of licensing. Certificates for duty-free import of such wares from the duchy of Schleswig are known from as early as 1751, when Eilert Schwan in Odense was issued a customs certificate for six dozen 'Folie Blumen,' among other items, made in Haderslev. In 1752 Margrethe Friis in Haderslev sent '5 Briefen gemachte Blumen' to Funen and Zealand, and in the following year Jens Callesen in the same location shipped '3 dusin seidene Blumen' to Jutland.[24] It is fortunate that in these documents the materials silk and foil are mentioned. The invention of foil flowers is also attributed to Séguin, who is said to have used coloured silver foil for a kind of flower which was in demand as hair adornments for ladies and for masquerade costumes.[25] In reality, he had probably only introduced them in France, as they were known in Italy far earlier and even in antiquity. In Denmark, they were mentioned in a royal decree from 1786 concerning 'Sumptuary Limitation,' commanding that 'All Italian and other flowers, so far as they have not with certainty been made here, shall, from 1 January 1786, be prohibited from being worn, likewise none may be imported nor any of foil be used on new clothes.'

The extensive manufacture of flowers in Denmark in the nineteenth century was inaugurated with the establishment of a large and important flower factory. From Riga, where for a number of years he had been engaged in factory operations, an English embroiderer and flower manufacturer by the name of Joseph Jonas (presumably Jones) arrived in Copenhagen in 1803-1804 with samples of his work. The poor-law authorities immediately showed interest in his plan for establishing an institute for young impoverished girls, whom he would train in 'artificial flower work and all kinds of embroidery,' and with which he thought to employ at least thirty girls.

The interest of the poor-law authorities was based on the prospect of a dignified and decent vocation for a large number of indigent women of the upper mid-

114 *Bridal bouquet* and *bridal wreath*. Feathers and steel wire. Frederikshavn, Denmark 1830-40s
Nationalmuseet, Brede (*cat. 346*)

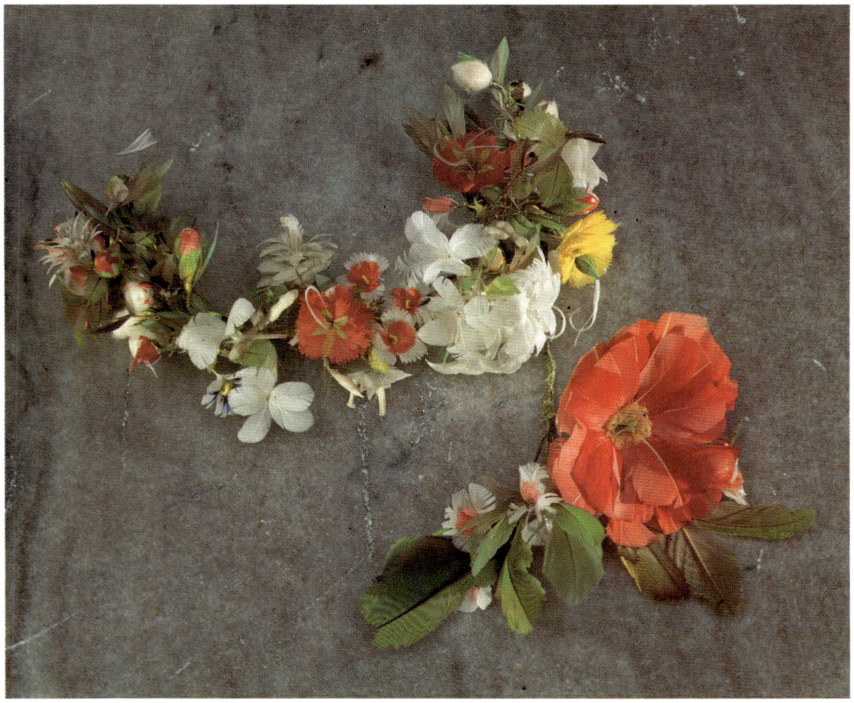

dle classes, so-called *pauvres honteuses*, that is self-respecting paupers who could not be referred to ordinary parish relief or to work in the poorhouses.

With various subsidies and loans from the Foundation for the Support of Industry (Resolution of 20 February 1805), a flower factory with press and dye-works was set up with thirty girls from the poor-law schools – in particular Frue Skole (Our Lady's School) – among whose pupils they had been selected by Jonas himself. Here, it was said, the most exquisite flowers were produced which in taste, delicacy, colour and quality could measure up to the best foreign products. The factory received orders not only from within the city but from abroad, and ladies frequently placed orders with their own specifications for flowers, festoons, floral baskets and so forth. Satisfaction with the prices was also expressed, likewise Jonas's efforts to meet every desire.

By sales abroad is probably meant the big annual trade fair in Kiel, the 'Kieler Umschlag,' where in 1806 an attempt was made to sell Danish industrial goods. Jonas's flowers attracted the public's special interest and occasioned a number of orders.[26]

The flowers were made partly of taffeta and partly of batiste or cambric of English make. Even during the war of 1807-14 it was possible for the factory to obtain material and maintain production, in spite of the embargo on English goods – and even after it had been expanded in 1808. The factory was damaged during the bombardment of Copenhagen in 1807 and Jonas lost very expensive instruments. Despite its losses, the factory moved into a newly purchased building in the city, where a new dye-workshop was set up and a factory for the manufacture of both flowers and embroidered English kid gloves, as well as other embroidery. In 1810 there were seventy-five poor-law authority children employed there, however there is no evidence that poverty-stricken bourgeois ladies fetched material there for home manufacture as the authority had anticipated. Nor has anything been preserved which can be attributed to Jonas's factory with any likelihood; one must be content with visualizing an exceedingly true-to-life and convincing product. This pertains especially to colour, since Jonas's skills as a dyer – an art he learned during travels in India and China – was highly praised. The instruction he provided also received the highest mention by the directors of the poor-law authority, who, in a report describe Jonas and his wife as proper, industrious, decent and thrifty people who had a firm hold on the children. The children were well instructed and stimulated to produce high quality work.

The factory again won honourable notice at an event in 1809, when some of the girls presented gifts to Queen Marie on the occasion of her entry into Copenhagen on 31 October. The gifts consisted of a diadem of gold, a 'ridicule' (bag), a notebook with tooled gold and embroidery, and a wreath of flowers – all made by the children at the factory.[27] Flower manufacturing continued until 1820 when Jonas died, and was carried on at different addresses by his widow until 1829 after which the name Jonas no longer appears in the city directory.[28]

Jonas's factory was not the only one in Copenhagen where flowers were manufactured, and probably not the only place where children were trained and employed in the industry. As early as 1778 it was proposed that little girls be permitted to perform the work which required the greatest manual dexterity, namely gathering the individual petals into flowers, because of their small, supple fingers.[29] There are also a number of small girls at work in the engraving in Diderot's *Encyclopédie* from 1765 (fig. 113). On the other hand, men were better suited for the heavy work of punching out the individual components.

In the nineteenth century, licenses were regularly issued to flower manufacturers who, for the most part, were women. Thus in 1816 Anne Dorthea Hansen was authorized to set up and operate a flower factory in Copenhagen with the right to hire the necessary workers and sell the flowers produced in large and small lots, on one condition, however: that she purchased the necessary materials from authorized dealers and did not import and sell foreign-made flowers. It was also required that trade tax on the sales be paid. Similar licenses were issued in the same year to Abraham Simonsen and in 1822 to Jette Simonsen, in 1827 to Sara Pedersdottir and Gustava Lund, and in 1834 to Carl Gottfried Lipke.[30]

All of the licenses applied to inhabitants of Copenhagen. The only exception was one issued in 1824 to Lactitia Carco and Lea Cotissos in Altona, and which was valid for duty-free importation into the duchies of Schleswig and Holstein of flowers they made out of feathers. This is the first mention of feathers as a material.

In the Danish Nationalmuseet there is an enchanting well-preserved set of feather flowers from the period between 1830 and 1840, consisting of a hair wreath and a corsage. Could they have been made in Altona by Lactitia and Lea? (fig. 114).

The manufacture of flowers continued throughout the century, also on an amateur basis. Or was it none other than *les pauvres honteuses,* who now stepped forth at the Industrial Association's exhibitions of manufactured and cottage industry wares? In 1844 three flower manufacturers were represented. Miss Fischer exhibited baskets and glasses with cloth roses or wild flowers; her works distinguished themselves above those of Madam Ritzau's samples of millinery flowers and other items, and above Lorenz Nielsen's outsized cloth rose intended for festoons. It had been made abroad and was adjudged 'without natural appearance.'[31]

Flower manufacturing was by this time largely carried out using semi-manufactured products: the individual petals and components were obtained from abroad, while the finishing treatment such as crimping, dyeing and assembling the flowers and then inserting them in decorations and garnitures, took place in the different workshops. In addition to ladies' finery the flowers were also used for bouquets in decorating rooms and salons.

The making of artificial flowers appears to have gained a certain status over the centuries within women's handicrafts and as a profession. In the first place, it was a neat and tidy occupation. Even noblewomen made flowers as a pastime. In the second place, there was an aura of beauty and poetry surrounding the product. Furthermore, it could not have been damaging to the profession that Goethe's wife, Christiane Vulpius, worked in a flower factory in Weimar at the time he met her. Incidentally, it was founded and run by the renowned publisher of *Journal der Luxus und der Moden,* Friedrich Justin Bertuch.[32] Nonetheless, in the very class-divided society of the time it was frowned on for women to work for wages – they should be supported. However, certain circumstances could temporarily subvert such ideals. One of those circumstances was the French Revolution, which meant that many who were formerly well-off had to adjust themselves to a modest income obtained through manual labour. This applied to Stéphanie Félicité de Genlis, who had been lady-in-waiting for the Duke of Orleans and had been taught artificial flowermaking by Joseph Wengel. After having fled the country she supported herself by making flowers, until she made a name for herself as an author. The Parisian modiste Rose Bertin presumably suffered a similar fate. She had been purveyor both to the Queen and to Louis XV's mistress, Madame Dubarry. According to a preserved bill, she supplied this trendsetting customer with a lilac bouquet of batiste.[33]

In Denmark both the bombardment of Copenhagen in 1807 and the national bankruptcy in 1814 were the cause of similar turns of fate, and as early as 1804 the poor-law authority in Copenhagen, as mentioned previously, had been aware of the plight of female citizens who needed reputable employment in order to survive.

Les pauvre honteuses often had to work surreptitiously in order to avoid the pity of the general public, and the attitude became more and more pronounced as the fateful events faded into the background. Flowermaking was a possible exception, or appeared to be endowed with a certain respectability. In any case this is what is meant when Mimi, in *La Bohème,* tells her lover Rodolfo that she makes flowers: 'Lilies and roses do I make; but the flowers which I produce alas, they have no scent.' She is thus making it clear to Rodolfo, and the audience, that she is a respectable girl.

Table of contents to catalogue

Catalogue entries prepared by

Saskia de Bodt: cat. 266, 275
Maria Fabricius Hansen: cat. 30, 40, 44, 57, 59, 98, 100, 101, 209, 262
Bettina von Meyenburg: cat. 1, 5
Peter Wagner: cat. 61, 62, 64-69, 72-75, 77-81
Hanne Westergaard: cat. 2-, 24, 25, 33, 34, 39, 253
Vibeke Woldbye: cat. 11, 14, 93, 95, 133, 142, 143, 145, 155, 170, 176, 194, 195, 203, 211, 212, 252, 270, 282, 311, 330, 332

Abbreviations used in the catalogue

beg.: beginning
ca.: circa
cat.: catalogue
cen.: century
fig.: figure
sign.: signed

diam.: diameter
dp.: depth
h.: height
l.: length
w.: width

EXH.: exhibition
INV.: inventory
LIT.: literature
PROV.: provenance

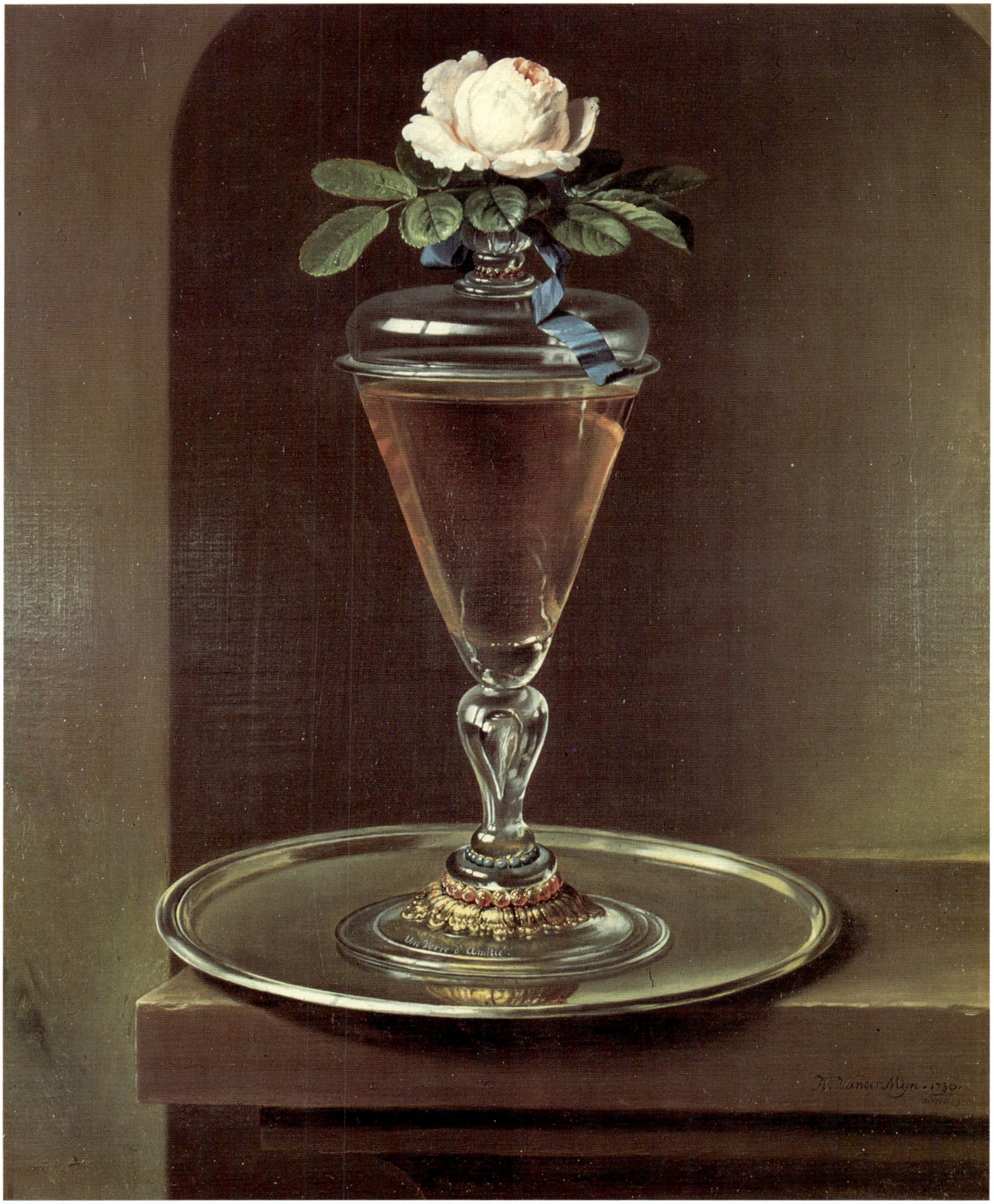
Un Verre d' Amitié
H. Vander Myn . 1730.

Paintings and drawings

1

Lucas van Valckenborch (before 1553-1597) *and* Georg Flegel (1566-1638)
'Spring'
One in a series of *The Four Seasons*'. Oil on canvas, 123 *x* 186.5 cm. Sign. 'LLV 1595'. Frankfurt, Germany 1595 (*fig. 37*)
Private collection, Sweden
EXH. *Bruegels tid. Nederländsk Konst* 1540-1620, Nationalmuseum, Stockholm 1984, no. 145, ill. p. 68; *Stilleben in Europa*, Westfälisches Landesmuseum für Kunst und Kulturgeschichte, Münster 1979, no. 145, ill. pp. 274, 276, 303, 558
LIT. Ingvar Bergström, 'Georg Flegel als Meister des Blumenstücks', *Festschrift Paul Pieper/Westfalen* 55, 1977, p. 137; Christie's. 29.11.1974, auction cat., fig. 37

In the 1590s, Lucas van Valckenborch, then living in Frankfurt, painted a series depicting the four seasons. Like *Winter*, *Spring* was painted in collaboration with Georg Flegel, an artist specialized in fruit and flower still lifes. *Spring* is known in five other versions.

The town in the background is Amsterdam. The garden with its leafless trees and people at work visualizes the early spring. The abundance of flowers in the baskets and the richness of the exotic bouquet on the table to the right represent an advanced stage of the season – according to humanism's nature symbolism a concerted homage to the defeat of winter and the approach of spring. Growing plants symbolize the life-giving force of nature's cycle.

The motif of a woman plucking flowers and herbs from baskets and mixing them as potpourri prior to making fragrant essences in the glasses on the table is typical of the pursuits of a noblewoman during the season in question, indicated here on the architrave of the house by representations of the three spring constellations, Aries, Capricorn and Gemini. The cycle of human life is in harmony with the changing of the seasons; in this work, landscape, genre and still-life painting are artistically merged to form a homogeneous whole.

2

Anthony van Dyck (1599-1641)
Self-portrait with sunflower
Oil on canvas, 60 *x* 73 cm. England ca. 1635-36 (*fig. 16*)
The Duke of Westminster, England
PROV. Unknown. There are a number of replicas and copies of this painting. The painting exhibited here, which is considered to be the original, was engraved by Wenzel Hollar in 1644.
EXH. Antwerp 1899; Royal Academy, London 1900
LIT. C. Brown, *Van Dyck*, 1982, p. 149; Sir L. Cust, *Anthony van Dyck. An Historical Study of his Life and Works*, 1900, p. 284, no. 208; G. Glück, *Van Dyck. Des Meisters Gemälde*, Stuttgart 1931, p. 496; Erik Larsen, *The Paintings of Anthony van Dyck*, I-2, 1988, no. 1019 and chapter 6; A. Schaeffer, *Van Dyck*, p. 401; R. Wark, 'A Note on van Dyck's Portrait with a Sunflower,' *Burlington Magazine*, vol. 98, 1956, p. 53 f

Van Dyck stayed in England on several occasions including the years 1632-41 as court painter to Charles I, who presented him with a portrait of himself on a gold chain in 1633.

Van Dyck has depicted himself half-length, standing at an angle with his face turned towards the beholder. Around his neck he wears the king's gold chain, which he raises with his left hand, pointing at himself with his forefinger. At the same time he points with the forefinger of his right hand at a tremendous sunflower which takes up most of the right side of the picture.

Several theories have been put forward regarding the symbolic content of the painting. Van Dyck does not present himself as a painter, but as a courtier. In English emblematic literature of the period, the sunflower often illustrates the relationship between subject and monarch, for just as the sunflower turns towards the sun for strength and energy, the subject turns towards the monarch. The most obvious interpretation of the self-portrait is the artist standing in the light of his patron's countenance, i.e., the glorious radiance of Charles I shines on Van Dyck.

3

Karel Slabbaert (ca. 1619-1654)
Botanist at his working table
Oil on canvas, 58.5 *x* 44.5 cm. Sign. 'Karel S(...)'. The Netherlands
Statens Museum for Kunst, Copenhagen (*Sp* 285)
LIT. *Catalogue of Old Foreign Paintings*, Statens Museum for Kunst, Copenhagen 1951, no. 664, ill.; Kurt J. Müllenmeister, 'Karel Slabbaert, ein Interieur und Bildnismaler aus Middelburg (1619-1654),' *Weltkunst*, vol. 42, no. 19, 1 October 1972, p. 1344; Werner Sumowski, *Gemälde der Rembrandt-Schüler*, I, Landau/Pfalz 1983, p. 502, ill. p. 517

4

Ottmar Elliger the Elder (1633-1679)
Fredrik III *and Sophie Amalie on horseback*
Set in a cartouche decorated with flowers. Oil on canvas, 80.6 *x* 62 cm. Ca. 1654 (*fig. 41*)
The Royal Collections, Rosenborg Palace, Copenhagen (7-22)
PROV. Inv. 1839. Acquired in 1837 from Frederiksborg Castle, Hillerød
EXH. *Sophie Amalie*, Rosenborg, Copenhagen 1986, cat. no. 9; *Dragter og Spil*, Rosenborg, Copenhagen 1988
LIT. E. F. S. Lund *Danske Malede Portrætter*, Copenhagen 1902, vol. 3, p. 74

5

Ottmar Elliger the Elder (1633-1679)
Ellybeth Mechtell and Angeneta Tacquet

6

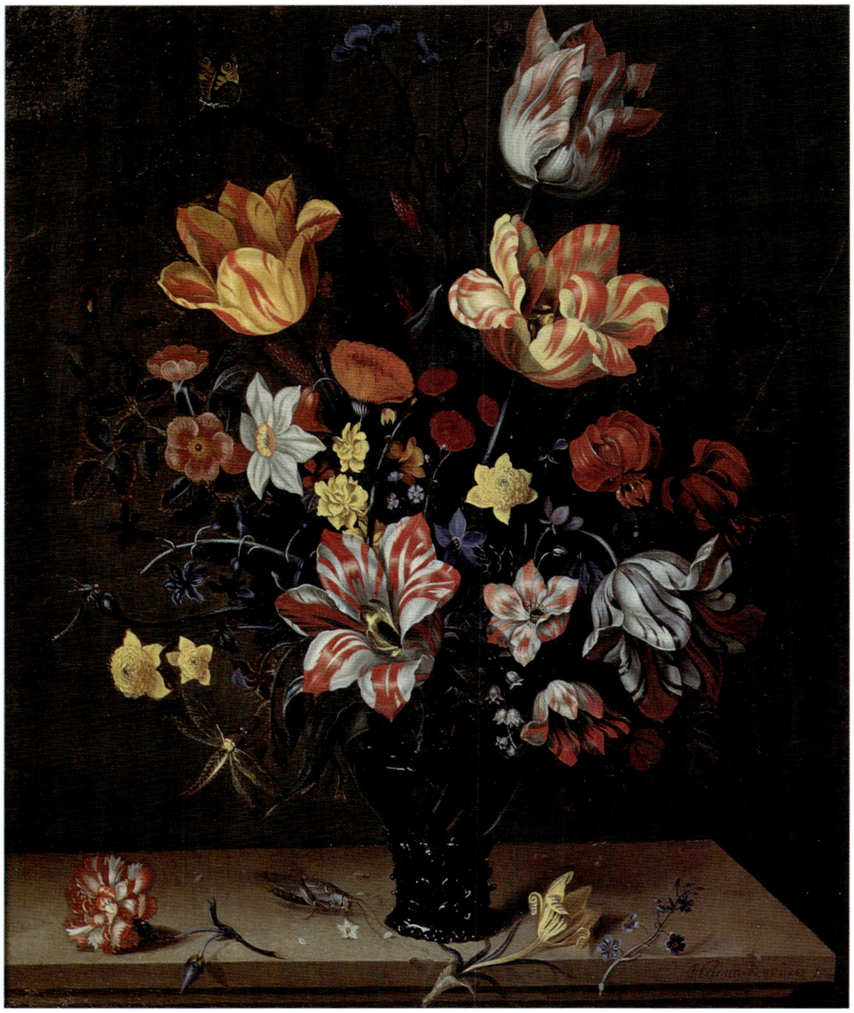

Oil on canvas, 131 *x* 115 cm. Sign. 'Ottmar Elliger pixt.', 1663
Det Nationalhistoriske Museum på Frederiksborg, Hillerød (A1746)

Ellybeth Mechtell (b. 1659) and her sister Angeneta Tacquet (b. 1661) as children in a garden. The grapes, insects and flowers around them provide an aesthetic decoration and also convey a deeper symbolism. White butterflies symbolize the spirit, the active life, and day (as opposed to night) and at the same time life after death, as represented by their metamorphosis from the larval stage to flying insects.

The painting is dated 1663. The girls are two and four years old respectively. The symbols taken from nature can be interpreted as religious and moral wishes for their future lives.

6
Helena Roouers
Vase with flowers
Oil on canvas, 55.5 *x* 46 cm. Sign. 'Helena Roouers fc. A 1663.'. The Netherlands (*ill.*)
Statens Museum for Kunst, Copenhagen (Stroe 16)
EXH. *Hollandsk Buket*, Kunstindustrimuseet, Copenhagen, 1969, cat. no. 42
LIT. *Catalogue of Old Foreign Paintings*, Statens Museum for Kunst, Copenhagen 1951, no. 596; Poul Gammelbo, *Dutch Still-Life Painting from the 16th to the 18th Centuries in Danish Collections*, Copenhagen 1960, p. 120, no. 173, ill. p. 121; Germaine Greer, *The Obstacle Race. The Fortunes of Women Painters and Their Work*, New York 1979, p. 240, ill. p. 241; Peter Mitchell, *European Flower Paintings*, London 1973, p. 220, fig. 312

7
H. van der Mijn (1684-1741)
Rose on a covered glass
Oil on canvas, 74 *x* 61 cm. Sign. 'H. Vander Myn.1730/august:31' and on the foot of the glass 'un verre d'amitié' (*ill.*)
Burghley House, Stamford, England (527)
EXH. *The Treasure Houses of Britain*. National Gallery of Art, Washington, Washington/New Haven 1985, cat. no. 297

8
Simon Verelst (1644-1721)
Glass vase with flowers
Oil on canvas, 101.5 *x* 79 cm. The Netherlands (*fig. 38*)
Statens Museum for Kunst, Copenhagen (670)
EXH. *Hollandsk Buket*, Kunstindustrimuseet, Copenhagen, 1969, cat. no. 44, ill.
LIT. *Catalogue of Old Foreign Paintings*. Statens Museum for Kunst, Copenhagen 1951, no. 750; Poul Gammelbo, *Dutch Still-Life Painting from the 16th to the 18th Centuries in Danish Collections*, Copenhagen 1960, p. 120, no. 174, ill. p. 121; Frank Lewis, *Simon Pietersz. Verelst 1644-1721*, Leigh-on-Sea 1979, p. 25, cat. no. 16, ill.

9
Maria Sibylla Merian (1647-1717)
Bouquet with insects
Gouache on vellum. Attached to copperplate, 35.8 *x* 26.6 cm. Germany
Statens Museum for Kunst, Den kongelige Kobberstiksamling, Copenhagen

19

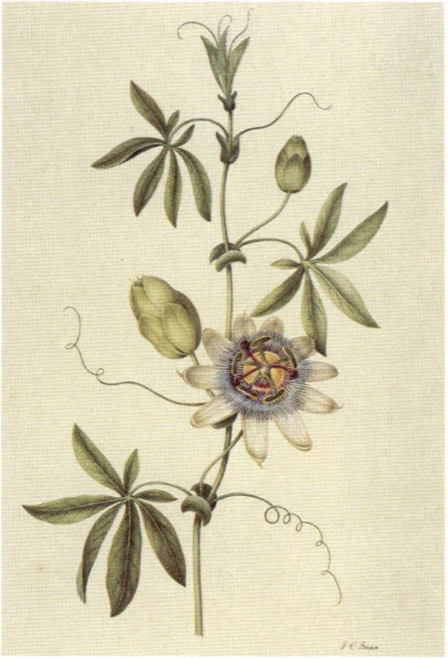

10
Jan Jepsen (1655-1700)
Moor girl and monkey
Oil on canvas, 98 x 78.5 cm. Denmark end of 17th century
The Royal Collections, Rosenborg Palace, Copenhagen (33-62)
PROV. Inv. 1718. 552.4

11
Alexander Roslin (1718-1793)
La Baronesse de Neubourg-Cromière
Oil on canvas, 91 x 74 cm. Sign. 'Roslin le Suèd 1756.' Paris 1756 (*fig. 111*)
Statens Konstmuseer, Nationalmuseum, Stockholm (NM2367)
LIT. Gunnar W. Lundberg, *Roslin. His Life and Work. Avec un resumé français et la catalogue des oeuvres*, Malmö 1957, no. 85

The portrait is a pendant to the portrait of her husband, Baron de Neubourg-Cromière, which is in a private collection in Scania, Sweden.

12
Peter Cramer (1726-1782)
Anna Marie Køster
Oil on canvas, 48 x 37 cm. Sign. 'Cramer 1762'. Denmark 1762 (*fig. 109*)
Det Nationalhistoriske Museum på Frederiksborg, Hillerød (A6646)

13
N. Lafrensen the Younger (1737-1807)
Ambassador, Baron Eric Magnus Staël von Holstein
Gouache, 25 x 20 cm. Sign. 'Lafenez [?]/1792'. Sweden 1792 (*fig. 17*)
Statens Konstmuseer, Nationalmuseum, Stockholm (NM1210)

14
I. C. Bayer (1738-1812)
Artichoke with butterflies
Gouache on vellum. Dark brown background, ca. 33 x ca. 26 cm. Sign. 'I:C:Baer pinx at naturam'. Copenhagen
Statens Museum for Kunst, Den kongelige Kobberstiksamling, Copenhagen (*Td*529,1)

Johann Christoph Bayer is primarily known as the illustrator of the botanical work *Flora Danica* and as the one who almost single-handedly decorated the porcelain service, which consisted of more than 1,800 pieces.

15
I. C. Bayer (1738-1812)
Digitalis
Gouache. Dark brown background, ca. 26.8 x ca. 18 cm. Copenhagen
Statens Museum for Kunst, Den kongelige Kobberstiksamling, Copenhagen (*Td*529,5)

16
I. C. Bayer (1738-1812)
Pea flower, asters
Gouache. Dark brown background, ca. 25.8 x 21.2/21.9 cm. Copenhagen
Statens Museum for Kunst, Den kongelige Kobberstiksamling, Copenhagen (*Td*529,6)

17
I. C. Bayer (1738-1812)
Milk tubes and forget-me-nots
Gouache. Almost black background, ca. 8.4 x ca. 11.9 cm. Copenhagen
Statens Museum for Kunst, Den kongelige Kobberstiksamling, Copenhagen (*Td*529,20)

18
I. C. Bayer (1738-1812)
Aster, blue
Gouache, ca. 32.2 x 23.3 cm. Sign. 'I:C:Baÿer'. Copenhagen
Statens Museum for Kunst, Den kongelige Koberstiksamling, Copenhagen (*Td*529,43)

19
I. C. Bayer (1738-1812)
Passion flower
Gouache, ca. 32.2 x ca. 23.2 cm. Sign. 'I:C:Bäÿer'. Copenhagen (*ill.*)
Statens Museum for Kunst, Den kongelige Kobberstiksamling, Copenhagen (*Td*529,44)

20
I. C. Bayer (1738-1812)
Carnation, red
Gouache, ca. 32.4 x 23.4 cm. Sign. 'I:C:Baÿer'. Copenhagen
Statens Museum for Kunst, Den Kongelige Kobberstiksamling, Copenhagen (*Td*529,45)

21
I. C. Bayer (1738-1812)
Tiger lily
Gouache, 32.6/32.2 x 23.5 cm. Sign. 'I:C:Baÿer'. Copenhagen
Statens Museum for Kunst, Den kongelige Kobberstiksamling, Copenhagen (*Td*529,46)

22
I. C. Bayer (1738-1812)
Lily, red
Gouache, ca. 32.4 x ca. 23.2 cm. Sign. 'I:C:Bäÿer'. Copenhagen
Statens Museum for Kunst, Den kongelige Kobberstiksamling, Copenhagen (*Td*529,47)

23
I. C. Bayer (1738-1812)
Moss rose
Gouache, 32.3/32.7 x 23.3 cm. Sign. 'I:C:Baÿer'. Copenhagen
Statens Museum for Kunst, Den kongelige Kobberstiksamling, Copenhagen (*Td*529,48)

24
Martinus Rørbye (1803-1848)
View from the artist's window
Oil on canvas, 38 x 29.8 cm. Denmark ca. 1825 (*fig. 18*)

26

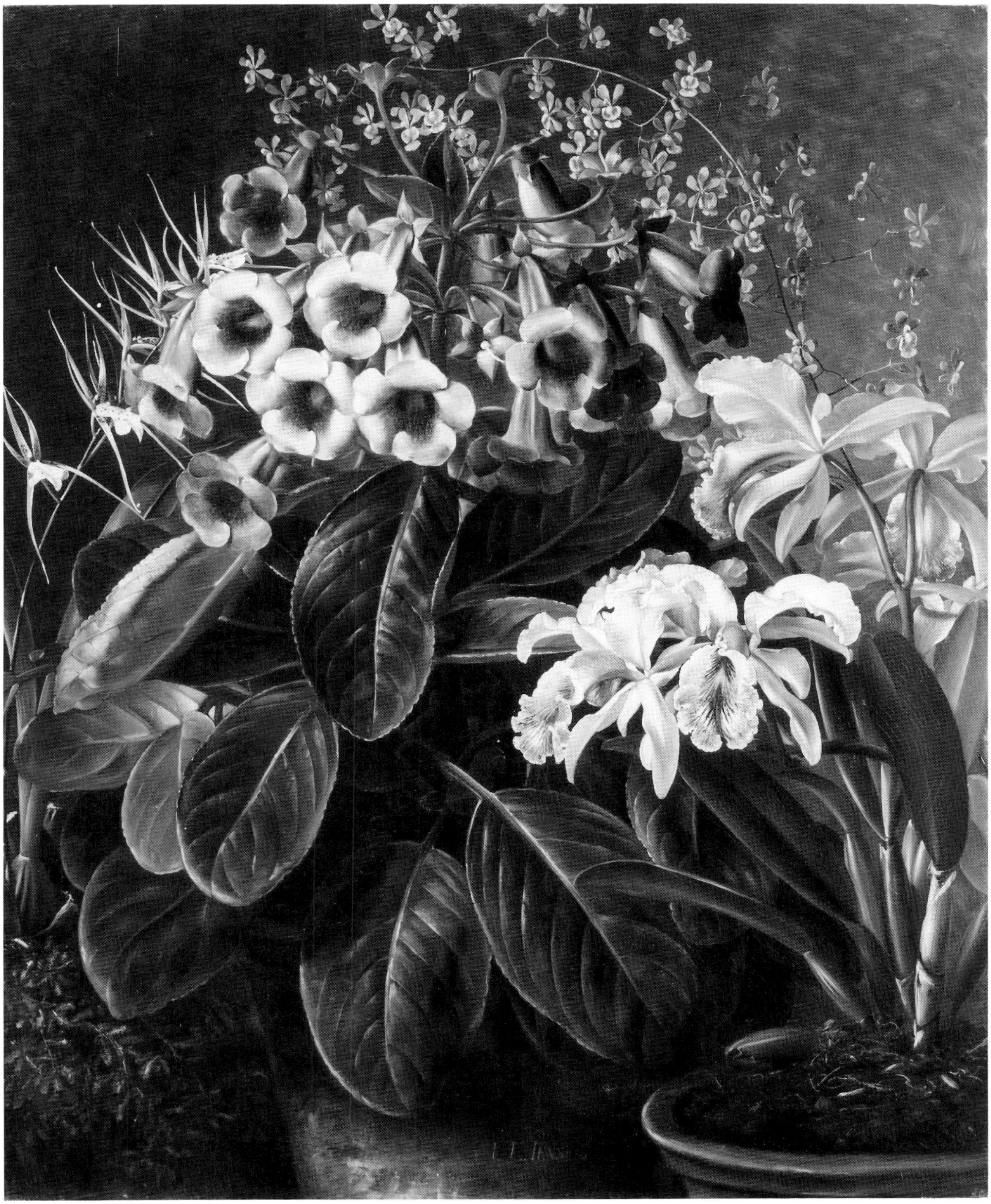

Statens Museum for Kunst, Copenhagen (7452)
EXH. The City Hall Exhibition, Copenhagen 1901, no. 1560; Kunstforeningen, Copenhagen 1905, no. 4; 1975, no. 135; The Thorvaldsen Museum 1981, no. 3; *Golden Age Painting in Denmark*, Moscow 1989
LIT. Ch. A. Been & E. Hannover, *Danmarks Malerkunst*, 1902-03, vol. I, p. 101; Tue & Bodil Gad, *Vinduet, et Biedermeiermotiv*, 1976, p. 74 f.; D. Helsted, E. Henschen, B. Jørnæs & T. Melander, *Martinus Rørbye 1803-1848*, Copenhagen 1981, p. 29

Through an open window in his parents' home in Amaliegade, Rørbye has depicted the view over Copenhagen harbour with the rigging sheer on the left and ships in dock on the right.

25
I. L. Jensen (1800-1856)
Vase with flowers
Oil on canvas, 87 *x* 74 cm. Sign. 'I. L. JENSEN SORENTO 1834' (*fig. 22*)
Statens Museum for Kunst, Copenhagen (285)
EXH. *Pittori Danese*, Rome 1977, no. 34; *Danish Painters in Rome*, Statens Museum for Kunst, Copenhagen 1978, no. 34, *Thorvaldsens græske vaser*, Thorvaldsen Museum, Copenhagen 1984-85 (no catalogue)
LIT. A. Greifenhagen, *Griechische Vasen auf Bildern des 19. Jahrhunderts*, Heidelberg 1978, p. 23

The flowers include *Magnolia grandiflora*, pomegranate flowers, poppies (*Papaver somniferum*), rhododendrons, ipomoea, hollyhock, knight's spore, probably a kind of wistaria (*Wisteria sinensis var. rosea*), roses and others such as *Alpinia speciosa*, *Siningaria speciosa*, *Strelitzia reginae*, *Tecome grandiflora* and *Cobaea speciosa*.

The figures on the vase, Dionysos and his companions, were taken by Jensen from a crater which had belonged to Thomas Hope since 1801.

The painting was bought by the Danish king Christian VIII, who himself collected antique vases and had supported I. L. Jensen in his youth.

26
I. L. Jensen (1800-1856)
Orchids and gloxinia in pots
Oil on canvas, 65 *x* 53.3 cm. Sign. 'I. L. Jensen'. Copenhagen (*ill.*)
Aarhus Art Museum, Aarhus (806)

27
I. L. Jensen (1800-1856)
Flower and fruit festoon
Oil on canvas. In two parts. Festoon made of bindweed, passion flowers, variegated dahlias, oak-leaves, wine leaves with bunches of grapes and sunflowers suspended around brass knobs in the shape of flowers. The two parts together 90 *x* 590 cm.
Baltica, Copenhagen

28
Constantin Hansen (1804-1880)
Study of a flower
Chicory. Watercolour, 22 *x* 12.5 cm. Denmark before 1835
Kunstindustrimuseet, Copenhagen (CHI)

29
J. Th. Lundbye (1818-1848)
Blooming amaryllis
Pen and Watercolour, 25.7 *x* 18.7 cm. Sign. 'Amaryllis formosissima' and 'd 19 april 1840'. Denmark 1840
Statens Museum for Kunst, Den kongelige Kobberstiksamling, Copenhagen (*Td*714,6)

30
J. Th. Lundbye (1818-1848)
Study of flowers
Pen, ink and watercolour, 27.3 *x* 19.8 cm. Plant names indicated: 'Catchfly, Avens, Walnut Leaf, Winter Green Periwinkle, Wild Sorrel' and 'Frvk [= Frederiksværk]', as well as the dates 26/5, 28/5, 40. Denmark 1840 (ill.)
Statens Museum for Kunst, Den kongelige Kobberstiksamling, Copenhagen (*Td*714,9)
EXH. *Von Abildgaard bis Marstrand*, Munich 1985, cat. 83, fig. 79

31
P. C. Skovgaard (1817-1875)
Spring flowers
White and blue anemones, yellow stars-of-Bethlehem, or buttercups. Watercolour, 30.5 *x* 25.5 cm. Denmark ca. 1855
Kunstindustrimuseet, Copenhagen (PCS7)

32
Studies of flowers etc., in botanical work
Bound botanical work from 1720 containing drawings (pencil and watercolour) of flowers produced by the Skovgaard family and friends from the end of the 19th century until modern times.
Private collection, Denmark

33
O. D. Ottesen (1816-1892)
Moss rose tree surrounded by summer flowers
Oil on canvas, 61 *x* 53 cm. Sign. 'O. D. Ottesen: 1864'. Denmark
Statens Museum for Kunst, Copenhagen (836)
EXH. *H. C. Andersens Blomster*, Statens Museum for Kunst, Copenhagen and the H. C. Andersen House, Odense 1978, no. 47
LIT. H. Westergaard: *H. C. Andersens Blomster. Haver. Buketter. Billeder*, Copenhagen 1978, p. 35; Blomstermaleren O. D. Ottesen, *Arbejdsbog og optegnelser*, H. Westergaard (ed.), Copenhagen 1979, p. 39

As an innovation in Danish flower painting, Ottesen introduced the idea of depicting plants in their natural surroundings, i.e., gardens, fields and woods.

34
O. D. Ottesen (1816-1892)
Flowers in a vase
Oil on panel, 77 *x* 57 cm. Sign. 'O. D. Ottesen 1869', Denmark (fig. 23)
Statens Museum for Kunst, Copenhagen (865)
EXH. *H. C. Andersens Blomster*, Statens Museum for Kunst, Copenhagen and the H. C. Andersen House, Odense 1978, no. 78
LIT. H. Westergaard: *H. C. Andersens Blomster. Haver. Buketter. Billeder*, Copenhagen 1978, p. 35; Blomstermaleren O. D. Ottesen, *Arbejdsbog og optegnelser*, H. Westergaard (ed.), Copenhagen 1979, p. 43

30

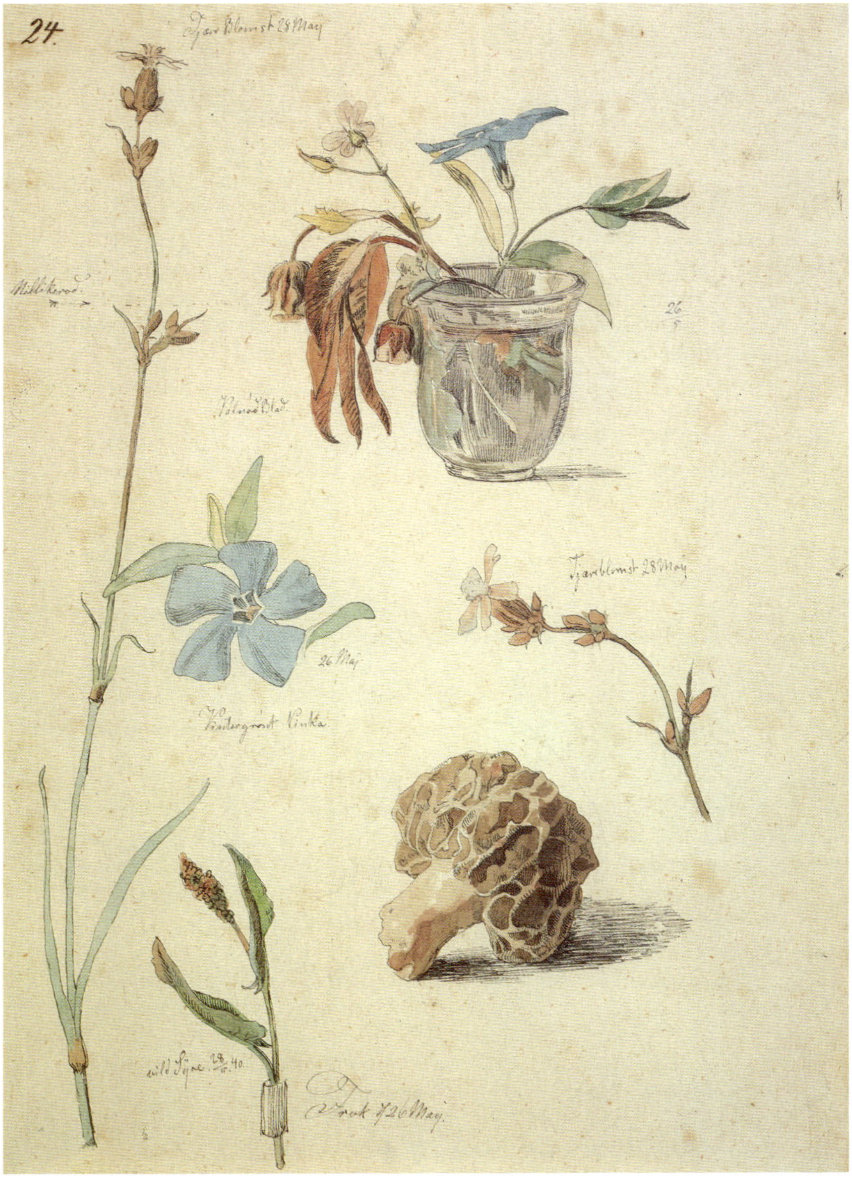

The original title of the painting was 'A vase with roses, cabbage-roses, carrot trace thishawe, Persian Yellow, Gloire de Dijon, General Jacqueminot and several other Flowers in a Window illuminated by the Sun (seen from outside).' The composition is considerably influenced by a flower painting by Jan van Huijsum acquired by the Statens Museum for Kunst in 1843, and which Ottesen, who since his youth had been interested in the work of Van Huijsum, copied in 1888.

35
Constantin Hansen (1804-1880)
Model for embroidery
Woodbine twig and butterfly. Watercolour, 39.5 *x* 34 cm. Sign. 'Const:Hansen 1872'. Denmark 1872
Kunstindustrimuseet, Copenhagen (CH39)

36
Constantin Hansen (1804-1880)
Plant ornament
Jasmine. Watercolour, 43 *x* 26.2 cm. Denmark
Kunstindustrimuseet, Copenhagen (CH70)

37
Lorenz Frølich (1820-1908)
Drawing framing a photograph of Hans Christian Andersen
Pen, brown ink, 16.2 *x* 11 cm. Sign. 'L Fr:76'. Denmark 1876 (*fig. 102*)
Statens Museum for Kunst, Den kongelige Kobberstiksamling, Copenhagen (*Td738a,66*)

38
Sophie Henck (1822-1893)
Copy of Jan van Huijsum's 'flower piece'
Oil on canvas, 82 *x* 62 cm. Denmark (*see fig. 20*)
Aarhus Art Museum, Aarhus (66)
EXH. *O. D. Ottesen og andre blomstermalere på H. C. Andersens Tid*, The Museum at Sønderborg Castle 1986, cat. no. 21, p. 15

39
Michael Ancher (1849-1927)
Girl with sunflowers
Oil on canvas, 101 *x* 95 cm. Sign. 'Michael Ancher 1889'. Skagen, Denmark 1889 (*fig. 27*)
Statens Museum for Kunst, Copenhagen (3820)
EXH. Charlottenborg, Copenhagen 1890, no. 16; Biennale Venice 1895, no. 7; Stockholm 1897, no. 925; *Kunstforeningens Mindeudstillinger*; 1928, no. 39, 1949, no. 25; *1880-erne i Nordisk Maleri*, Oslo, Stockholm, Helsinki, Copenhagen 1985-86, no. 6
LIT. Karl Madsen, *Skagens Malerne*, Copenhagen 1929, p. 40; Hanne Westergaard, 'Kunstnerkolonien på Skagen,' *1880-erne i Nordisk Maleri*, Uddevalla 1986, pp. 33-39

Ancher painted this picture shortly after a long sojourn in France (1888-89), where he might have heard about Van Gogh's sunflower paintings.

The young girl in the picture is Maren Brems. Shortly after her confirmation she found employment in the Ancher household. Wearing her new yellow dress, she is standing in the

43

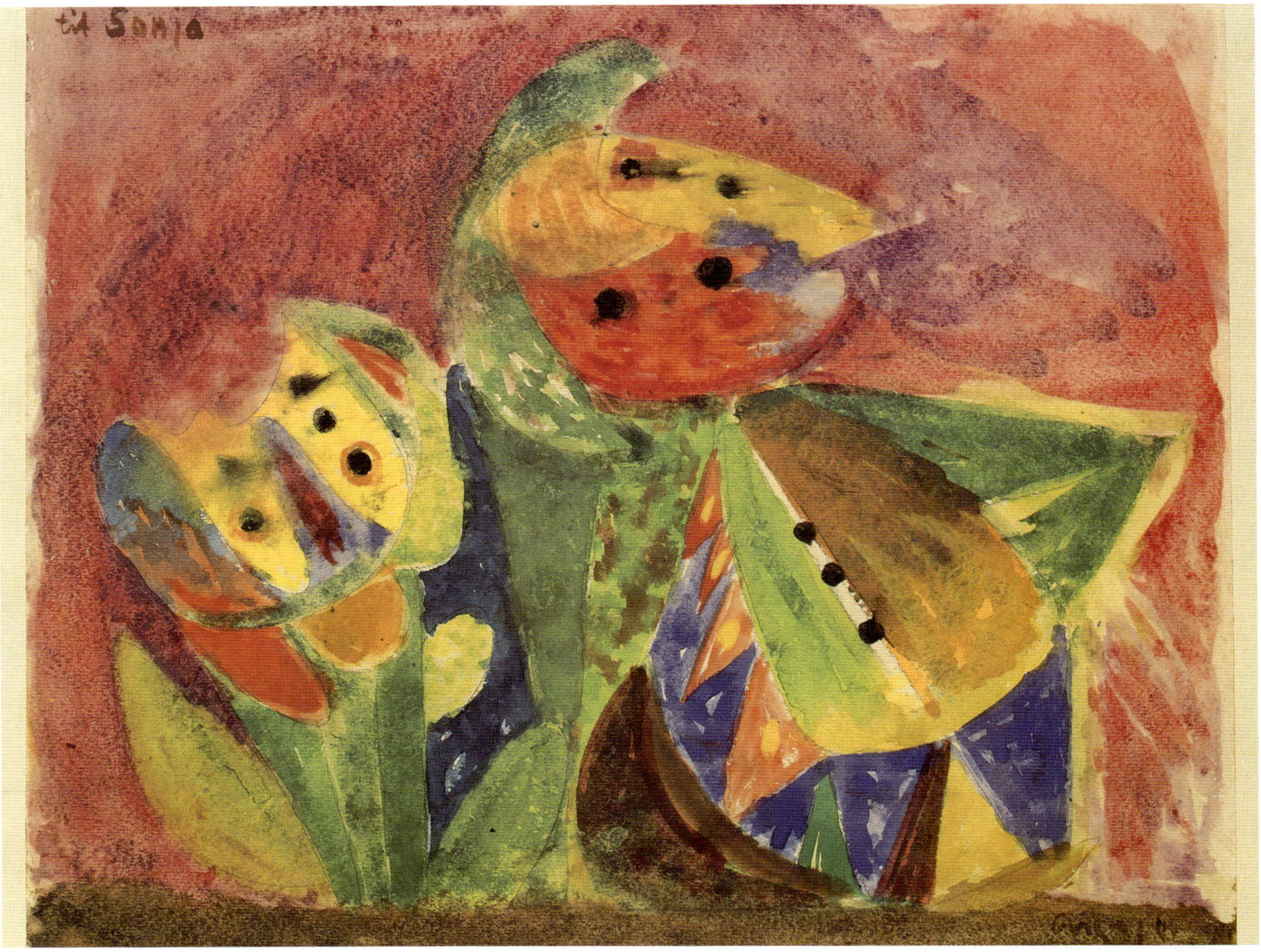

doorway between two rooms in the house at Markvej no. 2 in Skagen. The beholder's attention is drawn to the flowers which stand out against her dark apron and the white door.

40
Emil Nolde (1867-1956)
Anemones and blue lilies in a blue glass
Watercolour, 47.6 *x* 33.9 cm. Sign. 'Nolde'. Germany before ca. 1920
Statens Museum for Kunst, Den kongelige Kobberstiksamling, Copenhagen (*Tu*115*f*, 2)
LIT. Martin Urban, *Emil Nolde, Blumen und Tiere, Aquarelle und Zeichnungen*, Cologne 1965

Flower painting became one of Nolde's ways of liberating colour as a pure means of expression. The first series of flower and garden pictures was painted in oil around 1906-08, practically at the time of his association with the expressionistic group 'Die Brücke.' It was during this same period that Nolde became aware of the possibilities of watercolour as a medium, but he did not apply this technique to flower motifs until the years around World War I.

41
Emil Nolde (1867-1956)
Sunflowers
Watercolour, 34.8 *x* 45.1 cm. Sign. 'Nolde', Germany ca. 1932
Statens Museum for Kunst, Den kongelige Kobberstiksamling, Copenhagen (*Tu*115*f*, 8)

42
Emil Nolde (1867-1956)
Poppies
Watercolour, 46.2 *x* 34.3 cm. Sign. 'Nolde', Germany ca. 1934 (*fig. 63*)
Statens Museum for Kunst, Den kongelige Kobberstiksamling, Copenhagen (*Tu*115*f*, 9)

43
Asger Jorn (1914-1973)
Flower composition
Watercolour, 31 *x* 38 cm. Sign. 'Asger J. 44' and 'Til Sonja', Denmark 1944 (ill.)
Private collection

Prints and books

PRINTS

44
Albrecht Dürer (1471-1528)
Erasmus of Rotterdam
Engraving, 24.8 *x* 19.2 cm. Germany 1526
Statens Museum for Kunst, Den kongelige Kobberstiksamling, Copenhagen (Box VIII, 13)

Dürer has portrayed the erudite humanist sitting at his desk, pen and ink within reach and a pile of books in the foreground. The names of the artist and that of Erasmus of Rotterdam are presented on a tablet with inscriptions in Latin and Greek. An antique vase with lilies of the valley and violets is placed on the table in front of Erasmus – an indication of the Renaissance humanists' interest in antiquity as well as his delight in familiar plants and flowers.

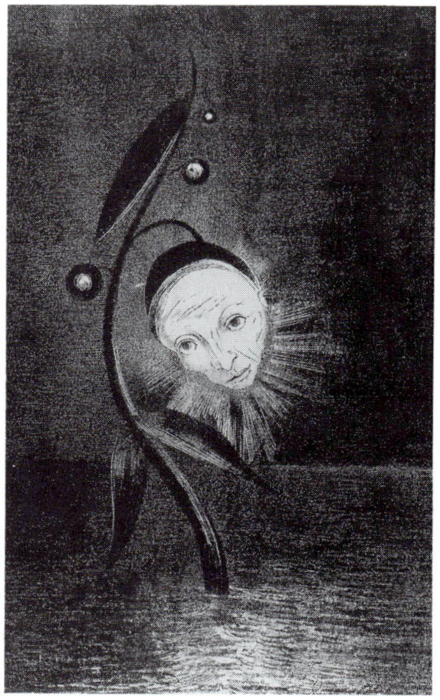

52

45
Adrian Collaert (ca. 1560-1618)
The sense of 'smell'
Engraving, 19.5 *x* 25.2 cm. The Netherlands (fig. 43)
Statens Museum for Kunst, Den kongelige Kobbersiksamling, Copenhagen (231*b*,135)

46
Johann Theodor de Bry (1562-1620)
Six vases with flowers
Engraving, ca. 30 *x* 22 cm. Germany
Statens Museum for Kunst, Den kongelige Kobberstiksamling, Copenhagen (91, 80-85)

47
Crispin de Pas (1589?-1670)
The sense of 'smell'
Engraving, 18.5 *x* 23.3 cm. The Netherlands
Statens Museum for Kunst, Den kongelige Kobberstiksamling, Copenhagen (300,83)

48
François Lefebure (mentioned ca. 1635-1657)
Sheets from *Livre de Fleurs et de Feuilles pour servir à l'Art d'orfèverie inventé par François Lefebure maistre orfèvre à Paris. Baltazar Moncornet fecit et excudit.* FLD *Ciartres excudit 1635*, Paris. Engraving, ca. 20.5 *x* 15.5 cm
Kunstindustrimuseet, Copenhagen

49
François Lefebure (mentioned ca. 1635-1657)
Design for jewellery
Engraving with 'peapod flowers' in a bouquet over a scene of a meal in a landscape with a city indicated as 'Paris,' 40.5 *x* 30 cm. Sign. 'françois le febure Inventor. Moncornet excudit avec privilege du Roy'. Paris
Kunstindustrimuseet (Den kongelige Kobberstiksamling, Statens Museum for Kunst, Copenhagen, Dep. 1922)

53

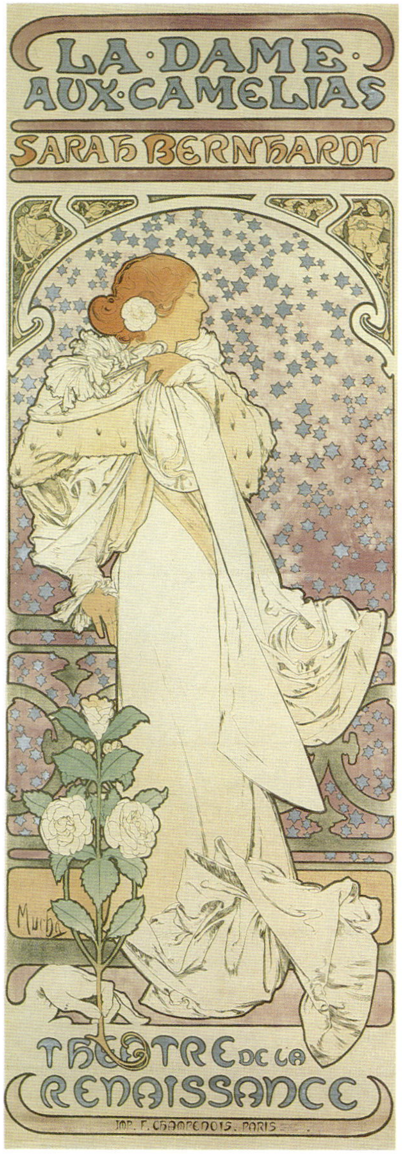

50
Gédéon Légaré (1615-1676)
Design for jewellery
Engraving. Flowers with 'peapod leaves' above a landscape, 41.2 *x* 30.5 cm. Sign. 'Gedeon Legare. F. L. D. Ciatres excudit Cum Privilegio Regis Christianiss'. France 17th century
Kunstindustrimuseet (Den kongelige Kobberstiksamling, Statens Museum for Kunst, Copenhagen, Dep. 1422)

57

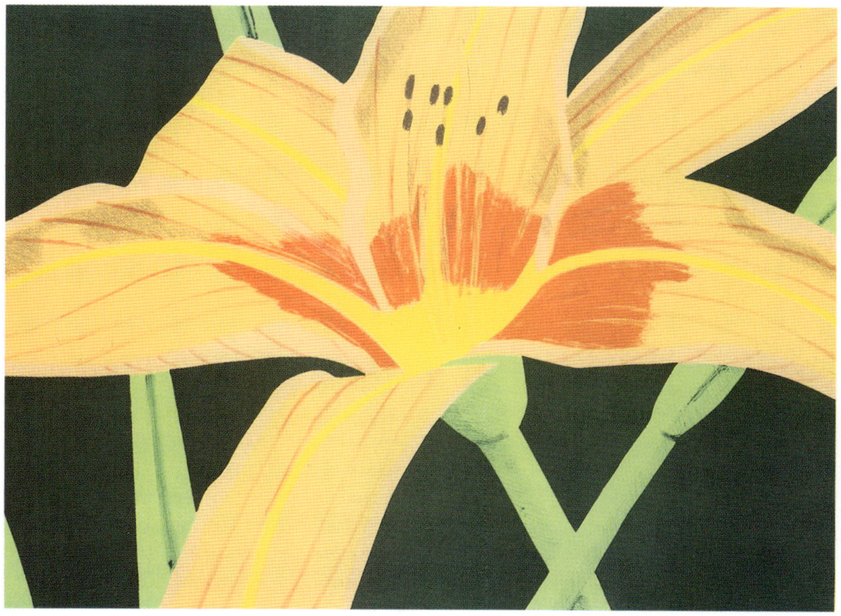

close-up views of flower motifs as in *Day Lily 2*, where the edge of the petals seems to indicate the limits of the field of vision. The simplification of the motif and the use of only a few, clear colours make *Day Lily 2* a typical example of pop art.

51
Wilhelm Altzenbach (d. after 1680)
Flower vase
Engraving, 34.7 x 25.2 cm. After Joh. Toussyn. Sign. 'Wilh Altzenbach fecit' and 'Gerhardt Altzenbach excudit'. Germany 17th century (fig. 42)
Kunstindustrimuseet, Copenhagen (373, 186)

52
Odilon Redon (1840-1916)
'La fleur du marécage, une tête humaine et triste'
Lithograph, 45.5 x 31.2 cm. From the series 'Hommage à Goya. 6 lithographs.' Print: Lemercier et Cie., Paris 1885 (*ill.*)
Statens Museum for Kunst, Den kongelige Kobberstiksamling, Copenhagen (613,4)

53
Alphonse Mucha (1860-1939)
'La Dame aux Camelias.' Sarah Bernhardt
Poster. Colour lithograph with silver, 207 x 77 cm. Print: F. Champenois, Paris 1896 (*ill.*)
Kunstindustrimuseet, Copenhagen

54
Agnes Slott-Møller (1862-1937)
'Summer. Summer Reading, Artistically Equipped'
Poster. Colour lithograph, 81.5 x 60 cm. Alfred Jacobsen's Litografiske Etablisement, Copenhagen
Kunstindustrimuseet, Copenhagen

55
Peter Blake (b. 1932) & Jann Haworth
The Beatles, 'Sgt. Peppers Lonely Hearts Club Band'
Record cover, 31.2 x 31.2 cm. EMI Records, England 1967 (*fig. 72*)
Private collection

56
Martin Sharp
Cream, 'Disraeli Gears'
Record cover, 31.2 x 31.2 cm. Polydor Records, England 1967 (*fig. 73*)
Private collection

57
Alex Katz (b. 1927)
Day Lily 2
Colour lithograph, 52. x 71 cm. Sign. with artist's signature and '85/90'. USA 1969
Galerie Börjeson, Malmö
LIT. Udo Kultermann, *Neue Formen des Bildes*, Tübingen (1969) rev. ed. 1976

In the 1960s, Katz worked with

58
Andy Warhol (1928-1987)
Flowers
Six screen-prints in different colours with flowers on a grassy background. From a series of ten sheets, 91 x 91 cm. Ed. Sunday B. Morning. New York 1970 (*fig. 66*)
Kunstbiblioteket, Lyngby

59
David Hockney (b. 1937)
'Godetia'
Engraving and aquatint in various colours on paper, 58.5 x 41.5 cm. Sign. 'David Hockney 73 – no. 16/100'. Ed. Petersburg Press, London 1973 (*ill.*)
Private collection

A vase with flowers is a common motif in the apparently quiet and peaceful interiors in Hockney's paintings. In a number of graphic works, for example *'Godetia,'* the flower vase has been isolated as the main motif of the composition. The colours of the bouquet are delicate but dense and form a collage-like contrast to the vase. The displacement of the centre of gravity of the flowers in relation to the vase and its position in the field of vision result in an almost imperceptible break of the superficial harmony that initially seems to characterize the picture, both technically and in terms of content.

60
Jean Baptiset Mondino
Prince, 'Lovesexy'
Record cover, 31.2 x 31.2 cm. Paisley Park Records, USA 1988
Private collection

59

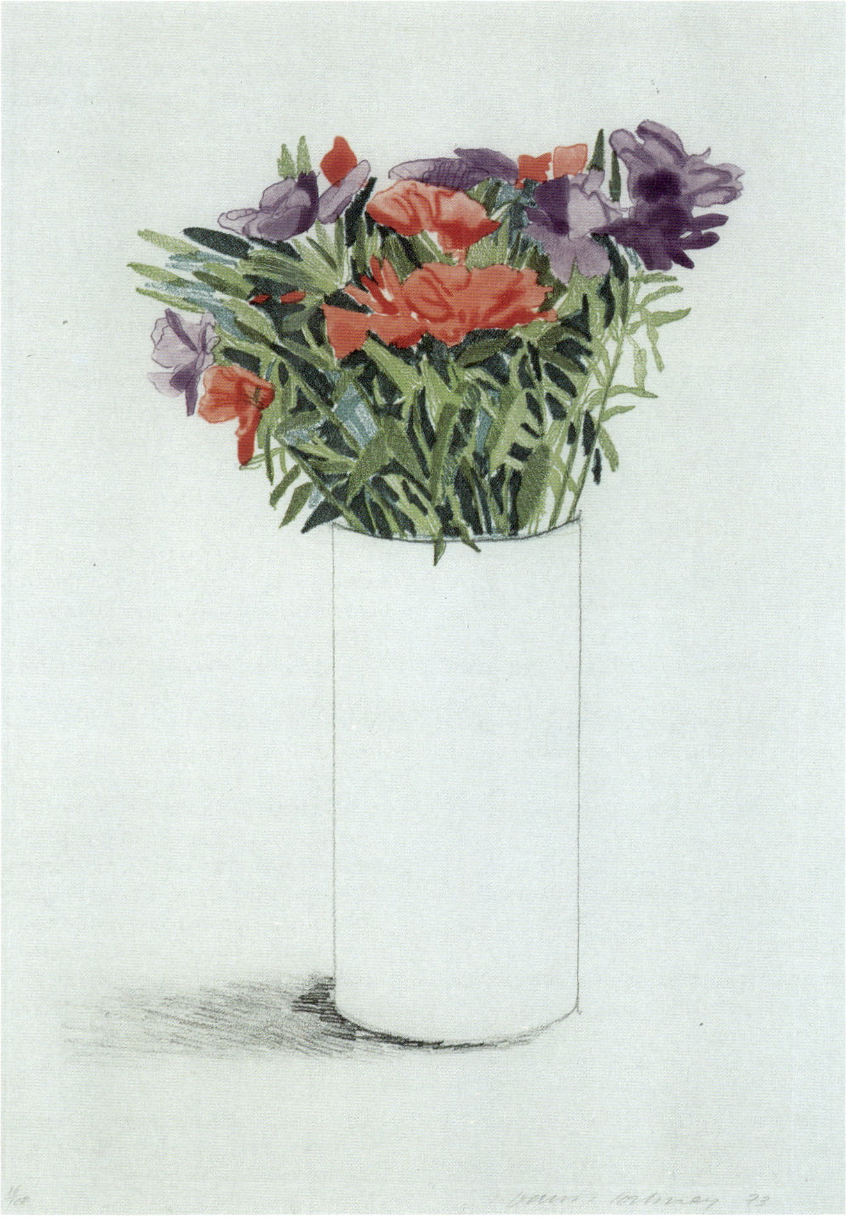

BOTANICAL BOOKS

61
Otto Brunfels (1488-1534)
Herbarum vivae eicones, vols. 1-3, Strasbourg 1530-36. Folio (*fig. 1*)
Botanisk Centralbibliotek, Copenhagen
LIT. Agnes Arber, *Herbals. Their Origin and Evolution. A Chapter in the History of Botany 1470-1670*, Cambridge 1938, pp. 206-09; Frans A. Stafleu & Richard S. Cowan, *Taxonomic Literature. A selective guide to botanical publications and collections with dates, commentaries and types*, vol. 1: KK (2nd ed.) Utrecht 1976, pp. 382-84

With the publication of this work the physician and botanist Otto Brunfels introduced a new era in the history of botany by including woodcuts of the majority of the plants mentioned. The pictures have been drawn from life, a fact indicated by the title 'living pictures of plants.' Apparently Brunfels was not familiar with the practice of pressing plants. The illustrator Hans Weiditz had accurately drawn the plant he saw, including withered leaves, instead of portraying the ideal plant, which became the custom later. A number of the beautifully coloured drawings are found in a herbarium by Felix Platter (1526-1614), one of the oldest large herbariums to have been preserved. *Herbarum vivae eicones* was a great success; it was printed in five editions in the course of ten years, and was translated into German under the title *Contrafeyt Kreuterbuch* (two editions) and also in a quarto edition in German.

62
Leonhard Fuchs (1501-1566)
De historia stirpium commentarii insignes..., Basel 1542. Folio (*figs. 2, 3*)
Botanisk Centralbibliotek, Copenhagen
LIT. Agnes Arber, *Herbals. Their Origin and Evolution. A Chapter in the History of Botany 1470-1670*, Cambridge 1938, pp. 64-70, 152-53; G. A. Pritzel, *Thesaurus Literaturae Botanicae Omnium Gentium*, Leipzig 1871-77, p. 115; Frans A. Stafleu & Richard S. Cowan, *Taxonomic Literature. A selective guide to botanical publications and collections with dates, commentaries and types*, vol. 1: A-G (2nd ed.) Utrecht 1976, pp. 894-95

Leonhard Fuchs, who was a physician and a philologist, was very interested in the identification of plants named by the authors of antiquity. The result of this interest was *De historia stirpium*, which contains 511 woodcuts of plants. In his description of the plants and their uses Fuchs follows the classics closely, thus the book's chief value is not its text. In his foreword Fuchs emphasizes the fact that every effort has been taken to obtain pictures that are as good and true to life as possible, and that the best artists have been used. They are portrayed at the end of the book: Albrecht Meyer drew the plants, Heinrich Füllmaurer transferred the drawings to wooden blocks and Veit Rudolph Speckle cut them. The illustrations are far better than those used by Brunfels and were reused and copied many times, the last time being in 1774. The book was published in German, French (three times) and in Dutch; an abridged edition in octavo appeared in several languages.

63
Pierre Vallet (b. ca. 1575)
Lilium purpureum – Lilium flavum. Woodcut. Two lilies, one of them hand-coloured, 29 *x* 17 cm. France ca. 1600 (fig. 4)
Kunstindustrimuseet, Copenhagen

64
Emmanuel Sweert (1552-?)
Florilegium... Tractans De Variis Floribus Et Aliis Indicis Plantis Ad Vivum Delineatum..., Frankfurt am Main 1612. Folio (*fig. 6*)
Botanisk Centralbibliotek, Copenhagen
LIT. Wilfrid Blunt, *The Art of Botanical Illustration*, London 1950, pp. 91-92; G. A. Pritzel, *Thesaurus Literaturae Botanicae Omnium Gentium*, Leipzig 1871-77

The Dutch-born gardener and botanist Emmanuel Sweert, who was the superintendent of Emperor Rudolph II's gardens, published this florilegium in 1612. On the title page it is stated that the plants illustrated can be purchased at the author's place of business in Frankfurt. In other words it is a kind of sales catalogue, though without prices. Many of the engravings have been copied from De Bry who in turn copied them from Vallet; the copies of copies are in most cases inferior. The quality also suffers from the fact that Sweert used various engravers with varying degrees of skill. Nevertheless, the book went through five editions until 1665.

65
Johann Theodor de Bry (1562-1620)
Florilegium novum, hoc est variorum maximeque rariorum florum... eicones. New Blumenbuch..., Oppenheim 1612-14. Folio
Botanisk Centralbibliotek, Copenhagen
LIT. Wilfrid Blunt, *The Art of Botanical Illustration*, London 1950, p. 91

Johann Theodor de Bry was a copperplate engraver and publisher in Frankfurt am Main. He exploited the interest in gardens around 1600 by publishing this picture book. Some of the pictures have been copied from a slightly older book, *Le Jardin du très Chrètien Henry* IV by Pierre Vallet, printed in 1608. Pierre Vallet was *brodeur ordinaire* at the royal court and also worked in the royal gardens. His book was meant as a collection of embroidery patterns (fig. 4). De Bry's book, which apart from the introduction and the names of the flowers has no text, may have been intended for the same purpose. The pictures, which have been copied from Vallet, are in reverse.

66
Basilius Besler (1561-1629)
Hortus Eystettensis, Sive Diligens et Accurata omnium Plantarum...Delineatio et ad Vivum Repraesentatio..., Eichstätt 1613. Folio
Botanisk Centralbibliotek, Copenhagen
LIT. Hans-Otto Keunecke, *Hortus Eystettenssis. Zur Geschichte eines Gartens und eines Buches. Eine Ausstellung der Universitätsbibliothek 1989* (Schriften der Universitätsbibliothek Erlangen-Nürnberg 20), Munich 1989; Joseph Schwertschlager, *Der Botanische Garten der Fürstbischöfe von Eichstätt* (Jahres-Bericht über das Bischöfische Lyceum zu Eichstätt für das Studienjahr 1889/90), Eichstätt 1890

The prince-bishop Johann Konrad von Gemmingen (1561?-1612) spent large sums of money on his garden in Eichstätt. His model was a garden in Nuremberg supervised by the famous physician and botanist Joachim Camerarius (1534-1598). The garden was probably laid out and begun in 1596-97. Work on the book, which commenced in about 1607, was entrusted to an apothecary, Basilius Besler. His brother, Hieronymous Besler, who was a Latinist, and Ludwig Jungermann (1572-1653), a professor in Giessen and Altdorf, assisted with the translation and preparation of the text. The work comprises 374 copperplate engravings depicting 1,084 plants. At least six engravers worked on the plates. The illustrations do not include important botanical details, and it is obvious that the decorative effect played a dominant role in the style of the plates. The garden was badly neglected during the Thirty Years' War, but the book was reprinted at least five times in the course of the 17th and 18th centuries. At the beginning of the 19th century the copperplates were melted down at the royal mint in Munich and thus ended up as small change.

67
Crispin de Pas (1589?-1670)
Hortus Floridus In quo rariorum et minus vulgariorum florum Icones..., Arnhem 1614. Quarto obliq. (*fig. 7*)
Botanisk Centralbibliotek, Copenhagen
LIT. Wilfrid Blunt, *The Art of Botanical Illustration*, London 1950, pp. 97-102; Jane Quinby, *Catalogue of Botanical Books in the Collection of Rachel McMasters Miller Hunt*. Vol.I, *Printed Books 1477-1700*, Pittsburgh 1958, pp. 217-220

Crispin de Pas was born into a family of copperplate engravers and completed his *Hortus Floridus* when still a young man. However, some of the engravings are signed by his brothers. An innovation is that most of the flowers are depicted growing out of the ground and being visited by insects. A gnawing mouse has also been included. The first part of the work is divided into four sections, one for each season, each with an engraved title-page showing the garden's flowers appropriate to the season. The title-page engraving shows an enclosed garden with flower parterres; the same picture is used for winter and spring, also for summer and autumn. The engravings depicting flowers are all accompanied by a Latin text giving information about their appearance, names, bibliographical references, etc. The work also has a second part (*altera pars*) in which both herbs and trees are illustrated. Here the quality of the engravings is inferior, which makes it reasonable to assume that this part was executed by Crispin de Pas when he was even younger. The book was published with a Latin text, but English, French and Dutch editions followed rapidly. In the copy exhibited the introductory texts are in French. At the beginning of the book the descriptions of the individual engravings are also in French (though not a translation of the Latin text), however the text accompanying the engravings is in Latin.

68
Matthaeus Merian (1593-1650)
Florilegium Renovatum et Auctum: Das ist Vernewertes und vermehrtes Blumenbuch..., Frankfurt am Main 1641. Folio (*fig. 5*)
Botanisk Centralbibliotek, Copenhagen
LIT. Wilfrid Blunt, *The Art of Botanical Illustration*, London 1950, p. 91; Jane Quinby, *Catalogue of Botanical Books in the Collection of Rachel McMasters Miller Hunt*. Vol. 1, *Printed Books 1477-1700*, Pittsburgh 1958, pp. 253-55

Matthaeus Merian the Elder married De Bry's daughter and took over his father-in-law's business in 1624. He published illustrations for the Bible and various geographical works. His accurate pictures of European towns in Martin Zeiler's *Topographia* were highly esteemed and still have great interest as cultural history. In 1641 he published his father-in-law's *Florilegium* expanded with copperplate engravings from G. B. Ferrari, *De Florum Cultura*, Rome 1633. Ferrari's book is a gardening book with pictures of garden plans, tools, etc., so Merian's publication is quite unambiguously a gardening book. By far the majority of De Bry's plates have been reused; only in a few cases have the names been altered. Ferrari's plates have been reversed after copying. Merian also borrowed the title plate from Ferrari. (See cat. 65.)

69
Maria Sibylla Merian (1647-1717)
Neues Blumenbuch. Allen Kunstverständigen Liebhabern zu Lust, Nutz und Dienst, mit Fleiss verfertiget, Nuremberg 1680. Folio (*fig. 10*)
Botanisk Centralbibliotek, Copenhagen
LIT. Wilfrid Blunt, *The Art of Botanical Illustration*, London 1950, pp. 127-29

Maria Sibylla Merian was the daughter of Matthaeus Merian the Elder and the granddaughter of J. T. de Bry. She displayed a talent for drawing at an early age and was given training in the subject. She eventually married her teacher, Johann Graff. Maria Sibylla took an interest as a child in the metamorphosis of insects, which she studied in depth, and at the end of the 1670s she commenced the publication of a work about the metamorphosis of European insects. In 1685 she agreed to a divorce and in 1698 set forth with one of her daughters on a voyage to Surinam in South America to study insects. In 1700 she returned to Europe, and the results of her journey were published in 1705 in *Metamorphosis Insectorum Surinamensium*. Maria Sibylla Merian always represented insects together with the plants on which they lived, thus her works have great botanical interest. In 1680 she published *Neues Blumenbuch* 'so wol zum Nachreissen und Mahlen/als dem Frauenzimmer zum Nähen/und allen Kunstverständigen Liebhabern zu Nuz und Lust.' She herself was skilled in these arts; the drawings are revised drawings after Nicholas Robert's *Fiori Diversi*, Rome 1640. The *Blumenbuch* was published under Maria Sibylla's married name, but she managed to mention who she is as the author's name is given as 'M. S. Gräffin, M. Merian des Ältern Tochter.'

70
Maria Sibylla Merian (1647-1717)
Six flower pictures
Gouache on parchment, ca. 34 *x* ca. 26 cm. Germany before 1685 (*fig. 11*)
The Royal Collections, Rosenborg Palace, Copenhagen (7.337, 7.338, 7.346, 7.356, 7.354)
PROV. Inv. Chr. V. 95.6
EXH. *Maria Sibylla Merian*, Rosenborg Palace, Copenhagen 1983

71
H. S. Holtzbecker (d. 1671)
Gottorfer codex
Gouache on parchment. Vols. 1 and 4. Mid-17th century (*fig. 9*)
Statens Museum for Kunst, Den kongelige kobberstiksamling, Copenhagen (*Tu*123, *Tu*126)
LIT. Helga de Cuveland, *Der Gottorfer Codex von Hans Simon Holtzbecker*, Worms 1989

72
Johann Christoph Volckamer (1644-1720)
Nürnbergische Hesperides, oder gründliche Beschreibung der edlen Citronat-, Citronen- und Pomerantzen-Früchte..., Nuremberg 1708-14. Folio
LIT. Wilfrid Blunt, *The Art of Botanical Illustration*, London 1950; Claus Nissen, *Die botanische Buchillustration. Ihre Geschichte und Bibliographie*. Vol. 1, *Geschichte*, Stuttgart 1951, p. 192

The wealthy Nuremberg merchant J. C. Volckamer, who owned a magnificent orangery, had *Nürnbergische Hesperides* published as a survey of the fruit trees that could be imported and cultivated around Nuremberg. The title Hesperides is a reference to the three Hesperides who, in their garden to the far west, had guarded the golden apples which Hera had received as a wedding present and which gave the gods eternal youth. In this case the golden apples are various citrus fruits, which are not only yellow but also come from the west. The names may also have been taken from an older book on the same subject,

G. B. Ferrari, *Hesperides sive de malorum aureorum cultura...* 1646. Other types of fruit trees and plants are also mentioned in this work, e.g., fig, pineapple and – surprisingly enough – auricula. Gardens, garden plants, greenhouses and orangeries, palaces, in fact even towns are mentioned and illustrated. The many copperplates were engraved by several artists: P. Decker the Elder and the Younger, L. C. Glotsch, B. Kenckel, C. F. Krieger, Joh. a Montalegre, W. Pfan and J. C. Steinberger.

73
Society of Gardeners
Catalogus Plantarum...A Catalogue of Trees, Shrubs, Plants and Flowers...which are propagated for Sale..., London 1730. Folio
Botanisk Centralbibliotek, Copenhagen
LIT. Wilfrid Blunt, *The Art of Botanical Illustration*, London 1950, pp. 132-34; Allan Stevenson, *Catalogue of Botanical Books in the Collection of Rachel McMasters Miller Hunt*. Vol. 2, *Printed Books 1701-1800*, Pittsburgh 1958, pp. 132-37

Before Carolus Linnaeus reformed the nomenclature of plants the same plant might well be known by several different names. This could result in people buying from a gardener a plant they already possessed under a different name. The gardeners of Chelsea therefore formed a little society, and in the course of monthly meetings they decided which names to use for the plants they offered for sale. They decided to publish a catalogue in three volumes with pictures of trees, bushes, plants and flowers and their corresponding names and descriptions. Only one volume came out, but the copperplates made for the remaining volumes were published together with the first volume. The engravings were made after drawings by Jacob van Huijsum (1687-1740) and others. The special interest of these plates lies in the fact that in seven of them the colours are printed by means of a kind of primitive mezzotint technique, whereas the fourteen remaining plates were, as usual, hand-coloured. It was the second time that this 'mock-mezzotint' method had been used in England. The first time was in John Martyn's *Historia Plantarum Rariorum...*, London 1728.

74
Carolus Linnaeus, from 1755 von Linné (1707-1777)
Flora Svecica, exhibens plantas per regnum Sveciae..., Stockholm 1745. Octavo
Danmarks Natur- og Laegevidenskabelige Bibliotek, UB 2, Copenhagen
LIT. Wilfrid Blunt, *The Complete Naturalist. A Life of Linnaeus*, London 1971, p. 44

In this list of Sweden's plants there is only one illustration, a picture of the plant that bears the author's name, *Linnaea borealis*. The plant was described for the first time by the Swiss botanist Caspar Bauhin in 1596 under the name *Campanula serpyllifolia*. Linnaeus formally changed the name in his *genera plantarum* (1736) after a description supplied by the Dutch botanist J. F. Gronovius (1690-1762). Linnaeus had published a drawing of the plant as early as in 1738 in his Lapland flora, *Flora Laponica*, where it is called 'planta nostra' ('our plant'). In *Critica Botanica* (1737) Linnaeus wrote: 'Linnaea was named by the celebrated Gronovius and is a plant of Lapland, low, insignificant, disregarded, flowering but for a brief space – from Linnaeus, who resembles it.'

75
Christoph Jacob Trew (1695-1769)
Plantae selectae, quarum imagines...pinxit Georgius Dionysius Ehret...publico usui dicavit D. Christophorus Iacobus Trevv...in aes incidit Ioannes Iacobus Haid..., Nuremberg 1750-73. Folio (fig. 12)
Botanisk Centralbibliotek, Copenhagen
LIT. Gerta Calmann, *Ehret. Flower Painter Extraordinary. An Illustrated Biography*, Oxford 1977, pp. 21-28, 95-97

C. J. Trew was a physician and collector in Nuremberg. He bought up botanical drawings (e.g., the originals for Besler's *Hortus Eystettensis*) and published several works on natural history. He came into contact with G. D. Ehret (1708-1770) through Peter Beurer, who was Trew's cousin. As Trew had seen a collection of Ehret's drawings and arranged their sale, they met in 1733, and Trew aroused Ehret's interest in botanically correct drawings of plants. For the rest of his life Trew sent paper to Ehret, who in return sent back drawings. Trew had the Augsburg engraver Johann Jacob Haid (1704-1767) engrave them. The engravings were published in ten installments with ten engravings in each, in all one hundred, of which the last came out after Trew's death under the supervision of B. C. Vogel (1745-1825), professor of botany in Altdorf. Trew himself prepared a scholarly text to accompany the plates in which he made use of Ehret's own observations; Ehret actually became a fine botanist. On the title page Trew acknowledged the contributions made by his colleagues by printing their names in equally large letters and letting them form part of the title along with his own. Furthermore, he honoured the illustrator by naming one of the plants after him, to this day called *Ehretia*.

76
Flora Danica
Copenhagen 1766-1874. Published by G. C. Oeder (1766-70) (*figs. 77, 88, 89*)
Kunstindustrimuseet, Copenhagen

77
Nikolaus Joseph Jacquin (1727-1817)
Collectanea ad botanicam, chemiam, et historiam naturalem spectantia..., vols. 1-5, Vienna 1786-96. Quarto
Botanisk Centralbibliotek, Copenhagen
LIT. Wilfrid Blunt, *The Art of Botanical Illustration*, London 1950, pp. 156-58; Bernice G. Schubert, 'Publication of Jacquin's *Icones plantarum rariorum*,' *Contributions from the Gray Herbarium of Harvard University*, no. 156, Cambridge, Mass. 1945, pp. 3-23

Upon his return from a voyage to the West Indies at Austrian expense, the Dutch-born Nikolaus Joseph Jacquin was put in charge of the botanical garden in Schönbrunn. Later he became professor at the University of Vienna and head of its botanical garden. Under his leadership many plants were collected from distant parts of the world, and he published a great many important botanical works. A splendid draughtsman himself, he assembled a group of good flower illustrators who worked on the publication of his very beautiful scientific works. The copperplates in *Collectanea* are anonymous.

78
Nicolas Robert (1614-1685)
Recueil des Plantes, dessinées et gravées par ordre du roi Louis XIV, Paris (1701) 1788. Folio (*fig. 8*)
Botanisk Centralbibliotek, Copenhagen
LIT. Wilfrid Blunt, *The Art of Botanical Illustration*, London 1950, pp. 108-12; G. A. Pritzel, *Thesaurus Literaturae Botanicae Omnium Gentium*, Leipzig 1871-77, p. 265

Nicolas Robert was appointed *peintre ordinaire de sa Majesté pour la miniature* in 1664 so that he could continue to portray beautiful and rare plants in the royal gardens just as he had portrayed those in the ducal ones in Blois. He also drew the illustrations for a textbook planned by the Académie royale des sciences. Only the first part, *Mémoires pour servir à l'Histoire des Plantes* with a text by Dionys Dodart (1634-1707) came out; it included thirty-nine plates by Robert. For the sequel, 319 copperplates were executed until 1692 after Robert's models. He engraved a number of them himself, the remainder being engraved by Abraham Bosse (1602-1676) and Louis de Châtillon (1639-1734). The work was delayed by Louis XIV's wars and the plates were not printed until 1701 – without text. They were admired – and rightly so – by Van Spaendonck, for example, which is presumably the reason why they were reprinted with some changes in 1788. On this occasion a list was added of the plants illustrated and a short account of the work's history.

79
Pierre-Joseph Redouté (1759-1840)
Les liliacées, vols. 1-8, Paris 1802-16. Folio (*fig. 14*)
Botanisk Centralbibliotek, Copenhagen
LIT. Frans A. Stafleu, 'Redouté – Peintre de Fleurs,' in George H. M. Lawrence (eds.) *A Catalogue of Redoutéana exhibited at the Hunt Botanical Library*, Pittsburgh 1963, pp. 1-32

Redouté's reputation was so great that the illustrated work on the lily family and related plants which he published appeared under his name and not under those of the botanists who had contributed to it (A. P. de Candolle, F. de la Roche and A. Raffenau-Delile). The 503 plates, which were published in eighty installments, were engraved using the stipple method; in 1796 Redouté carried the development of this method a step further so that by applying different colours to the copperplate, several colours could be printed during one printing. On the other hand, the plates had to be reinked after every pull. Plates printed in colour in this way were then finished by hand. Redouté was awarded a prize for this method by Louis XVIII, though he had to defend his copyright in court. The method was also used for A. P. de Candolles *Plantarum historia Succulentarum* (Paris 1799-1832). It never became widely used, as it was extremely expensive. *Les liliacées* was published partly as an ordinary folio edition and partly (from 1807) in a large folio (broadsheet) on which the plates were finished by the master himself.

80
Etienne Pierre Ventenat (1757-1808)
Jardin de la Malmaison, Paris 1803-05. Folio (*fig. 13*)
Botanisk Centralbibliotek, Copenhagen
LIT. Winfried Baer & Walter Lack, *Pflanzen auf Porzellan. Kat. Botanischer Garten und Botanisches Museum Berlin-Dahlem*. Berlin 1979, pp. 59-61

The social and artistic recognition which flower illustrators achieved in the course of the 18th century reached its zenith with Pierre-Joseph Redouté (1759-1840), who found an extravagant patroness in Napoleon's first wife, Joséphine. Her immense horticultural interest resulted in the laying out of expensive gardens at Malmaison and Navarre and in the publication of books. A commission to publish a book about the plants in the garden at Malmaison was entrusted to the priest and botanist Etienne Pierre Ventenat and P.-J. Redouté. The copperplate engravings were done by the stipple method, which Redouté had learned from F. J. Bartolozzi in England in 1787. In order to hasten the completion of the work, sixteen engravers were employed. The book contained 120 engravings, which together with the text were published in 20 installments in a total of 200 copies. The engravings, as well as other engravings by Redouté, were used as patterns for porcelain services manufactured in Sèvres and Berlin.

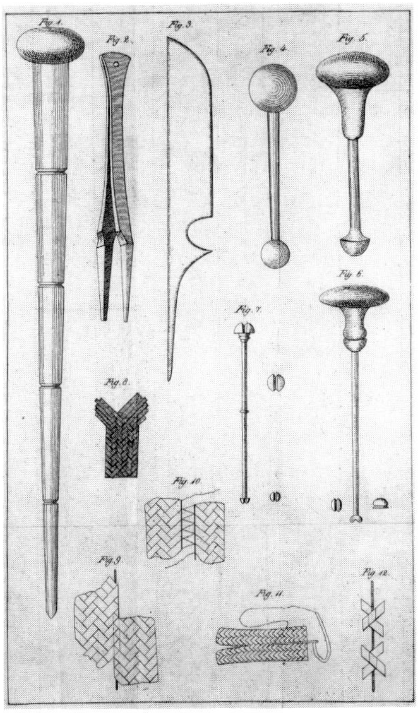

87

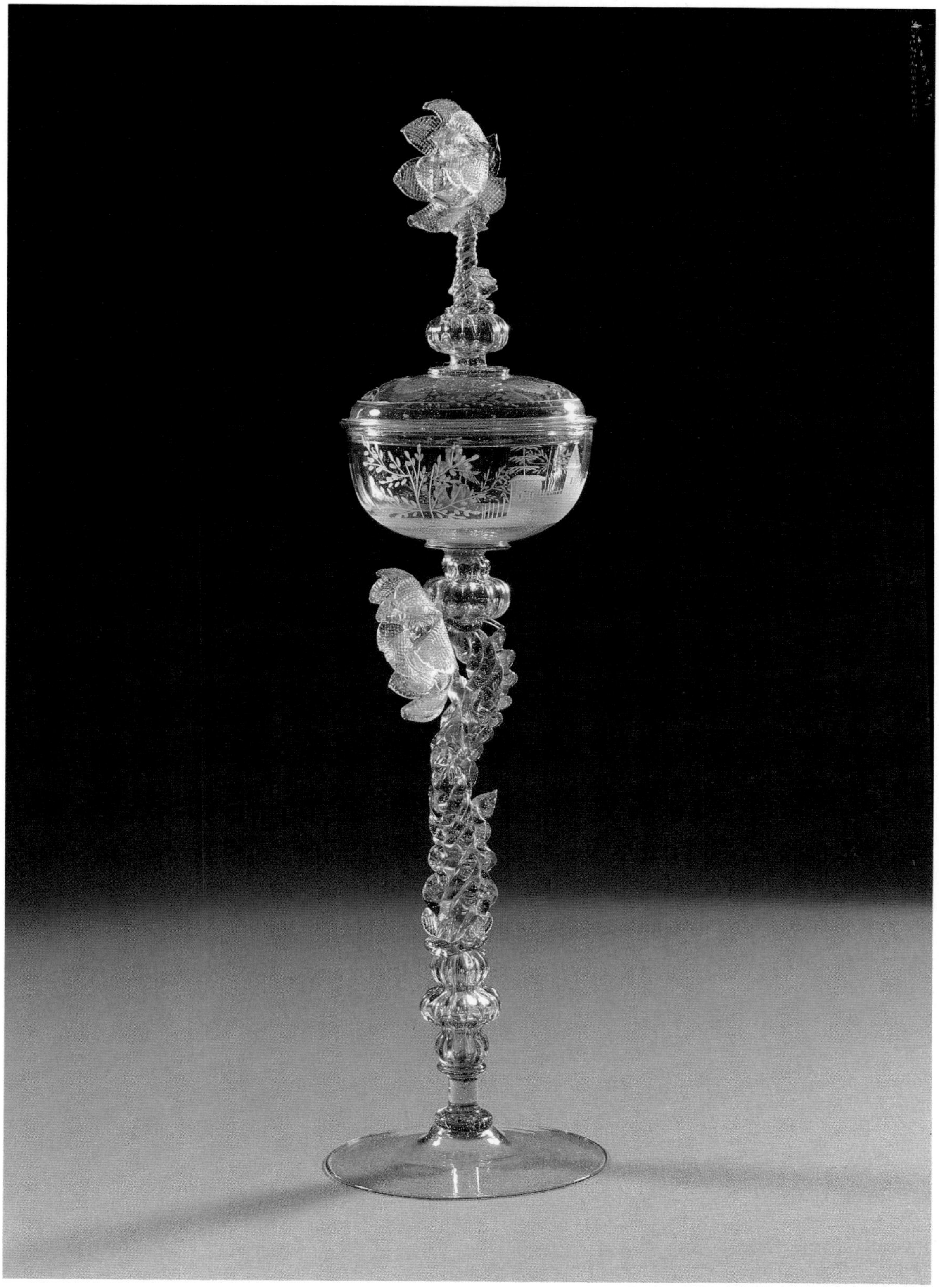

91

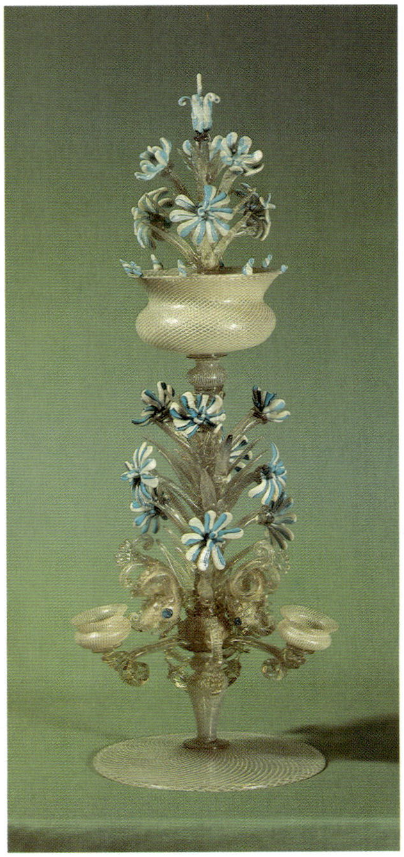

81
Pierre-Joseph Redouté (1759-1840)
Les roses, vols. 1-3, Paris 1817-24 Folio
Royal Copenhagen Museum, Copenhagen
LIT. Frans A. Stafleu, 'Redouté – Peintre de Fleurs,' in George H. M. Lawrence (eds.) *A Catalogue of Redoutéana exhibited at the Hunt Botanical Library*, Pittsburgh 1963, pp. 1-32

This, the most famous of all Redouté's work, was also inspired by the Empress Joséphine, whose real name was Marie-Josèphe Rose. Several hundred types of rose were cultivated in the gardens at Malmaison (the empress retains an important place in the history of rose cultivation), and it was there that Redouté began his work. The descriptions were written by the botanist Claude-Antoine Thory (1759-1827). The three volumes containing a total of 170 copperplate engravings were published in 30 installments; the stipple method of engraving was used, the colouring being finished by hand. As in the case of *Les liliacées*, two editions were produced: normal folio copies and five large folio (broadsheet) copies, the latter with two sets of plates, black-and-white and coloured. Later *Les roses* was also published several times in octavo format, in certain cases supplemented by new plates. However, the quality of the plates in the octavo editions is inferior to that in the folio volumes.

OTHER BOOKS

82
Rosina Adami (married Chemnitz) (1742-1797)
Pattern book
Contains examples of various handicrafts. Copenhagen second half of the 18th century
Kunstindustrimuseet, Copenhagen (57/1986)

83
Versuch von Rissen Blumen und Grotesken nebt anderen

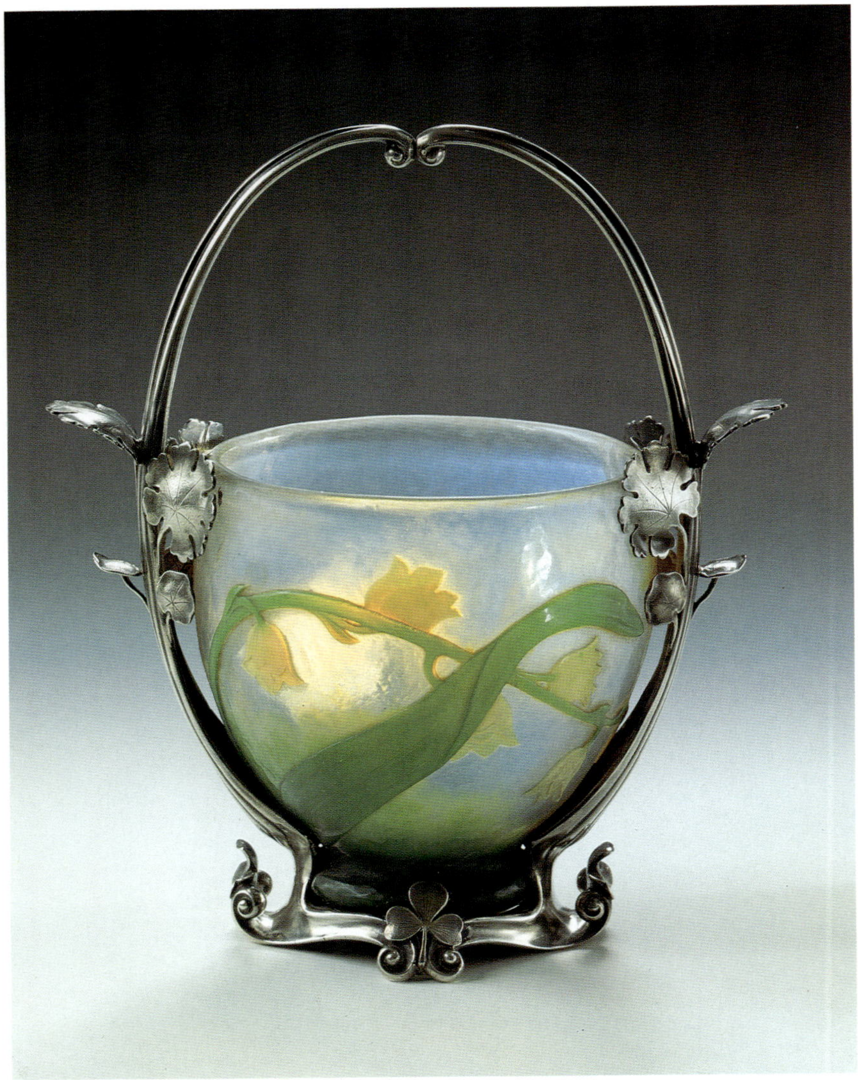

94

93

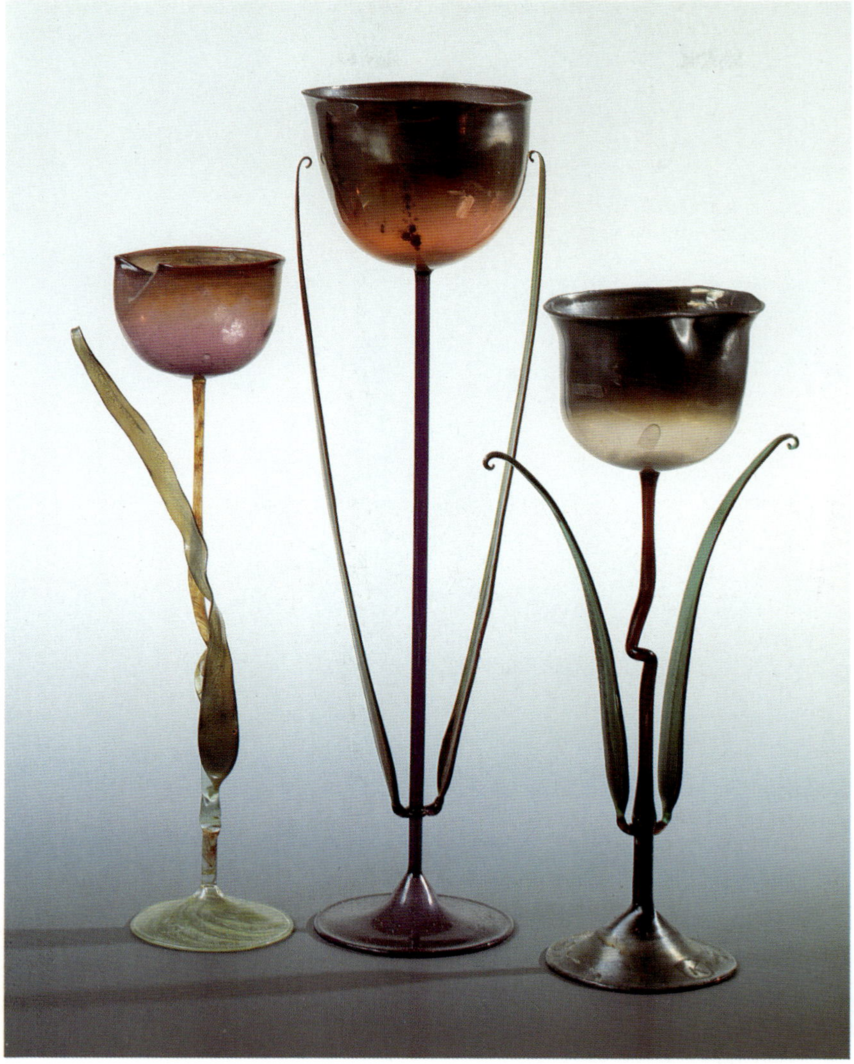

Verzierungen mit ihren Entwurfen, Umrissen, Schatten und Licht nach neuer Invention nebt einer Anweisung zu derselben Zeichning. Für unterschiedliche Liebhaber, absonderlich für alle und iede Künstler und Professionisten, Frankfurt und Leipzig 1770
Kunstindustrimuseet, Copenhagen

84
Johan Friedrich Netto
Zeichen-Mahler und Stickerbuch für Damen, Leipzig 1795
Kunstindustrimuseet, Copenhagen

85
N. Truslew (1762-1827)
Flora Copenhagen 1804
Kunstindustrimuseet, Copenhagen

86
'Un Amateur'
Le jardinier fleuriste dédié aux dames, Paris 1823
Kunstindustrimuseet, Copenhagen

87
H. C. Lund
Anvisning i at forfærdige de smukkeste kunstige Blomster, Copenhagen 1827 (*ill.*)
Kunstindustrimuseet, Copenhagen

88
Oluf Olufsen Bagge
Samling af Brodeermønstere, Copenhagen ca. 1830
Kunstindustrimuseet, Copenhagen

89
J.-J. Grandville (1803-1847)
Les fleurs animées. Texte par Taxile Delord, Paris s.d. (*fig. 101*)
Private collection, Copenhagen

Glass

90
Goblet and cover with roses
White glass. The stem contains a thread of red glass. Stem and cover decorated with applied flowers. Engraved, h. 43 cm. Bohemia or the Netherlands 1675-1700 (*ill.*)
The Royal Collections, Rosenborg Palace, Copenhagen (22.627*a-b*)
PROV. Inv. 1718.202.54

91
Centrepiece
Filigree glass *a reticello*, white glass with white threads and opaque white and light blue glass, h. 51 cm. Venice, Italy ca. 1700
The Royal Collections, Rosenborg Palace, Copenhagen (22-462)
INV. 1718.177.23
LIT. Gudmund Boesen, *Venetianske Glas på Rosenborg*, Copenhagen 1960, cat. no. 26

Given to Frederik IV, King of Denmark in 1709 in Venice.

92
Rummer with cover
White glass engraved with scattered flowers and leaves, h. 47.5 cm., diam. 19 cm. Kungsholms Glasbruk, Sweden ca. 1725-50
Kunstindustrimuseet, Copenhagen (B52/1915)

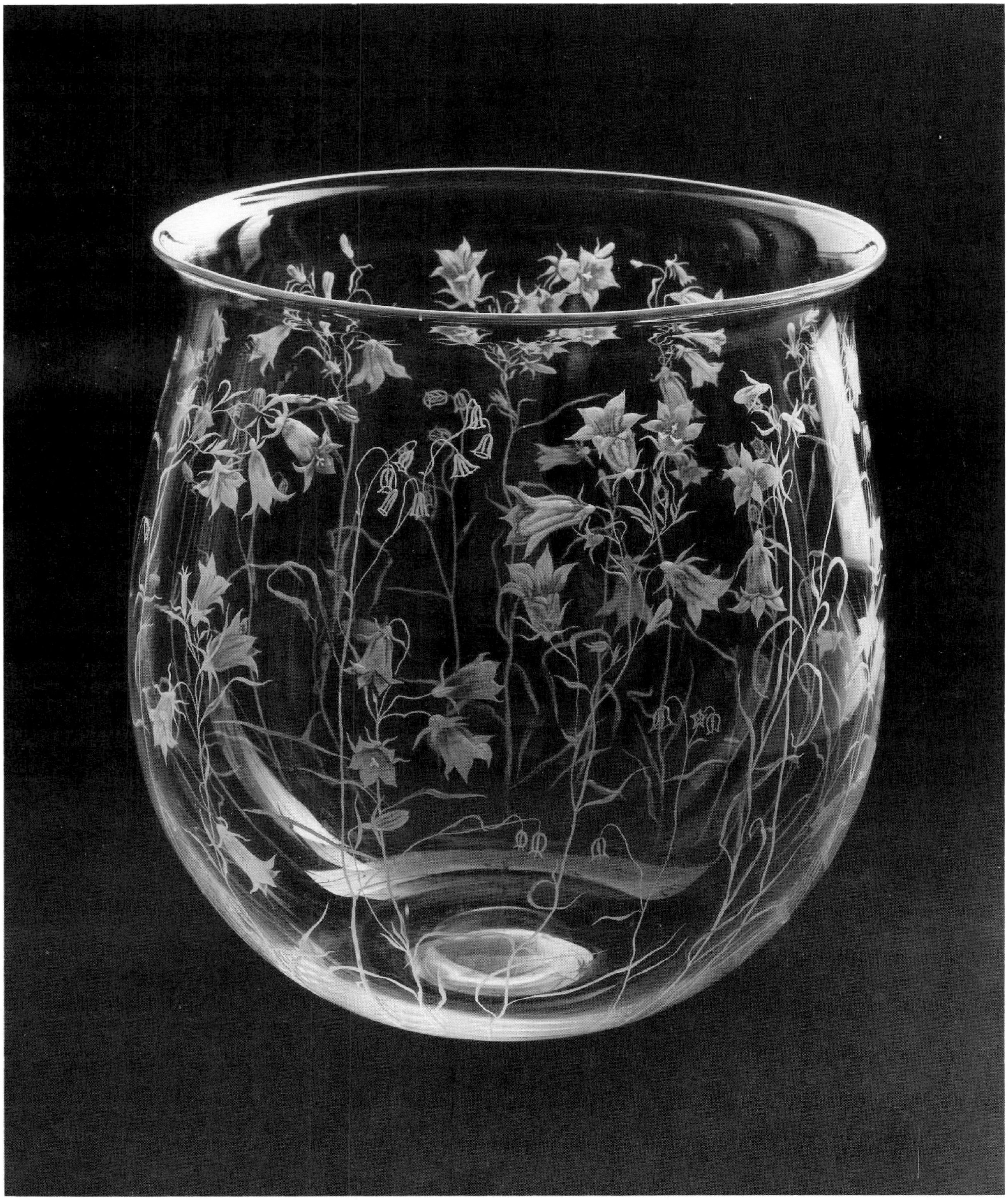

102

98 99 100

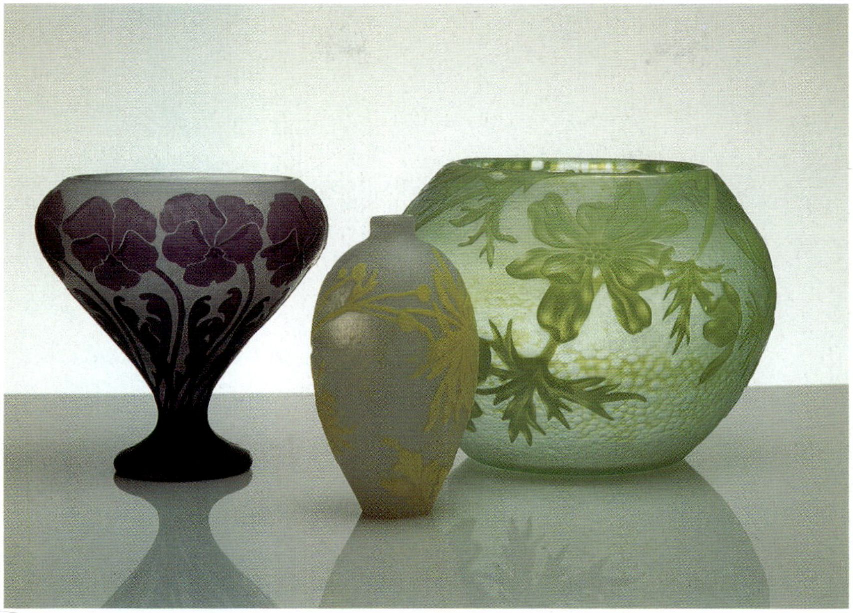

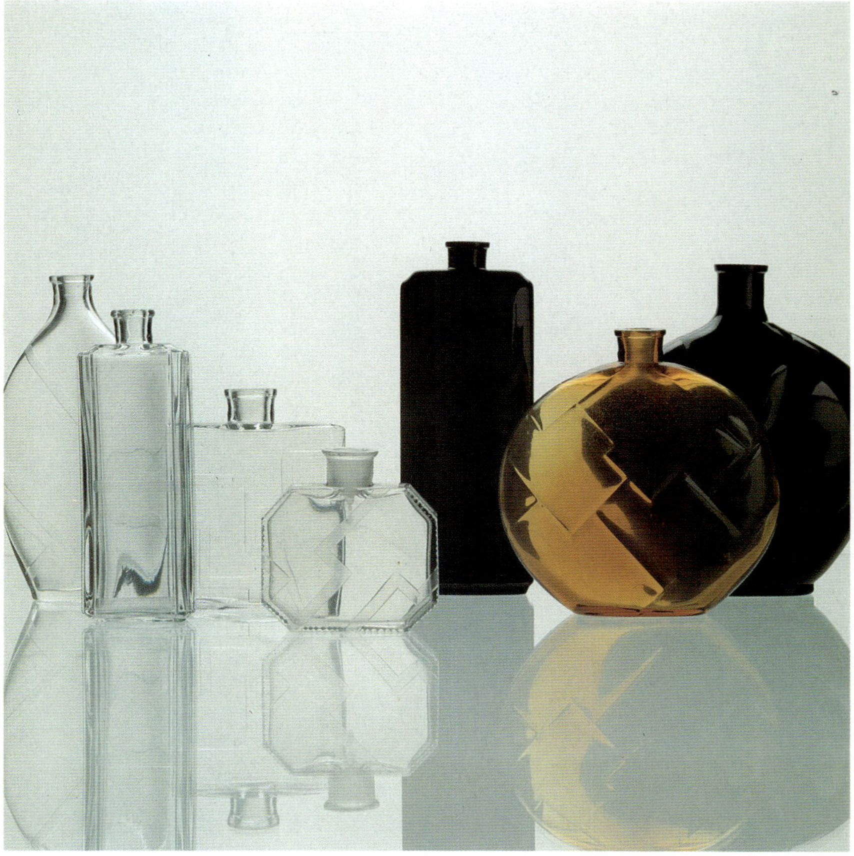

101

93
Karl Koepping (1848-1914)
Five 'Blumengläser'
Coloured glass shaped as flowers, h. ca. 20-30 cm. Ilmenau, Thüringen, Germany 1896 (*ill.*)
Kunstindustrimuseet, Copenhagen (805-809)
LIT. Jørgen Schou-Christensen, 'Glaskunst omkring år 1900,' *Det Danske Kunstindustrimuseum. Virksomhed 1964-1968*, Copenhagen 1969, pp. 161-182 (ill.)

The first director of the Danish Kunstindustrimuseet, Pietro Krohn, acquired a total of twelve glasses directly from the artist in 1896. These incredibly fragile glasses, exhibited for the first time at S. Bing in Paris, Christmas 1895, were executed in collaboration with the German glassmaker Friedrich Zimmermann in Wiesbaden. However, the actual pieces dating from late 1896 were made at the Lehrwerkstatt für Glasinstrumentenmacher in Ilmenau. The glasses were made of test tubes and glass rods used in chemical laboratories which can be melted over a gas flame.

94
Lucien Bonvallet (1861-1919)
Sugar bowl
Coloured overlay glass with lilies of the valley in natural colours. The bowl is mounted with silver shaped as plant stalks with foliage, h. 18.5 cm, w. 15 cm. The glass is signed in engraving painted with gold: 'Daum Nancy', framed by lilies of the valley. Made by Daum Frères, Nancy. The silver mounting is signed 'CARDEILHAC', Cardeilhac's sign, 'Minerva Head 1'. Made by Cardeilhac, Paris, France ca. 1900 (*ill.*)
Kunstindustrimuseet, Copenhagen (880)
LIT. Pietro Krohn (et al.), *Det danske Kunstindustrimuseum. De første fem Aars Virksomhed*, Copenhagen 1901, p. 21, fig. 18

Bought at the World Exhibition in Paris 1900.

107

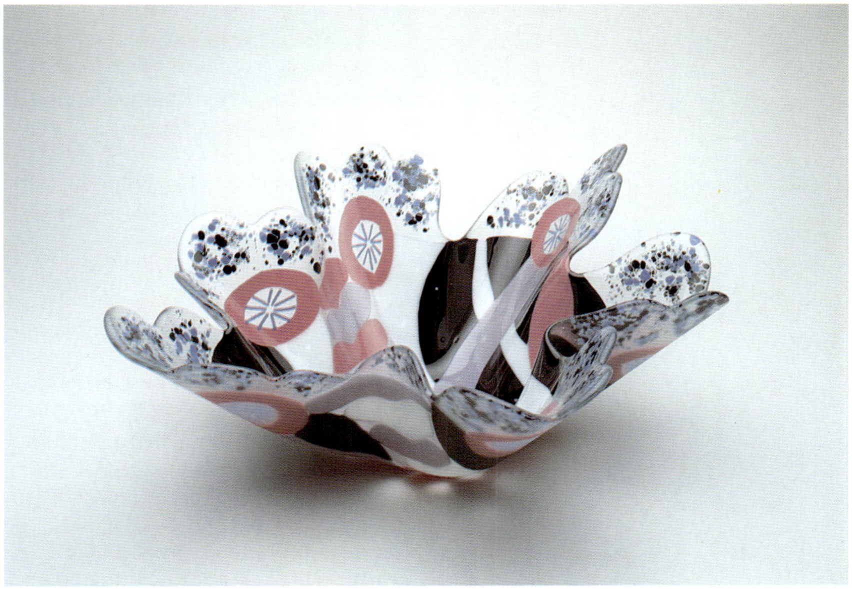

95
Emile Gallé (1846-1904)
Vase
Opalescent glass in various colours. Decorated with carved narcissi in relief, partly etched and engraved. On one side engraved and gilded: 'Une âme qui revient ... Ch. Baudelaire' (from the poem 'Le Flacon' by Baudelaire), h. 15 cm. Signed 'A Madame Emile Hannover Emile Gallé de Nancy 1891' engraved and gilded. Nancy, France 1891 (fig. 61)
Kunstindustrimuseet, Copenhagen (B48/1923)
EXH. *Émile Gallé. En glaskonstens mästare*, Malmö 1966, p. 14, cat. 57.
LIT. Émile Gallé, *Le Décor Symbolique*, Académie de Stanislas, Nancy 1900, p. 15; Emil Hannover, 'Nekrolog over Gallé,' *Tilskueren*, 1904, p. 932; Jørgen Schou-Christensen, 'Glaskunst omkring 1900,' *Det danske Kunstindustrimuseum. Virksomhed 1964-1969*, Copenhagen 1969, pp. 166 ff.

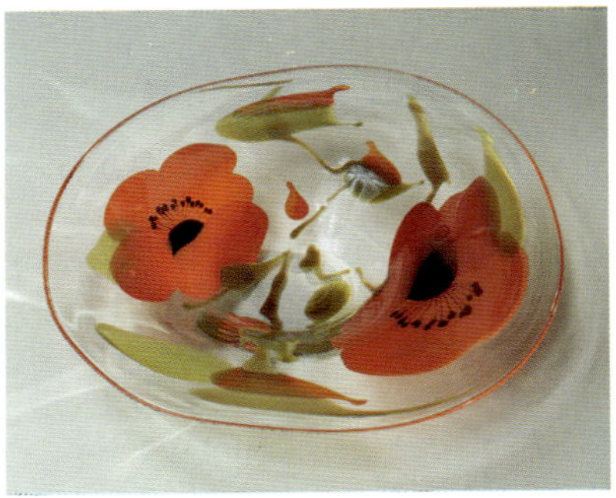

108

Already in 1892, the first director of the Danish Kunstindustrimuseet, Pietro Krohn, bought glass from Émile Gallé, probably at the suggestion of Emil Hannover, who was to become his successor. Hannover and Gallé had established a friendship by correspondence, which resulted in Gallé making a present of this vase to Mrs. Hannover in 1891. The vase was delivered in a specially-made wooden box and accompanied by a prose poem written on a thin wooden sheet. The vase is one of the main works in his 'speaking glass' (*Verres parlants*) production. The subject of the vase must be 'un dernier bouquet d'Ophélie.' Gallé described Ophelia's flowers as the ultimate flower symbol.

96
Émile Gallé (1846-1904)
Vase, 'Les Tulipes'
Opal glass with melted green colour. Decorated with tulips in enamel colours outlined with gold, h. 33 cm. Sign. 'Emile Gallé fecit' and a flower as well as the letters 'EG' painted in gold on the neck. Nancy, France 1891-92
Kunstindustrimuseet, Copenhagen (1047)
EXH. *Émile Gallé. En glaskonstens mästare*, Malmö 1966, p. 16, cat. 66; *Émile Gallé*, Museum Bellerive, Zürich 1979, cat. no. 76; *Nancy 1900*, Münchner Stadtmuseum, 1980, cat. no. 277 a

97
Daum Frères
Vase
Overlay glass with red poppies and dark leaves on a frosted white ground, h. 17 cm. Signed 'DAUM Nancy'. Nancy, France end of 1890s
Nationalmuseum, Dept. of Decorative Arts, Stockholm (NM12/1900)

98
G. Wennerberg (1863-1914)
Vase
White and yellow overlay glass. Cut decoration with chrysanthemum, h. 14.9 cm. Sign. 'Kosta G Wennerberg 95'. Kosta Glasbruk, Sweden 1900 (*ill.*)
Nationalmuseum, Dept. of Decorative Arts, Stockholm (NM14/1901)
EXH. *Svenske Jugendglas. Överfångsglas 1898-1918*, Nationalmuseum, Stockholm 1980, cat. 22
LIT. Eva Nordenson, *Nationalmusei årsbok, vol.* 14, Stockholm 1967, ill. p. 28; Bengt Nyström, 'Jugendglas à la Wallander och Wennerberg,' *Fataburen 1975*, Lund 1976, pp. 47-66, fig. 9

Two years before the World Exhibition in Paris in 1900, Wennerberg was employed as a designer at Kosta. He designed a number of items of modern ornamental glassware decorated with flowers using the overlay technique inspired by French Art Nouveau styles, primarily those of Emile Gallé and the Daum brothers. The chrysanthemum vase was one of those exhibited in Paris in 1900.

99
G. Wennerberg (1863-1914)
Vase
Light green overlay glass. Cut decoration with wild flowers, h. 17 cm. Sign. 'Kosta G Wennerberg 142 A. E. B'.

111

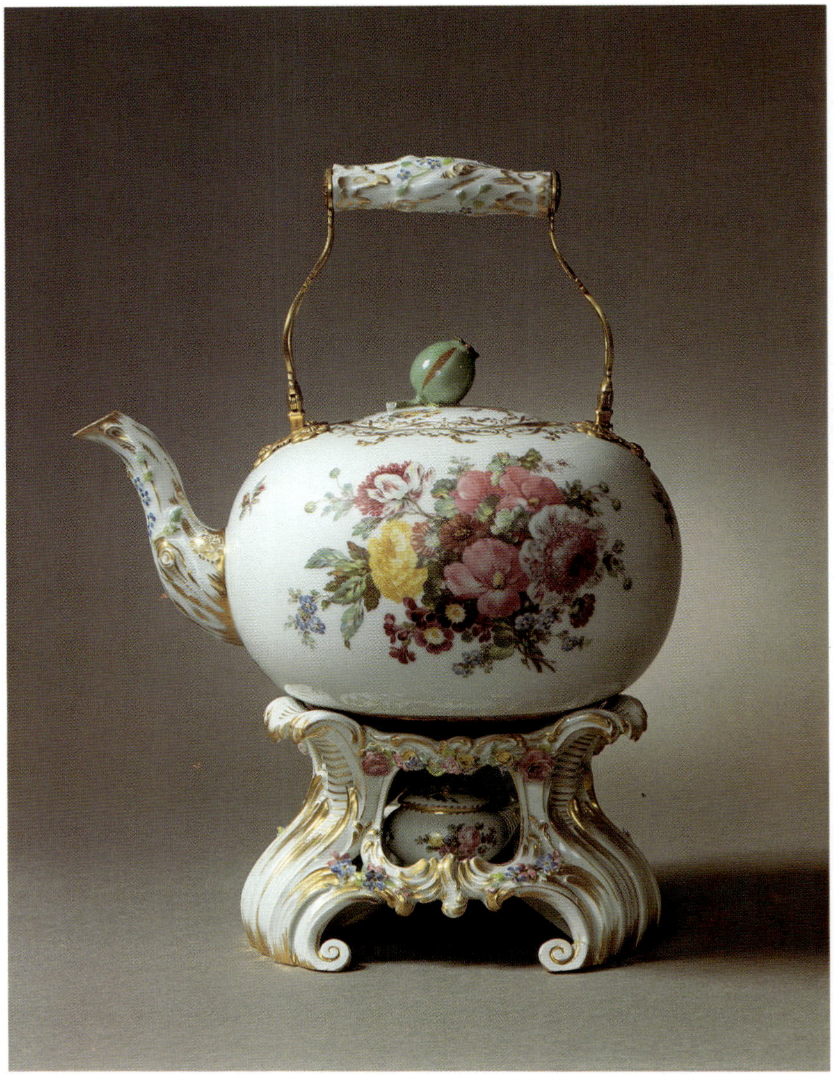

The cutting was executed by Axel Enoch Boman. Kosta Glasbruk, Sweden 1900 (*ill.*)
Nationalmuseum, Dept. of Decorative Arts, Stockholm (NM5/1901)
EXH. *Svenskt Jugendglas. Överfångsglas 1898-1918*, Nationalmuseum, Stockholm, cat. 22

100
Karl Lindeberg (1877-1931)
Vase
Purple overlay glass. Etched decoration with pansies, h. 16.2 cm. Sign. 'Kosta K Lindeberg'. Kosta Glasbruk, Sweden ca. 1910 (*ill.*)
Nationalmuseum, Dept. of Decorative Arts, Stockholm (NM119/1961)
EXH. *Svenskt Jugendglas, Överfångsglas 1898-1918*, Nationalmuseum, Stockholm 1980, cat. 94

While the shape of the vase was copied from Emile Gallé, the decoration differs from the rich and colourful French style. By combining a simple colour scheme with a slightly stylized motif, Lindeberg emphasizes the precise, shallow silhouette effect obtained by etching.

101
Edvin Ollers (1888-1959)
Four perfume bottles
White, black and amber glass. Blown in a mould and pressed. One of the bottles has an engraved decoration, h. max. 13.8 cm. Sign. 'Ollers'. Limmareds Glasbruk, Sweden 1919-40 (*ill.*)
Nationalmuseum, Dept. of Decorative Arts, Stockholm (NM126/1960, 128/1960, 129/1960, 115 *b*/1973)
EXH. *Svensk glas 1915-1960*, Nationalmuseum, Stockholm 1987, p. 57, cat. 192, pl. 7
LIT. Dag Widman, 'Edwin Ollers – en av 1917 års män,' *Form*, vol. 56, 1960, pp. 197-201

Edvin Ollers, originally a painter, made his debut in 1917 in the field of decorative art with a series of good, everyday glassware for Kosta Glasbruk. He designed a series of perfume bottles for Limmared's Glasbruk to be presented at the Stockholm Exhibition of 1930. The circular, flat bottles are inspired by Chinese snuffboxes, and the pressed or engraved patterns on the bottles are designed in the ornamental, geometric style of the time. The bottles were designed for a stopper or a cork, but as bakelite had its breakthrough as cover material at that time, the interest in Oller's bottles soon diminished.

102
Lisa Bauer (b. 1920)
Bowl
White glass with engraved decoration of harebell, h. 28.2 cm, diam. 27 cm. Sign. 'Kosta L. B.-Sig.P./T C.' and 'Lisa Bauer'. The bowl was designed by Sigurd Persson and blown by Bengt Heintze. Kosta Glasbruk, Sweden 1972
Nationalmuseum, Dept. of Decorative Arts, Stockholm (NM2/1974)

103
Eva Englund (b. 1937)
Bowl
Glass. Graal technique with black rim and foot. Decorated with rose twigs in blue and yellow, h. 20.5 cm, diam. 26 cm. Sign. 'ORREFORS, Graal.V.201-74 Eva Englund'. Orrefors, Sweden 1974
Nationalmuseum, Dept. of Decorative Arts, Stockholm (NM49/1975)

104
Aase Voss Schrader (b. 1913)
Bowl
White glass. Cut and engraved decoration with umbelliferous plants, birds, etc. Sign. with the artist's monogram and 77. The decoration was ordered by the Kunstindustreet, Copenhagen and executed on a glass from Hovmannstorps Glasbruk, Sweden 1977
Kunstindustrimuseet, Copenhagen (34/1977)

105
Corina Teunissen van Manen (b. 1950)
Dish 'Botanomancy'
White glass with diamond-engraved decoration: two hands reaching for each other among blooming flowers. Poem by Frank Murphy, h. 3.5 cm, diam. 35.7 cm. Sign. 'corina tvm 1977'. The Netherlands 1977
Kunstindustrimuseet, Copenhagen (31/1980)
EXH. *Moderne hollandsk textilkunst og glas*, Kunstindustrimuseet (travelling exhibition), Copenhagen 1980, pp. 50-51

106
Ulla Forsell (b. 1944)
Dish
Blue glass with white daisies, h. 5.2 cm, diam. 39 cm. Sign. 'ULLA FORSELL'. Artist's workshop, Sweden 1978
Kunstindustrimuseet, Copenhagen (64/1978)

107
Richard Lalonde (b. 1950)
Bowl
Composed by melting various pieces of glass together and then casting the melt in a mould. The surface is sandblown and polished, h. 16.5 cm, diam. 44 cm. USA 1984
Museum Boymans-van Beuningen, Rotterdam (1886)

108
Finn Lynggaard (b. 1930)
Dish
White glass with poppies in coloured, flashed glass, h. 8.5 cm, diam., 46.3 cm. Engraved: 'F.L.85'. Ebeltoft, Denmark 1985 (*ill.*)
Kunstindustrimuseet, Copenhagen (112/1985)

114

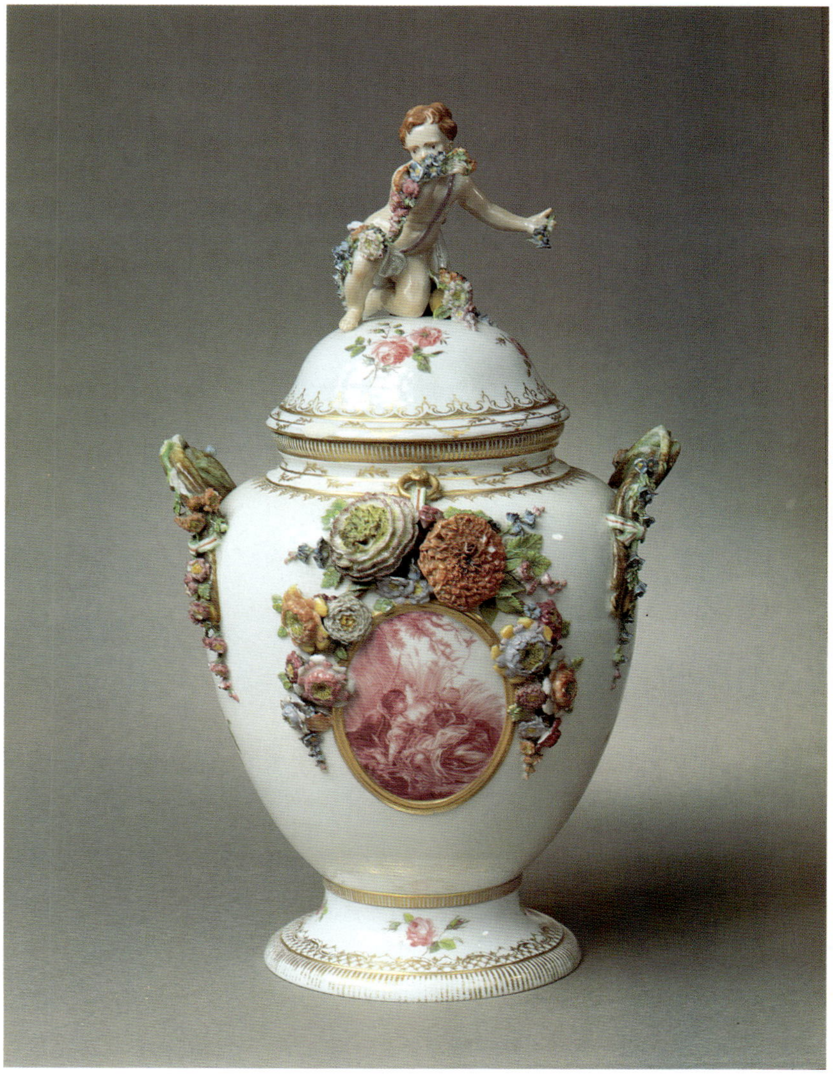

Ceramics Denmark

109
Tureen with cover and stand
Soft-paste porcelain with handles shaped as branches and the knob as a flower. The tureen is decorated with scattered bouquets and flowers in various colours, h. 12 cm, w. 20 cm. Marked with King Frederik V's monogram. The Fournier Factory, Copenhagen ca. 1765
Kunstindustrimuseet, Copenhagen (A2/1921)

110
Perfume bottle
Porcelain decorated in various colours and gold, h. 7 cm. Royal Copenhagen Porcelain Manufactory, Copenhagen 1775-86
Kunstindustrimuseet, Copenhagen (A68/1922)
LIT. *Det danske Kunstindustrimuseum. Virksomhed 1922*, Copenhagen 1923, p. 59

111
Teapot with chafing dish and spirit lamp
Porcelain. Spout and handle moulded with rocailles painted in gold. The knob in the shape of a capsule. The body is decorated with a bouquet and

124

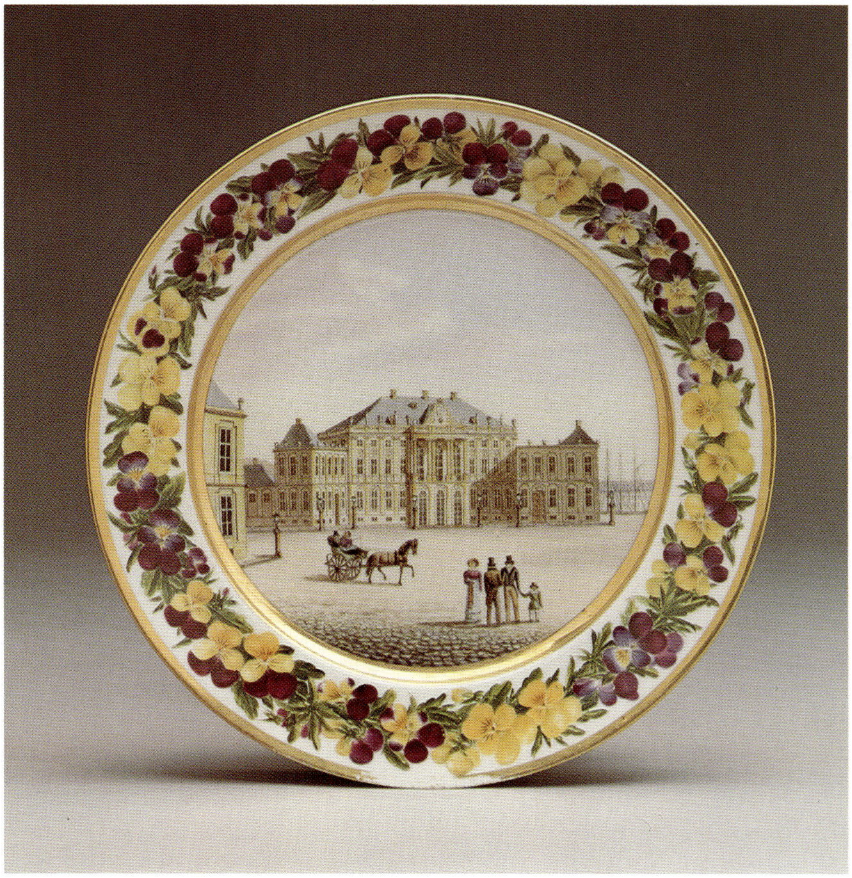

scattered flowers in various colours. The chafing dish is moulded with three scrolls and applied flowers in various colours. Copied after a Meissen model, h. 38 cm. Royal Copenhagen Porcelain Manufactory, Copenhagen ca. 1779 (ill.)
The David Collection, Copenhagen (KP151)
LIT. *Dansk kunst og kunsthåndværk. Davids Samling*, Copenhagen 1983, cat. no. 16

112
Potpourri vase
Porcelain. Decorated with flower festoons and small leaves in various colours, h. 36 cm. Marked with the three blue wavy lines. Royal Copenhagen Porcelain Manufactory, Copenhagen ca. 1780
Kunstindustrimuseet, Copenhagen (54/1953)
LIT. *Det danske Kunstindustrimuseum. Virksomhed 1949-1954*, Copenhagen 1956, fig. 89; Erik Lassen, *Keramik* Copenhagen 1968, p. 171, fig. 74

113
Two flower boxes
Porcelain. Flower bouquets in various colours, h. 10 cm, l. 20 cm. Marked with the three blue wavy lines and 'M 2'. Royal Copenhagen Porcelain Manufactory, Copenhagen ca. 1780
Kunstindustrimuseet, Copenhagen (A46/1908)

114
Potpourri vase
Porcelain. Applied flowers painted in various colours. Two medallions with pastoral scenes; one copied from an engraving by Ph. Caresme, *La bergère couronné*, the other from J. E. Nilson's engraving after Boucher: *Les Amants Surpris*, h. 40.5 cm. Marked with the three blue wavy lines. Royal Copenhagen Porcelain Manufactory, Copenhagen 1780-85 (*ill.*)
Kunstindustrimuseet, Copenhagen (703/1962)
LIT. Bredo L. Grandjean, *Kongelig dansk porcelain*, Copenhagen 1962, pl. 114 (shown with other cover); Bredo L. Grandjean 'Nogle nyerhvervelser i dansk porcelæn,' *Det danske Kunstindustrimuseum. Virksomhed 1959-1964*, Copenhagen 1964, pp. 71-80 (ill.)

115
Box
Porcelain. Decorated with flower bouquet in various colours, h. 10.6 cm, w. 23 cm, dp. 14.8 cm. Marked with the three blue wavy lines. Royal Copenhagen Porcelain Manufactory, Copenhagen 1780-90
Kunstindustrimuseet, Copenhagen (176/1954)

116
Buttons
Porcelain. Interlacing pattern in relief painted with flowers in various colours and gold, diam. 1.8 cm. Royal Copenhagen Porcelain Manufactory, Copenhagen 1780-1800
Kunstindustrimuseet, Copenhagen (B38/1924)

117
Dish from the 'Juliane Marie' service
Porcelain. Oval with wavy pierced rim decorated with draped ribbons in relief. Painted with bouquets in various colours and gold, h. 3.5 cm, l. 26.5 cm, w. 22 cm. Royal Copenhagen Porcelain Manufactory, Copenhagen ca. 1785
The David Collection, Copenhagen (KP51*a*)
LIT. *Dansk kunst og kunsthåndværk. Davids Samling*, Copenhagen 1983, cat. no. 70

118
Plate from the 'Flora Danica' service
Porcelain. Decorated on the 'Pearl Model' by I. C. Bayer (1738-1812), who, in 1768-76, provided the drawings for G. C. Oeder's botanical work *Icones Florae Danicae*. Royal Copenhagen Porcelain Manufactory,

Copenhagen 1790-1803 (fig. 78)
The Royal Collections at Rosenborg Palace and Kunstindustrimuseet, Copenhagen
LIT. Bredo L. Grandjean, *Flora Danica*, Copenhagen 1950; Ole Villumsen Krogh (ed.), *Flora Danica og det danske hof*, Copenhagen 1990

The service was probably originally meant as a present for Empress Catherine II of Russia.

119
Flower stand
The handles are in the form of lions. Decorated with *caillouté* in gold on *bleu-de-rois* ground. On both sides, panels with figures and a basket with flowers painted in various colours, h. 17 cm. Marked with the three blue wavy lines. Royal Copenhagen Porcelain Manufactory, Copenhagen end of 18th century
Kunstindustrimuseet, Copenhagen (673)
LIT. Bredo L. Grandjean, 'Nogle nyerhvervelser af dansk porcelæn,' *Det danske Kunstindustrimuseum. Virksomhed 1959-1964*, p. 76, fig. 31

The handles are copied from an engraving in E. A. Petitot's *Suite des Vases*, 1764.

120
Coffeepot
Porcelain with a turned wooden handle. Decorated with flower festoons and scattered flowers in various colours. Knob in the shape of a pink rose bud, h. 9.2 cm. Marked with the three blue wavy lines. Royal Copenhagen Porcelain Manufactory, Copenhagen, end of 18th century
Kunstindustrimuseet, Copenhagen (630)

121
Perfume bottle
Porcelain, in the shape of a rocaille. Metal stopper and gilt mounts. Decorated with landscapes in colours, h. 9.5 cm. Marked with the three blue wavy lines. Royal Copenhagen Porcelain Manufactory, Copenhagen end of 18th century
Kunstindustrimuseet, Copenhagen (187/1954)

122
Perfume bottle
Porcelain. In the shape of a rocaille decorated with various colours, h. 9.5 cm. Sign. with wave mark. Royal Copenhagen Porcelain Manufactory, Copenhagen end of 18th century
Kunstindustrimuseet, Copenhagen (A4/1918)

123
Dish
Porcelain. Decorated with flowers in various colours, l. 26 cm, w. 19 cm. Marked with the three blue wavy lines. Royal Copenhagen Porcelain Manufactory, Copenhagen end of 18th century
Kunstindustrimuseet, Copenhagen (A1/1919)

124
I. L. Jensen (1800-1856)
Dish
Porcelain. In the centre, a view of King Frederik VIII's Palace at Amalienborg Square, Copenhagen. I. L. Jensen decorated the rim with pansies, diam. 23 cm. Marked with the three blue wavy lines, crown (royal ownership) and 'J.' (Jensen). Royal Copenhagen Porcelain Manufactory, Copenhagen (*ill.*)
Royal Copenhagen Museum, Copenhagen (0.48)

125
I. L. Jensen (1800-1856)
Sample dish
Porcelain. Decorated with flowers by I. L. Jensen. On the reverse is a label 'Malet af Jensen. Prøvedecor af Lyngbye. 1827,' (Painted by Jensen. Sample décor by Lyngbye. 1827), diam. 22 cm. Marked with the three blue wavy lines and 'J.' (Jensen). Royal Copenhagen Porcelain Manufactory, Copenhagen 1927
Royal Copenhagen Museum, Copenhagen (0.120)

Three different borders in engraved gold, probably designed by the Danish architect G. F. Hetsch and painted by Lauritz Rasmus Lyngby, employed 1824-56.

126
Elise Thomsen
Cup and saucer
Porcelain. Decorated with flowers in various colours: roses, violets, forget-me-nots, pansies, etc. The rims with a palmette border and beading. In the centre of the saucer the monogram 'W. A. P.'. Cup: h. 9.9 cm, saucer: diam. 14.9 cm. Marked with the three blue wavy lines. The model was designed by G. F. Hetsch. Royal Copenhagen Porcelain Manufactory, Copenhagen ca. 1830
Kunstindustrimuseet, Copenhagen (39/1970)

127
I. L. Jensen (1800-1856)
Jewel box
Porcelain. Flower painting by I. L. Jensen, cameo ornaments by the painter Zweidorff, and ground colour by L. Foght. The bronze mounts were executed by Jørgen Dahlhoff, h. 15.5 cm, w. 33.5 cm, dp. 26 cm. Royal Copenhagen Porcelain Manufactory, Copenhagen 1836 (*fig. 21*)
The Royal Collections, Rosenborg Palace, Copenhagen (16-2)
EXH. *Kongelig Porcelæn på Rosenborg*, Copenhagen 1982, cat. no. 134

128
Part of service, jug, cup and saucer
Porcelain. Decorated in blue and gold with cornflowers and golden spike. Jug: h. 27.5 cm. Cup: h. 8.5 cm. Marked: (Jug) 'F' (for L. Foght) and (cup) 'A'. Royal Copenhagen Porcelain Manufactory, Copenhagen ca. 1835
Royal Copenhagen Museum, Copenhagen

129
C. F. Liisberg (1860-1909)
Vase
Porcelain. Applied white and grey peonies on a dark blue underglaze ground painted by Arnold Krog, h. 22 cm. Marked with the three blue wavy lines and the artists' monograms. Royal Copenhagen Porcelain Manufactory, Copenhagen 1887
Kunstindustrimuseet, Copenhagen (B149/1907)

136

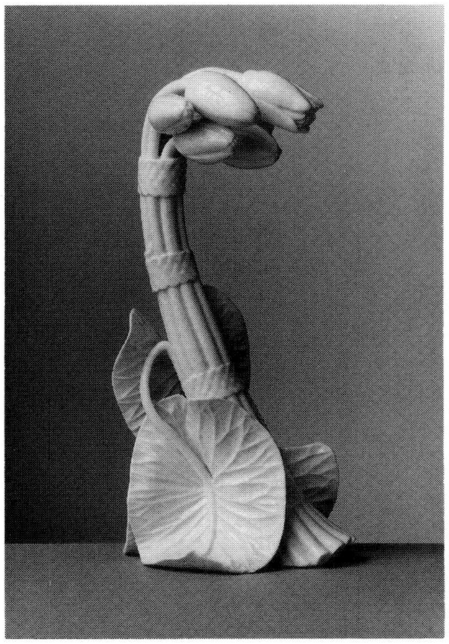

130
Arnold Krog (1856-1931)
Dish
Porcelain. Blooming peonies painted in blue underglaze by F. A. Hallin, diam. 39.5 cm. Marked with the three blue wavy lines and Hallin's monogram. Royal Copenhagen Porcelain Manufactory, Copenhagen ca. 1888
Kunstindustrimuseet, Copenhagen (A61/1911)

131
Arnold Krog (1856-1931)
Dish from the 'Tiffany' service
Porcelain. Decorated with red carnations, diam. 21.5 cm. Marked with the three blue wavy lines, a crown, 'Denmark' and '60/2517'. Royal Copenhagen Porcelain Manufactory, Copenhagen 1892-1900
Royal Copenhagen Museum, Copenhagen

132
Pietro Krohn (1840-1905)
Vase with cover
Porcelain. Lilies of the valley, partly in relief, h. 19 cm. Marked 'B & G'. The Bing & Grøndahl Porcelain Manufactory, Copenhagen 1888-89
Kunstindustrimuseet, Copenhagen (8/1911)
LIT. Erik Lassen, *En københavnsk porcelænsfabriks historie. Bing & Grøndahl 1853-1978*, Copenhagen 1978, p. 21, fig. 17

133
Pietro Krohn (1840-1905)
Three cups and saucers, 'Potentil' (cinquefoil), *'Åkande'* (water lily), and *'Narcisse'* (narcissus)
Porcelain. In the shape of flowers. Painted in underglaze colours, h. 6 cm, 8.5 cm, and 5.5 cm. respectively. Marked 'B & G'. The Bing & Grøndahl Porcelain Manufactory, Copenhagen 1888-91 (fig. 28)
Kunstindustrimuseet, Copenhagen (66/1947, 78/1947, 129 *a-b*/1988)
LIT. Erik Lassen, *En københavnsk porcelænsfabriks historie. Bing & Grøndahl 1852-1978*, Copenhagen 1978, p. 21, fig. 16; C. Nyrop, 'Plantemotiver i Gjenstande fra Bing & Gröndahls Porcelænsfabrik' *Tidsskrift for Kunstindustri*, 1894, pp. 53-56

134
Arnold Krog (1856-1931)
Dish
Porcelain. Four water lily leaves surrounding a flower to form a flower stand. Modelled by Erik Nielsen. Blue and pink underglaze colours, diam., ca. 30 cm. Sign. 'AK', the three blue wavy lines, '12K', '5094' and Denmark with a crown 'Arnold Krog December 1894'. Royal Copenhagen Porcelain Manufactory, Copenhagen 1894
Nationalmuseum, Dept. of Decorative Arts, Stockholm (NM1327/1895)
LIT. Dyveke Helsted 'Arnold Krog og porcelænet' *Den Kongelige Porcelænsfabrik 1775-1975*, Copenhagen 1975, p. 53

135
Two plates
Porcelain. The rims are decorated, one with lilies of the valley, the other with auriculas and daisies, diam. 22 cm. Sign. '128' (0.101) and '122' (0.106), Royal Copenhagen Porcelain Manufactory, Copenhagen after 1894
Royal Copenhagen Museum, Copenhagen (0.101, 0.106)

136
Elisabeth Drewes Kofoed (b. 1877)
Water lilies
Porcelain. Sculpture, undecorated, h. 43.5 cm. Marked ED, N.8, three towers, B&G. COPENHAGEN. The Bing & Grøndahl Porcelain Manufactory, Copenhagen 1898 (*ill.*)
Royal Copenhagen Museum, Copenhagen
LIT. Erik Lassen, *En dansk porcelænsfabriks historie. Bing & Grøndahl 1853-1978*, Copenhagen 1978, fig. 31

137
Effie Hegermann-Lindencrone (1860-1945)
Jar
Porcelain. Partly pierced to form a blooming hawthorn. Underglaze painting and gold, h. 17 cm. Marked 'B & G' and the artist's monogram. The Bing & Grøndahl Porcelain Manufactory, Copenhagen 1899
Kunstindustrimuseet, Copenhagen (1214)

138
Arnold Krog (1856-1931)
Teapot, milk jug, and sugar bowl, from the 'Marguerite' service
Porcelain. Handles and knobs in the shape of insects. Daisies and clover leaves in low relief painted in underglaze in greyish brown and white. Teapot: h. 10 cm, diam. 19.5 cm. Milk jug: h. 4 cm, diam. 10.8 cm. Sugar bowl: h. 6 cm, diam. 15.5 cm. Marked with the three blue wavy lines. Royal Copenhagen Porcelain Manufactory, Copenhagen ca. 1900
Kunstindustrimuseet, Copenhagen (1130, 1145, 1146)

Ceramics Other European Countries

139
Tile picture
Tin-glazed earthenware. Ten tiles decorated in various colours with five tulips, h. 25 cm, w. 62.5 cm. Hoorn?, the Netherlands ca. 1640 (fig. 46)
Museum Boymans-van Beuningen, Rotterdam (A5030)

142

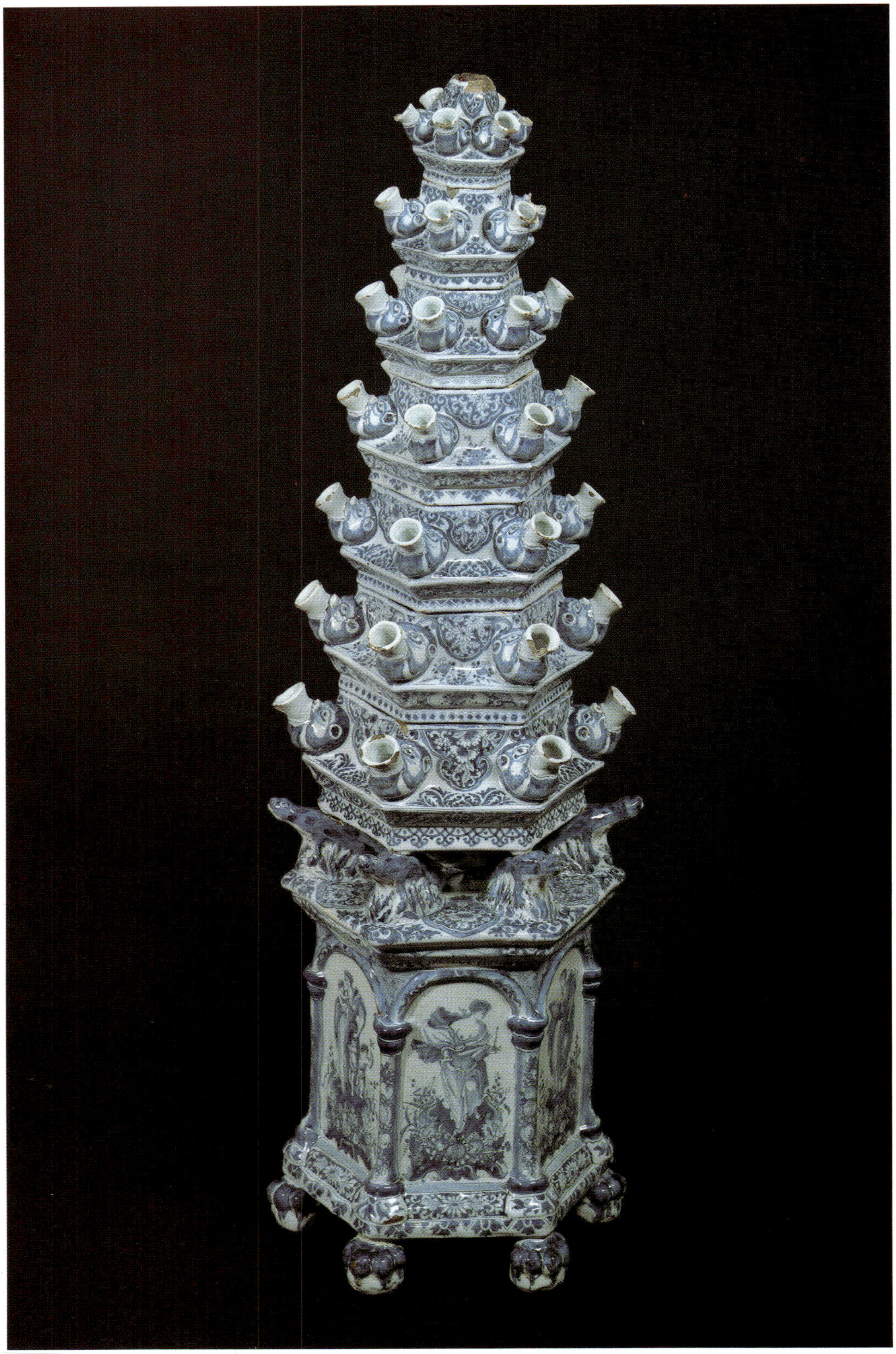

143

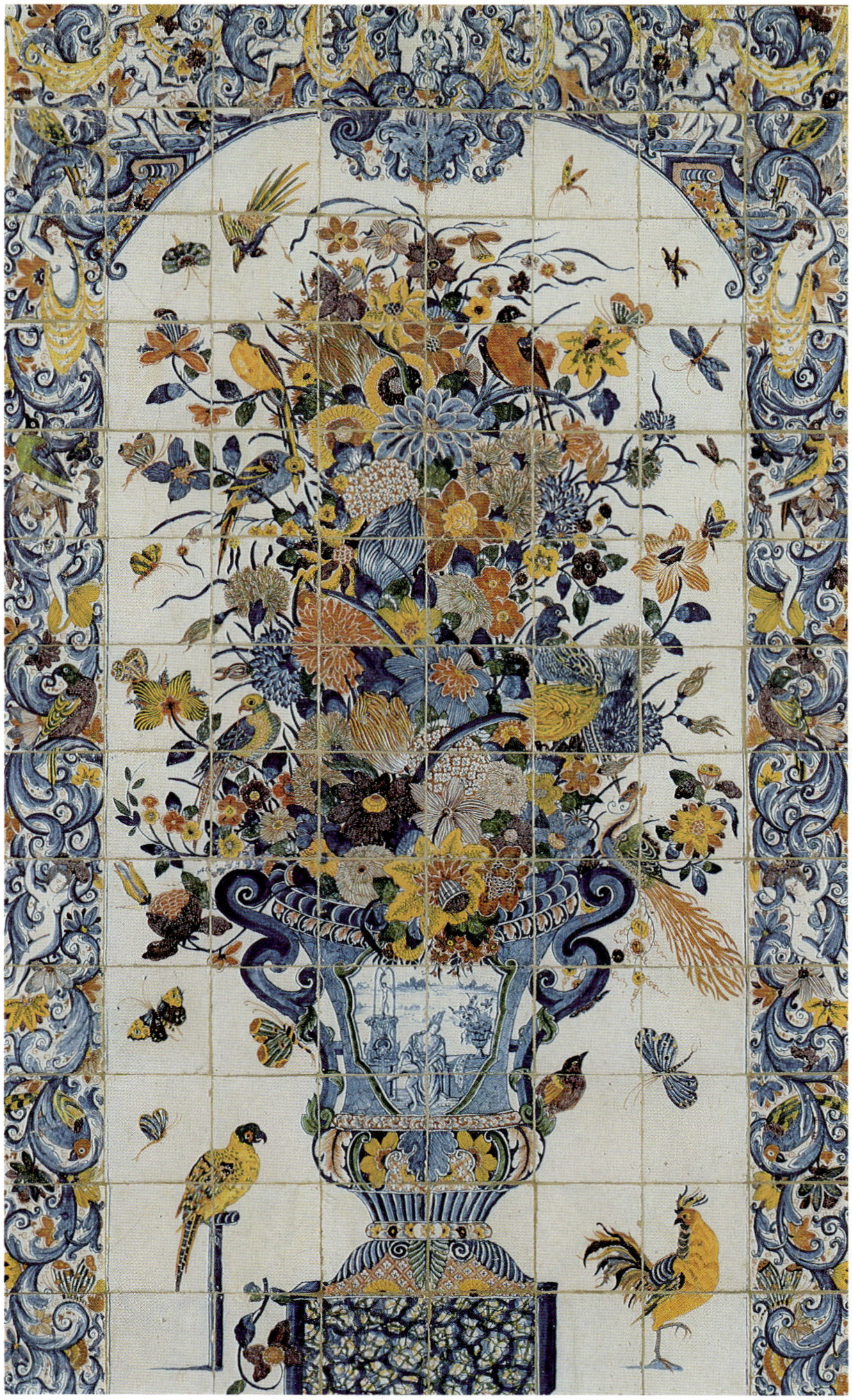

LIT. A. Berendsen (et al.), *Fliesen*, Munich 1964, p. 134, ill. p. 136; C. H. de Jonge, *Nederlandse tegels*, Amsterdam 1971, ill. p. 36, ill. p. 137; G. Kaufmann, *Bemalte Wandfliesen*, Munich 1973, ill. p. 142

Probably after an original by Judith Leyster.

140
Albrecht Cornelis de Keiser (1650-1684)
Tulip vase
Tin-glazed earthenware. Decoration in blue, h. 38 cm. Sign. 'AK' in monogram. Delft, the Netherlands mid-17th century (*ill.*)
Kunstindustrimuseet, Copenhagen (B106/1910)

141
Jug
Tin-glazed earthenware. Biblical scene in various colours in a green wreath with pink roses. Foot and cover of gilt silver, h. 24.2 cm, w. 15 cm. Sign. on the handle 'WR.' Foot and cover marked with the Nuremberg hallmark and Jacob Pfaff's maker's mark (master in 1675, died 1780). Nuremberg, Germany ca. 1690
Kunstindustrimuseet, Copenhagen (B52/1944)

142
Adriaen Kocks (d. 1701)
Flower pyramid
Tin-glazed earthenware consisting of eight tiers intended to contain water with nozzles for holding flowers. Blue and white decoration; on the base are scenes with allegorical figures, h. 104.1 cm. Sign. 'AK', 'De Grieksche A'. Delft, the Netherlands end of 17th century (*ill.*)
The Duke of Devonshire and the Chatsworth House Trust, England
PROV. Probably bought by the first Duke of Devonshire (1640-1707)
LIT. Michael Archer, 'Pyramids & Pagodas for Flowers,' *Country Life*, 22 Jan. 1976, pp. 166-169

In spite of its name, tulip vases were used for other flowers. Most of the flower pyramids were delivered to the British customers in the years 1688-1710 after the culmination of the 'tulipomania.'

143
Tile picture of a flower vase
Tin-glazed earthenware. Consisting of 104 square tiles decorated in various colours, h. 183 cm, w. 104 cm. Probably from the De Roos Factory, Delft, the Netherlands 1720-25 (*ill.*)
Kunstindustrimuseet, Copenhagen (44/1960)

LIT. Erik Lassen, 'En blomstervase af hollandske fliser,' *Det danske Kunstindustrimuseum. Virksomhed 1959-1964*, Copenhagen 1964, pp. 49-57

144
Teapot
Tin-glazed earthenware. Globular with a tapering spout, the handle in the shape of a branch, the knob in the shape of a fruit. Decorated with flowers in green, manganese and blue on a yellow ground, h. 12.5 cm, l. 19 cm. Veuve Perrin, Marseilles, France ca. 1750 (*ill.*)
The David Collection, Copenhagen (FK163)
LIT. *C. L. Davids Samling II*, Copenhagen 1963, pp. 56 f.

145
Dish
Tin-glazed earthenware. Oval, silver form. Decorated in various colours with one large and three minor bouquets and scattered flowers. The rim is lined with brown, l. 54 cm, w. 40 cm. Mark of Joseph Hannong. Strasbourg, France ca. 1760-70
The David Collection, Copenhagen (FK143)
LIT. *C. L. Davids Samling* II, Copenhagen 1963, pp. 64-65

Strasbourg's famous tradition of flower painting reached its peak in the years between 1760 and 1770, i.e., when Joseph Hannong was director of the factory. Usually, the bouquet is

146

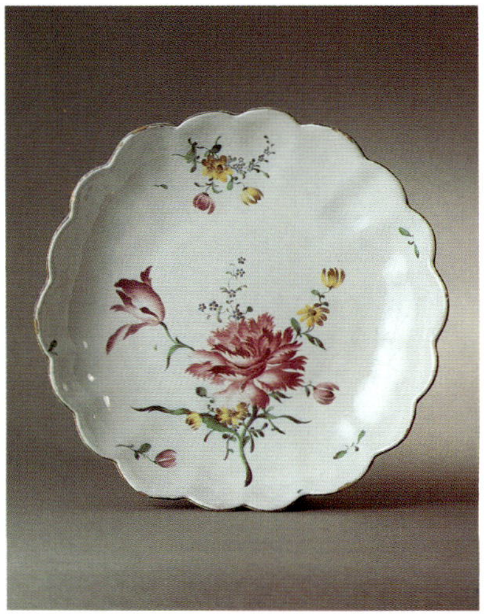

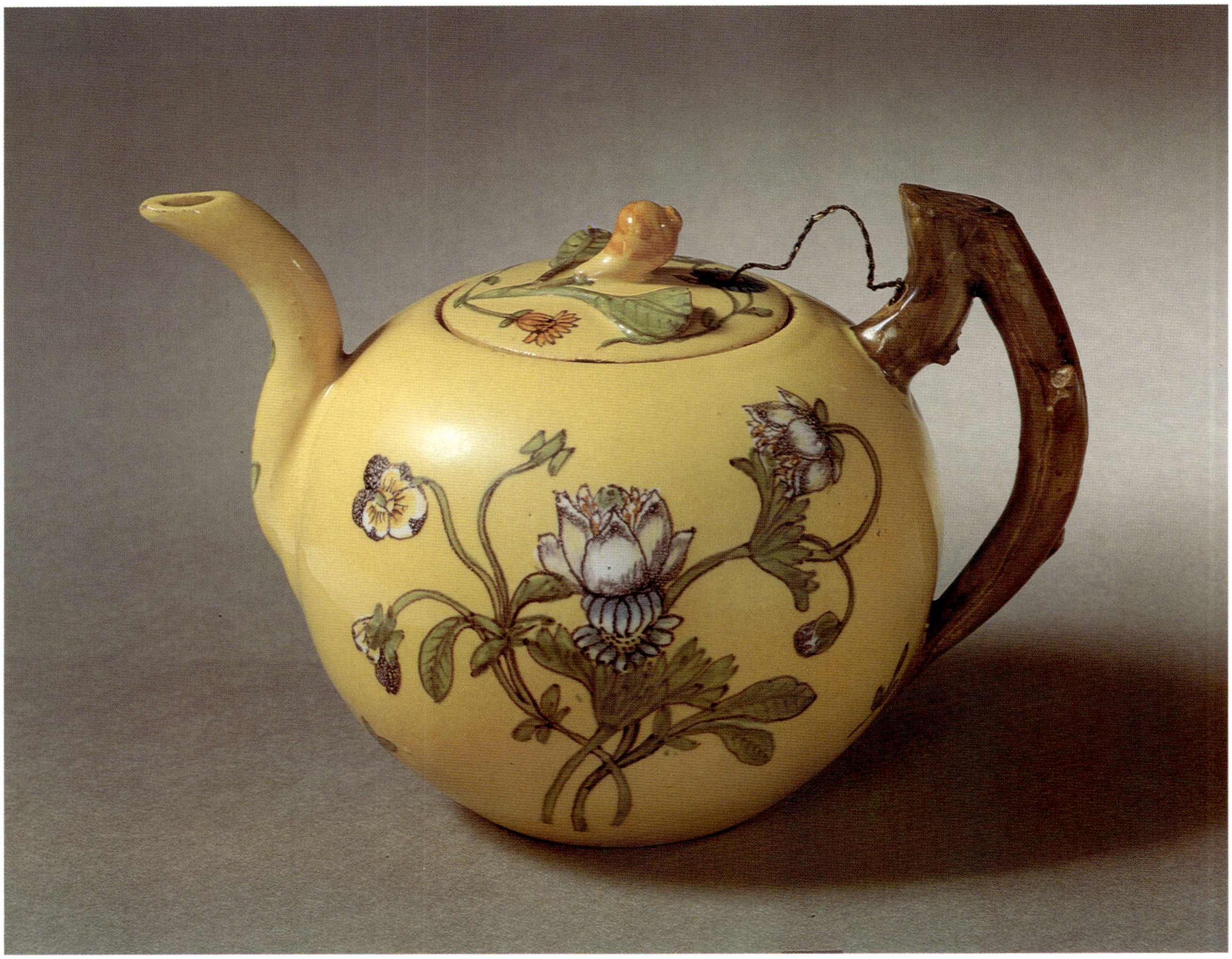

144

140

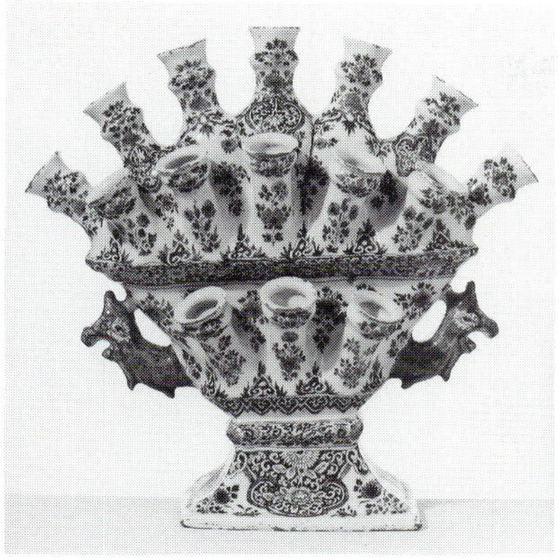

150

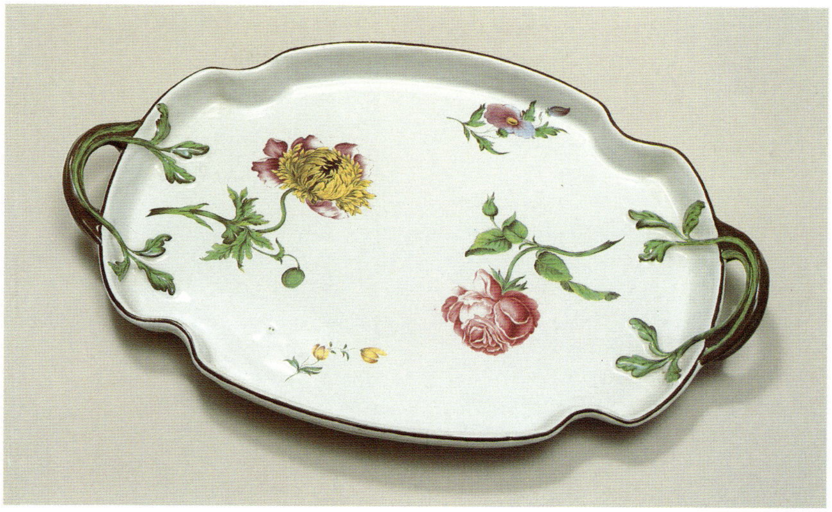

composed around one big flower, generally a tulip or a rose, and the petals are given form by incredibly fine, delicate strokes.

146
Dish
Tin-glazed earthenware. Round with wavy rim. The dish is decorated with one large and one minor bouquet and scattered flowers, diam. 25 cm. Mark of Joseph Hannong. Strasbourg, France 1760-70 (*ill.*)
The David Collection, Copenhagen (FK145)

147
Sauceboat
Tin-glazed earthenware. Decorated with bouquets and scattered flowers in various colours, h. 9.5 cm, l. 21 cm, w. 16 cm. Mark of Joseph Hannong. Strasbourg, France 1762-81
Kunstindustrimuseet, Copenhagen (63/1951)

148
Dish
Tin-glazed earthenware. Oval. Decorated in various colours, birds and flowers on the rim. In the centre, a large bouquet, l. 48.3 cm. Sign. 'Rörstrand'. Rörstrand, Sweden 1758-59
Nationalmuseum, Dept. of Decorative Arts, Stockholm (NM215)

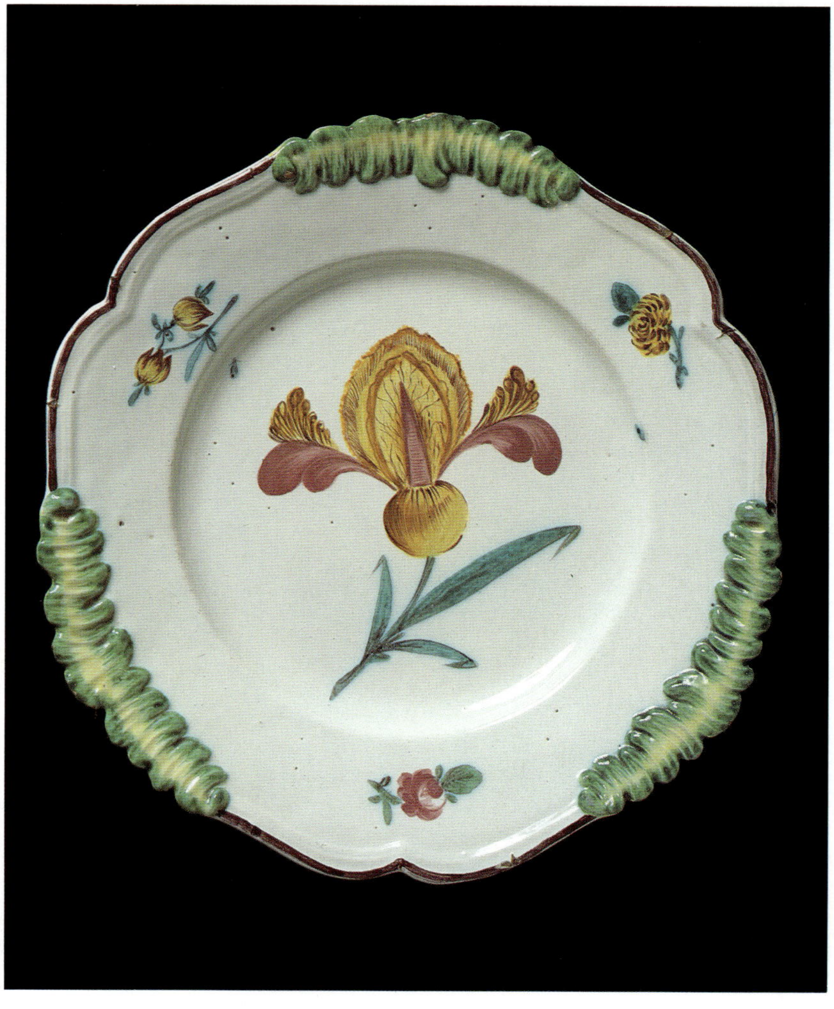

154

155

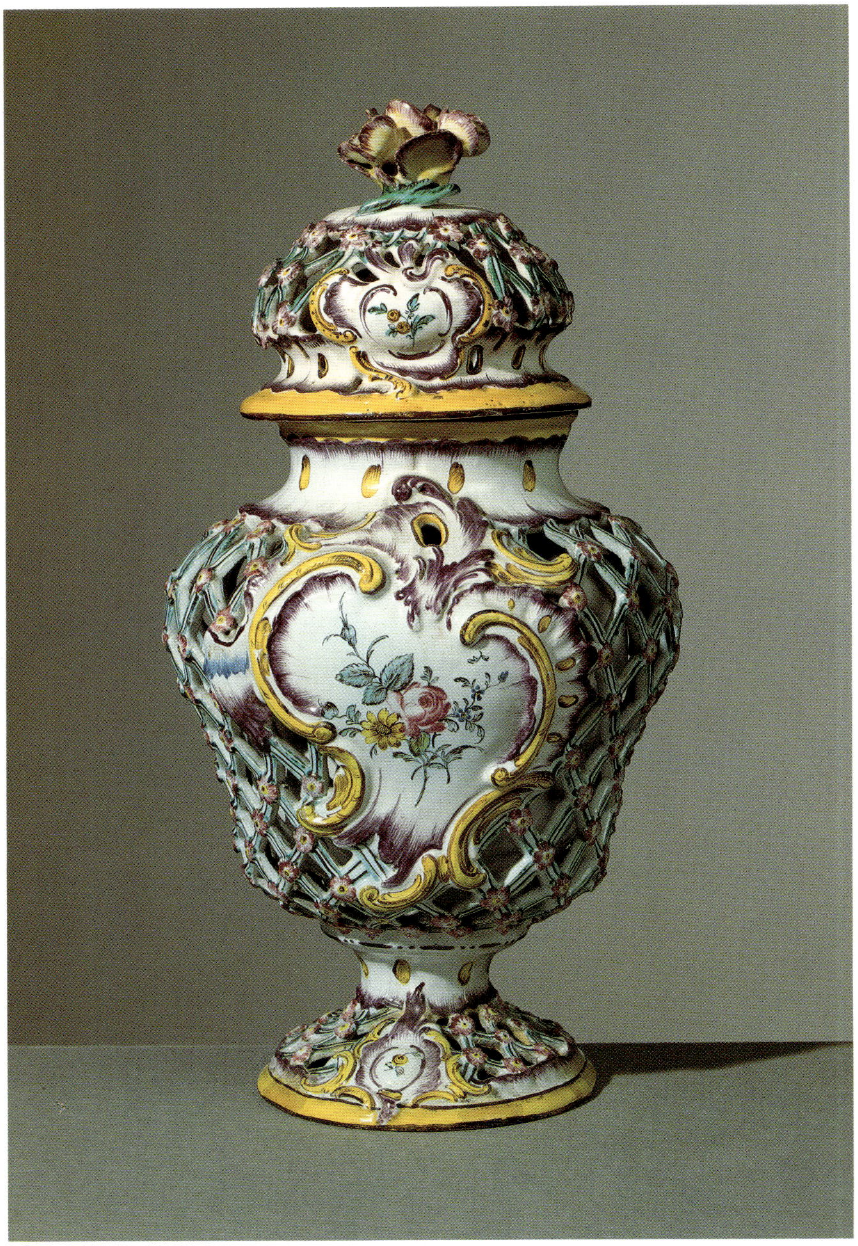

149
Bidet
Tin-glazed earthenware. Decorated with flowers in various colours. On the rim is a festoon with trilobate, yellow flowers, h. 15.5 cm, w. 28 cm, l. 48 cm. Sign. 'Rörstrand 23/4 1765'; signed by Carl Erik Löfström. Rörstrand, Sweden 1765
Nationalmuseum, Dept. of Decorative Arts, Stockholm (292/1921)
LIT. Helena Dahlbäck Lutteman, *Svenskt porslin. Fajans, porslin och flintgods 1700-1900*, Västerås 1980, ill. p. 90

150
Tray
Tin-glazed earthenware. Oval with handles shaped like twigs. Decorated with flowers in various colours, l. 41 cm, w. 30 cm. Dated 9 July 1774. Sign. with three crowns and 'MB 9/7 74 4B'.
Marieberg, Sweden 1774
Nationalmuseum, Dept. of Decorative Arts, Stockholm (NMCXV993)

151
Plate
Tin-glazed earthenware. The centre decorated with a bouquet in various colours, the rim with partly printed flower twigs in blue and a few painted in colours, diam. 24 cm. Sign. 'R-1/5'.
Rörstrand, Sweden ca. 1770
Nationalmuseum, Dept. of Decorative Arts, Stockholm (NM201)

152
Potpourri vase
Tin-glazed earthenware. Applied branches, flowers, and fruit as well as painted flowers and scattered leaves in various colours, h. 34.4 cm. Marked 'K/T/R'. Decorated by J. A. Rühl.
J. S. F. Tännich period, Kiel, Germany 1763-66
Kunstindustrimuseet, Copenhagen (32/1955)

153
Dish
Tin-glazed earthenware. Decorated with scattered flowers in various colours, diam. 39 cm. Marked: 'Kiel T No. 5'.
J. S. F. Tännich period, Kiel, Germany ca. 1765
Kunstindustrimuseet, Copenhagen (B132/1910)

154
Dish
Tin-glazed earthenware. Moulded rim decorated in green, in the centre a yellow flag, diam 24 cm. Marked 'RF'.
Otto Fick, Reval ca. 1770 (*ill.*)
Kunstindustrimuseet, Copenhagen (A2/1923)

155
Potpourri vase
Tin-glazed earthenware. Double walled. The external wall, the cover, and the foot are executed in trellis work; the knob in the shape of a flower. Panels decorated with bouquets in various colours, h. 37 cm, diam. 20 cm. Marked 'S tff/B/A' for painter J. A. G. Adler and director Johann Buchwald. Stockelsdorff, Germany second half of 18th century (*ill.*)
Kunstindustrimuseet, Copenhagen (71/1952)

Potpourri vases, in tin-glazed earthenware as well as in porcelain,

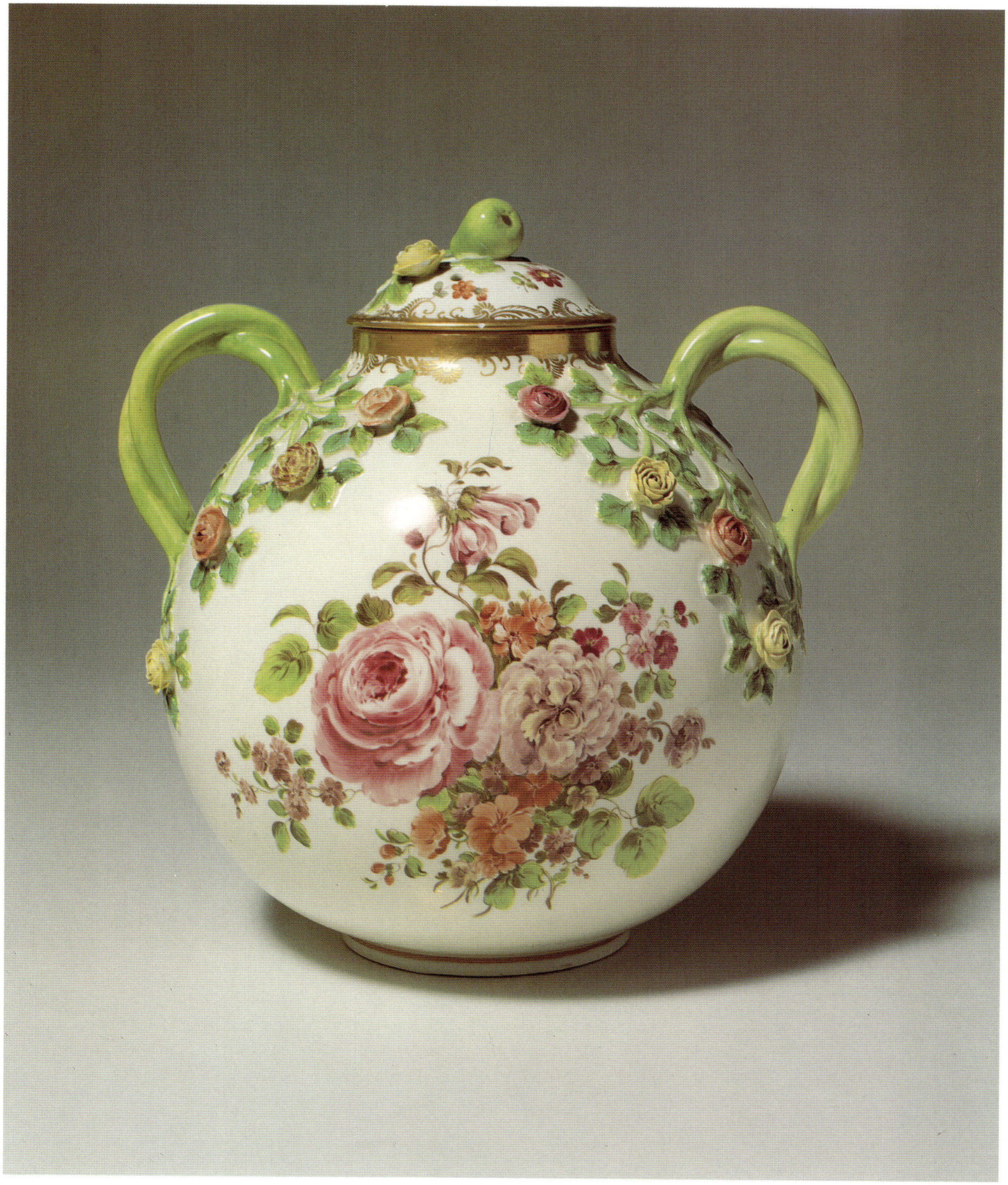

172

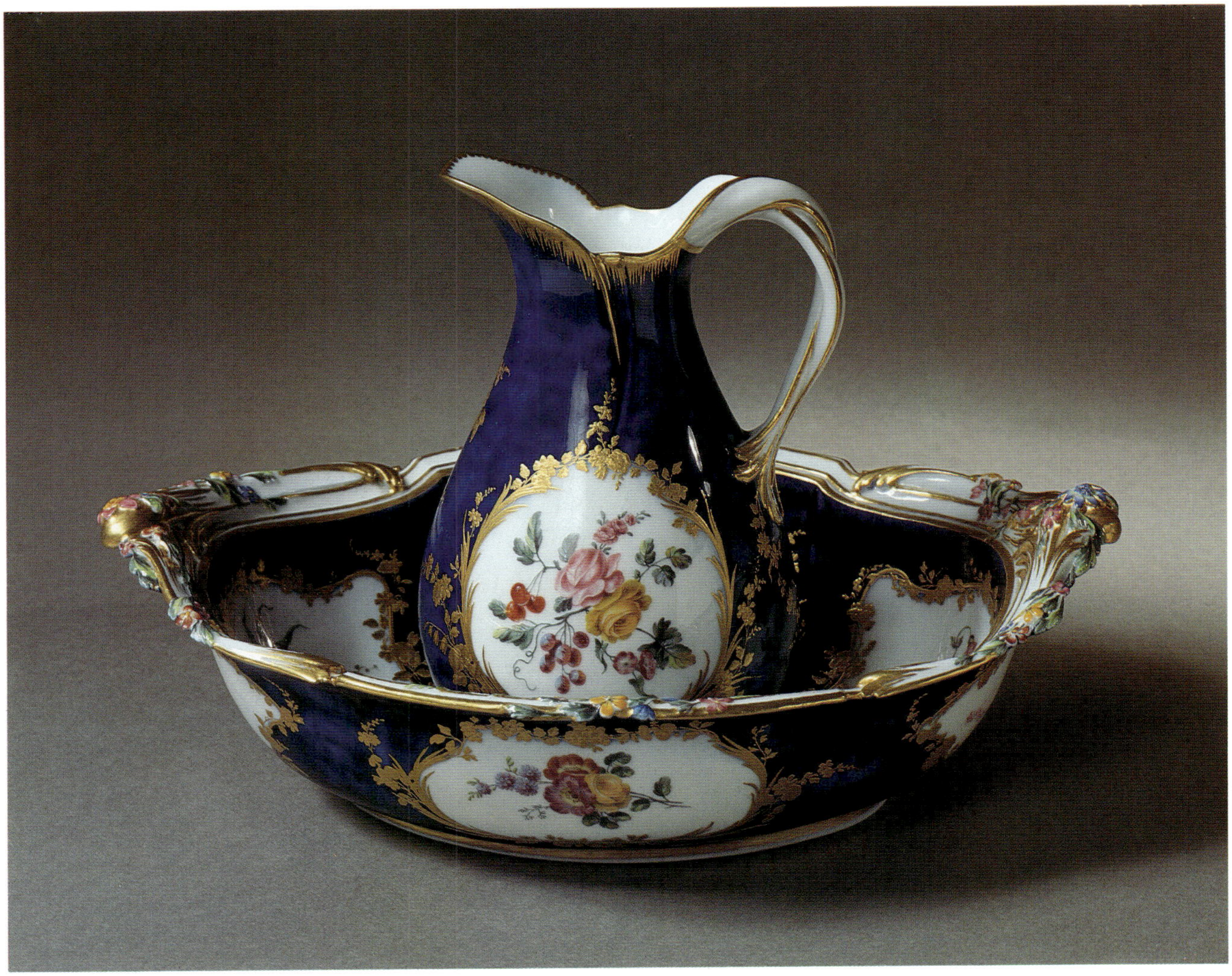

were popular for decorative and practical purposes, especially from the middle of the 18th century on. A potpourri (from French: rotten jar) is a mixture of fragrant, dried flowers, herbs and spices. Usually, the vases had two covers; an interior closed one and an external pierced one through which the scent could penetrate once the interior cover had been removed.

156
Perfume bottle
Porcelain decorated with harbour scenes in various colours and gold, h. 7.5 cm. Meissen?, Germany ca. 1730
Kunstindustrimuseet, Copenhagen (75/1953)

157
Snuffbox
Porcelain. The exterior decorated with applied forget-me-nots, h. 6 cm, w. 7.4 cm. Meissen, Germany 1735-40
Kunstindustrimuseet, Copenhagen (B193/1939)
PROV. The Lady Carnavon Rothschild Collection
LIT. Axel Heine, *Porcelæns-Tabatièren i det 18. Aarhundrede*, Copenhagen 1937. No. 29; V. Slomann, 'Tobak og Tabatièrer,' *Tilskueren*, 1939, p. 415, fig. 3

158
Snuffbox
Porcelain. The exterior decorated with scattered flowers in relief painted in various colours, h. 3.8 cm, l. 8.1 cm. Meissen, Germany mid-18th century
Kunstindustrimuseet, Copenhagen (B120/1939)
LIT. Axel Heine, *Porcelæns-Tabatièren i det 18. Aarhundrede*, Copenhagen 1937, no. 57

159
Snuffbox
Porcelain. The exterior decorated with scattered flowers and bouquets in relief painted in various colours, h. 4.3 cm, diam. 8.8 cm. Meissen, Germany mid-18th century
Kunstindustrimuseet, Copenhagen (B215/1939)
LIT. Axel Heine, *Porcelæns-Tabatièren i det 18. Aarhundrede*, Copenhagen 1937, no. 53

174

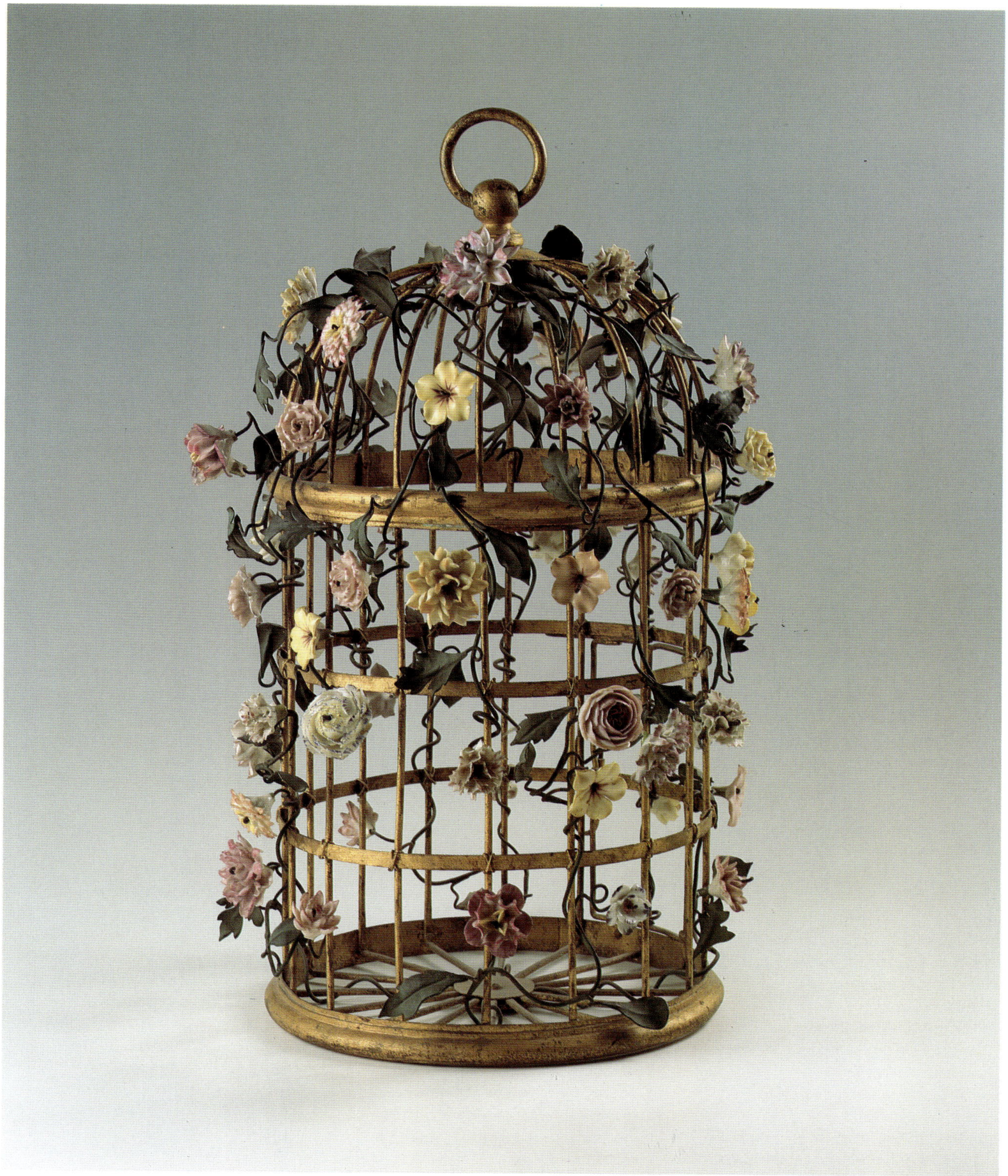

165

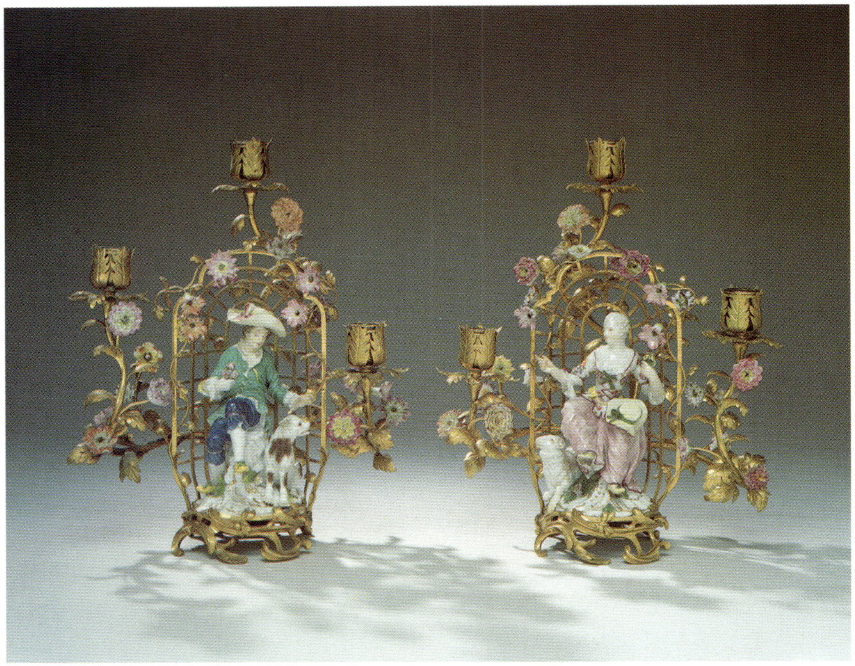

The decoration *blaue deutsche Blumen* seems to have been used as of 1745 at the earliest.

160
Snuffbox
Porcelain. The exterior decorated with flowers and plait in relief. The interior of the lid is decorated with a basket with flowers in various colours through which a woman's face is seen, h. 4.9 cm, w. 9.7 cm. Meissen, Germany mid-18th century
Kunstindustrimuseet, Copenhagen (B229/1939)
LIT. Axel Heine, *Porcelæns-Tabatièren i det 18. Aarhundrede*, Copenhagen 1937, no. 80

161
Snuffbox
Porcelain. Purple scale pattern with gold plait and panels of scattered flowers and fruit painted in various colours. The interior of the lid decorated in various colours with a flower vase on a table, h. 3.9 cm, b. 7.9 cm. Meissen, Germany ca. 1760
Kunstindustrimuseet, Copenhagen (B227/1939)
LIT. Axel Heine, *Porcelæns-Tabatièren i det 18. Aarhundrede*, Copenhagen 1937, no. 80

162
Teapot with cup and saucer
Porcelain. Multicoloured flowers on a yellow ground. Teapot: h. 9 cm, cup: h. 3 cm, saucer: diam. 12 cm. Mark of crossed swords. Meissen, Germany, mid-18th century
Kunstindustrimuseet, Copenhagen (A51-52-1919)

163
Cup and saucer
Porcelain. Colourful flower twigs, butterflies, and insects on a yellow ground. Cup: h. 7.3 cm, saucer: diam. 15 cm. Mark of crossed swords. Meissen, Germany 1750s
Nationalmuseum, Dept. of Decorative Arts, Stockholm (NM64/1984)
EXH. *Aron Andersson Collection*, Nationalmuseum, Stockholm 1984, no. 50

164
Dish
Porcelain. Decorated in blue underglaze with *blaue deutsche Blumen*, scattered flowers and insects. Mark of crossed swords and 'M' (painter's mark), h. 6 cm, diam. 33.5 cm. Meissen, Germany mid-18th century
Kunstindustrimuseet, Copenhagen (7/1983)

165
Two candlesticks
Gilt bronze and porcelain. A porcelain shepherd and shepherdess painted in various colours sitting under an espalier of gilt bronze leaves and porcelain flowers, h. 33 cm, w. 27 cm. The porcelain was produced in Meissen, Germany ca. 1760, the bronze mounting in France or Germany in the same period *(ill.)*
Nationalmuseum, Dept. of Decorative Arts, Stockholm (NM67-68/1965)

166
Dish
Porcelain. Bouquet and scattered flowers painted in various colours and gold, h. 7.8 cm, diam. 33.5 cm. Marked with the Frankenthal factory mark. Frankenthal, Germany 1759-62
Kunstindustrimuseet, Copenhagen (179/1984)

167
Tureen with cover
Porcelain. Decorated with gold stripes and scattered flowers in various colours, h. 24 cm. Marked with the Frankenthal mark. Frankenthal, Germany 1770-75
Kunstindustrimuseet, Copenhagen (1*a*-*b*/1990)

168
Covered cup and saucer
Porcelain. Decorated in various colours with flower monogram G on cup and saucer. The cover is decorated with scattered flowers and a medallion with the letter G. Cup: h. 9.4 cm, saucer: diam. 13.2 cm. Mark of crossed swords above a star and the number '4'. Meissen, the Marcolini period, Germany 1780-1816
Kunstindustrimuseet, Copenhagen (138)

169
Potpourri vase
One of a pair. Porcelain. Handles in the shape of branches fastened to the body with applied twigs and roses. The

173

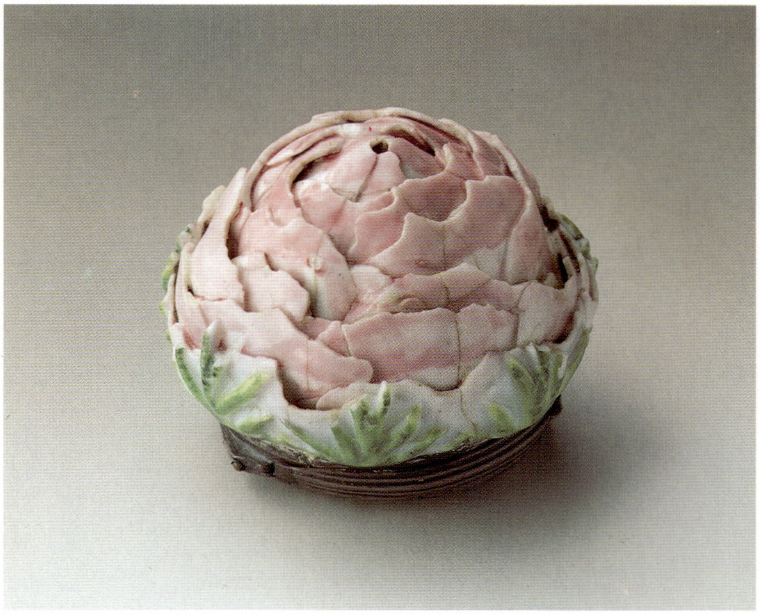

186

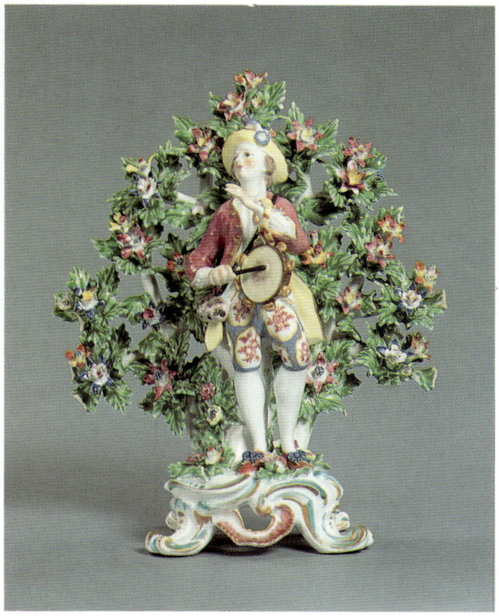

knob in the shape of a green pear and a yellow rose. Decorated with rich bouquets in various colours, h. ca. 25 cm. Vienna ca. 1760 (*ill.*)
Nationalmuseum, Dept. of Decorative Arts, Stockholm (NM294/1950)

170
Cup and saucer
Porcelain. Decorated in various colours and gold with *Linnaea borealis* L. Cup: h. 7.5 cm, saucer: diam. 7.9 cm. China, Ch'ien-Lung ca. 1754 (*fig. 75*)
Linnémuseet, Uppsala (A21)
LIT. Winfried Baer & H. Walter Lack, *Pflanzen auf Porzellan*, cat. Botanischer Garten und Botanisches Museum Berlin-Dahlem, Berlin 1979, p. 25 ff., pl. 1, cat. no. 1

On a journey to China, Per Osbeck, a Swedish pupil of Carolus Linnaeus (1707-1778), ordered a tea service as a present for his famous teacher. The service was decorated with a tiny plant, *Linnea borealis* L., which Linnaeus had discovered on a trip to Lapland and later gave his own name. However, most of the service was broken during transportation from Gothenburg to Uppsala. Some years later, a new service was ordered from China via the Swedish East India Company, most of which is preserved in the Linnémuseet. The decoration was copied from the engraving of *Linnea borealis* L., in Carolus Linnaeus's *Flora Svecica* (Leiden 1745, cat. 74).

171
Flower branch
Soft-paste porcelain. Branch made of painted metal and vellum mounted with three carnations made of soft-paste porcelain. Largest diam. 6.5 cm. Vincennes, France ca. 1750

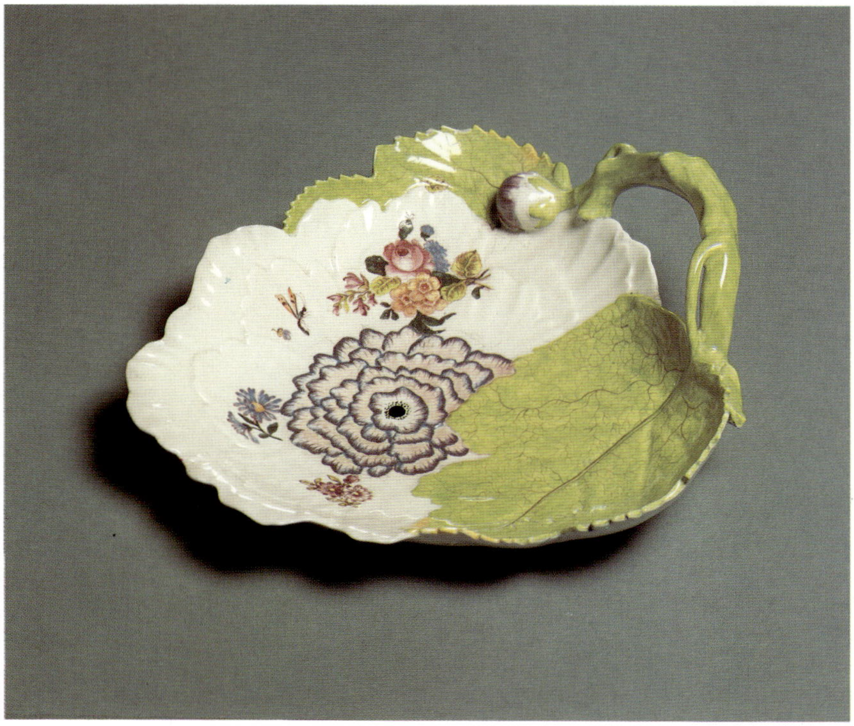

181

188

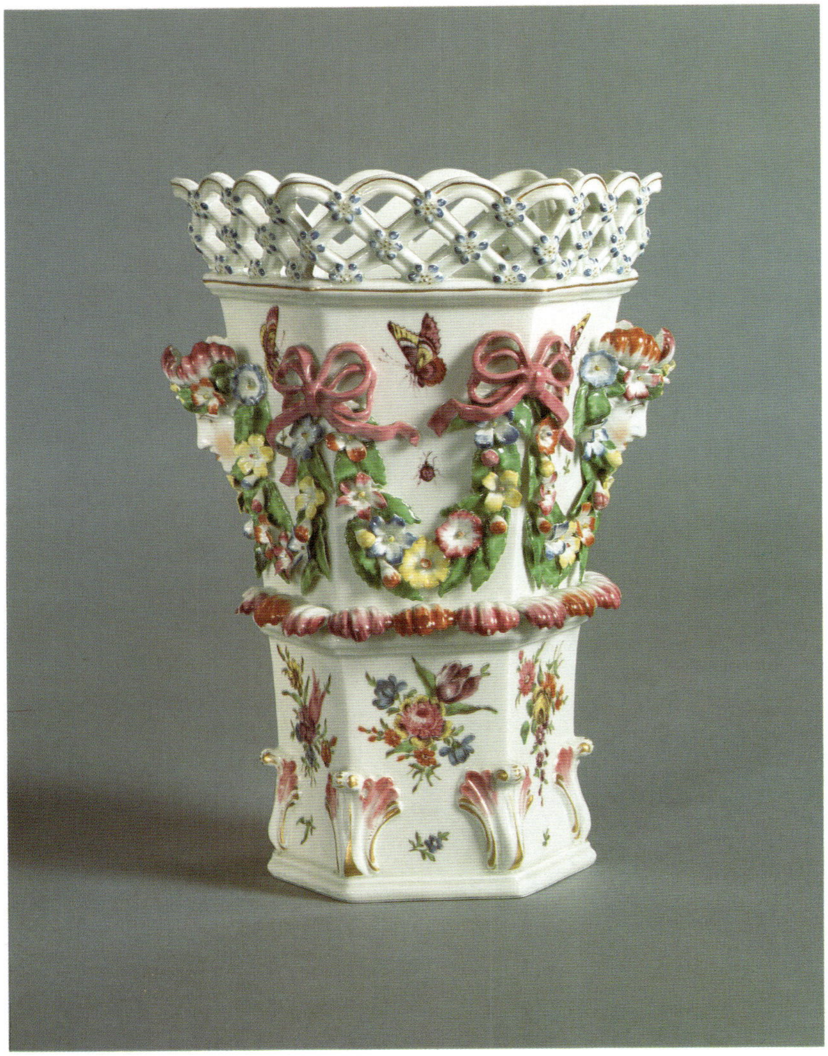

The David Collection, Copenhagen (20/73)

172
Basin with ewer
Soft-paste porcelain. Dark blue ground *bleu lapis* with white panels in reserve decorated with flowers in various colours. The rim of the basin is ornamented with small flowers in relief. Ewer: h. 19 cm, basin: l. 32.5 cm. Marked with the date letter 'A' for 1753. Vincennes, France 1753 (*ill.*)
The David Collection, Copenhagen (64/74)
LIT. Svend Eriksen, *Fransk porcelæn/French Porcelain. Davids Samling/The David Collection*, Copenhagen 1980, cat. no. 35-36

173
Snuffbox
Soft-paste porcelain. In the shape of a rose painted in various colours, h. 4.5 cm. Mennecy, France, mid-18th century (*ill.*)
Musée des Arts Décoratifs, Paris (32878)

174
Bird cage
Gilt iron decorated with vines of green leaves and porcelain flowers. France, mid-18th century. The porcelain flowers were probably made at Vincennes (*ill.*)
Musée des Arts Décoratifs, Paris (53447)

175
Cup and saucer
Soft-paste porcelain. Rhomboid pattern in dark blue and gold, decorated with flowers in various colours. Cup: h. 6.1 cm, saucer: diam. 13.3 cm. Sèvres factory mark and the date letter E for 1757
Nationalmuseum, Dept. of Decorative Arts, Stockholm (NM172/1984)
EXH. *Aron Andersson Collection*, Nationalmuseum, Stockholm 1984, no. 141

176
Plate
Porcelain. Decorated with flower baskets, cupids in oval medallions and garlands in various colours. Blue rim decorated with gold. In the centre flower monogram 'CL', diam. 24.4 cm. Sèvres factory mark and the date letter for 1773
Kunstindustrimuseet, Copenhagen (40/1971)

177
Bouillon bowl with dish, 'Ecuelle et son plateau'
Porcelain. The handle of the bowl shaped as an olive branch. Dark blue ground with oval panels in reserve painted with roses in pink and green. Foliage and bows decorated in gold. Total h. 10.6 cm. Bowl and dish marked with Sèvres factory mark, date letter for 1776, painter's mark for Chappuis ainé and gilder's mark for Guillaume Noël
Kunstindustrimuseet, Copenhagen (120*a-c*/1984)

178
Cup and saucer
Soft-paste porcelain. *Oeil de perdrix* ground in blue with laurel wreaths in gold and pink roses in reserves. Green festoons. Cup: h. 6.1 cm, saucer: diam. 13.6 cm. Sèvres factory mark and date letter G for 1759, painter's mark 'F' in blue for Micaud
Nationalmuseum, Dept. of Decorative Arts, Stockholm (NM173/1984)
PROV. Collection C. U. Palm
EXH. *Aron Andersson Collection*, Nationalmuseum, Stockholm 1984, no. 142

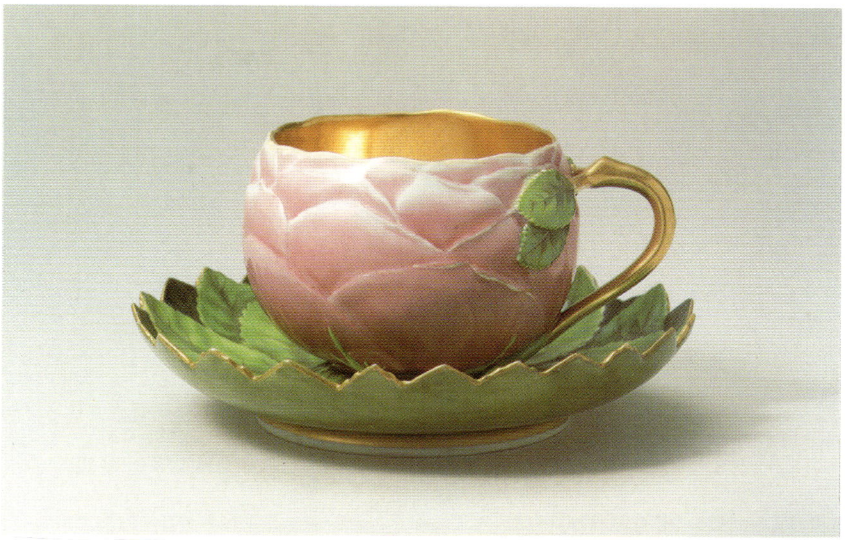

179
Cup and saucer
Soft-paste porcelain. Cup: h. 6 cm, saucer: diam. 12 cm. Sèvres factory mark with date letter for 1788. Decorated by J.-P. Fumez. Sèvres, France 1788
The David Collection, Copenhagen (9/65)

180
Cup and saucer
Porcelain. Festoons of yellow and purple violets and ribbons with ornaments in black and gold on a grey ground. Cup: h. 6.2 cm, saucer: diam. 12.7 cm. Sign. with La Courtille's mark. Paris ca. 1800 (*ill.*)
Nationalmuseum, Dept. of Decorative Arts, Stockholm (NM1406/1885)

181
Dish
Soft-paste porcelain in the shape of a flower with leaves and twig handle painted with scattered flowers in colours, l. 23.3 cm, w. 21.5 cm. Sign. 'Red Anchor'. Chelsea, England ca. 1753-54 (*ill.*)
The Board of Trustees of the Victoria & Albert Museum, London (C.239*a*-1935)
LIT. J. L. Dixan, *English Porcelain of the 18th Century*, London 1952

182
Dish
Soft-paste porcelain. Bouquet and scattered flowers in various colours as well as four scenes from Aesop's *Fables*, l. 43 cm, w. 34.4 cm. Sign. 'Red Anchor'. Chelsea, England 1753-58
Kunstindustrimuseet, Copenhagen (151/1984)

183
Mug
Soft-paste porcelain. Decorated with a botanical plant; coral tree, *Erythrina sp.*, painted in various colours, h. 14 cm, w. 15 cm. Sign. 'Red Anchor'. Chelsea, England ca. 1755 (*ill.*)
The Board of Trustees of the Victoria & Albert Museum, London (174-1940)

184
Plate, 'Acanthus Spinosus'
Soft-paste porcelain painted in various colours with a botanical plant copied from P. Miller, *Figures of... Plants described in the Gardeners Dictionary*, 1755-60, vol. I, pl. VII, diam. 21.5 cm. Chelsea, England ca. 1755-58 (*fig. 76*)
The Board of Trustees of the Victoria & Albert Museum, London (C58-1949)
PROV. Gift of Mr. H. E. Barker. Previously in Col. and Mrs. Dickson's Collection
LIT. Bellamy Gardner, *Sir Hans Sloane's Plants on Chelsea Porcelain*, Trans. E. P. C., vol. 4, 1932; J. V. G. Mallet, *A Chelsea Talk*, Trans. E. C. C., vol. 6 pt. I (1965); Patrick Synge-Hutchinson, 'G. D. Ehret's Botanical Designs on Chelsea Porcelain,' *Connoisseur*, Oct. 1958

185
Tureen with cover and dish
Soft-paste porcelain shaped as primrose leaves with applied primroses on body and knob painted in various colours. Tureen: l. 16.6 cm, w. 8.7 cm, cover: l. 14.5 cm, w. 9 cm, dish: l. 27 cm, w. 3.5 cm. Chelsea, England ca. 1756
The Board of Trustees of the Victoria & Albert Museum, London (C.192-B-1977)

186
Figure, 'Drummer Boy'
Porcelain. Decorated in various colours and gold, h. 23.3 cm, w. 20.5 cm, dp. 12 cm. Marked 'A', 'Red Anchor' and 'Dagger'. Bow, England ca. 1760-65 (*ill.*)
The Board of Trustees of the Victoria & Albert Museum, London (C.46-1947)

187
Plate
Porcelain. Surface covered with tulips, roses, etc., painted in various colours and lined with gold, diam. 23 cm. Sign. 'Gold Anchor'. Chelsea, England ca. 1765-72
The Board of Trustees of the Victoria & Albert Museum, London (2948-19)
LIT. W. B. Honey, *Old English Porcelain*, London 1948

188
Vase
Porcelain. Hexagon with open lattice work rim. Applied flower festoons and painted bouquets in various colours, h. 22.5 cm, w. 18 cm. Worcester, England 1770 (*ill.*)
The Board of Trustees of the Victoria & Albert Museum, London (C.368-1935)
LIT. Franklin A. Barrett, *Worcester Porcelain*, London 1953

189
Two plates
Porcelain. Decorated in various colours with botanical plants: *a* jasmine and *b*

tulip tree. Sign. on reverse side 'Jasminum Officinale. Common Jessamine' and 'Liriodendron Tulipeferia. Common Tulip Tree', diam. 22 cm. Sign. with crown above crossed bars, 'D', and '115'. Derby after 1794 (*fig. 79*)
Private collection, Germany
Original: *a Jasminum Officinale* in *Curtis's Botanical Magazine*, vol. 1, pl. 31, 1 Febr. 1787; *b Liriodendron Tulipefera* in *Curtis's Botanical Magazine*, vol. 8, pl. 175, 1794

190
Coffeepot
Black jasper ware. Enamel decoration in various colours, 'Chrysantemum pattern,' h. 15.7 cm. Stamped 'WEDGWOOD' and horizontal 'A'. Josiah Wedgwood & Sons, England 1804-10
Kunstindustrimuseet, Copenhagen (95*a-b*/1983)

191
Dish
Tin-glazed earthenware with printed brown decoration, diam. 32 cm. Stamped 'WEDGWOOD'. England 1808-11 (*ill.*)
The Board of Trustees of the Victoria & Albert Museum, London (C.139-1963)
LIT. Una des Fontaines, 'The Darwin Service and the First Printed Floral Patterns at Etruria,' *Proceedings of the Wedgwood Society*, 1966, no. 6, pp. 69-90

192
Plate
Tin-glazed earthenware decorated with *Cyclamen persicum* in various colours, diam. 21.5 cm. Marked with stamped 'S' and painted 'Round Leav'd Cyclamen'. Possibly decorated by Thomas Pardoe. Staffordshire or Swansea, England, beginning of 19th century
The Board of Trustees of the Victoria & Albert Museum, London (3699-1901)

Transferred from the Jermyn Street Collection (Museum of Practical Geology).

193
Plate
Porcelain decorated in various colours with botanical plant: *Solenandria cordifolia* VENT. The rim decorated with a gilt frieze of stylized palmettes and acanthus leaves. The name of the plant painted on the reverse side, diam. 22.6 cm. Sceptre mark and painter's mark. Königliche Porzellanmanufaktur, Berlin (KPM) 1803-13
Private collection, Germany
LIT. Winfried Baer & H. Walter Lack, *Planzen auf Porzellan*, cat. Botanischer Garten und Botanisches Museum Berlin-Dahlem, Berlin 1979, p. 79, cat. no. 124

Copied after: P.-J. Redouté in

191
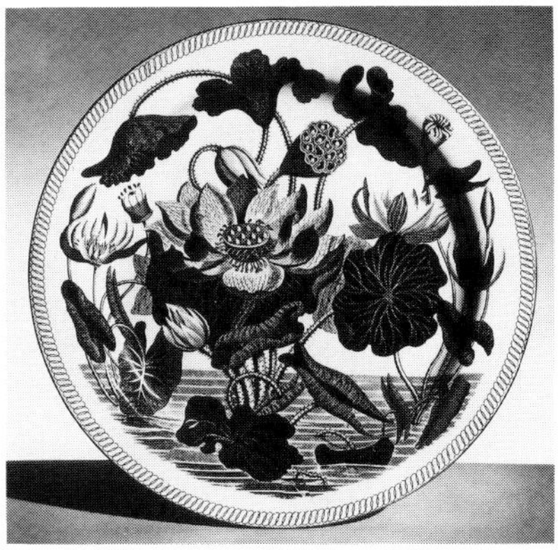

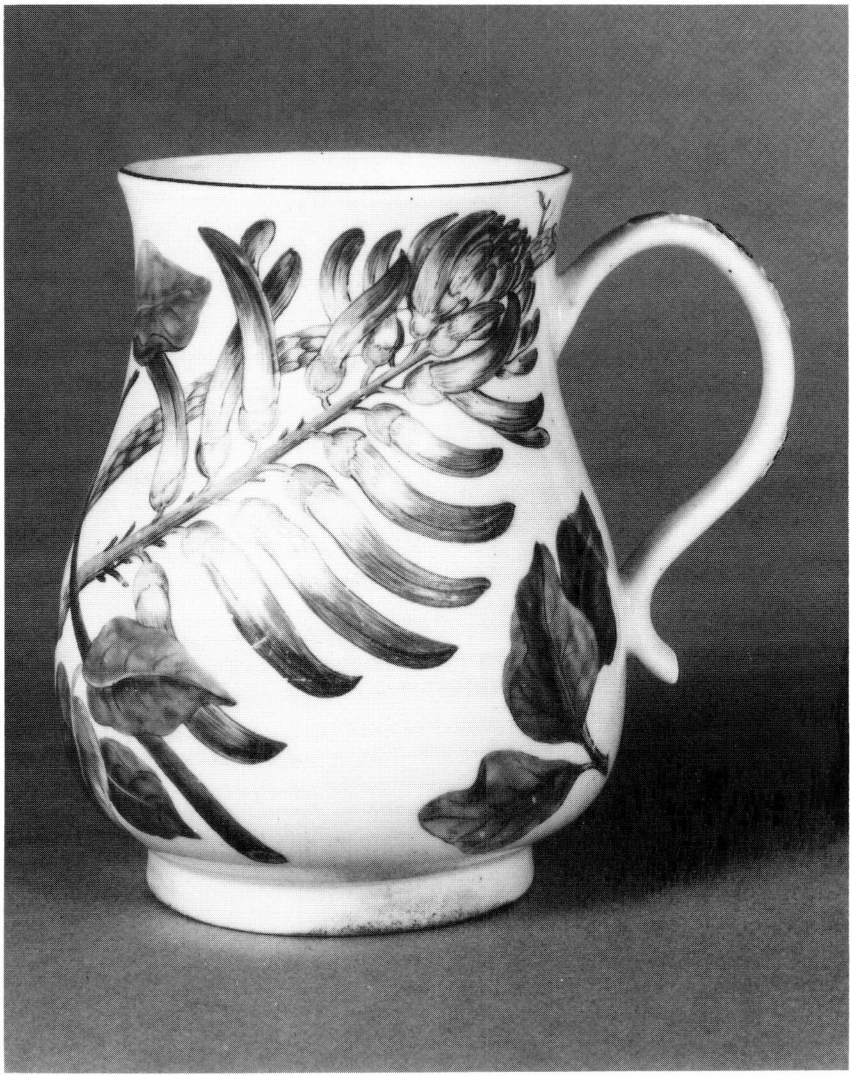
183

180

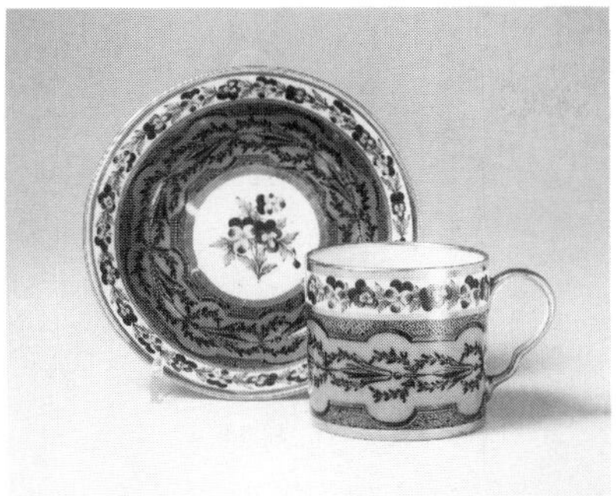

E.-P. Ventenat, *Jardin de la Malmaison*, 1804, pl. 69, part 12

194
Dessert plate
Porcelain decorated with botanical plant *Pelargonium echinatum* in various colours. The name of the plant and 'Cap de bonne espérance' painted in black on reverse side, diam. 23.7 cm. Sceptre mark. Königliche Porzellanmanufaktur, Berlin (KPM) 1806-07 (fig. 81)
Schloss Charlottenburg, Berlin-Porzellansammlung Belvedere, Berlin (KS VIII/1740)
LIT. Winfried Baer & H. Walter Lack, *Pflanzen auf Porzellan*, cat. Botanischer Garten und Botanisches Museum Berlin-Dahlem, Berlin 1979, p. 65 ff.

Shortly after Napoleon's entry into Berlin on 25 October 1806, a dinner service was ordered for the Empress Joséphine. This was a replacement for a precious Sèvres service with motifs from P.-J. Redouté, which the French empress had presented to her adopted daughter Stéphanie. The Berlin service is almost entirely decorated after Redouté's colour prints in E.-P. Ventenat, *Jardin de la Malmaison*, Paris 1804.

195
Part of a tea service
Porcelain. Consisting of tray, teapot, milk jug, cup and saucer, egg cup and plate. Decorated with botanical plants in various colours. Tray, octagonal: *Aitonia capensis, Azalea indica, Banksia ericaefolia, Bauera rubioides, Dryandralongifolia, Lambertia formosa, Roxburgia gloriosa, Solandra grandiflora*, l. 37.2 cm, w. 29.5 cm. Teapot: *Dionaca muscipula, Sarracenia*, h. 16 cm. Milk jug: *Jacquinia aurantiaca*, h. 13.5 cm. Cup: *Diosma fragrans*, h. 12.5 cm. Saucer: *Linnea borealis*, diam. 16.5 cm. Plate, octagonal: *Protea pulchella*, diam. 23 cm. Egg cup: *Bossiaea prostrata*, h. 6 cm. Sceptre mark. Königliche Porzellanmanufaktur, Berlin (KPM) 1817-23 (*fig. 82*)
Schloss Charlottenburg, Berlin-Porzellansammlung Belvedere, Berlin (B280/7,8,9,11*a-b*,15-17)
LIT. Georg Himmelheber, *Kunst des Biedermeier 1815-1835*, Munich 1988, cat. no. 202, pl. 89; Winfried Baer & H. Walter Lack, 'Pflanzen aus Kew auf Porzellan aus Berlin,' *Willdenowia 16*, 1986, p. 285 ff.

Most of the plants depicted grow outside of Europe, mainly in Australia. The names of the plants are painted in black on the reverse of the various parts. The majority of the decorations are copied from *Curtis's Botanical Magazine* and *Andrews's Botanist's Repository*. Most of the plants were grown in the Royal Gardens at Kew, and the service is thought to have been produced for one of the leading botanists, Sir Joseph Banks, member of the Horticultural Society in London and the Linnean Society, possibly with Alexander von Humboldt as an intermediary.

196
Cup and saucer
Porcelain. The cup in the shape of a heart, the knob in the shape of a flame. Decorated with floral letter 'W' and scattered flowers in various colours. The handle is shaped as a ribbon tied around the cup. The saucer has a *trembleuse*, h. 13 cm. Sceptre mark. Berlin, Germany, beginning of 19th century
Kunstindustrimuseet, Copenhagen (B4/1920)

197
Cup and saucer
Porcelain. The cup is shaped as a pink rose, the saucer as green rose leaves. Cup: h. 6 cm, saucer: diam. 14 cm. Mark of crossed swords. Meissen, Germany, mid-19th century (*ill.*)
Nationalmuseum, Dept. of Decorative Arts, Stockholm (s.n.)
EXH. *En ros är en ros, är en ros*, Kulturen, Lund 1988

198

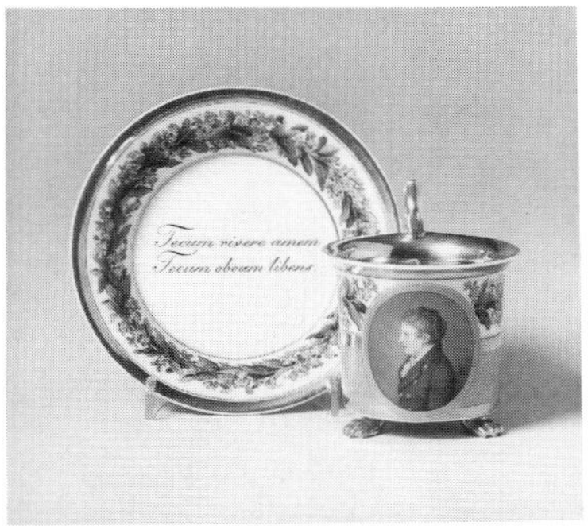

198
Cup and saucer
Porcelain. Portrait of the boy Lars Johan Hierta in profile. Decorated with forget-me-nots along the rim of cup and saucer. In the centre a text in black: 'Tecum vivere amen/Tecum obeam libens'. Cup: h. 9 cm, saucer: diam. 13 cm. Mark of crossed swords. Stamped '7'. Meissen, Germany 1817 (*ill.*)
Nationalmuseum, Dept. of Decorative Arts, Stockholm (NM4/1951)
LIT. Leif Kihlberg, *Lars Hierta i helfigur*, Stockholm 1968, pp. 80-81

199
Cup and saucer
Porcelain. Portrait of Carin E. Hierta in profile. Decorated with roses along the rim of cup and saucer. In the centre a quotation from Gustav Philip Creutz' *Atis og Camilla*. Cup: h. 9 cm, saucer: diam. 13 cm. On the reverse side an inscription: 'C. E. H. Dresde 1817'. Mark of crossed swords. Meissen, Germany 1817
Nationalmuseum, Dept. of Decorative Arts, Stockholm (NM5/1951)
LIT. See cat. no. 198

200
Plate
Porcelain. Decorated in various colours with the botanical plant *Thea Bohea*

204

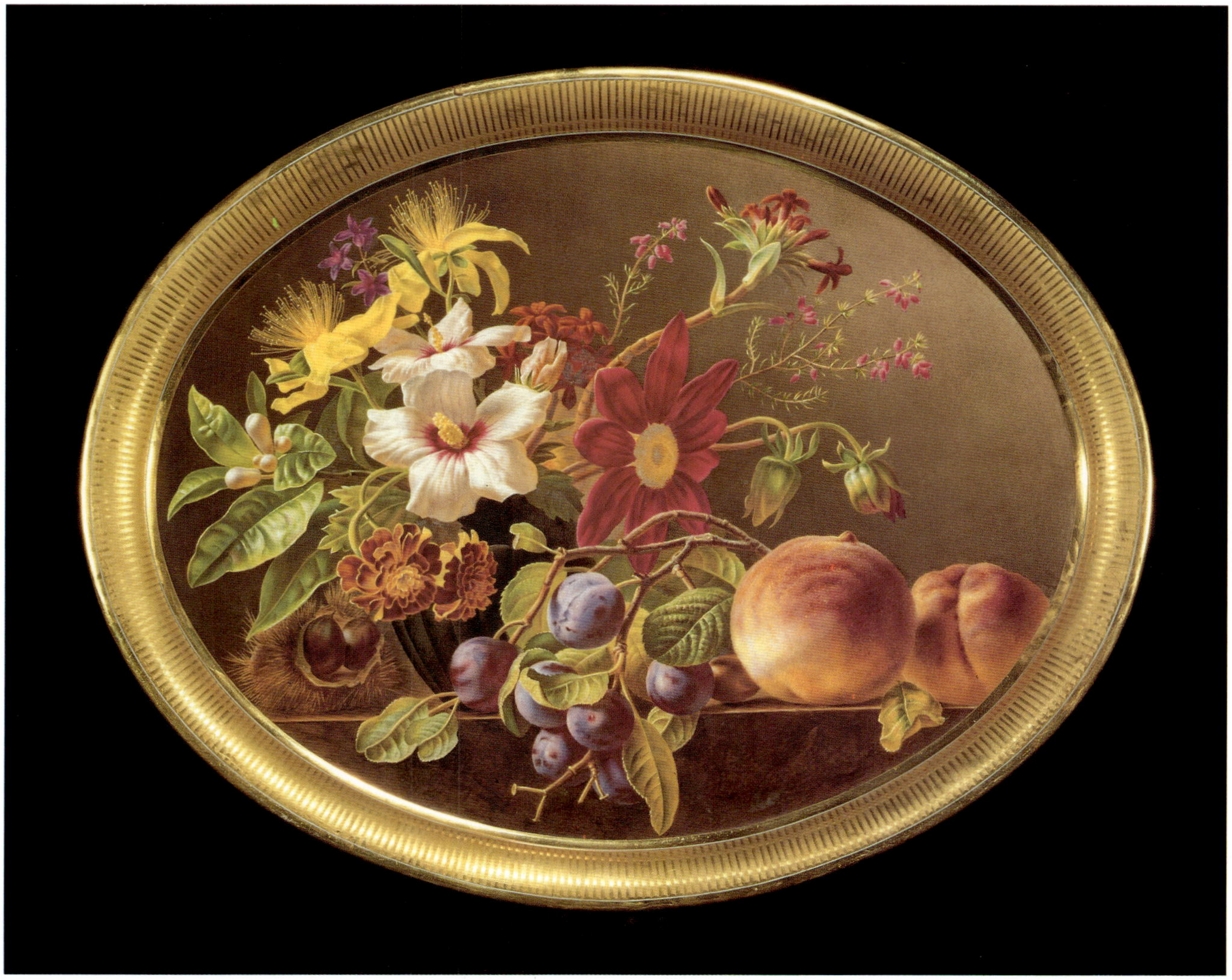

on a brown ground. The rim decorated with a double gold lining, diam. 24.5 cm. Shield mark, stamp marked '45', and date mark '803'. K.K. Wiener Porzellanmanufaktur after 1803
Private collection, Germany
LIT. Winfried Baer & H. Walter Lack, *Pflanzen auf Porzellan*, cat. Botanischer Garten und Botanisches Museum Berlin-Dahlem, Berlin 1979, p. 105, cat. no. 228

201
Plate
Porcelain. Decorated with the botanical plant *Alstroemeria pulchella* in various colours on a black-brown ground. Cream-coloured rim lined in polished gold. On the reverse painted: 'Alstroemeria pulchella,' diam. 24.2 cm. Shield mark, painter's mark '38' (Josef Wundsam), stamp mark '46' and the date mark '821'. K.K. Wiener Porzellanmanufaktur 1821 (fig. 83)
Private collection, Germany
LIT. Winfried Baer & H. Walter Lack, *Pflanzen auf Porzellan*, cat. Botanischer Garten und Botanisches Museum Berlin-Dahlem, Berlin 1979, p. 104 ff.

202
Easter egg
Porcelain decorated in various colours with flower basket and watering can in a landscape. Top and bottom painted with gold, h. 7.7 cm. The Imperial Porcelain Manufactory, St. Petersburg, Russia ca. 1820
Nationalmuseum, Dept. of Decorative Arts, Stockholm (NM214/1984)
EXH. *Aron Andersson Collection*, Nationalmuseum, Stockholm, no. 176

203
Plate
Porcelain decorated in various colours with botanical plant *Rosa Linnea* DC lined with polished gold. The rim is decorated with a stylized, matt gilded leaf design, diam. 23 cm. Sign. below the plant 'Rozier Blanc de neige'. Marked 'Archangelski 1826' and stamped 'x'. Prince Jussupoff's Porcelain Manufactory, Arkhangelskoye 1826
Private collection, Germany
LIT. Winfried Baer & H. Walter Lack,

210

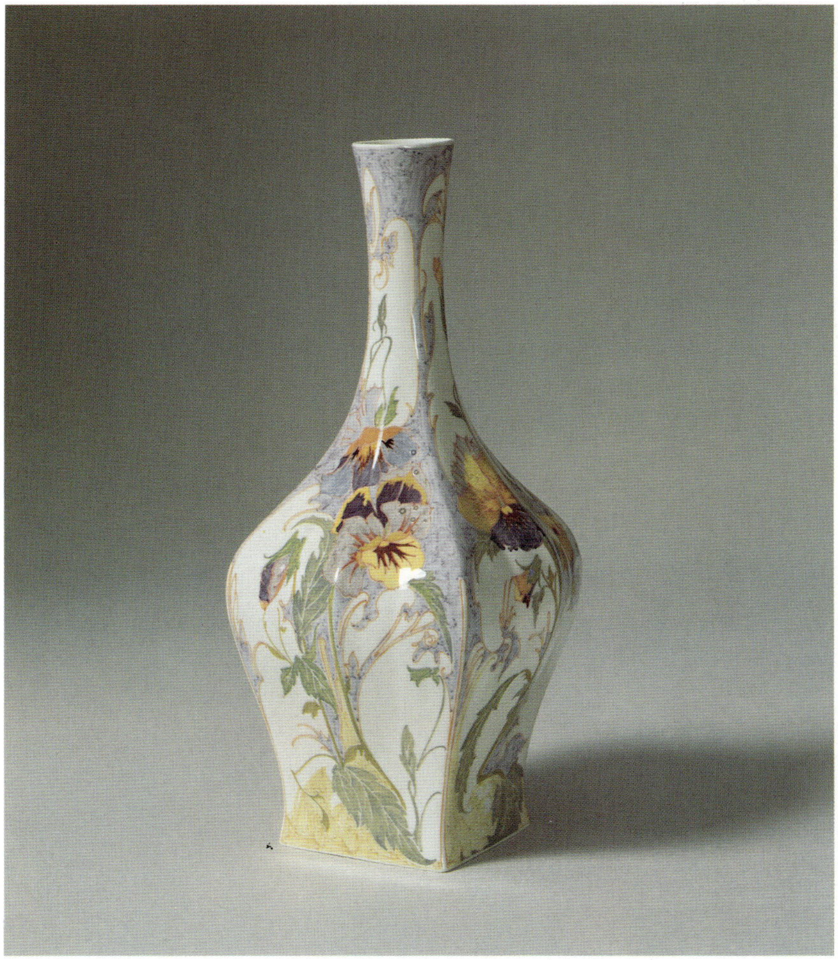

208

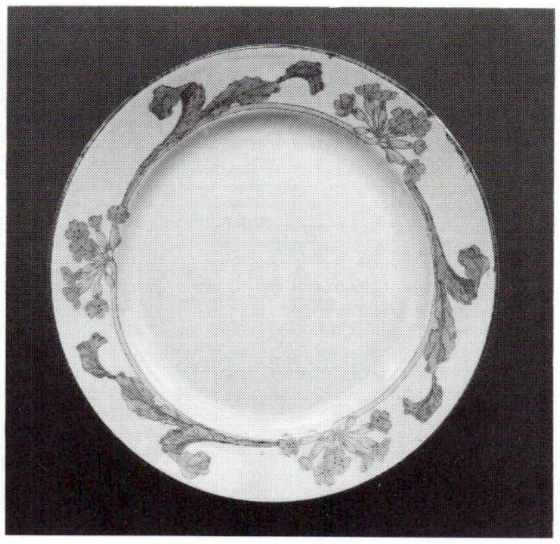

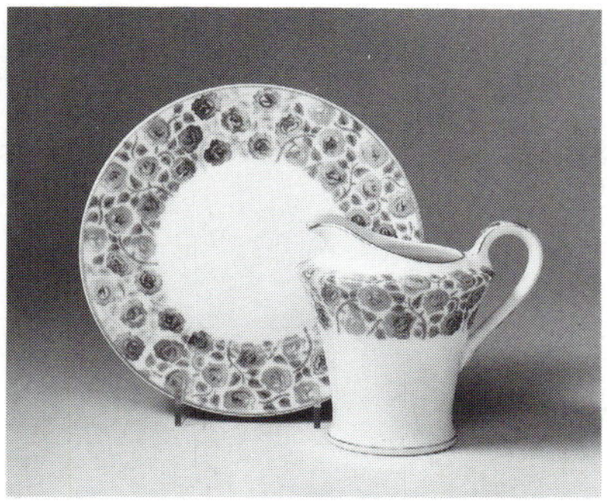

211

Pflanzen auf Porzellan, cat. Botanischer Garten und Botanisches Museum Berlin-Dahlem, Berlin 1979, p. 86 f., cat. no. 144
Original: P.-J. Redouté, *Les roses*, 18, Paris 1820

Prince Jussupoff, who was highly esteemed at Catherine the Great's court, was director general of the Imperial Porcelain Manufactory at St. Petersburg 1792-1802. In 1814, he founded his own private manufactory on his estate Arkhangelskoye north of Moscow, where he manufactured decorated services for his own use on white porcelain from Sèvres and Limoges, among others. The plate is part of a series decorated after Redouté, *Les roses*.

204
Tray
Porcelain. Decorated with a vase with flowers and fruit in various colours, w. 43.8 cm. Sèvres factory mark and 'L' as well as another engraved mark. France ca. 1830 (*ill.*)
The Royal Collections, Rosenborg Palace, Copenhagen (23-1300)

205
Cup and saucer
Porcelain decorated with multicoloured flower festoons enclosed in blue squares. Cup: h. 5 cm, saucer: diam. 13 cm. Sign. 1840 'Chateau des Tuileries' 'SV LP47' (saucer), 'SV LP40 540' (cup), Sèvres, France 1840
Nationalmuseum, Dept. of Decorative Arts, Stockholm (CXV 476)
EXH. *Porslin från Sèvres*, Nationalmuseum, Stockholm 1982, no. 133

206
Vase
Tin-glazed earthenware. White-glazed body with a large, applied yellow iris, h. 20.5 cm. Gustavsberg, Sweden 1897 (*fig. 25*)
Nationalmuseum, Dept. of Decorative Arts, Stockholm (NM28/1897)
EXH. *Gustavsberg 150 år*, Nationalmuseum, Stockholm 1975, ill. p. (IV)

207
G. Wennerberg (1863-1914)
Plate, 'Lilies of the valley'
Bone china. The rim decorated with lilies of the valley in relief painted in various colours, diam. 17.7 cm. Gustavsberg, Sweden 1897
Gustavsberg Museum, Gustavsberg
EXH. *Stockholmsutställningen 1897*;

212

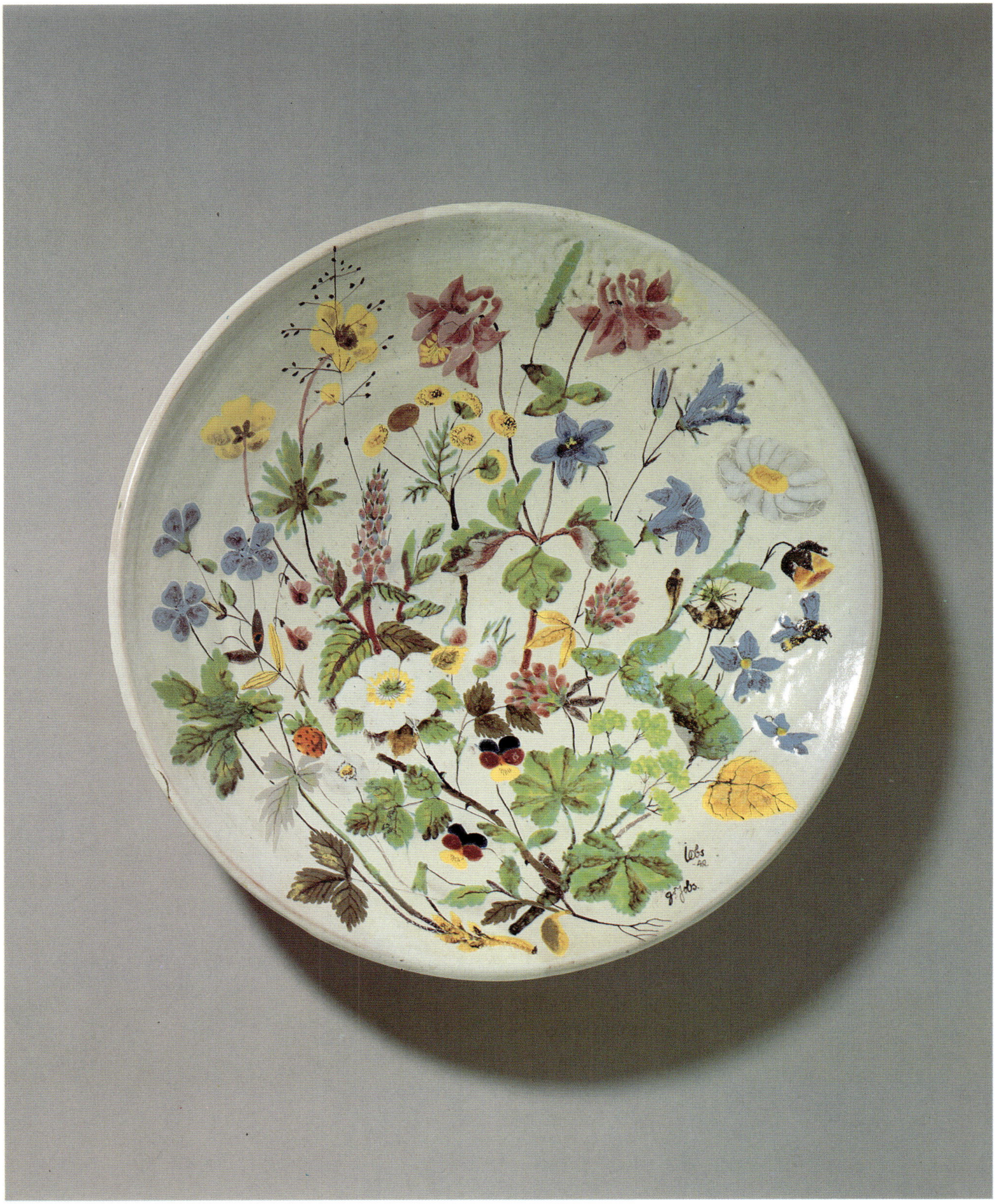

215

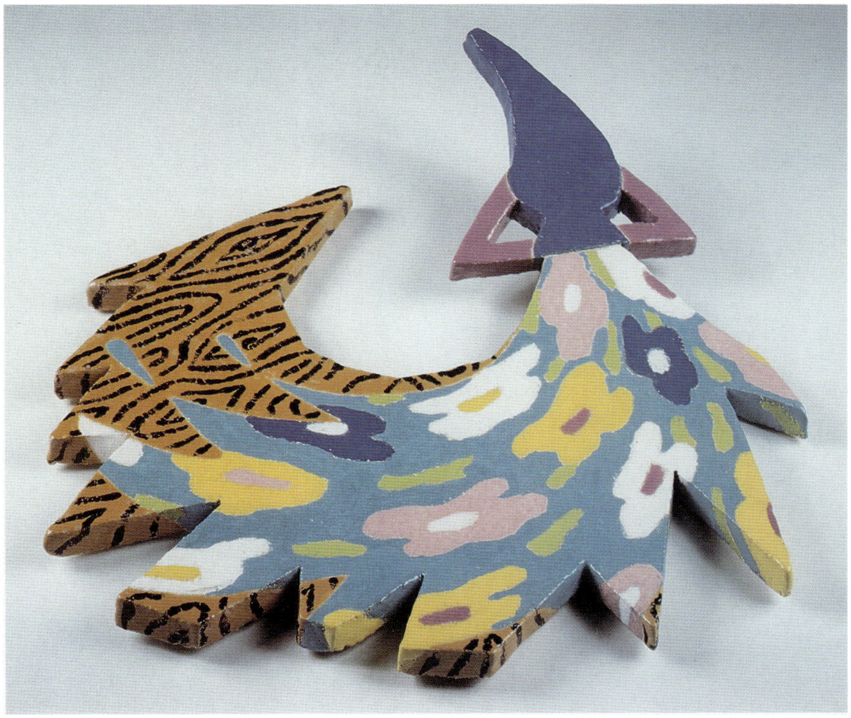

Gustavsberg 150 år, Nationalmuseum, Stockholm 1975, no. 105
LIT. Inga Arnö-Berg, *Serviser från Gustavsberg*, Västerås 1971, ill. opposite p. 65; Helena Dahlbäck Lutteman, *Svenskt porslin. Fajans, porslin och flintgods 1700-1900*, Västerås 1980, ill. p. 187; Eva Nordenson, 'Sekelskifte,' *Nationalmusei årsbok*, vol. 14, Stockholm 1967, ill. p. 25; Elisabet Stavenow-Hidemark, *Svensk Jugend*, Nordiska Museet, Stockholm, ill. p. 49

208
G. Wennerberg (1863-1914)
Plate, 'Gullvifva'
Bone china. Rim decorated with primroses partly painted and partly printed in various colours, diam. 21.5 cm. Gustavsberg, Sweden 1897 *(ill.)*
Nationalmuseum, Dept. of Decorative Arts, Stockholm (NM121/1966)
EXH. *Stockholmutställningen 1897*; *Gustavsberg 150 år*, Nationalmusem, Stockholm 1975, ill. p. (IV)
LIT. Inga Arnö-Berg, *Serviser från Gustavsberg*, Västerås 1971, ill. opposite p. 65; Helena Dahlbäck Lutteman, *Svenskt porslin. Fajans, porslin och flintgods 1700-1900*, Västerås 1980, ill. p. 187; Eva Nordenson, 'Sekelskifte,' *National-musei årsbok*, vol. 14, Stockholm 1967, ill. p. 24; Elisabet Stavenow-Hidemark, *Svensk Jugend*, Nordiska Museet, Stockholm, ill. p. 49

209
Alf Wallander (1862-1914)
Part of 'Iris' service
Chocolate pot, cup and saucer. Porcelain decorated with irises in blue, brown and pink, and with green leaves, all in low relief. Pot: h. 21.5 cm, cup: h. 7.5 cm, saucer: diam. 24 cm. Marked Rörstrand with three crowns. Rörstrand, Sweden 1897
Nationalmuseum, Dept. of Decorative Arts, Stockholm (NM871-872/1927)
LIT. Bo Lagercrantz, *Iris, Vineta och Gröna Anna. Rörstrandserviser 1860-1960*, Västerås *1960*; Helena Dahlbäck Lutteman, *Svenskt porslin. Fajans, porslin och flintgods 1700-1900*, Västerås 1980, ill. p. 186; Bengt Nyström, *Konsten til industrin. Alf Wallander och Gunnar Wennerberg som konstindustriella formgivare*, Lund 1982, ill. pp. 22, 37

210
S. Schellink (1876-1958)
Vase
Porcelain, so-called 'eggshell porcelain,' decorated with pansies in purple, yellow and green, h. 26.5 cm, diam. 12.5 cm. The form is designed by Jurriaan Kok. Marked with factory mark for Rozenburg and Schellink's mark. Rozenburg, The Hague ca. 1905 *(ill.)*
Nationalmuseum, Dept. of Decorative Arts, Stockholm (NM69/1972)

211
Jean Dufy (1888-1964)
Milk jug and small plate, 'Pivoines'
Porcelain with printed decoration of roses and leaves in blue and pink. Jug: h. 10.8 cm. Plate: diam 17.2 cm. Sign. 'Théodore Haviland/Limoges/FRANCE/Exposition des A. D./Paris 1925 Jean Dufy'. Designed for Théodore Haviland, Limoges, France for the World Exhibition in Paris 1925 *(ill.)*
Nationalmuseum, Dept. of Decorative Arts, Stockholm (NM71-72/1979)
LIT. Tamara Préaud & Serge Gauthier, *Ceramics of the Twentieth Century*, Oxford 1982, no. 79

212
Gocken Jobs (b. 1914) *and* Lisbet Jobs-Söderlund (b. 1909)
Dish
Tin-glazed earthenware decorated with wild flowers and grasses in various colours, diam. 46.5 cm. Sign. 'G Jobs-jobs 42'. Artist's workshop in Leksand, Sweden 1942 *(ill.)*
Nationalmuseum, Dept. of Decorative Arts, Stockholm (NM21/1986)
EXH. *Jobs keramik och textil*, National-museum, Stockholm 1986, no. 23

213
Pablo Rueda Lara (b. 1945)
'Sunflower'
Earthenware partly glazed in white and blue, h. 12.5 cm, diam. 36 cm. Marked with artist's signature and '79', 'HEUSDEN IX-IIX'. The Netherlands 1979
Museum Boymans-van Beuningen, Rotterdam (A5168)

214
Marco Zanini (b. 1954)
Vase with flower, 'Tanganyka'
Stoneware. The vase with matt, purple glazing. Separate flower decorated with dark blue, red and orange glazes. Total h. 53 cm, diam. at foot 32 cm. Designed for Memphis, Milan, Italy 1982
Kunstindustrimuseet, Copenhagen (134*a-b*/1984)

215
Marijke van Os (b. 1950)
Sculpture, 'Bouquet Cabalero'
Earthenware. Bouquet decorated in strong colours, h. 16.5 cm, diam. ca. 66 cm. Sign. 'M. VAN OS 1985'. The Netherlands 1985 (*ill.*)
Museum Boymans-van Beuningen, Rotterdam (A5323)

216
Marijke van Os (b. 1950)
Sculpture, 'Amphora with bouquet'
Glazed earthenware. Vase with flowers. Decorated in strong colours, h. 58 cm, w. 32 cm, diam. (foot) 12 cm. Sign. '1990 M. van Os'. The Netherlands 1990
Marijke van Os, The Hague

217
Jan van der Vaart (b. 1931)
Tulip pyramid
Porcelain. Seven tiers. Transparent glaze, h. 93 cm, largest diam. 27 cm. Sign. 'v d Vaart 87' and wheel. The Netherlands 1987
Museum Boymans-van Beuningen, Rotterdam (A6321A-G)

218
Jan van der Vaart (b. 1931)
Tulip pyramid
Stoneware. Four tiers. Bronze-coloured glaze, h. (each part) 19 cm, w. 20 cm, dp. 20 cm. Sign. 'v. d. Vaart 89 IX, 90 3X' and wheel. The Netherlands 1989-90
Museum Boymans-van Beuningen, Rotterdam (A6324A-E)

219
Jan van der Vaart (b. 1931)
Tulip pyramid
Stoneware. Five tiers, star-shaped with seven holes. Blue glaze, h. (each part) 18.5 cm, diam. 19 cm. Sign. 'v. d. Vaart 89, v. d. Vaart 90 IX' and wheel. The Netherlands 1989-90
Museum Boymans-van Beuningen, Rotterdam (A6324A-E)

220
Janice Tchalenko (b. 1942)
Bowl and plate 'Black Rose'
Stoneware decorated with big black roses. Bowl: h. 7 cm, diam. 14 cm. Plate: diam. 27 cm. Dart Pottery, Dartington, England ca. 1988
Kunstindustrimuseet, Copenhagen (263*a-b*/1989)
LIT. 'Dart Pottery – Colour from the Quarry,' *Ceramic Review*, vol. 116, 1989, p. 24 ff.

221
Janice Tchalenko (b. 1942)
Teapot and small plate
Stoneware decorated with a red, a yellow, and a blue stylized flower with green stem. Teapot: h. 15.5 cm, plate: diam. 18.7 cm. Dart Pottery, Dartington, England ca. 1988
Private collection, Copenhagen

Metal work 'Objets de vertu'

222
Wheeled spurs
Iron, gold and enamel. Decorated with enamel flowers and leaves and the front of a lion. The wheel is shaped as a five-pointed star, h. 13.5 cm, w. 8 cm. Denmark 1640s? (*fig. 94*)
The Royal Collections, Rosenborg Palace, Copenhagen (7-166)
PROV. Inv. 1696. 77 no. 17
EXH. *Christian IVs Skatte*, Rosenborg Palace (*Christian IV and Europe*, Steffen Heiberg ed.), Copenhagen 1988, cat. no. 585
LIT. Jørgen Hein, 'Goldemail,' *Kunst & Antiquitäten*, 1988, no. 2

223
Almanac
Paper on cylinder of enamelled gold. Coloured flowers on a white ground. The handle of the roller in the shape of a forget-me-not, h. 3.2 cm, w. 1.7 cm. Title: *Almanach Curieux Pour l'Année 1647 De l'Imprimerie de Thomas la Carriere, ruë S.Iacq.près S.Yuce.* France 1647 (*fig. 94*)
The Royal Collections, Rosenborg Palace, Copenhagen (3-97)
PROV. Inv. 1696, 50 no. 9
EXH. *Trésors des Rois de Danemark*, Petit Palais, Paris 1978, no. 26; *Christian IVs Skatte*, Rosenborg Palace (*Christian IV and Europe*, Steffen Heiberg ed.), Copenhagen 1988, cat. no. 721
LIT. Jørgen Hein, 'Goldemail,' *Kunst & Antiquitäten*, 1988, no. 2

224
Princess Magdalene Sibylla's gold pitcher
Gold studded with rubies and diamonds on lid and foot. Pear shaped body. Bossed and scalloped six-foil foot and cover. Handle with cast herma, and thumbpiece of a cast work satyr's mask. Engraved flowers, among others: tulips and carnations. Under the spout, an engraving with Princess Magdalene Sibylla's crowned monogram flanked by the date 1650, h. 24.7 cm. Under the base, engraved '248,' 'C' [?] and 'TA 744'. Denmark ca. 1650 (*fig. 95*)
Kunstindustrimuseet, Copenhagen (715/1962)
EXH. *Christian IVs Skatte*, Rosenborg Palace. (*Christian IV and Europe*, Steffen Heiberg ed.), Copenhagen 1988, cat. no. 723
LIT. Erik Lassen, 'En dansk prinsesses guldkande,' *Det danske Kunstindustrimuseum. Virksomhed 1959-1964*, Copenhagen 1964, pp. 41-47

In 1634, Princess Magdalene Sibylla was married to King Christian IV's son, the prince elect. After the prince's death, she remarried in 1652 and left Denmark.

225
Sophie Amalie's hunting sword
With two knives, scabbard and sword

226

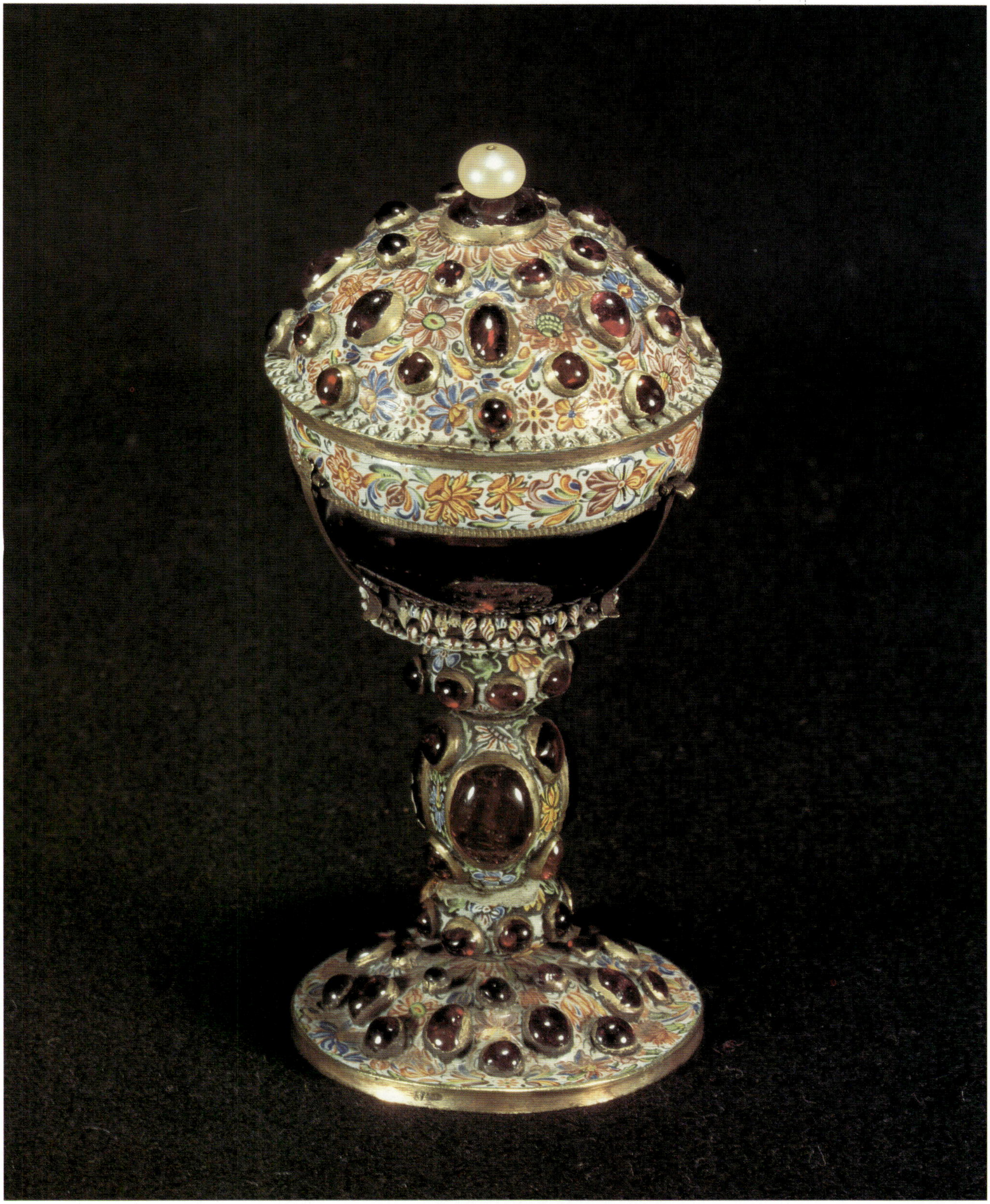

238

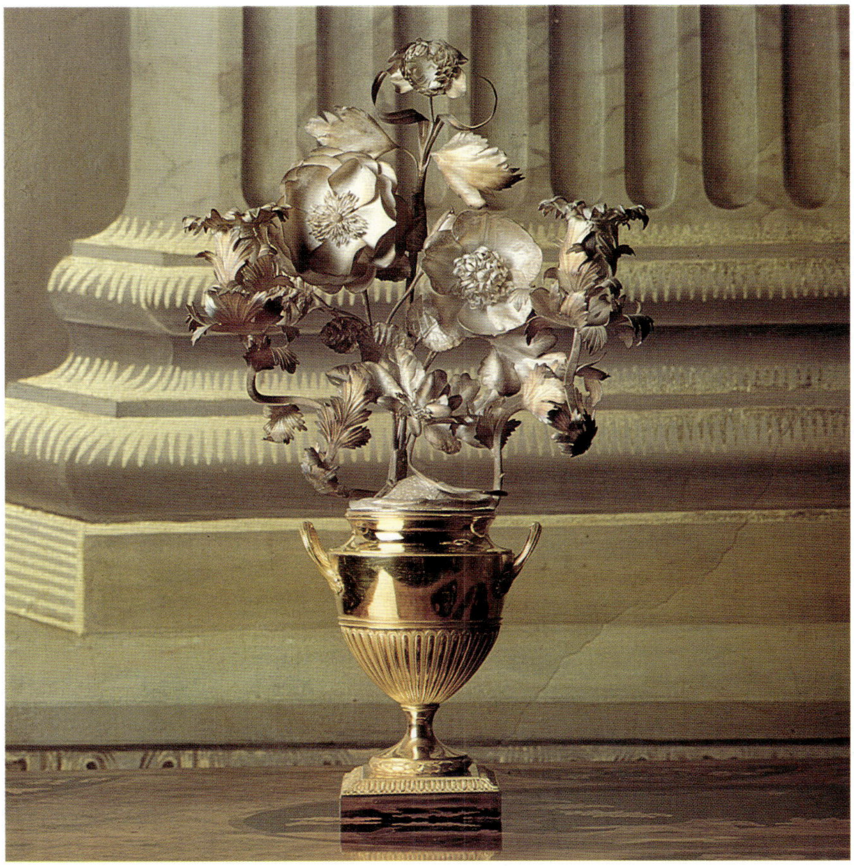

239

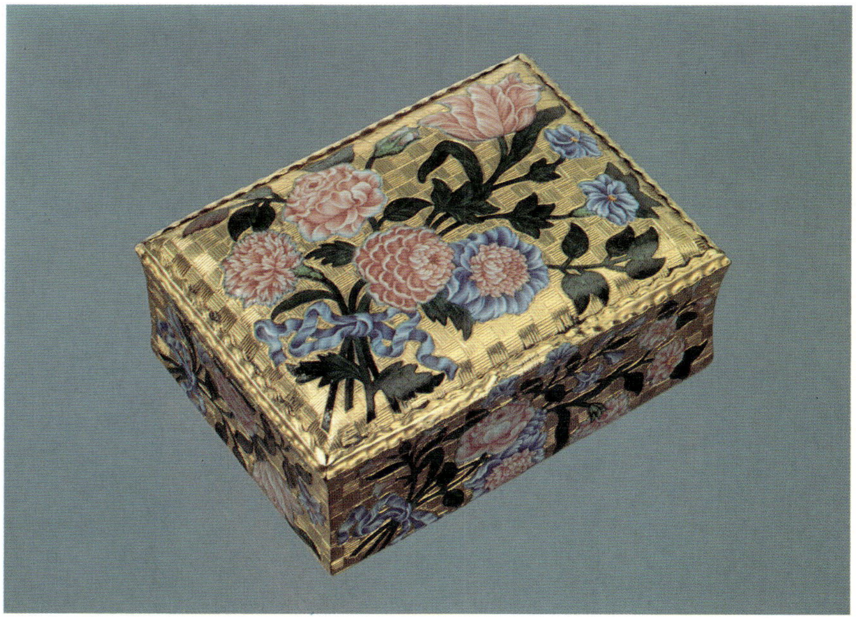

belt. Steel, gold, enamel, rhinoceros horn and leather. The leather scabbard is mounted with a locket and chape of gold with multicoloured flower enamel and with crowned initials SA in palm branches. Total l. 76.6 cm. The blade is sign. with three stamped double crosses as well as with a mark with two crossed swords. Northern Europe (Copenhagen/Hamburg) ca. 1650 (*fig. 94*)

The Royal Collections, Rosenborg Palace, Copenhagen (7.219*a-b*)

PROV. Inv. 1696. 76.5

EXH. *Trésors des Rois de Danemark*, Petit Palais, Paris 1978, cat. no. 70; *Sophie Amalie*, Rosenborg Palace, Copenhagen 1986, cat. no. 192

LIT. A. Hoff, H. D. Schepelern & Gudmund Boesen, *Royal Arms at Rosenborg*, Copenhagen 1956, no. 28

226

Dionysio Miseroni (1607-1661) *and* Hanns Reinhardt Taravell

Cup and cover

Garnets set in enamelled gold with multicoloured flowers on a white ground, ornamented with garnets and pearls, h. 10.7 cm, w. 5.3 cm. Bowl of cup, probably an antique garnet, cut by Dionysio Miseroni in Prague. The setting is probably made by Hanns Reinhardt Taravell. Prague ca. 1650-55 (*ill.*)

The Royal Collections, Rosenborg Palace, Copenhagen (5-241)

PROV. Inv. 1718. 51.8

EXH. *Trésors des Rois de Danemark*, Petit Palais, Paris 1978, cat. no. 57

LIT. R. Distelberger, 'Dionysio und Ferdinand Eusebio Miseroni,' *Jahrbuch der Kunsthistorischen Sammlungen in Wien*, vol. 75, Vienna 1979, p. 139

227

Paul Prieur (1620-1682?)

Walking stick

Narwhal tusk. Knob and chape of enamelled gold with multicoloured flowers set with rubies, l. 103.6 cm. The narwhal tusk was turned by Bendix Grodtschilling. Ca. 1663 (*fig. 94*)

The Royal Collections, Rosenborg Palace, Copenhagen (7-217)

233

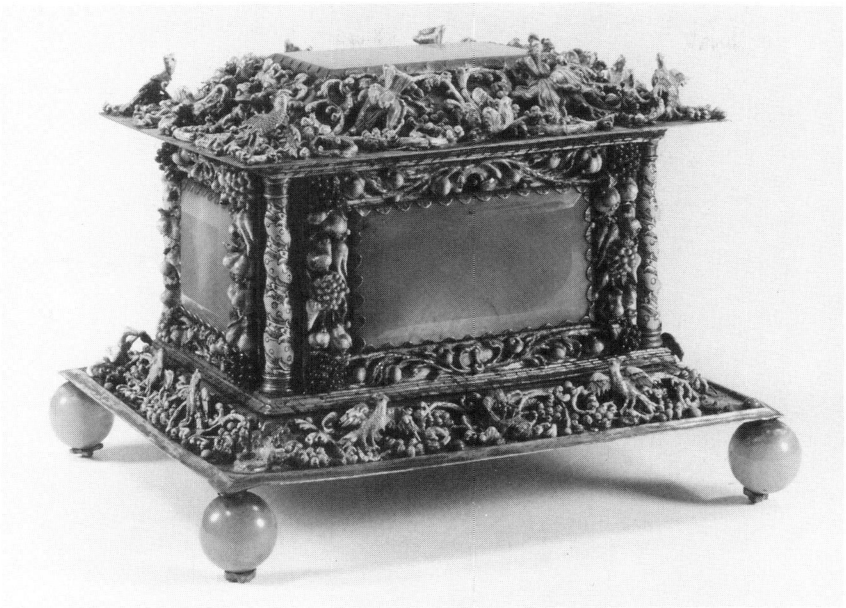

234

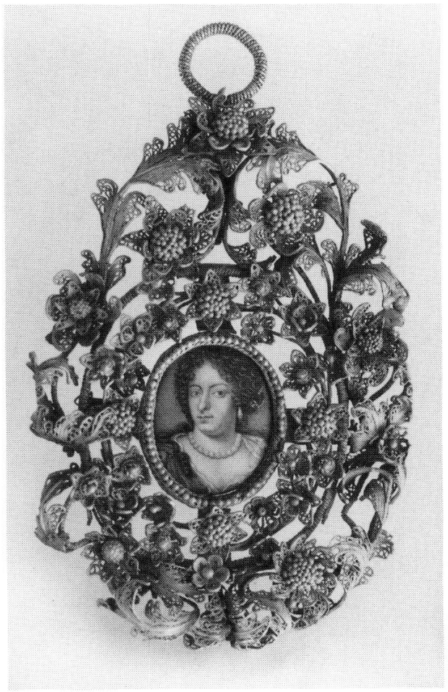

PROV. Green Cabinet, no. 27, 1696
EXH. *Sophie Amalie*, Rosenborg, Copenhagen 1986, cat. no. 197
LIT. Mogens Bencard, 'Enhjørninger, narhvaler og gamle grønlændere,' *Museerne i Viborg Amt*, vol. 13, 1985, pp. 115-116

228
D. van Werckhoven (d. 1692)
Two candlesticks
Silver. Domed foot, twisted shaft with strong bead. Chased and embossed flower motifs, h. ca. 32 cm, diam. (foot) 22.5 cm. Leiden, the Netherlands 1668
Museum Boymans-van Beuningen, Rotterdam (MBZ294, 295)
EXH. *Leids Zilver*, Stedelijk Museum De Lakenhal, Leiden 1977, p. 164, no. 24

229
Nécessaire
Gold. Flowers in openwork. Containing clasp knife, a pair of compasses, pince-nez, scissors, writing blades (ivory) and pencil holder. Engraved flowers on scissors and knife, h. 9.2 cm. Ca. 1675
The Royal Collections, Rosenborg Palace, Copenhagen (13-183)
PROV. Acquired in 1859 from the Regalia Chamber. Mentioned in the inventory list of the Chamber in 1784

230
Wolfgang Spitzenberg
Bowl
Silver. Chased and embossed flower decoration. Under base, the letters 'M' and 'S' engraved in monogram, h. 9.5 cm, diam. 15.5 cm. Maker's mark and hallmark for Hamburg. Germany ca. 1675
Kunstindustrimuseet, Copenhagen (A105/1915)

231
Two vases with covers
Silver filigree. Stylized flowers and leaves partly in relief, h. 15 cm and 15.5 cm respectively. Denmark 1675-1700?
The Royal Collections, Rosenborg Palace, Copenhagen (12-192, 12-196)
PROV. Acquired 1783 from the estate of Princess Charlotte Amalie (lit. o no. 225). Part of a set of vases to be placed on a cabinet. Charlotte Amalie (1706-1783) may have inherited the set from her mother, King Frederik IV's Queen, Louise (d. 1720) or from her grandmother, King Christian V's Queen, Charlotte Amalie (d. 1714).

232
Jørgen Goldschmidt (mentioned 1674-94)
Covered bowl
Silver. Chased and embossed with flowers. In the centre of the cover an oval panel with the engraved face-to-face monogram 'CA' (?), flanked by '1683' and framed by two bundled flower branches. The interior of the cover decorated with the pricked face-to-face monogram 'OM' flanked by 'Anno 1741' and below '50Ld'. Cast handles, h. 12.6 cm, l. incl. handles 30.5 cm. Maker's mark and Copenhagen hallmark 16- (possibly 1680)
Kunstindustrimuseet, Copenhagen (17/1964)
LIT. Erik Lassen, *Dansk Sølv*, Copenha-

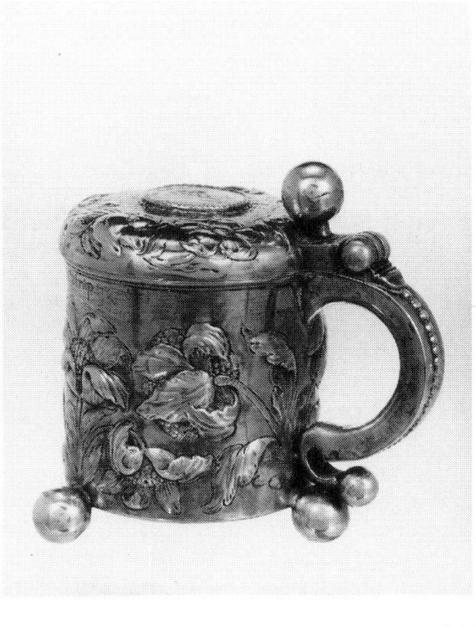

237

241

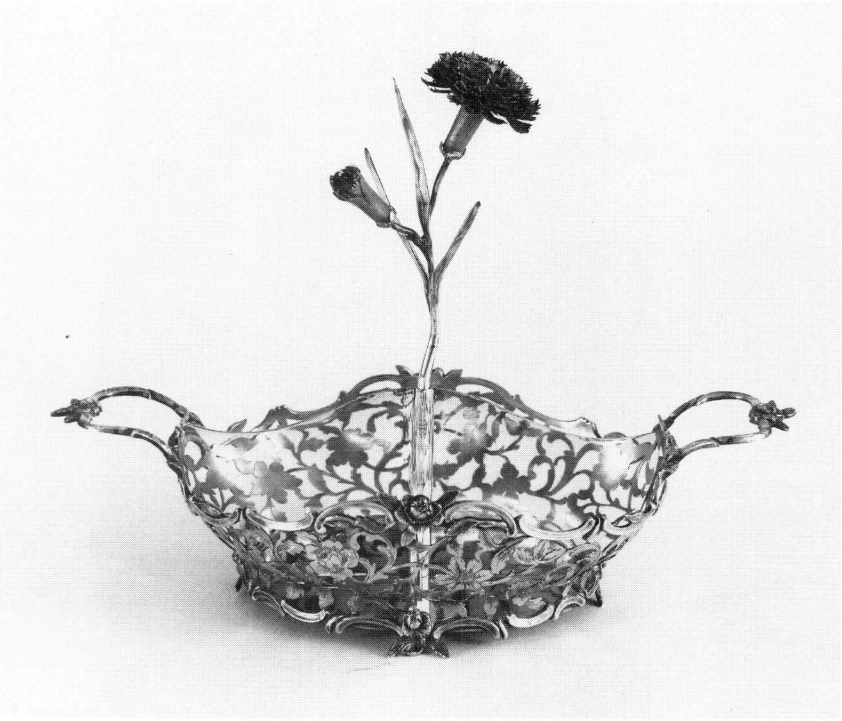

gen 1964, fig. 80-81; *Konsul George Jorck og hustru Emma Jorck's Fonds beretning 1963-67*, pp. 28-29 (ill.)

233
Hans Jakob Mair (1641/64-1718)
Box
Gilt silver and agate set with semiprecious stones and enamelled flowers in various colours, 20.1 cm. Maker's mark and hallmark for Augsburg. Germany ca. 1680 (*ill.*)
The Royal Collections, Rosenborg Palace, Copenhagen (5-215)
PROV. Inv. 1797.71.1 (Acquired from the estate of Princess Charlotte Amalie, 1783)

234
Pierre Signac (ca. 1624-1684)
Ulrika Eleonora
Enamel miniature in silver filigree frame with applied flowers and leaves. Frame: h. 14.5 cm, w. 9.8 cm. ca. 1680 (*ill.*)
The Royal Collections, Rosenborg Palace, Copenhagen (6-599)

235
Johan Hieronimus Weischer (ca. 1645-1705)
Covered box
Silver. Chased flower festoon. Cover decorated with leaves surrounding a rosette. Initials 'B. M. A. D.' engraved, h. 6.4 cm, diam. 7.9 cm. Hallmark for Viborg and maker's mark. Denmark ca. 1680-90
Kunstindustrimuseet, Copenhagen (3/1949)
PROV. Manor St. Restrup, Jutland

236
Sacharias du Vignon
Dish
Silver. Round with flowers in relief, including tulips, diam. 34.4 cm. Sign. with 'rampant lion', and maker's mark and Rotterdam hallmark for 1687. On reverse, inscription 'Dit.is.de.kerc-ke.schotel. van poortegal. 1687'. Rotterdam, the Netherlands 1687
Museum Boymans-van Beuningen, Rotterdam (BZ25)
EXH. *Oude kerkelijke kunst*, s'-Hertogenbosch 1913, cat. no. 672; *Vier eeuwen Nederlands zilver*, Gemeentemuseum The Hague 1952, cat. no. 434; *Meesters in zilver*, Rotterdams Historisch Museum, Rotterdam 1966, cat. no. 32

237
Mogens Thommesen Løwenhertz (ca. 1669-1734)
Tankard on three globular feet
Silver. Moulded handle with globular tumbler. Chased flower decoration. The cover is decorated with a Danish coin from 1691. Interior silver gilt, h. 13 cm. Sign. with monogram 'MTL'. Horsens, Denmark ca. 1700 (*ill.*)
Kunstindustrimuseet, Copenhagen (B147/1910)

238
Vase with flowers
Silver flowers in a silver gilt vase, h. 49 cm, w. 42 cm. Italy end of 17th century; vase, late 18th century (*ill.*)
Burghley House, Stamford, England
PROV. Mentioned in inventory list 1688 in 'my ladyes closett'

239
Jacob Henriksen a Møinichen (ca. 1722-1788)
Snuffbox
Gold. Bouquets of roses, carnations and tulips in red, white and blue enamel on gold ground imitating basketwork, h. 3 cm, l. 6.4 cm, w. 4.6 cm. Sign. with Copenhagen hallmark for 1758, and maker's mark IM 1754 (*ill.*)
Kunstindustrimuseet, Copenhagen (21/1954)
LIT. Erik Zahle, 'To danske gulddåser og andre pretiosa,' *Det danske Kunstindustrimuseum. Virksomhed 1949-1954*, Copenhagen 1956, pp. 27-35

240
Perfume bottle
Enamel. Stopper and furnishings of gilt bronze. Woman with flower in hand sitting in a landscape with ruins, h. 7.5 cm. Copenhagen ca. 1780
Kunstindustrimuseet, Copenhagen (A58/1910)

241
Arnoldus Warneke van Amersfoort (1744-after 1795)
Basket
Silver. Openwork with engraved and applied flowers. Across the basket is a strap to which a carnation is attached, h. 17 cm, w. 22.8 cm, dp. 11.8 cm. Sign. with date mark and 'L'. Amster-

dam, the Netherlands 1770 (*ill.*)
Museum Boymans-van Beuningen, Rotterdam (MBZ 74)
LIT. K. A. Citroen, *Amsterdamse zilversmeden*, Amsterdam, no. 77

242
Christian Werum (ca. 1735-1792)
Tea service: tea urn, pot and sugar bowl
Silver with chased flower decoration. The knobs in the shape of flowers. Tea urn: h. 33 cm, l. 23 cm, w. 19 cm. Teapot: h. 17 cm, w. 10.5 cm, l. 19 cm. Sugar bowl: h. 8.5 cm, w. 13.8 cm, l. 23.5 cm. Sign. with maker's mark and Copenhagen hallmark for 1771
Kunstindustrimuseet, Copenhagen (92*a-c*/1987)

243
Rebeccah Emes and Edward Barnard (in apprenticeship 1781, d. ca. 1853-55)
Teapot
Silver, 'Indian Style.' Chased and punched flower motif. Knob shaped as a flower, h. 15.5 cm, l. 29 cm, w. 19 cm. Maker's mark, 'Lion Passant', 'Leopard's Head', 'King's Head', and date mark. London 1827-28
Kunstindustrimuseet, Copenhagen (85/1987)

244
Jules-Paul Brateau (1844-1923)
Cup with tray, 'Le Trèfle' (trefoil)
Pewter. Flowering trefoil in relief on punched ground. Below the rim of the cup 'Numero Deus Impare Gaudet' (Virgil, *Bucolica*, VIII, 75). Cup: h. 17.2 cm, tray: diam. 19.5 cm. Marked with Jules Brateaus' mark. Paris 1887
Kunstindustrimuseet, Copenhagen (862,866)

245
Frans Zwollo (1872-1945)
Cup
Silver. Lilies of the valley with leaves. Chased, embossed and engraved, h. 16.5 cm, diam. 11 cm. Marked '1898 F. Zwollo Fec.', 'rampant lion', Minerva Head, date mark, 'H', maker's mark. Amsterdam 1898
Museum Boymans-van Beuningen, Rotterdam (MBZ114F)
EXH. *F. Zwollo*, The Hague 1932; *De tijd wisselt van spoor*, Singer Museum, Laren 1932, cat. no. 5; *Frans Zwollo sr en zijn tijd*, Museum Boymans-van Beuningen, Rotterdam 1982, cat. no. 5 (travelling exh.)
LIT. W. Koonings, *19de eeuws zilver*, Zeist 1964, fig. 50

246
Lucien Bonvallet (1861-1919)
Candelabrum
Silver. Shaped as a stylized plant, h. 38 cm. Sign. 'CARDEILHAC PARIS', Cardeilhac's mark and 'Mercury Head 1'. Made by Cardeilhac, Paris ca. 1900
Kunstindustrimuseet, Copenhagen (882)
PROV. Acquired at the World Exhibition in Paris 1900
LIT. Pietro Krohn (et al.), *Det danske Kunstindustrimuseum. De første fem Aars Virksomhed*, Copenhagen 1901, p. 10, fig. 9

247
Lucien Bonvallet (1861-1919)
Sugar bowl with lid and spoon
Silver. Thistles soldered and engraved. Flowers in ivory, h. 19 cm, diam. 15.5 cm. Spoon: l. 18.3 cm. Sign. 'CARDHEILHAC PARIS', Cardeilhac's mark, 'Minerva Head 1', stamped with 'Mercury Head 1'. Paris ca. 1900
Kunstindustrimuseet, Copenhagen (878)
LIT. Pietro Krohn (et al.), *Det danske Kunstindustrimuseum. De første fem Aars Virksomhed*, Copenhagen 1901, p. 9, fig. 8

248
Lucien Gaillard (b. 1861)
Frame
Silver. Etched with hemlock motif, h. 17.8 cm, w. 13.5 cm. Paris, France ca. 1900
Kunstindustrimuseet, Copenhagen (885)
PROV. Acquired at the World Exhibition in Paris 1900

249
Hans Stoltenberg-Lerche (1867-1920)
Ewer
Pewter. Tulips in high relief. Handle in the shape of stems and leaves, h. 20.5 cm, w. 24 cm. Stamped '33 KAYSERZINN 4220'. Made after model from 1898 at Kayserzinn, Krefeld-Cologne, Germany ca. 1900
Kunstindustrimuseet, Copenhagen (852)

262

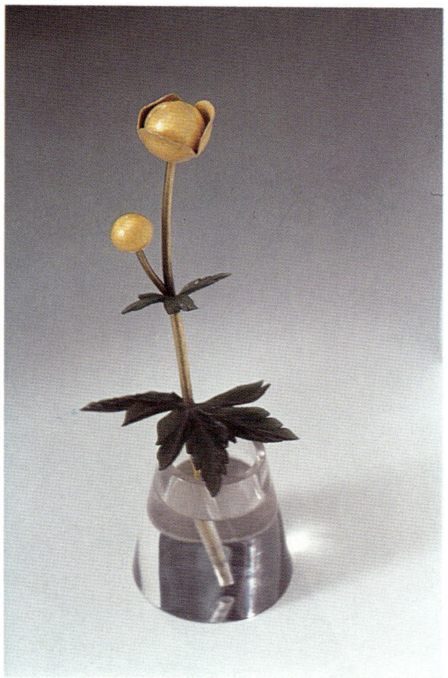

PROV. Acquired at the World Exhibition in Paris 1900

Furniture

250
Table
Gilded wood. Top made of scagliola with flowers and plants, w. 131.5 cm, dp. 67 cm. Denmark 1660s
The Royal Collections, Rosenborg Palace, Copenhagen (6-8)
PROV. Inv. 1718.5.23.
The stand possibly older than the top, which may have been rescued from the fire at Sophie Amalienborg Palace, 1689

251
Tea table
Oak veneered with maple. Four twisted legs on ball feet connected with crosses. Top in the shape of a tray. Inlaid flowers (roses, carnations, etc.,) with branches and leaves of green-painted bone, h. 74.5 cm, w. 82 cm, dp. 57.5 cm. Denmark or the Netherlands end of 17th century
The Royal Collections, Rosenborg Palace, Copenhagen (9-113)
LIT. Peter Thornton, *Seventeenth*

258

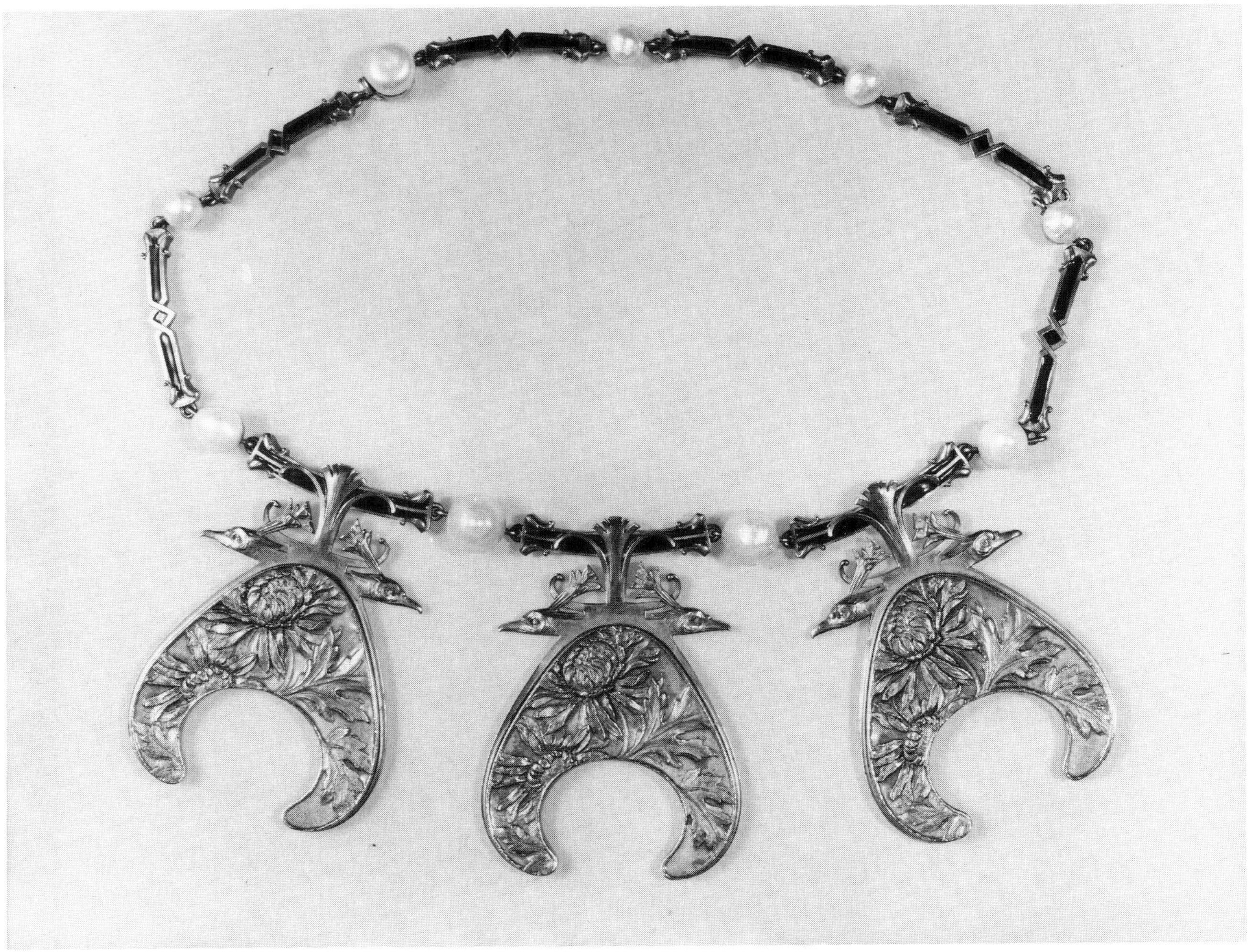

260

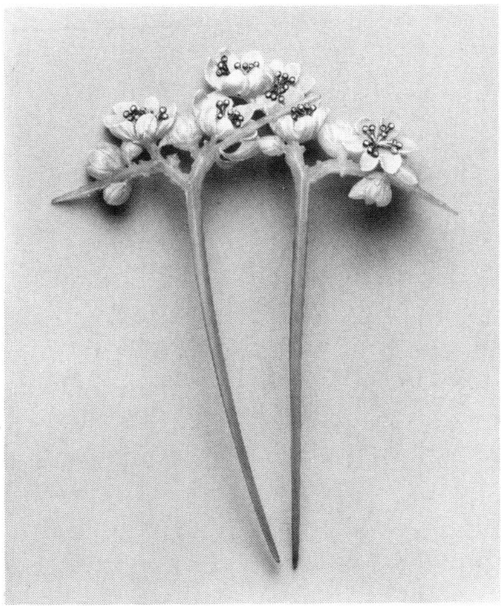

Century Interior Decoration in England, France, and Holland, New Haven/London 1978, p. 230

The table was either made in Copenhagen by a Dutch furniture maker or imported from the Netherlands.

252
Tulip cabinet
Ebony veneered onto oak and cedar. The exterior of the cabinet doors decorated with inlaid tulips in mother-of-pearl. The interior decorated with tulips painted in oil, h. 183 cm, w. 132/122 cm, dp. 42 cm. The Netherlands second half of 17th century (*fig. 48*)
Museum Boymans-van Beuningen, Rotterdam (*Div.*M 17)

The drawers decorated with tulips may have contained tulip bulbs, which were considered an investment, especially in the 1620s.

253
Marie Krøyer (1867-1940)
Sofa
Stained pinewood decorated with sunflowers, ribbons and bows in poker work. The cushion made of leather, h. 86.5 cm, l. 122 cm, dp. 55 cm. Part of a set consisting of a sofa, two arm chairs, a table and a stool. The stool is sign. 'Marie Krøyer fec. 1899'. The Skaw, Denmark possibly 1899
Nationalmuseet, Brede (1225/1984)
EXH. *1880-erne i nordisk maleri*, Statens Museum for Kunst (not in catalogue), Copenhagen 1986; *P. S. Krøyers*

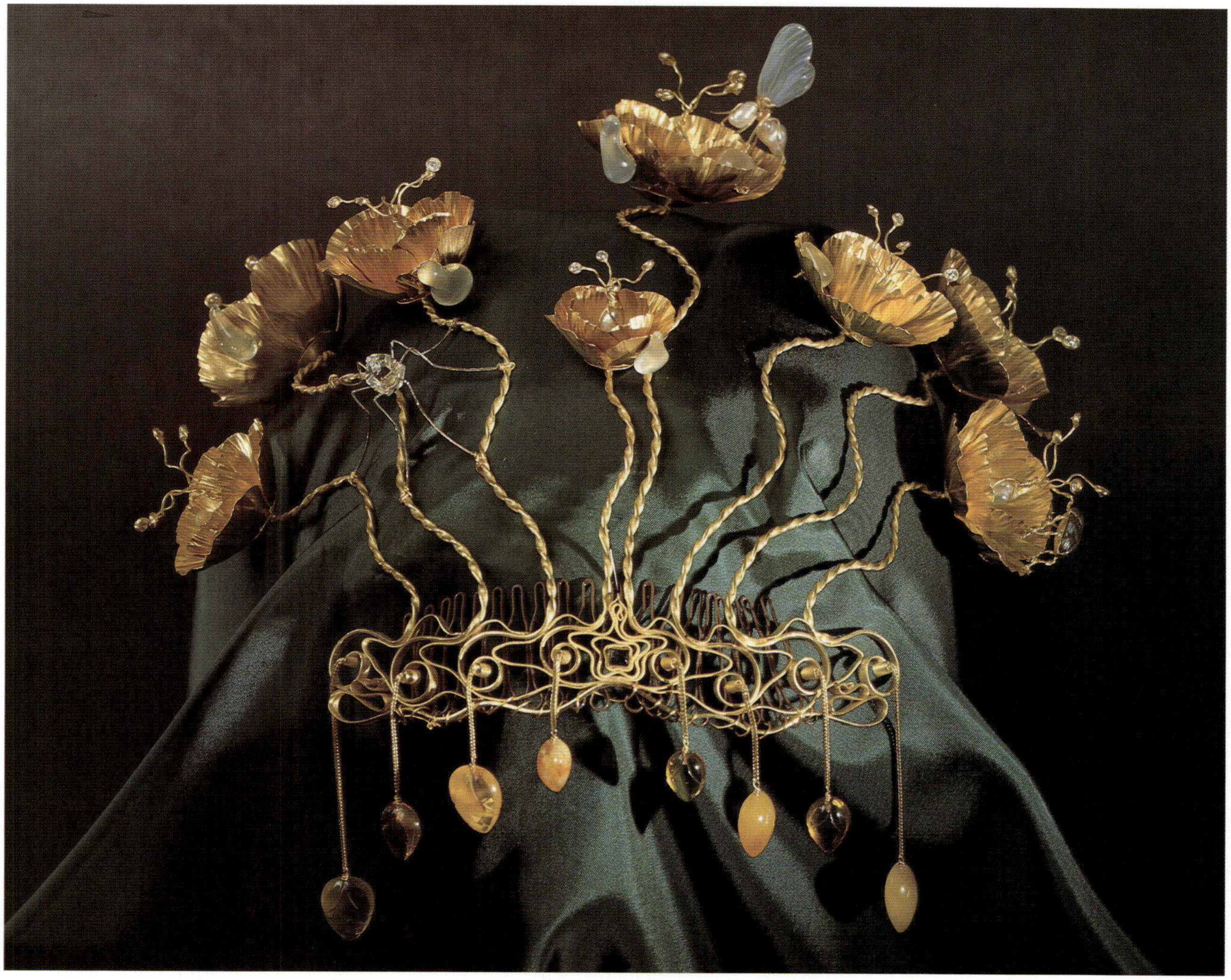

fotografier, The Hirschsprung Collection, Copenhagen and the Skaw Museum 1990

In 1894, the Danish painter P. S. Krøyer, assisted by the architect Ulrik Plesner set up a summer house in the Skaw Plantation. He and his wife, the painter Marie Krøyer, tastefully decorated the home and designed a suite of furniture in 1898-99 consisting of a rigid sofa, two square and one semicircular chairs – all with tall backs and leather cushions – as well as a stool and a table.

Marie Krøyer was particularly interested in the Arts and Crafts Movement. The furniture is inspired by English furniture from that period, especially Charles Rennie Mackintosh's designs, which could be studied in the magazine *The Studio*. Marie Krøyer's furniture is decorated with summer plants and flowers dominated by sunflowers.

254
Émile Gallé (1846-1904)
Ladies writing desk, 'Bureau Pensée' (Pensée: Heartsease)
Walnut inlaid with walnut burrwood, palisander, ebony, mahogany, maple, and exotic wood. Decorated with heartseases. The bronze knobs shaped as heartseases. Sign. in inlaid wood 'Gallé Exposn 1900', h. 108 cm, w. 72 cm, dp. 52 cm. Nancy, France 1900 (*fig. 51*)
Kunstindustrimuseet, Copenhagen (1023)

PROV. Acquired at the World Exhibition in Paris 1900

255
Louis Majorelle (1859-1926)
Chair
Pinewood veneer, legs and uprights to the back made of walnut. The forelegs and the uprights to the back are in the shape of flower stems with finials in the shape of poppy capsules. The seat and back are upholstered in leather decorated with carved and printed pattern of poppies, h. 102 cm, w. 38 cm, dp. 38 cm, h. of seat 48 cm. Nancy, France ca. 1900 (*fig. 26*)
Kunstindustrimuseet, Copenhagen (31/1965)

266

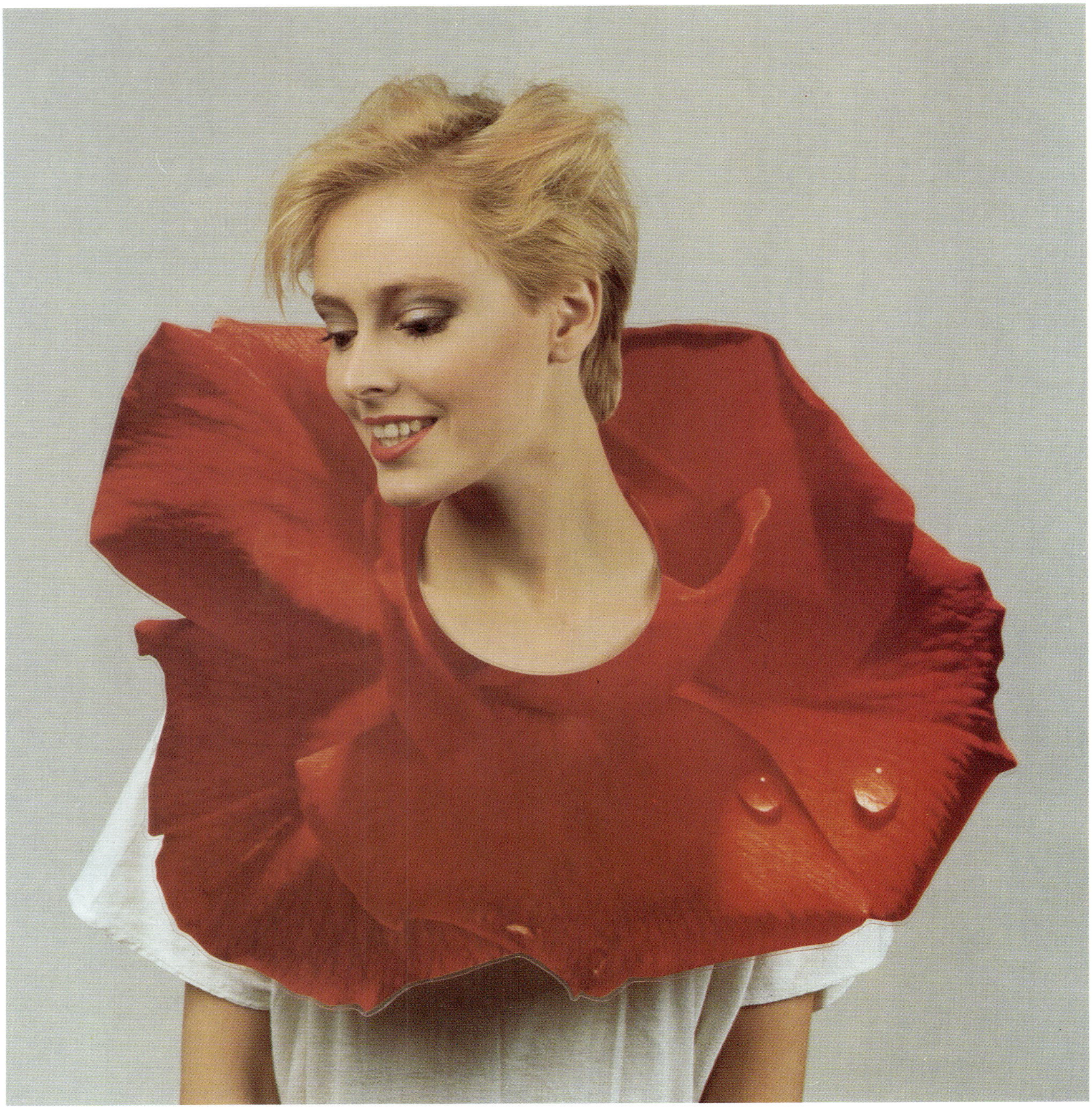

Jewellery

256
Pendant, cameo with Noah's Ark
Onyx carved with the embarkation of Noah's Ark. Mounted in gold. On the reverse, in champlevé enamel polychrome flowers as well as a crowned 'K' for Kirsten Munk, h. 3.7 cm, w. 4.9 cm. Attributed to Alessandro Masnago or his workshop, Milan ca. 1575, the mounting in Denmark ca. 1640 (*fig. 94*)
The Royal Collections, Rosenborg Palace, Copenhagen (3-123)
PROV. Inv. 1718.43.9
EXH. *Sophie Amalie*, Rosenborg, Copenhagen 1986, cat. no. 166; *Christian* IV*s skatte*, Rosenborg (*Christian* IV *and Europe*, Steffen Heiberg, ed.), Copenhagen 1988, cat. no. 629

257
Portrait cameo of Emperor Ferdinand III *(1637-1657)*
Ivory on conch shell, gold and enamelled flowers, h. 3.1 cm, w. 2.2 cm. Inscription on reverse side: 'FERDI ROM IMP SE AVGE HUN BO REX'. After a medal by George Schweigger ca. 1650, artist unknown.
The Royal Collections, Rosenborg Palace, Copenhagen (3-132)
PROV. Mentioned in the estate of Princess Sophie Hedevig 1735
EXH. *Christian* IV*s skatte*, Rosenborg, (*Christian* IV *and Europe*, Steffen Heiberg, ed.), Copenhagen 1988, cat. no. 615

258
René Lalique (1860-1945)
Necklace, 'Chrysanthèmes'
Gold, enamel and pearls. Three pendants with chrysanthemums in relief, cast and chased on a light green enamel ground, h. 6 cm, l. 38.2 cm. Sign. 'LALIQUE'. Paris ca. 1897-99 (*ill.*)
Musée des Arts Décoratifs, Paris (36254)
EXH. *L'Art de vivre*, Cooper Hewitt Museum, New York 1989
LIT. Sigrid Barten, *René Lalique. Schmuck und Objets d'art 1890-1910. Monographie und Werkkatalog*, Passau 1977, cat. 340; Y. Brunhammer, 'René Lalique,' *Administration des Monnaies et Médailles*, bull. 58, 1er trimestre 1978, ill. p. 78

259
Lucien Bonvallet (1861-1919)
Buckle
Silver. Thistle in open work with blossom of yellow bone, h. 5.5 cm, w. 9 cm. Sign. 'CARDEILHAC', Cardeilhac's mark, Minerva Head 1, Mercury Head. Paris ca. 1900
Kunstindustrimuseet, Copenhagen (886)
PROV. Acquired at the World Exhibition, Paris 1900
LIT. Pietro Krohn (et al.), *Det danske Kunstindustrimuseum. De første fem Aars Virksomhed*, Copenhagen 1901, p. 13, fig. 12

260
Lucien Gaillard (b. 1861)
Comb
Coloured horn carved with hawthorn flowers in mother-of-pearl and gold, h. 12 cm. Sign. 'L.GAILLARD'. Paris ca. 1900 (*ill.*)
Musée des Arts Décoratifs, Paris (11323)
PROV. Acquired from Lucien Gaillard at the Salon, Paris 1904

261
Edgar Bensé (d. 1923)
Brooch
Platinum and brilliants. Two big and two smaller water lily leaves and a flower, h. 8.3 cm, w. 8 cm. Paris ca. 1900
Kunstindustrimuseet, Copenhagen (B19/1933)

Edgar Bensé was a Danish goldsmith who worked in Paris.

262
Henrik Wigström (1862-1923) *and* Carl Fabergé (1846-1920)
Globe flower
Vase of rock crystal. Stem of gold, blossom and bud of translucent, yellow enamel on gold. Leaves made of nephrite, h. 14.5 cm. Marked: '72 zolotnik', Fabergé's maker's mark and workshop mark for Henrik Wigström. St. Petersburg, Russia 1908-17 (*ill.*)
Nationalmuseum, Dept. of Decorative Arts, Stockholm (NM123/1976)
EXH. *Carl Fabergé och hans samtida*, Konstindustrimuseet, Helsinki 1980, no. 58; *Carl Fabergé – Vorbild und Nachfolge*, Bayerisches Nationalmuseum, Munich 1986
LIT. Géza von Habsburg-Lothringen & A. von Solodkoff, *Fabergé. Court Jeweller to the Tsars*, Studio Vista/ Christie's, London 1979, pl. no. 109, p. 89; A. K. Snowman, *The Art of Carl Fabergé*, London (1953) 2nd rev. ed. 1962, pl. 49

During the last decades of the 19th century and until the Russian Revolution in 1917, the Russian court jeweller, Carl Fabergé, created a number of exquisite and exclusive goldsmith works and *objets d'art*. Particularly special are his flower vases with a single stem with one or more flowers or berries placed in a vase of rock crystal which is cut in such a way that the flower seems to be in water. These works are technically unique,

275

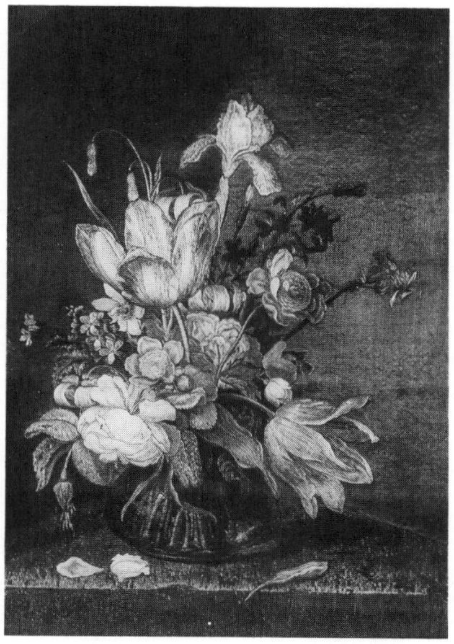

and the combination of metals, enamel, stones, pearls, etc., highly sophisticated. In his work as a goldsmith, Fabergé was inspired by the art of the past and his flowers have their origin in the 18th century. Around the turn of the century, Fabergé was also influenced by French Art Nouveau, and his interest in Japanese art is reflected in a number of flower arrangements.

263
Torben Hardenberg (b. 1949)
Necklace 'Carnivorous plant with insects'
Silver, gold and small diamonds. Blooming plant. A fly contemplating another, smaller fly being eaten, h. 8 cm, w. 9 cm. Sign. 'Hardenberg'. Copenhagen 1979. Mounted on a 'display' of plexiglass
Private collection, Sweden

264
Torben Hardenberg (b. 1949)
Two brooches, 'Summer Night' and 'Winter Day'
Cornucopia of gold. 'Summer Night' with rubies and small brilliants. 'Winter Day' with sapphires and small brilliants. Both: h. 5 cm, w. 6 cm. Copenhagen 1990
Torben Hardenberg, Copenhagen

265
Arje Griegst (b. 1938)

269

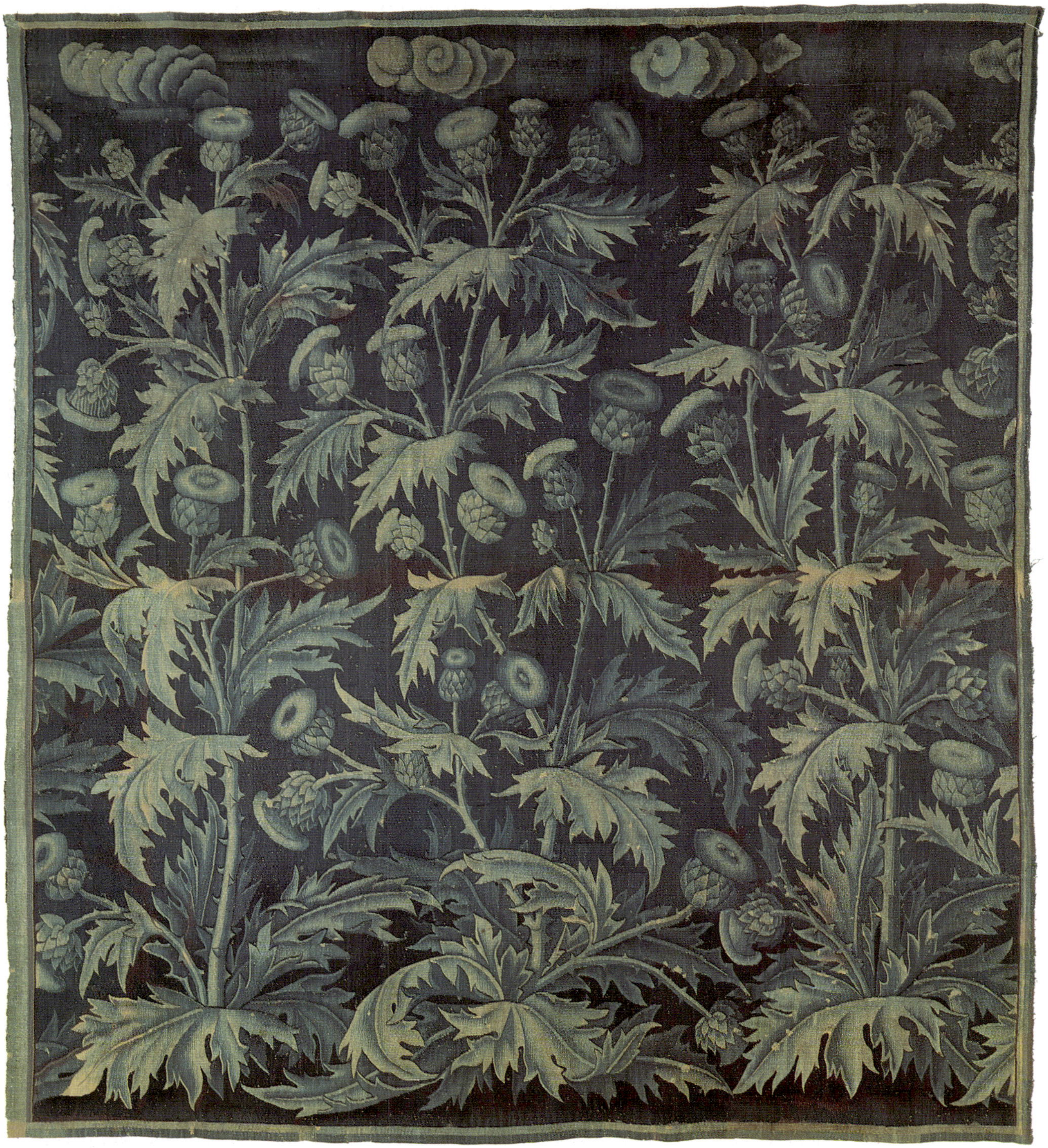

Hair ornament
Gold, moonstone, diamonds, oriental pearls, carved opal. Flowers with dewdrops and insect, h. 23 cm, b. 22 cm. Copenhagen 1976 (*ill.*)
Her Majesty Queen Margarethe of Denmark
LIT. Henrik Sten Møller, *Arje Griegst – en verden i guld- a world in gold*, Copenhagen 1982

266
Gijs Bakker (b. 1942)
Necklace, 'Dewdrop'
Laminated photography. Large, red rose leaf with two dewdrops. Largest diam.

270

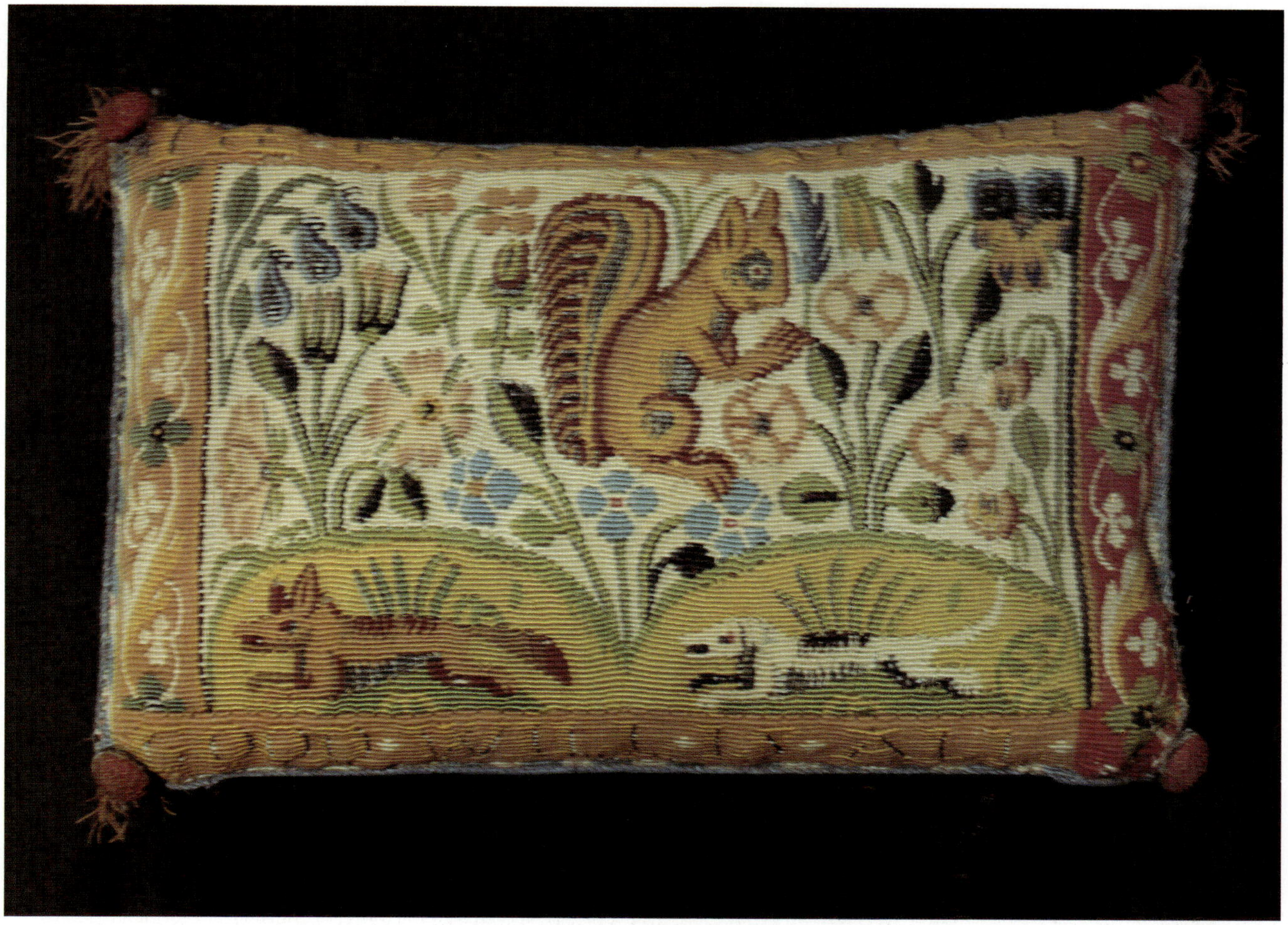

57 cm. The Netherlands 1982 (*ill.*)
Stedelijk Museum, Amsterdam (KNA6530)
LIT. Liesbeth den Besten, 'Edelsmeedkunst,' *Holland in vorm. Nederlandse vormgeving 1945-1987*, G. Staal & H. Wolters (eds.), The Hague 1989 (with bibliography); G. Stall, *Gijs Bakker vormgever. Solo voor een solist*, The Hague 1989, p. 34

In the 1960s and 1970s, the Dutch jeweller Gijs Bakker became internationally known for his pioneering work. Around 1962, he and Emmy van Leersum (1930-1986) began reacting against the idea of jewellery as a mere status symbol. The two artists questioned the form (utility) and material (expensiveness), and joined the geometric-abstract school within the visual arts (Ad Dekkers). In the course of the 1970s, they adopted a more conceptual means of expression inspired by 'body art.' The jewellery exhibited here can be seen as a reaction against this attitude. In *Dewdrop* from 1982, a necklace explicitly meant to be worn by a woman, Gijs Bakker confronts the (false) romanticism forever present between man and woman and expressed in the use of jewellery. In his own words, *Dewdrop* is an ironic ode to woman. The *Bouquet Brooch* from 1988 – in a double sense – is a cheap piece of jewellery consisting of a bouquet from a postcard embedded in plastic to which an expensive tourmaline has been attached (cat. 267) and can be seen as a continuation of *Dewdrop*. (Source: Interview with Gijs Bakker, 17 July 1990)

267
Gijs Bakker (b. 1942)
'Bouquet Brooch'
Gold and laminated photography with tourmaline, h. 11 cm, w. 11 cm. The Netherlands 1989
Central Museum, Utrecht (2636)
EXH. *Gijs Bakker, vormgever*, Helen Drutt Gallery, New York 1989; *Gijs Bakker*, Centraal Museum, Utrecht 1990
LIT. Gert Stall, *Gijs Bakker vormgever. Solo voor een solist*, The Hague 1989 p. 46

268
Gijs Bakker (b. 1942)
Comb
Gold and laminated photography, h. 5 cm, w. 2.3 cm. Sign. 'Gijs Bakker '89'. The Netherlands 1988
Museum Boymans-van Beuningen, Rotterdam (VI.2-1465)

Created for the travelling exhibition,

271

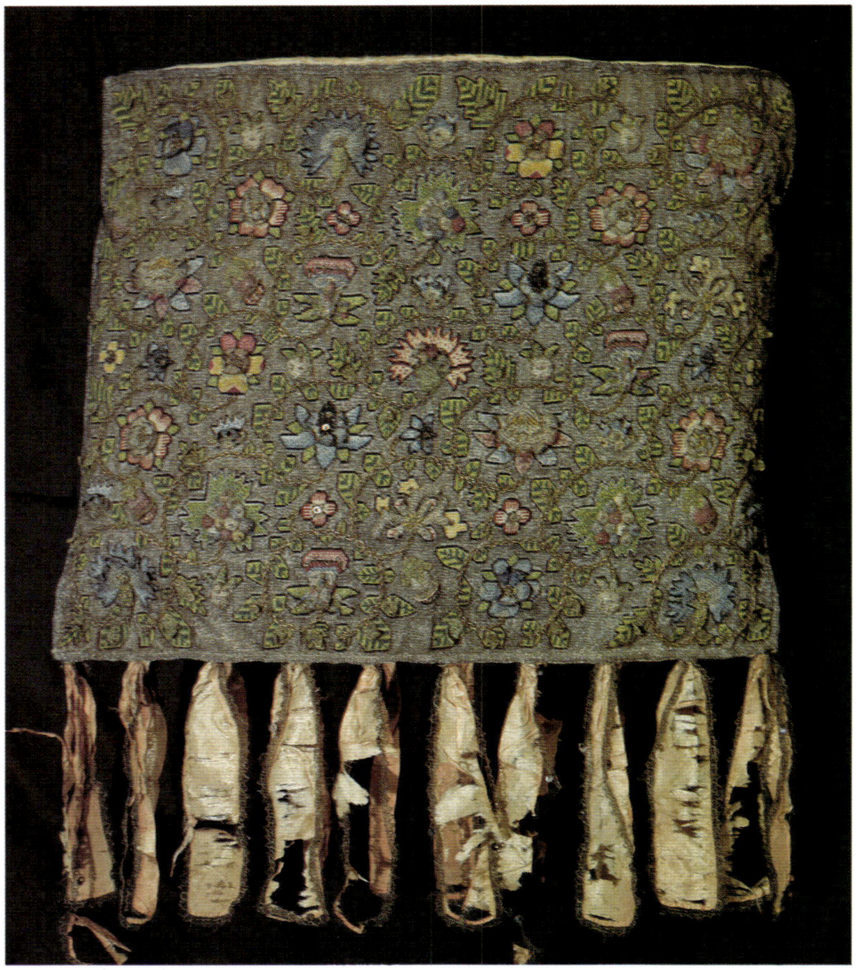

Kammen, an art collection of combs, Museum Boymans-van Beuningen, Rotterdam 1989

Textiles

269
Verdure, artichokes
Tapestry. Woven in wool and silk. Tall artichokes on a blue background. Above stylized clouds, h. 272 cm, w. 249 cm. France beginning of 16th century (*ill.*)
Kunstindustrimuseet, Copenhagen (B54/1938)
LIT. Betty Kurth, 'En ukendt fransk Gruppe af Verdurer fra Overgangen til det 16. Aarh.,' *Kunstmuseets Aarsskrift*, vol. 27, 1940, pp. 48-60, fig. 6

270
Pillow
Wool, silver thread. Tapestry woven. The centre of the pillow depicts a squirrel sitting on a white background with multicoloured flowers. A dog is chasing a fox in front of two small hills. Border of stylized flowers and leaves. At the top and bottom: 'The Gift is Small' and 'Goodwill is All', h. 17.7 cm, w. 25.4 cm. The Sheldon Manufactory, England ca. 1600 (*ill.*)
S. Franses Ltd., London

The Sheldon Manufactory in Warwickshire, named after its founder William Sheldon (d. 1570), provided mainly the county's noblemen with cushion covers woven in a simple, but charming style.

271
Pillow
Silk, gold and silver threads. Embroidered on a silver ground with flower festoons in red, blue, yellow and green silk as well as gold thread. The flowers are partly made in stumpwork, h. 35.5 cm, w. 40.6 cm. England ca. 1580-90 (*ill.*)
S. Franses Ltd., London

272
Anna Cathrine? (King Christian IVs daughter, 1618-1633)
Flower piece
Silk embroidery on silk ground. White vase decorated with blue flowers. Bouquet of tulips, carnations and other flowers in many colours. 46.5 *x* 36.4 cm. Sign. 'Anna C'. Denmark beginning of 17th century
The Royal Collections, Rosenborg Palace, Copenhagen (3-42)
PROV. Inv. 1718.552.2

273
Anna Cathrine? (King Christian IVs daughter, 1618-1633)
Flower piece
Silk embroidery on silk ground. Vase with bouquet in many colours. 46.4 *x* 36.3 cm. Sign. 'Anna C'. Denmark beginning of 17th century?
The Royal Collections, Rosenborg Palace, Copenhagen (7-373)
PROV. Inv. 1718.552.2

274
Gloves
Leather with silk cuffs. Embroidered with silk and gold thread and with pearls, l. 24 cm. The Netherlands first half of 17th century
Rijksmuseum, Amsterdam (2921)
EXH. *Kralen, Pitten en Schelpen*, Koninklijk Instituut voor de Tropen, Amsterdam 1953; ... *op de Raempte off mette Brodse* ..., Amsterdams Historisch Museum , Amsterdam 1987
LIT. E. Gibson, 'Some Gloves from the Collection of Mr Robert Spence,' part I-II, *The Connoisseur*, vol. 55, 1919, p. 88 & LVIII, 1920, p. 19

275
Wijnant Haelwech (1618-after 1650)
Flower piece

Embroidered in blue, red, yellow and green shaded silk on dark grey silk. Glass vase in a niche with bouquet of roses, fritillaries, tulips, buttercups, anemones, narcissus, hyacinths, irises and others. In the background, a few fallen leaves and an insect. 51 *x* 36.5 cm. Sign. 'W. HAELWECH 1650'. The Netherlands 1650 (*ill.*)
Rijksmuseum, Amsterdam (RBK1957-70)
LIT. Saskia de Bodt, ... *op de Raempte off mette Brodse ... Nederlands borduurweerk uit de zeventiende eeuw*, Haarlem 1987, pp. 11-21, 88-90; Charlotte Paludan, *Alverdens Broderier, Kunstindustrimuseet*, Copenhagen 1983, cat. no. 24, pp. 17, 19

The flower piece is made completely in the Dutch 17th-century flower still-life tradition and in its technical perfection comparable to the best painted flower pictures. This flower piece is part of a group of embroidered pictures with flower motifs all made in the Netherlands around the middle of the 17th century. The small embroidery signed by F. van Pae(p) and dated 7 December 1650 bearing the coat of arms of the Amsterdam family Valckenier (cat. 276) belongs to the same group.

Little is known about Wijnant Haelwech; he was born in Amsterdam on 25 February 1618, son of the embroiderer Adrianus Haleweg or Haelwech. On 5 October 1639, he declared that he was making embroidery, but that he intended to learn the art of painting as well. Nevertheless, he still called himself embroiderer at his wedding in 1645. In the flower piece from 1650, his training as a painter is reflected in the partly painted niche in which the vase is placed. (Genealogical information kindly provided by Dr. W. Bruijnesteijn, Arnhem.)

276
Flower piece
Coloured and shaded silk embroidery on brownish satin. Vase with tulip, fritillary and wild flower on a table. On the vase, the device and name 'C VALCKENIER', on the edge of the table, 'F V PAE [p?] 1650 7/12'. 26 *x* 21 cm. Ivory frame. The Netherlands 1650 (*fig. 49*)
Kunstindustrimuseet, Copenhagen (A115/1915)
EXH. *Alverdens broderier. Kunstindustrimuseet*, Copenhagen 1983, cat. no. 24, ill. p. 18

277
Table cover
Wool and silk. Tapestry woven. In the centre, a representation of *Christ at Emmaus* in a wreath of fruit and surrounded by scattered flowers. Border with the evangelists' symbols between festoons of fruit. 200 *x* 300 cm. Possibly Delft or Gouda, the Netherlands mid-17th century (*fig. 47*)
Her Majesty Queen Margarethe of Denmark
LIT. Ernst Fischer, *Flamskvävnader i Skåne*, Lund 1962, fig. 1; Vibeke Woldbye, 'Hollandske blomstertæpper i Danmark,' *Det danske Kunstindustrimuseum. Virksomhed 1964-1969*, Copenhagen 1969, pp. 51-78, cat. no. 5

278
Top sheet
Edging decorated with white embroidery. Vine of tulip, rose, carnation, and grape between narrow flower braiding. Lace border, h. 19 cm, w. 270 cm. Denmark, 17th century
Kunstindustrimuseet, Copenhagen (B36/1917)
EXH. *Alverdens broderier i Kunstindustrimuseet*, Copenhagen 1983, cat. no. 185, ill. p. 60

279
Purse
Crocheted gold thread. Flowers, h. 6.4 cm, w. 7.3 cm. Denmark? 1650-75?
The Royal Collections, Rosenborg Palace, Copenhagen (3-100)
EXH. *Sophie Amalie*, Rosenborg, Copenhagen 1986, cat. no. 123-132
LIT. M. Bencard and J. Hein, 'Three Cabinets on Stands from the Seventeenth Century,' *Furniture History*, vol. 21, 1985, p. 150

In 1784 the purse is mentioned, together with twelve others, as being kept in 'The Black Tresor' of the Rosenborg Regalia Chamber.

280
Purse
Silk. Iris embroidered with silk in various colours, h. 11 cm, w. 12 cm. Friesland probably last quarter of 17th century
Rijksmuseum, Amsterdam (1113)
PROV. Koninklijk Kabinet van Zeldzaamheden, 1875

281
Hermann Weigberg
Flower piece
Silk embroidery on paper. Anemone, tulip and hyacinth in various colours. Identical on both sides. 18.8 *x* 13.3 cm. Copied from Maria Sibylla Merian, *Neues Blumenbuch*, Nuremberg 1680, vol. 3, pl. 4: *hyacinth*, pl. 6: *anemone*. Copenhagen 1680s?
The Royal Collections, Rosenborg Palace, Copenhagen (10-270)
PROV. 1696 in the Miniature Chamber, p. 95, no. 8 '... Christian den Femte, af Monsr. Weigberg præsenteret'

282
Tapestry
Wool and silk. Tapestry woven. Earlier mounted on the back of a chair. Partly naturalistic flowers (including rose, lily, and carnation) on dark blue ground, h. 72.2 cm, w. 64.7 cm. (with frame). Soho, England ca. 1720
S. Franses Ltd., London

During the directorship of Joshua Morris (1720-30) the Soho manufactury produced a number of woven tapestries and chair covers with flower motifs after French models. The origin of these is the tapestry-woven Dutch table covers from the mid-17th century.

283
Arm chair with embroidered cover
Stained beechwood carved with female herms, scrolls and foliage together with King Fredrik IV's monogram. Made by the furniture maker Johan Weis. Cover embroidered in wool and

295

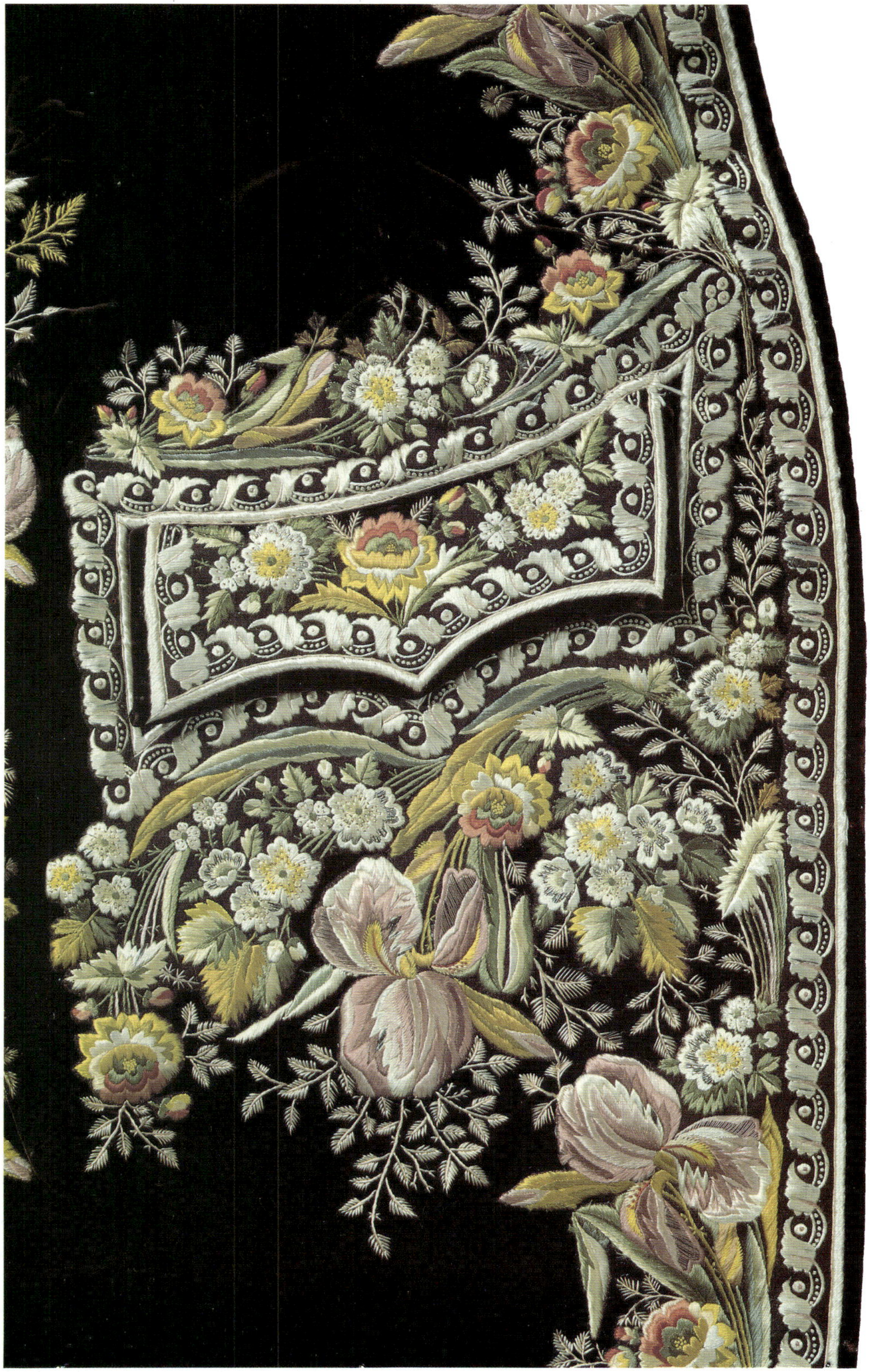

silk with flowers and human figures in gros and petit point by Queen Charlotte Amalie and her ladies-in-waiting, h. 130 cm. Copenhagen 1718
The Royal Collections, Rosenborg Palace, Copenhagen (21.3)
PROV. Inv. 1718.8.
LIT. Tove Clemmensen, *Signerede arbejder af københavnske snedkere i Københavns Snedkerlaug gennem fire hundrede år*, Copenhagen 1954, p. 212

From a suite of furniture consisting of six arm chairs and twelve chairs with high backs embroidered by Queen Charlotte Amalie and ladies-in-waiting (two are signed).

284
Silver brocade
Peonies and lilies as well as pines and stone sarcophagus on silver ground, l. 58 cm, w. 55 cm. Lyon, France ca. 1730-35
Kunstindustrimuseet, Copenhagen (A47/1927)

285
Silk brocade
Multicoloured bouquets and flower festoons in bows as well as blue lace ribbons. Reused for christening robe, l. 92 cm, w. 53.5 cm. France? mid-18th century
Kunstindustrimuseet, Copenhagen (A83/1915)

286
Silk brocade
Multicoloured, almost naturalistic floral sprigs and floating vines on a ribbed ground. Spitalfields?, England mid-18th century
Kunstindustrimuseet, Copenhagen (B51/1912)

287
Silk brocade
Multicoloured flowering vines and floating leaves and lace pattern on a ribbed ground, l. 95 cm, w. 50.5 cm. Lyon, France mid-18th century
Kunstindustrimuseet, Copenhagen (2126)

311

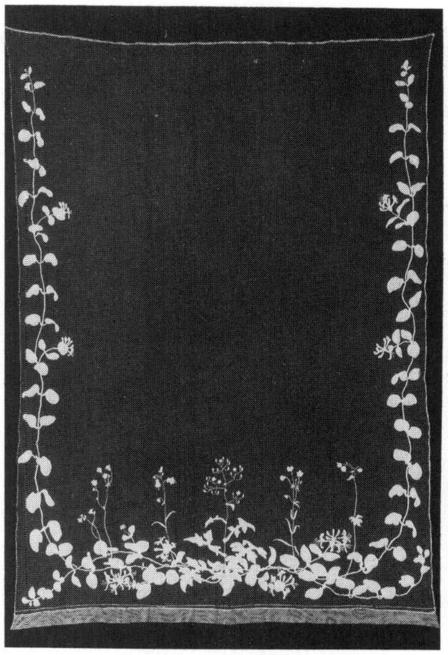

288
Silk brocade
Flower- and fruit-bearing branches over a floating single-coloured vine pattern on a ribbed ground, l. 98 cm, w. 54 cm. Lyon, France ca. 1750-60
Kunstindustrimuseet, Copenhagen (A44/1927)

289
Silk brocade
Slender vines and flower bouquets as well as single-coloured ribbons and thin vines on taffeta, l. 86 cm, w. 48.5 cm. Lyon, France ca. 1770-80
Kunstindustrimuseet, Copenhagen (A23/1927)

290
Ph. de Lasalle (1723-1805)
Panel. Silk brocade
Flower basket carried by two pigeons encircled in a flower wreath, h. 170 cm, w. 54.5 cm. Lyon, France ca. 1780
Kunstindustrimuseet, Copenhagen (3/1984)

291
Front for dress
Silk damask, embroidered with twisted silk. Bouquets of roses, lilies, carnations, tulips, etc., wrapped with ribbons and light flowering vines, l. 55 cm. China for the European market ca. 1760-70
Kunstindustrimuseet, Copenhagen (B47/1918)
EXH. *Alverdens broderier i Kunstindustrimuseet*, Copenhagen 1983, cat. no. 443

292
Gauze ribbon
Broché pattern of flower twigs in pink and white and waving bands, l. 77 cm, w. 6 cm. France? ca. 1760-70
Kunstindustrimuseet, Copenhagen (39/1986)

293
Waistcoat, uncut
Embroidered *à disposition* with silk on ribbed cream-coloured silk. Pattern of scattered flowers and bouquets, l. 103 cm. France ca. 1780-90
Kunstindustrimuseet, Copenhagen (2333)
EXH. *Alverdens broderier i Kunstindustrimuseet*, Copenhagen 1983, cat. no. 81

294
Waistcoat
Silk serge embroidered with spun silk in various colours and with silver thread, spangles and cups. Pattern of palmettes with bouquets, l. 70 cm. Denmark ca. 1780-1800
Kunstindustrimuseet, Copenhagen (20/1945)
EXH. *Alverdens broderier i Kunstindustrimuseet*, Copenhagen 1983, cat. no. 76

295
Men's coat, incomplete
Chestnut-brown velvet. Embroidered on panel of brown cloth with spun silk in various colours. Flower motifs with iris, anemone, and hawthorn along the front edge and slits as well as on the pockets. Lyon?, France 1780-1810 (*ill.*)
Kunstindustrimuseet, Copenhagen (13/1955)
EXH. *Alverdens broderier i Kunstindustrimuseet*, Copenhagen 1983, cat. no. 77, ill. p. 40

296
Panel for wall lining
Silk brocade with multicoloured flowers

321

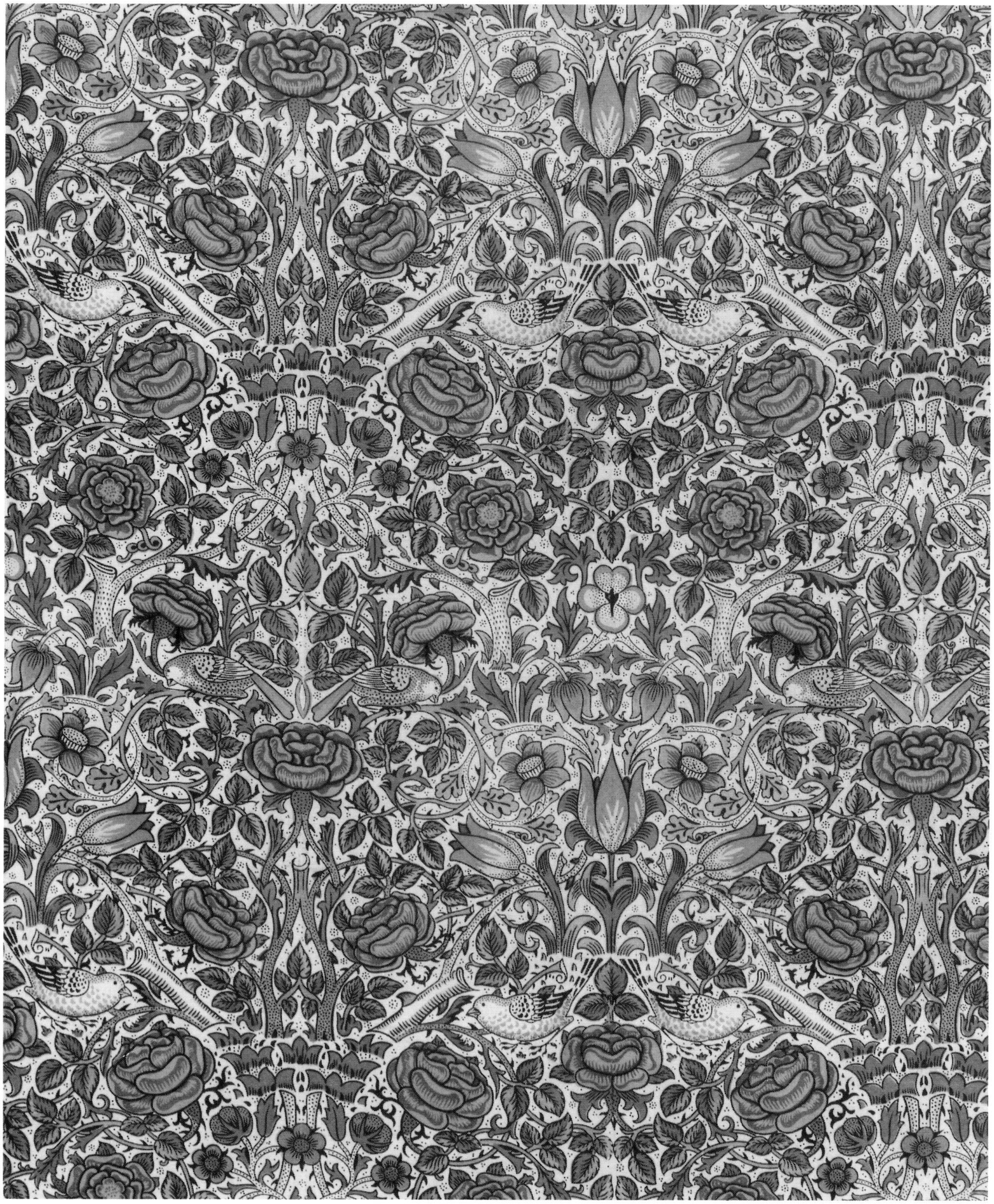

and ivy vines as well as bronze-coloured trophies and bees on an ivory-coloured ribbed ground, l. 411 cm, w. 75.8 cm. France ca. 1800
Kunstindustrimuseet, Copenhagen (D1252)

297
Border for wall lining, 'Dessin du Rose'
Silk brocade with rose garlands and bronze latticework as well as classicistic bands on a ribbed ground, l. 50 cm, w. 38 cm. Made for the Palais de Meudon, France ca. 1800
Kunstindustrimuseet, Copenhagen (D1253)

298
Pocketbook
Four-leaved with flap. Atlask embroidered in spun silk with motifs of stock, primrose, rose, forget-me-not, the initials 'ML' and '1792', h. 17.5 cm. Denmark 1792
Kunstindustrimuseet, Copenhagen (B86/1935)
EXH. *Alverdens broderier i Kunstindustrimuseet*, Copenhagen 1983, cat. no. 104

299
Pocketbook
Four-leaved. Atlask embroidered in spun silk. Wreaths on each leaf of forget-me-not and ivy with heartseases and the inscriptions 'Tendresse/AKH/19.Januari' and 'Regret/HH/1.Januari', h. 15.2 cm. Denmark ca. 1800-10
Kunstindustrimuseet, Copenhagen (38/1946)
EXH. *Alverdens broderier i Kunstindustrimuseet*, Copenhagen 1983, cat. no. 109

300
Pocketbook
Two-leaved with pockets and flap. Black atlask embroidered with spun silk. Interior flaps decorated with oval medallions with bindweed and primrose respectively, h. 17.5 cm. Denmark ca. 1800-20
Kunstindustrimuseet, Copenhagen (U2338)

328

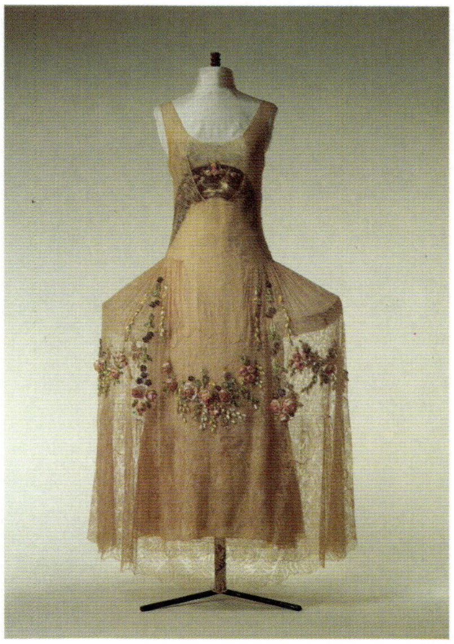

301
Pocketbook
Four-leaved with flap. Black silk serge embroidered with spun silk. Flower motifs, e.g., poppies and others, and the inscription 'Blomster spire om dit Fjed – I din Sjæl boe salig Fred', h. 17.3 cm. Denmark ca. 1800-20
Kunstindustrimuseet, Copenhagen (U1782)
EXH. *Alverdens broderier i Kunstindustrimuseet*, Copenhagen 1983, cat. no. 117

302
Pocketbook
Black atlask embroidered with silk. Oval medallions with bindweed and primrose, h. 17.3 cm, w. 10.5 cm. Denmark ca. 1820
Kunstindustrimuseet, Copenhagen (U2338)

303
Workbag
Atlask embroidered with chenille and set with gauze flowers painted with watercolour. The lower part pretends to be a basket with roses, stock, chrysanthemum, anemones, bindweed and daisy, h. 21 cm, w. 15 cm. Denmark 1820-30
Kunstindustrimuseet, Copenhagen (B90/1935)
EXH. *Alverdens broderier i Kunstindustrimuseet*, Copenhagen 1983, cat. no. 123

304
Briefcase
Silk serge embroidered with black silk. Vase with flowers, h. 27 cm, w. 31 cm. Denmark ca. 1830
Kunstindustrimuseet, Copenhagen (B45/1913)
EXH. *Alverdens broderier i Kunstindustrimuseet*, Copenhagen 1983, cat. no. 129

305
'Ridicule'
Bag. Taffeta embroidered with chenille and appliqué flowers of silk crêpe. The lower part imitating a basket with fuchsia and white roses, h. 22 cm, w. 18 cm
Kunstindustrimuseet, Copenhagen (U1894)
EXH. *Alverdens broderier i Kunstindustrimuseet*, Copenhagen 1983, cat. no. 121

306
A pair of ladies' slippers
Embroidered in coloured wool with cross and floss stitches on tabby canvas. Roses and primroses, l. 25 cm. Denmark or Sweden ca. 1840
Kunstindustrimuseet, Copenhagen (24/1984)

307
Silk gauze ribbon
Jacquard woven. Brocaded flower pattern, l. 114 cm, w. 7.5 cm. Switzerland? ca. 1840-50
Kunstindustrimuseet, Copenhagen (U2160 *b*)

308
Silk ribbon
Jacquard woven. Brocaded and welt-patterned shawl motif with pink and brown flowers on a taffeta ground, l. 122 cm, w. 8.2 cm. Switzerland? ca. 1840-50
Kunstindustrimuseet, Copenhagen (U2234)

335

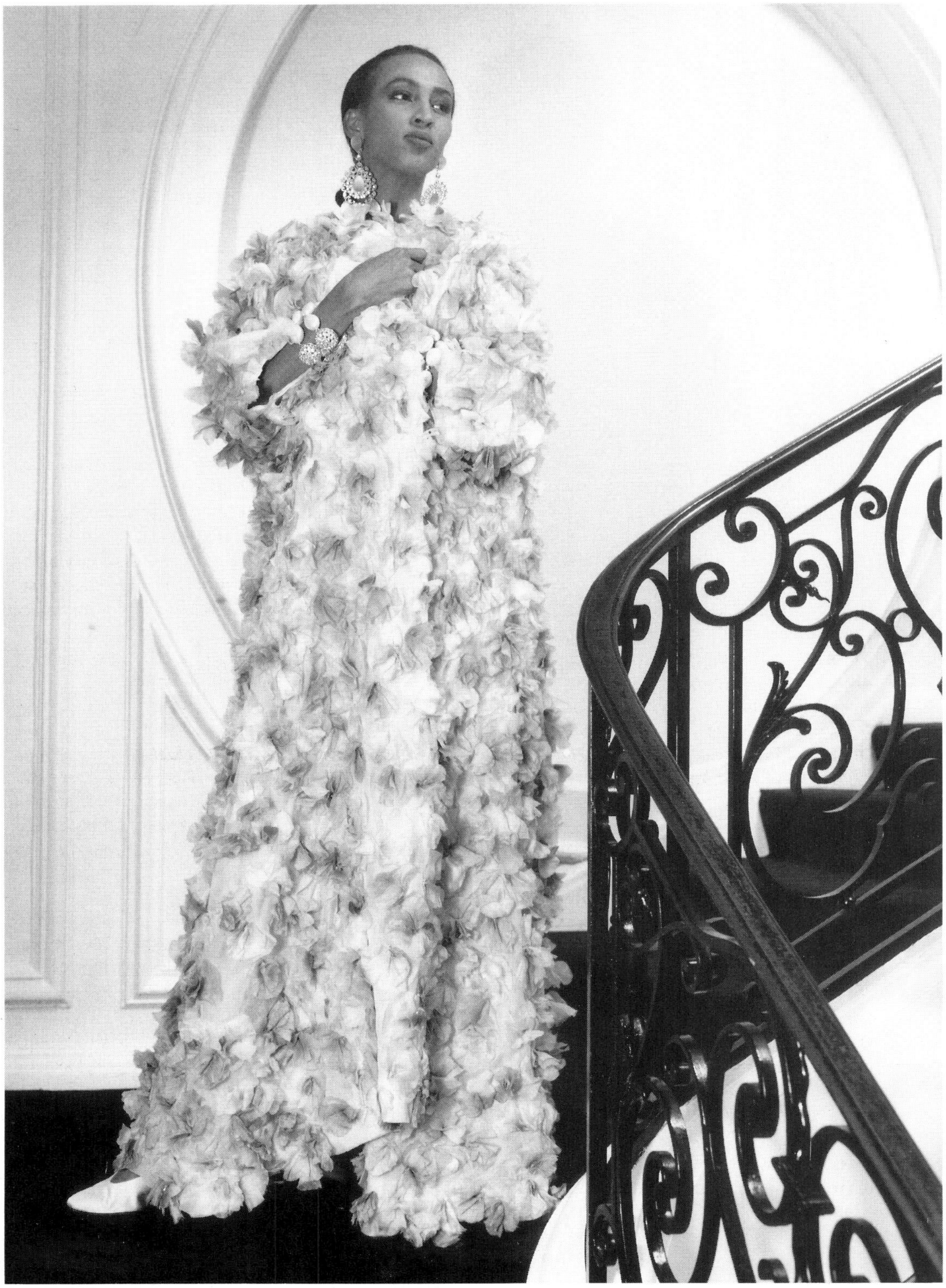

325, 326

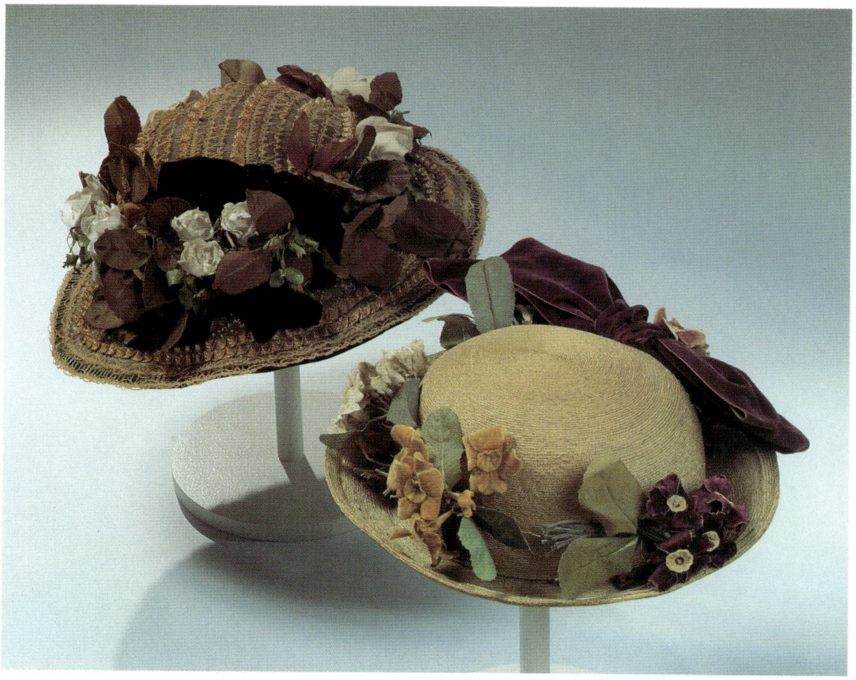

309
Album
Casette with leaflets of which five are embroidered with spun silk in various colours and decorated with gold pearls. Flower motifs, h. 15 cm, w. 9.5 cm. Sign. 'Geschenk für C. Pommerenck bei ihrer Abreise aus Oldenburg den 3. April 1842', Germany 1842
Kunstindustrimuseet, Copenhagen (44/1982)
EXH. *Alverdens broderier i Kunstindustrimuseet*, Copenhagen 1983, cat. no. 135

310
Two girls' caps for Bornholm headgear
Atlask embroidered with spun silk and chenille. Bouquets of 'Bornholm rose,' h. 15-16 cm. Bornholm, Denmark 19th century
Kunstindustrimuseet, Copenhagen (109/1958, 5/1978)
EXH. *Alverdens broderier i Kunstindustrimuseet*, Copenhagen 1983, cat. no. 321

311
Georgia Skovgaard (1828-1868) *and* P.C. Skovgaard (1817-1875)
Bridal veil
Tulle embroidered with woodbine and field flowers. Made for the wedding of Georgia Skovgaard to the painter P.C. Skovgaard, Denmark 1851 (ill.)
Private collection, Denmark
LIT. Lise Osvald, 'Broderi og kærlighed,' *Herculanum paa Sjælland*, Mirjam Gelfer-Jørgensen (ed.), Copenhagen 1988, pp. 221 ff.

The veil is embroidered by the bride, daughter of the botanist J.F. Schouw, and her friends. P.C. Skovgaard designed the decoration. This inspired a cooperative effort between Georgia Skovgaard and several Danish artists who became interested in designing patterns for embroidery. She initiated a Danish embroidery tradition still very much alive today. At the same time, the bridal veil represents a new attitude to the beauty of wild plants, which inspired Danish landscape painters at the time.

312
Silk ribbon
Jacquard woven with brocaded bouquets and rose sprigs on satin ground, l. 29 cm, w. 8.5 cm. Switzerland second half of 19th century
Kunstindustrimuseet, Copenhagen (U1948,4)

313
Silk ribbon
Jacquard woven. Brocaded flower vines on taffeta ground, l. 42 cm, w. 3.6 cm. Czechoslovakia? second half of 19th century
Kunstindustrimuseet, Copenhagen (150*b*/1949)

314
Hat with poppies
Straw, metal, textile, l. 26 cm, w. 24 cm. Crown w. 27 cm. Denmark 1870s
Nationalmuseet, Brede (4159/1949)

315
William Morris (1834-1896)
'The Honeysuckle Design'
Cotton with printed decoration. Poppies and honeysuckle in pale red, copper red, pale blue and black on a blue ground, h. 100.5 cm, w. 94 cm. Designed 1876, made in England ca. 1894
Kunstindustrimuseet, Copenhagen (2181)

316
Cotton velvet
Printed decoration. Large red-brown flowers and buds on long stems, l. 103 cm, w. 80.5 cm. England ca. 1895
Kunstindustrimuseet, Copenhagen (2143)

317
Lindsay P. Butterfield (1869-1948)
'Crown Imperial'
Silk. Printed decoration, Crown Imperial and five-leaved small flowers in white and pink on a copper-red ground, l. 99 cm, w. 88 cm. England ca. 1895
Kunstindustrimuseet, Copenhagen (2173)

318
Felix Aubert (b. 1866)
Fabric, 'Iris d'eau'
Cotton satin. Printed decoration. White irises in water with ripples, l. 80.5 cm, w. 71 cm. Pilon et Cie., Paris 1897 (fig. 56)

332

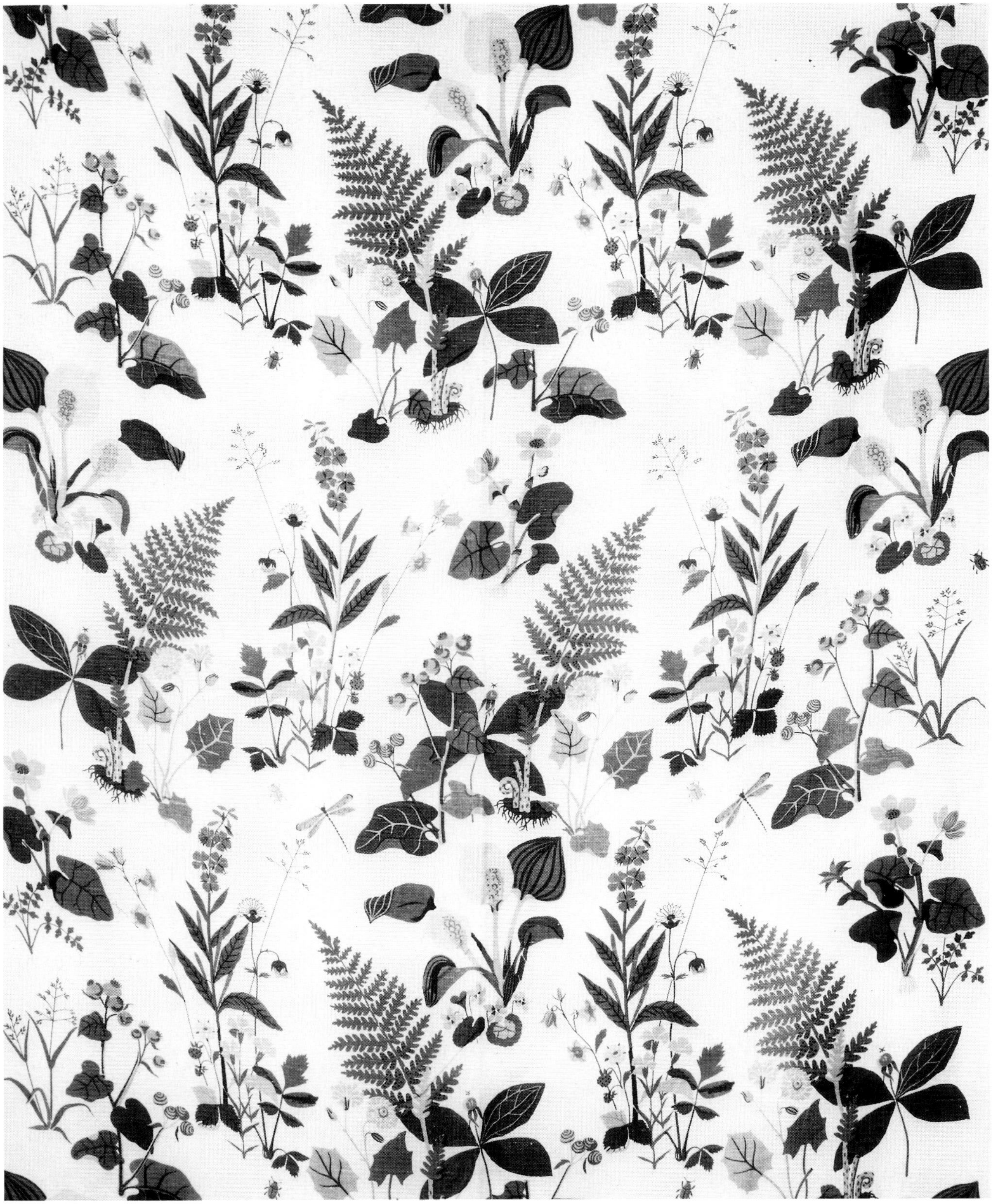

338

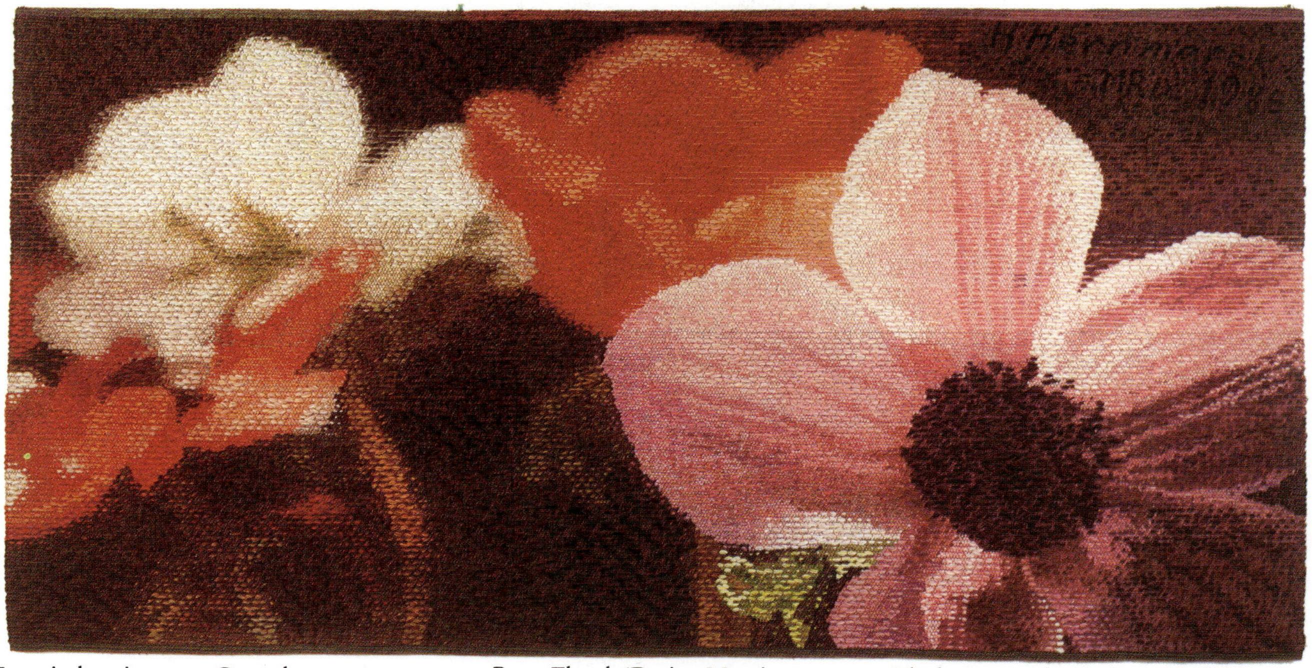

Kunstindustrimuseet, Copenhagen (2177)

319
Fabric, cotton velvet
Printed decoration. Large-lobed tulips on a subtly patterned ground, l. 79.5 cm, w. 73 cm. England ca. 1895 (*fig. 54*)
Kunstindustrimuseet, Copenhagen (2149)

320
Thomas Wardle
Cotton
Printed decoration. Yellow tulips with leaves, l. 69 cm, w. 49.5 cm. Silver Studios, England ca. 1895
Kunstindustrimuseet, Copenhagen (2172)

321
William Morris (1834-1896)
'Strawberry Thief'
Cotton with printed decoration; rose branches with bluish-green leaves, tulips, narcissi, and yellow and red birds. Sign. 'Reg.d. Morris & Company, 449 Oxford Street', h. 97 cm, w. 97.5 cm. Designed 1876-83, made in London, England ca. 1895
Kunstindustrimuseet, Copenhagen (2203)
LIT. Peter Floud, 'Dating Morris Patterns,' *Architectural Review*, no. 750, July 1959

322
Felix Aubert (b. 1866)
Fan leaf
Silk lace. Bindweed in green, blue and brown, l. 51 cm. Made for La Maison Moderne, Paris, France ca. 1900
Kunstindustrimuseet, Copenhagen (1027)
PROV. Acquired at the World Exhibition in Paris 1900

323
Johann Hrdclicka (1857-1907)
Collar
Needle lace of white flax thread. Hemlock, w. 49 cm. Vienna ca. 1900
Kunstindustrimuseet, Copenhagen (1011)
PROV. Acquired at the World Exhibition in Paris 1900
LIT. Pietro Krohn (et al.), *Det danske Kunstindustrimuseum. De første fem Aars Virksomhed*, Copenhagen 1901, p. 25, fig. 22

324
Kristian Møhl-Hansen (1876-1962)
Alga, pillow
Black serge with atlask appliqué and embroidery in satin stitch in green and white, pale yellow and plied green silk, h. 55 cm, w. 55 cm. Made at Clara Wæver, Copenhagen 1905
Kunstindustrimuseet, Copenhagen (1180)
EXH. *Alverdens broderier i Kunstindustrimuseet*, Copenhagen 1983, cat. no. 59, ill. p. 34

325
Hat with applied roses
Straw and textile, h. 10 cm, l. 39 cm, w. 35 cm. Copenhagen 1890s (*ill.*)
Nationalmuseet, Brede (391/1938)

326
Hanne Davidsen
Hat with primroses
Straw and textile, h. 11 cm, l. 35 cm, w. 31 cm. Copenhagen 1908-10 (*ill.*)
Nationalmuseet, Brede (437/1923-W203*e*)

Hanne Davidsen was court milliner in Copenhagen.

327
Valdemar Andersen (1875-1928)
Ladies' jacket
Undyed spun silk embroidered with

cotton yarn in lavender, black and other colours. Vine pattern in Vienna style, h. 94 cm. Embroidered at Permin's embroidery atelier and tailored by Wessel & Vett (Magasin du Nord), Copenhagen 1909
Kunstindustrimuseet, Copenhagen (B12/1942)
EXH. *Alverdens broderier i Kunstindustrimuseet*, Copenhagen 1983, cat. no. 95, ill. p. 44

328
Boué Soeurs
'Robe de style,' evening dress or war crinoline
Peach-coloured lace and silk chiffon with braiding of silver lamé. Decorated with silk and silver ribbons, embroidered with thick, twisted silk and thin metal thread. Appliqué rose buds and frills of roses and flowering vines made of silk ribbon in pink and peach, h. ca. 140 cm. Paris ca. 1923 (ill.)
Kunstindustrimuseet, Copenhagen (128/1989)
LIT. Beyfus, *Think pink*, Octagon, Spink & Son Ltd, Spring 1989, vol. 26, no. 1. ill. p. 32; *Grand Couturiers*, Musée du Costume de la Ville de Paris, 1965, cat. no. 3; Caroline Rennolds Milbank, *Couture. Great Fashion Designers*, London 1985, p. 73; *Moments de Mode*, Musée des Arts de la Mode, Paris 1986, cat. no. 77; Naomi Tarrant, *Haute Couture at Spink*, Spink & Co. London 1989, cat. no. 15

329
Marie Gudme Leth (b. 1895)
'Hortensia'
Fabric printed in four colours on Dutch linen. The pattern consists of a flower bouquet with iris, hydrangea, tulips, daffodils, bleeding heart, carnation, rose and others as well as scattered forget-me-nots and small butterflies, w. 132 cm. Repeat h. 50 cm. Artist's workshop, Copenhagen 1942
Kunstindustrimuseet, Copenhagen (29/1978)
EXH. *Stentøj og stoftryk af Nathalie Krebs og Marie Gudme Leth*, Kunstindustrimuseet, Copenhagen 1978

339

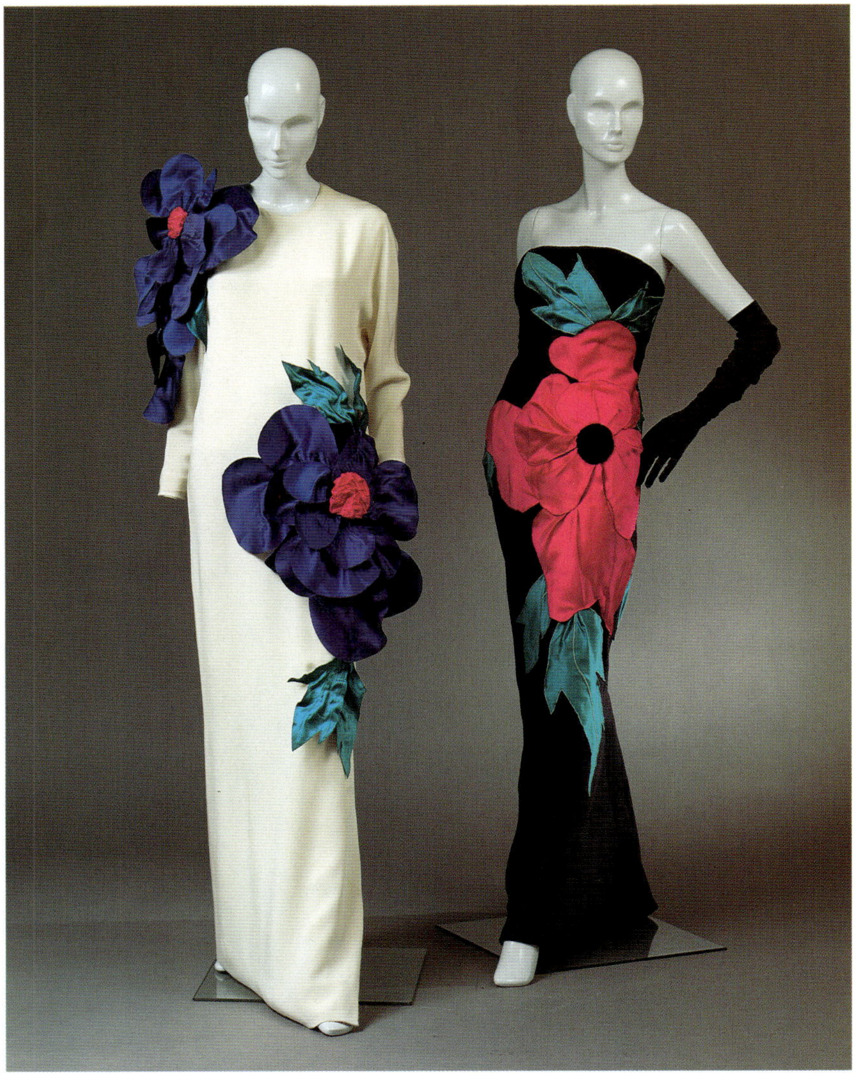

330
Josef Frank (1885-1967)
Fabric
Flax. Printed decoration *Svenska Vårblommor*. Tulips, crocuses, primroses and others in colours, repeat h. 52 cm, w. 130 cm. Designed by Josef Frank and made for the Svenskt Tenn Co., Sweden before 1945
Nationalmuseum, Dept. of Decorative Arts, Stockholm (NM80/1945)

In 1932, the Austrian architect Josef Frank began his affiliation with the company Svenskt Tenn, for which he designed a large number of patterns for printed fabrics. These are now considered classics within Swedish textile art.

331
Arne Jacobsen (1902-1971)
Fabric
Printed pattern with rows of hyacinth glasses, h. 250 cm, w. 127 cm. A/S Olesen, Copenhagen
Private collection, Denmark

332
Gocken Jobs (b. 1914)
Fabric
Flax. Printed decoration *Trollslända*. Naturalistic flowers, berries, and foliage as well as dragonflies and dung

beetles on uncoloured ground, repeat h. 100 cm, w. 130 cm. Made for NKS Textilkammare in Ljungbergs Textiltryck, Floda, Sweden 1945
Nationalmuseum, Dept. of Decorative Arts, Stockholm (NM79/1965)

In 1945, Gocken and Lisbet Jobs launched a series of printed textiles for the NKS Textilkammere. This was the beginning of a wide production, later to be continued in the family's own workshop at Leksand in Dalarna, Jobs Handtryck. The flower motifs were taken directly from the sisters' ceramics. However, in the textiles a new monumentality was achieved in the pattern repeats of up to 1 meter. The Jobs sisters' naturalistic flowers represent the very essence of a Swedish summer idyll and possess a fresh, innocent joy in nature, devoid of banality.

333
Gocken Jobs (b. 1914)
Fabric
Flax. Printed decoration, *Stugrabatt*. Naturalistic flowers in various colours: amaryllis, hare bell, larkspur, sunflower, fronds, and others on an uncoloured ground, repeat h. 100 cm, w. 130 cm. Sign. on edging: 'Gocken Jobs «Stugrabatt»'. Designed 1951, made in Jobs Handtryck, Leksand, Sweden 1958
Nationalmuseum, Dept. of Decorative Arts, Stockholm (NM109/1958)
EXH. *Jobs keramik og textil*, Nationalmuseum, Stockholm 1986, cat. no. 2, rep. in colour on cover

Cf., cat. no. 232

334
Christian Dior (1905-1957)
Hat
Set with artificial lilies of the valley in narrow diagonal rows, h. ca. 10.5 cm. Sign. on label: 'Christian Dior/Paris/Made in France'. Paris ca. 1955
Kunstindustrimuseet, Copenhagen (122/1989)

335
Cristóbal Balenciaga (1895-1972)
Evening coat

351

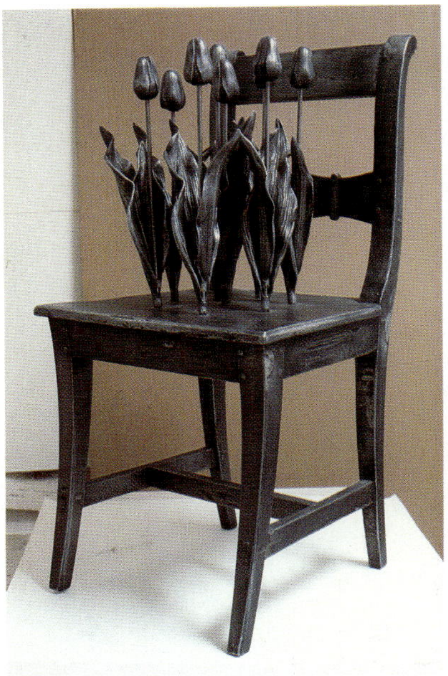

White organza with appliqué pink silk flowers. Paris 1964 (*fig. 64 and p. 190*)
Hubert de Givenchy, Paris
LIT. *Hommage à Balenciaga*, cat. Musée Historique des Tissus de Lyon, 1985, cat. no. 147

336
Maija Isola (b. 1927)
Fabric, 'Unikko'
White tabby woven cotton. Printed pattern of stylized poppies in red colours with black stems. Sign. on edging: 'MAIJA ISOLA «UNIKKO.» MARIKANYAS. MARITEXTIL.SUOMI-FINLAND', w. 140 cm, l. 360 cm. Designed for Maritextil, Finland ca. 1965 (*fig. 67*)
Kunstindustrimuseet, Copenhagen (1/1975)

337
Anna Polesny
International Levi's
Blue jeans shorts. Flower embroidery in colours, h. 38 cm, w. 52 cm. Embroidered sign. 'ANNA'. USA 1973 (*fig. 71*)
Julie Schafler Dale, New York
EXH. Museum of Contemporary Crafts, New York; The M. H. de Young Memorial Museum, San Francisco; The Los Angeles Municipal Art Gallery; The Madison Art Center in Madison, Wisconsin; Arizona State University at Tempe, Arizona

338
Helena Hernmarck (b. 1941)
Tapestry, 'Anemones'
Wool. Tapestry woven with anemones in red and purple, h. 137 cm, w. 275 cm. Sign. 'H Hernmarck MDW 1985'. Assisting weaver Mollie Doe Wensberg. USA 1985 (*ill.*)
Helena Hernmarck, Ridgefield
EXH. Birmingham Alabama Public Library 1986; Bellas Artes, Santa Fé, New Mexico 1986; *Images in Contemporary Tapestry 1988*, Northern Arizona University Art Gallery, Flagstaff, Arizona 1988; *Textile Show*, Oxford Gallery, Rochester, New York 1989; Hurlbutt Gallery, Greenwich Library 1989

339
Erik Mortensen (b. 1926) *and* Balmain
Dress
Haute couture. Dark blue fourreau with appliqué flower of shocking-pink satin. The Summer Collection, Paris 1985 (*ill.*)
Erik Mortensen, Paris
EXH. Else Bülow, *Erik Mortensen, Balmain – Alvar Aalto*, Nordjyllands Kunstmuseum, Ålborg 1989, cat. 10

340
Erik Mortensen (b. 1926) *and* Balmain
Dress
Haute couture. White silk crêpe with appliqué flowers of blue satin. The Summer Collection, Paris 1985 (*ill.*)
Erik Mortensen, Paris
EXH. Else Bülow, *Erik Mortensen, Balmain – Alvar Aalto*, Nordjyllands Kunstmuseum, Ålborg 1989, cat. 11

Miscellaneous

341
Vase with flowers and fruits
Porcelain, silk and wax, h. of vase 47 cm. The vase made in Japan 1660-70 (fig. 109)
The Royal Collections, Rosenborg Palace, Copenhagen (1-57)
PROV. Inv. 1718.362.5
LIT. Mogens Bencard, 'Med en dyne nedrevet,' *Skalk*, 1981, no. 5, pp. 12-15

343

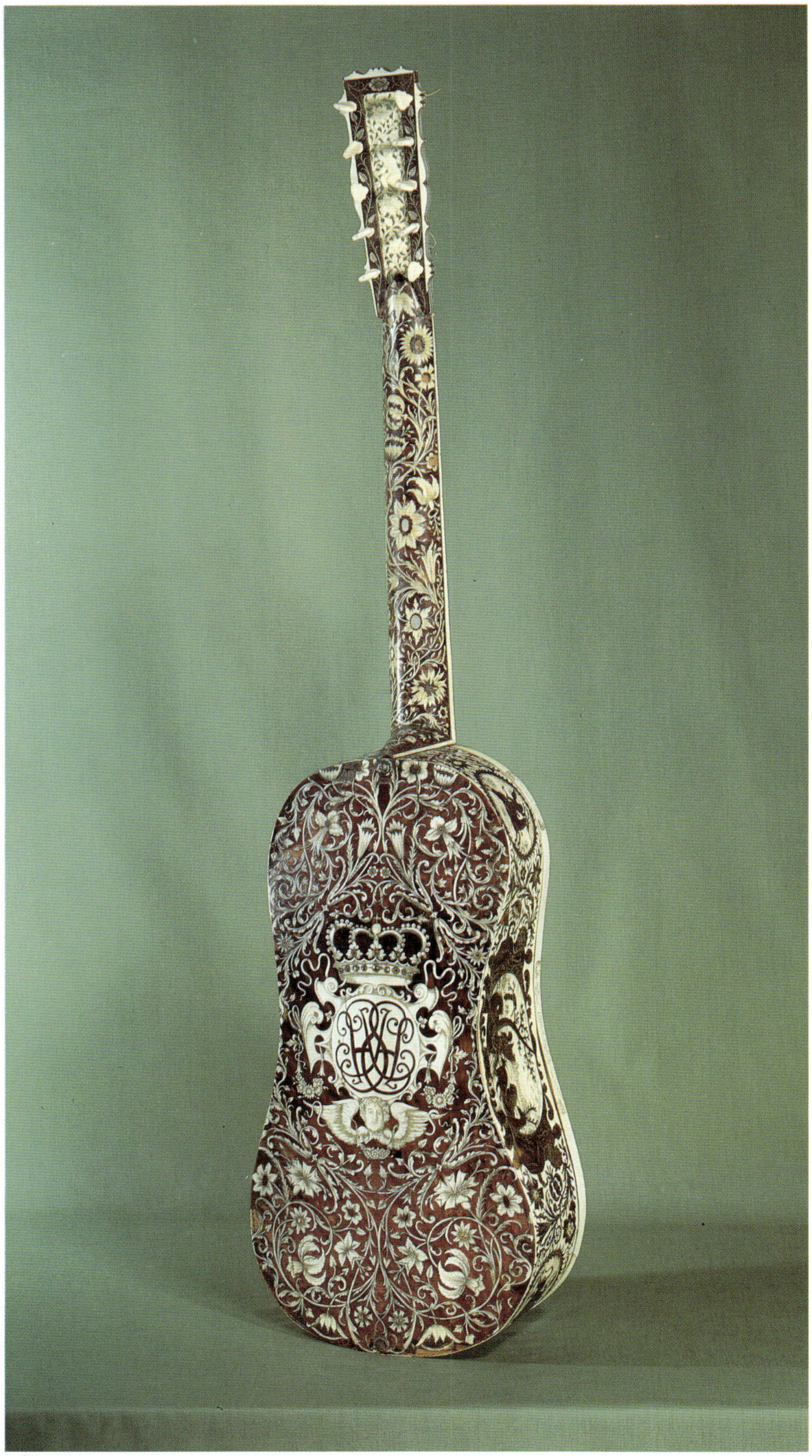

342
Two vases with flowers
Vases made of knitted silver thread. Flowers of silk and silk thread in red and yellow with green leaves, most of them edged with silver thread, h. 22.5 cm and 21 cm respectively. Copenhagen 1690s
The Royal Collections, Rosenborg Palace, Copenhagen (7-251, 7-252)
PROV. 1824 from the Royal Kunstkammer, Kk, 1737, 782, 599

Presented to King Christian v by the female midget Elschen on New Year's Eve 1697.

343
Joachim Tielke
Guitar
Tortoise veneered and inlaid ivory with naturalistic flowers and garlands, allegorical figures and a cartouche with Sophie Hedevig's (King Frederik iv's Sister, 1677-1737) monogram, l. 98 cm, largest w. 25.2 cm. Hamburg 1703 (*ill.*)
The Royal Collections, Rosenborg Palace, Copenhagen (11-21)
PROV. 1849 from the Lord Chamberlain's Department
LIT. Mogens Bencard, *Musical Instruments at Rosenborg*, (Paper at Cimcim Conference 1982, Copenhagen); Günther Hellwig, *Joachim Tielke*, Frankfurt am Main 1980, no. 114

344
Magnus Berg (1666-1739)
Ivory relief, 'Smell'
Part of a series of the senses. Woman smelling a rose in her right hand. In her left hand, a lily, 11.1 *x* 9.9 cm. Sign. 'Magnus Berg fecit'.Copenhagen before 1731
The Royal Collections, Rosenborg Palace, Copenhagen (12-341)
PROV. 1867 from the Statens Museum for Kunst. Kk 1713, 700.364/21
EXH. *Magnus Berg 1666-1739*, Rosenborg Palace, Copenhagen 1989
LIT. L. Dietrichson, *Magnus Berg*, 1912, pp. 128, 204; Åshild Paulsen, *Magnus Berg*, Oslo 1989, no. E 34

345
Basket with flowers in box
Wood, glass, and textile, h. 56 cm, w. 48 cm, dp. 8.5 cm. Sign. 'D. Lassen 1829'. Denmark 1829
Nationalmuseet, Brede (2/1910-L 444 *a*)

346
Bridal bouquet and bridal wreath
Feathers and wire. Bouquet: h. 19 cm. Wreath: l. 25 cm. Frederikshavn, Denmark 1830-40s (*fig. 114*)
Nationalmuseet, Brede (1605-1606/1945)

347
Photograph of newly married couple and bridal wreath in box
Photograph, pearls, wood, metal, paper, textile, h. 41.5 cm, w. 37 cm, dp. 7.5 cm. Tune Parish, Denmark 1867
Nationalmuseet, Brede (1001/1989)

348
Ville Vallgren (1855-1940)
Bronze statuette, 'Calla'
Redish-brown and green patina, h. 27 cm. Sign. 'Vallgren'. Sweden 1897
Kunstindustrimuseet, Copenhagen (1000)
EXH. *Almänna Konst- och Industriutställningen 1897*, Stockholm, cat. no. 1549

349
Perfume bottle, 'Coque d'or'
Bow-shaped. Cobalt-coloured glass, partly gilded. Glass stopper ground in. Guerlain, Paris 1937
Torben Hardenberg, Copenhagen
LIT. *Baccarat. Les flacons à parfum*, Paris 1986, no. 770

350
Silver rose
From Richard Strauss' *and* Hugo von Hofmannsthal's opera *Der Rosen Kavalier*
Søren Frandsen's scenography, Det kongelige Teater, Copenhagen 1976, l. 41 cm. Box: h. 8-13 cm, l. 47 cm, w. 12-24 cm
The Royal Theatre, Copenhagen

351
Raimo Kanerva (b. 1941)
'The Tulip Chair'
Chair of aluminum with tulips growing from the seat, h. 72 cm. Finland ca. 1980 (*ill.*)
Galerie Börjeson, Malmö, Sweden

352
Lars Ravn (b. 1959)
Sculpture, flowers in a vase
Wrought iron and glass, h. ca. 250 cm. Copenhagen 1990
Lars Ravn, Copenhagen

353
Torben Hardenberg (b. 1949)
Fountain, 'Novalis' Blue Pavillon'
Triangular basin of zinc, upper part of copper. Trellis work mounted with cast fantastic figures, flowers and insects painted in various colours, h. ca. 200 cm. Copenhagen 1990
Torben Hardenberg, Copenhagen

Notes and bibliographies to articles

Peter Wagner
Flower gardens, flower fashions and illustrated botanical works

pp. 8-23

1 John Prest, *The Garden of Eden. The Botanic Garden and the Re-Creation of Paradise*, New Haven/London 1981
2 Hans-Otto Keunecke, 'Hortus Eystettensis. Zur Geschichte eines Gartens und eines Buches', *Schriften der Universitätsbibliothek Erlangen-Nürnberg*, vol. 20, Munich 1989
3 Peter Wagner, 'Otto Sperling's uddannelse og virksomhed som botaniker', *Medicinsk Forum*, vol. 41, Copenhagen 1988, pp. 169-181
4 Wilfrid Blunt, *The Art of Botanical Illustration*, London 1950, pp. 106, 112-113
5 Helga de Cuveland, *Der Gottorfer Codex von Hans Simon Holtzbecker*, Worms 1989
6 Blanche Henrey, *British Botanical and Horticultural Literature before 1800. I. The Sixteenth and Seventeenth Centuries. History and Bibliography*, London 1975, p. 77
7 Blunt, *op.cit.*, p. 111
8 Prest, *op.cit.*, p. 92 ff.
9 Blunt, *op.cit.*, pp. 127-129
10 Vibeke Woldbye, 'Hollandske Blomstertæpper i Danmark', *Det danske Kunstindustrimuseum. Virksomhed 1964-1969*, Copenhagen 1969, pp. 51-78
11 Lys de Bray, *The Art of Botanical Illustration. The Classic Illustrators and Their Achievements from 1550 to 1900*, Bromley 1989, p. 43
12 *Ibid.*, p. 40 ff.; Blunt, *op.cit.*, p. 117 ff.; I. Bergström, *Stillebenmåleri under 1600-talet*, Göteborg 1947
13 Anne Fox Maule & Peter Wagner, 'Renaissance til revolution', *Naturens Historiefortællere 1. Udviklingsideens historie. Fra Platon til Darwin*, Niels Bonde (et al. ed.), Copenhagen 1985, pp. 125-155; J. J. Rousseau, 'Lettres élémentaires sur la botanique', *Collection complète des œuvres de J. J. Rousseau citoyen de Genève. Tome quatorzième, contenant le IV. volume de melange*, 1782. J. Aubry published the engraved illustrations 1789. Translated into English, French and Danish, *Botanik for Fruentimmere i Breve til Fru L***, 2. ed., Copenhagen 1790
14 Prest, *op.cit.*, p. 102 ff.
15 Gerta Calmann, *Ehret. Flower Painter Extraordinary. An illustrated Bibliography*, Oxford 1977
16 Blunt, *op.cit.*, pp. 173-182
17 Peter Wagner, 'Det kongelige værk Flora Danica, *Flora Danica og det danske hof*, Ole Villumsen Krog (ed.), Copenhagen 1990, pp. 14-43
18 Blunt, *op.cit.*, pp. 156-158
19 *Ibid.*, pp. 184-188
20 David Elliston Allen, 'Natural History and Visual Taste: Some Parallel Tendencies', *The Natural Sciences and the Arts. Aspects of Interaction from the Renaissance to the 20th. Century. An International Symposium. Acta Universitatis Upsaliensis. Figura Nova Series 22*, Uppsala 1985, pp. 32-45
21 Allen, *op.cit.*, pp. 41-42
22 Winfried Baer, 'Zur Geschichte der botanisch-wissenschaftlichen Dekore auf Porzellan', Winfried Baer & Walter Lack, *Pflanzen auf Porzellan. Austellung zum 300 jährigen Bestehen des Botanischen Gartens Berlin*, Berlin 1979, pp. 19-24

Hanne Westergaard
The immortal motif

pp. 24-36

SELECTED LITERATURE

Budde Christensen, Johan Lange, Jette Dahl Møller, Michael Sterll, *Oldemors potteplanter*, cat. Botanisk have, Copenhagen 1988

Sven Delblanc, 'Den giftiga blomman. Erotiska motiv i Strindbergs ålderdomsdiktning', *Studier tillägnade Gunnar Tideström*, Uppsala 1965-66

Emil Hannover, 'At bygge Bo og at bo i Hygge', (1897), *Vort Hjem*, 1901, (*Smaaskrifter VII 1899-1901*, pp. 260-284)

Lisbeth Hertel, 'Karen Blixens blomster', *Karen Blixens blomster. Natur og kunst paa Rungstedlund*, Copenhagen 1983

Frank Høifødt, 'Smertens blomst – et supplement', *Kunst og Kultur*, vol. 4 1989

Mindeblade om Professor, Blomstermaler Johan Lauritz Jensen, Copenhagen 1856

Hanne Westergaard, *H. C. Andersens blomster. Haver. Buketter. Billeder*, Copenhagen 1978

Idem, *O. D. Ottesen. Arbejdsbog og optegnelser*, Copenhagen 1979

H. C. Andersen, *Eventyr og fortællinger*, many editions

Herman Bang, *Elna*, Copenhagen 1883

Idem, *Sommerglæder*, Copenhagen 1902

Charles Baudelaire, *Les fleurs du mal*, 1857

The Poetical Works of Rupert Brooke, Geoffrey Keynes (ed.), London 1946

Gabriele D'Annunzio, *Piacere*, 1889

Emma Gad, *Takt og Tone*, Copenhagen 1918

Poul Henningsen, *Kulturkritik 1-4*, Copenhagen 1973
Anthony Hope, *The Prisoner of Zenda*, 1894
I. P. Jacobsen, 'Kender du Pan?', *Arabesk* I (1868), *Digte og Udkast*, Vilh. Møller & Edv. Brandes (eds.), Copenhagen 1886
Idem, *Niels Lyhne* begun 1874, Copenhagen 1880
Idem, *Mogens og andre Noveller*, Copenhagen 1882
Marcel Proust, *A la recherche du Temps perdu*, 1913-27
Oscar Wilde, *The Picture of Dorian Gray*, 1891

Bettina von Meyenburg
'Saying it with Flowers'

pp. 37-56

SELECTED LITERATURE

Francis Bacon, *Gesta Grayorum*, London 1592
Pieter Biesboer, 'Tulipa Turcarum – über die Tulipomania in Europa', *Europa und der Orient*, Berlin 1989, pp. 288-294
Wilfrid Blunt, *Tulipomania*, Harmondsworth 1950
Idem, *The Art of Botanical Illustration*, London 1950
Stefan Bursche, *Tafelzier des Barock*, Munich 1974
Joachim Cameriarius II, *Symbolorum et emblematum ex re herbaria*, Nuremberg 1593
Alice Coats, *The Treasury of Flowers*, London 1975
R. Colie, 'Still Life, Paradoxes of Being', *The Renaissance Tradition of Paradox*, Princeton 1966, p. 272 ff.
Johanna Dittmar, *Blumen und Blumensträusse als Opfergabe im alten Ägypten*, Munich 1986
John Fisher, *The Origins of Garden Plants*, 1982
Alain Gruber, *Blumen*, cat. Abegg-Stiftung, Riggisberg 1986
Marie-Louise Hairs, *Les peintres flamands de fleurs au 17ème siècle*, Brussels 1985
Dieter Hennebo, *Gärten des Mittelalters*, Munich 1987
P. Hulton & L. Smith, *Flowers in Art from East and West*, cat. British Museum, London 1975
Th. Dacosta Kaufmann, *L'Ecole de Prague*, Paris 1985
Jarmila Kraclova, 'Die Gärten Rudolfs II in Prag', *Leids Kunsthistorisch Jaarboek 1982*
Jacob Masen, *Speculum imaginum veritatis occultae*, Cologne 1650
Abbé Picinelli, *Mondo symbolico*, Milan 1654
John Prest, *The Garden of Eden*, London 1981
L. J. Ringbom, *Paradis terrestre. Myt och verklighet*, Åbo Akademi s.d.
Cesare Ripa, *Iconologia*, Padua 1624-25
Joachim von Sandrart, *Academie der Bau-, Bild- und Mahlerey-Künste*, Nuremberg 1675-94
Simon Schama, *The Embarrassment of Riches*, London 1987
Norbert Schneider, *Stilleben, Realität und Symbolik der Dinge*, Cologne 1989
Sam Segal, 'The Flower Pieces of Roelandt Savery', *Leids Kunsthistorisch Jaarboek 1982*
Idem, *Tulips by Anthony Claesz*, Maastricht 1987
Idem, *A Prosperous Past – The Sumptuous Still Life in the Netherlands 1600-1700*, cat. Fogg Art Museum, Cambridge 1988
Stilleben, cat. Westfälisches Landesmuseum, Münster 1979
A. L. Storck, 'Tulipes sauvages et cultivées', *Série documentaire 13 des Conservatoire et Jardin botanique*, Geneva 1984
Emmanuel Sweerts, *Florilegium*, Frankfurt 1612
Alain Tapié, *Symbolique et botanique*, cat. Musée des Beaux Arts, Caen 1987
Piero Valeriano, *Hieroglyphica sive de sacris*, Milan 1654
Vibeke Woldbye, 'Hollandske blomstertæpper i Danmark', *Det danske Kunstindustrimuseum. Virksomhed 1964-1969*, Copenhagen 1969, pp. 51-78
Vibeke Woldbye & Bettina von Meyenburg (ed.), *Konkylien og Mennesket*, cat. Kunstindustrimuseet, Copenhagen 1983

Saskia de Bodt
An encyclopaedia of forms

pp. 57-73

1 For a survey of the aesthetic theories concerning ornament and naturalism in (proto) Art Nouveau, cf., Stephan Tschudi Madsen, *Sources of Art Nouveau*, Oslo 1956, pp. 164-187 ('The cult of plant and line')
2 Émile Gallé, 'Le mobilier contemporain orné d'après la nature', *Revue des arts décoratifs*, Nov. & Dec. 1900, in Émile Gallé, *Écrits pour l'Art. Floriculture, Art décoratif, Notices d'exposition (1884-1889)*, Paris 1980, pp. 237-276. Annoted after the article: 'Émile Gallé ne devait pas écrire la dernière partie de cette étude'.
3 Gillian Naylor, *William Morris by Himself. Designs and Writings*, London/Sydney (1988) 1989, p. 205
4 John Ruskin, a.o. *Modern Painters*, vols. 5-7
5 Gallé, *op.cit.*, 1908
6 Quoted by Ian Bradley, *William Morris and his World*, London 1978, pp. 37-38
7 Graham Shankland, 'William Morris, Designer', *William Morris. Selected Writings*, Asa Briggs (ed.), Harmondsworth (1962) 1973
8 *Fantin-Latour*, cat. Grand Palais, Paris 1982 (several exhibitors), p. 21
9 *Georgiana Burne-Jones*, *Memorials of Edward Burne-Jones*, London/New York 1906, vol. I, p. 287
10 A. M. W. Stirling, *William de Morgan and his Wife*, New York 1902, pp. 199, 207, 318
11 From 'The Defence of Guinevere and other Poems' (1858), Briggs (ed.), *op.cit.*, Harmondsworth (1962) 1973, pp. 48-55
12 Burne-Jones, *op.cit.*, vol. I, p. 196
13 *Ibid.*, vol. I, p. 212
14 Aymer Vallance, *William Morris. His Art, his Writings and his Public Life*, London (1897) 1986, p. 49
15 'I hate the country – apples only can keep me in good spirits. Topsy's [Morris's] garden is perfectly laden with them' (1860). Cf., Burne-Jones, *op.cit.*, vol. I, p. 211
16 *Oxford and Cambridge Magazine*,

1865, in *William Morris: Selected Writings*, G. D. H. Cole (ed.), London 1946, pp. 275-276

17 On old-fashioned gardens and the attitude of William Morris and John Ruskin, see Michael Waters, 'Old-Fashioned Gardens' & 'Floral Codes', *The Garden in Victorian Literature*, Cambridge 1988, pp. 48-71, 109-148

18 *The Collected Works of William Morris*, May Morris (ed.), vols. 1-24, London 1910-1915, vol. 22, pp. 87-90

19 For a modern critical survey of the most important European garden theorists, cf., Clemens Alexander Wimmer, *Geschichte der Gartentheorie*, Darmstadt *1989*

20 Cf., catalogue section of Linda Parry, *William Morris Textiles*, London 1983

21 Barbara Morris, *Inspiration for Design. The Influence of the Victoria and Albert Museum*, London 1986, pp. 83-93

22 Cf., Peter Floud, 'Dating Morris Patterns', *Architectural Review*, July 1959, s.p.; Parry, *op.cit.*, p. 54 ff.; B. Morris, *op.cit.*, p. 104 ff.

23 L. F. Day, 'The Art of William Morris', *Art Journal* (special number), London 1899, p. 17

24 John Ruskin, 'Lecture VII: Colour', *Lectures on Art*, London 1906, pp. 217-221

25 Emma Lazarus, 'A Day in Surrey with William Morris', *The Century Illustrated Magazine*, vol. 32, no. J, July 1886. Quoted by Parry, *op.cit.*, p. 44

26 Kelmscott House, 7 May 1883, written to his daughter Jenny. Cf., Naylor, *op.cit.*, p. 203

27 Cf., A. R. Dufty, *Kelmscott. An Illustrated Guide*, London 1977; *idem*, *William Morris and Kelmscott*, London 1981

28 Cf., Burne-Jones, *op.cit.*, vol. 2, p. 86

29 Vallance, *op.cit.*, p. 191

30 Naylor, *op.cit.*, p. 101

31 'The Beauty of Life', (lecture 1880), Naylor, *op.cit.*, pp. 209-210

32 Burne-Jones, *op.cit.*, vol. 1, pp. 153, 155, 175

33 *Ibid.*, vol. 1, p. 261

34 *Ibid.*, vol. 1, p. 225

35 *Ibid.*, vol. 2, p. 227

36 *Ibid.*, vol. 2, p. 177

37 *Ibid.*, vol. 2, pp. 118-120

38 'The Garden', *Blackwood's Magazine*, vol. 73, 1854, p. 142. Quoted by Waters, *op.cit.*, p. 96

39 Philippe Garner, *Émile Gallé*, London 1976, pp. 11-34

40 Gallé, *op.cit.*, 1980, p. 239

41 *Ibid.*, introduction

42 Émile Gallé, 'L'Horticulture et les versants méridionaux des Alpes. Notes de voyage', *Bulletin de la Société d'horticulture de Nancy*, December 1877, February & April 1878, in Gallé, *op.cit.*, 1980, pp. 3-56

43 Francoise-Thérèse Charpentier, *Émile Gallé*, Nancy 1978, p. 30. Information given by a former gardener and Lucille Perdrizet-Gallé, daughter of Émile Gallé. My thanks are due to Mr. Dingenus van de Vrie for this reference

44 Émile Gallé, *Bulletin de la Société d'horticulture de Nancy*, April 1892, in Gallé, *op.cit.*, 1980, pp. 61-63

45 Émile Gallé, 'Le salon de floriculture à Nancy juillet 1893', *Bulletin de la Société d'horticulture de Nancy*, October 1893; Gallé, *op.cit.*, 1980, pp. 64-75

46 Philippe Garner, *op.cit.*, p. 25

47 Descriptions by Emile Gallé for 'Le vase Pasteur' and 'Le vase Prouvé', *op.cit.*, 1980, pp. 148-154, 183-185

48 Maurice Guillard (et al.), *Claude Monet at the Time of Giverny*, cat. Centre Culturel du Marais, Paris 1983, pp. 16-17. Letter of June 5th 1883

49 The different phases of the 'flower-tunnel' are described in *Claude Monet at the Time of Giverny*, 1983, pp. 14-15

50 Letter presumably from February 1900. Cf., *Monet by Himself*, Richard Kendall (ed.), London/Sydney 1989, p. 187

51 Max Sauerlandt in *Jahrbuch der Stiftung Seebühl Ada und Emil Nolde*, Flensburg 1959, p. 18

52 Emil Nolde, *Reisen, Achtung, Befreiung. 1919-1946*, Cologne 1967, p. 9

53 *Ibid.*, p. 28

Maria Fabricius Hansen
Flowering welfare

pp. 74-81

SELECTED LITERATURE

Julie Schafler Dale, 'Anna Polesny', *Art to Wear*, New York 1986, pp. 203-205

Bente Hansen (et al. ed.), *Dengang i 60'erne. – Billeder fra dengang, tekster fra i dag*, Copenhagen 1978

Jennifer Harris (et al.), *1966 and All That. Design and the Consumer in Britain 1960-1969*, London 1986

Hommage à Balenciaga, cat. Musée Historique des Tissus de Lyon, 1985

Kynaston McShine, *Andy Warhol. A Retrospective*, cat. The Museum of Modern Art, New York 1989

John Szarkowski, *Irving Penn*, cat. The Museum of Modern Art, New York 1984

Jens Erik Sørensen & Hans-Olof Boström (ed.), *'Covers' – Pladeomslag 1950-1981*, cat. Aarhus Kunstmuseum, Århus 1981

Winfried Baer
Botanical décors on porcelain

pp. 82-92

1 Wilfrid Blunt, *The Art of Botanical Illustration*, London 1950; *idem*, *The Compleat Naturalist. A Life of Linnaeus*, London 1971; K. Gerstenberg, 'Die naturwissenschaftliche Richtung in der deutschen Blumenmalerei', *Zeitschrift für Kunstwissenschaft*, vol. 7, 1953, p. 85; A. Lane, 'Flower Painting on Pottery and Porcelain', *The Geographical Magazine*, vol. 18, May 1945-April 1946, p. 522; C. Nissen, *Die Botanische Buchillustration. Ihre Geschichte und Bibliographie*, Stuttgart 1951, vol. 2; *idem*, 'Die naturwissenschaftliche Abbildung', *Gutenberg-Jahrbuch*, 1944, no. 49; P. Hulton & L. Smith, *Flowers in Art from East and West*, cat. British Museum, London 1979

2 A. Arber, 'Goethe's Botany', *Chronica Botanica*, Leiden 1946, vol. 10, pp. 63-126

3 F. H. Hoffmann, *Das Porzellan der*

europäischen Manufakturen im XVIII. *Jahrhundert*, Berlin 1932, pp. 459-462; R. Rückert, *Meissener Porzellan 1710-1810*, cat. Bayerisches Nationalmuseum, Munich 1966, p. 129; H. Jedding, *Europäisches Porzellan. Von den Anfängen bis 1800*, Munich 1971, vol. I

4 W. Mrazek & W. Neuwirth, *Wiener Porzellan 1718-1864*, cat. Österreichisches Museum für Angewandte Kunst, Vienna 1970, p. 41

5 Blunt, *op.cit.*, 1950, p. 167; C. Hansen & A. Fox Maule, 'Pehr Osbeck's Collections and Linnaeus's Species Plantarum (1753)', *Botanical Journal of the Linnean Society*, vol. 67, Oct. 1973, no. 3, pp. 190, 191, 211; B. Gyllensvärd, *Oriental Ceramics, the World's great Collections*, Museum of Far Eastern Antiquities, Stockholm, Tokyo 1976, vol. 9, no. & fig. 99; Blunt, *op.cit.*, 1971, pl. 8, p. 238, figs. 185-186; W. Baer & H. W. Lack, *Pflanzen auf Porzellan. Ausstellung zum 300jährigen Bestehen des Botanischen Gartens Berlin*, Berlin 1979, pp. 25-29, pl. I

6 Examples in Franks-Collection, British Museum, and in Victoria & Albert Museum, both in London. Cf., J. Ayers & D. S. Howard, *China for the West: Chinese Porcelain and other Decorative Arts from the Mottadedeh Collection*, London/New York 1978, vol. I, pp. 304-305

7 B. Gardener, 'Sir Hans Sloane's Plants on Chelsea Porcelain', *Transactions of the English Porcelain Circle*, vol. 4, 1932, p. 22; *idem*, 'Sir Hans Sloane's Chelsea Porcelain Heirlooms in the Possession of Major R. C. H. Sloane Stanley', *Transactions of the English Ceramic Circle*, vol. 2, 1939, no. 6, pp. 26-27; F. S. Mackenna, 'Botanical Painting on Chelsea Porcelain', *Apollo*, vol. 56, July 1952, no. 329, p. 7; G. Calmann, *Ehret, Flower Painter Extraordinary*, Oxford 1977; Baer & Lack, *op.cit.*, 1979, pp. 29-33, figs. 10-11

8 C. Scherer, *Das Fürstenberger Porzellan*, Berlin 1909, p. 24; S. Ducret, *Fürstenberger Porzellan*, Braunschweig 1965, vol. I, p. 82, vol. 2, p. 132; B. Frfr. v. Wolff Metternich, *Fürstenberg Porzellan, ein Brevier*, Braunschweig 1976, p. 22; Baer & Lack, *op.cit.*, 1979, pp. 33-36, figs. 15-20

9 E. J. Soil de Moriamé & L. Deplace de Formanoir, *La manufacture impériale et royale de porcelaine de Tournay*, Tournai 1937; *Exposition de porcelaine de pâte tendre*, cat. Musée de Mariémont, 1958, no. 247; A.-M. Marien-Dugardin, *Porcelaines de Tournai*, cat. Musées Royaux d'Art et d'Histoire, Brussels 1959; *idem, Porcelaines de Tournai du* XVIIIe *siècle. Trésors inconnus du Musée de Mariémont 4*, Morlanwelz 1969; H. Jedding, *Europäisches Porzellan. Von den Anfängen bis 1800*, Munich 1971, vol. I, p. 11-170; M. Jottrand, 'Le peintre de fleurs G.-D. Ehret et la porcelaine de Tournai', *Les Cahiers de Mariémont*, vol. 3, 1972, pp. 25-47; Baer & Lack, *op.cit.*, 1979, pp. 36-40, figs. 23-25

10 A. Hayden, *Kopenhagener Porzellan*, Leipzig 1913, pp. 105-120; V. Christensen, 'The Flora Danica Service', *The Connoisseur*, July 1935, pp. 28-29; B. L. Grandjean, *The Flora Danica Service*, Copenhagen 1950; Baer & Lack, *op.cit.*, 1979, pp. 41-49, figs. 27, 29, 37, 39, 40, 44, 45 & pl. 2; O. Villumsen Krog (ed.), *Flora Danica og det danske hof*, Copenhagen 1990

11 F. B. Gilhespy, *Derby Porcelain*, London 1961; F. A. Barrett & A. L. Thorpe, *Derby Porcelain 1750-1848*, London 1971; A. Stevenson (ed.), *Catalogue of Botanical Books in the Collection of Rachel McMasters Miller Hunt*, Pittsburgh/Penns. 1961, vol. 2 (1), p. 110 (Hunt Botanical Library); Baer & Lack, *op.cit.*, 1979, pp. 49-50, fig. 52

12 A. George, *Exhibition of Derby Porcelain painted by William 'Quaker' Pegg 1775-1851*, London 1977; Baer & Lack, *op.cit.*, 1979, pp. 50-52, fig. 54

13 *Christie's Review of the Season 1987*, col. pl. p. 377 (below)

14 Cf., J. Murdoch & J. Twichett, *Painters and the Derby China Works*, cat. Victoria & Albert Museum, London 1987

15 'Manufacture nationale de Sèvres', *Archives*, Carton Pb 1, Caisse 1 (Travaux des ateliers 1800-1808); O. Marschall v. Bieberstein (ed.), *Eine Adoptivtochter Napoleon I., Stephanie, Grossherzogin von Baden*, Leipzig 1902; F. Walter, *Stephanie Napoleon. Lebensweg und Weggenossen*, 1789-1860, Baden-Baden [1948]; P. Verlet, S. Grandjean & M. Brunet, *Sèvres*, Paris 1953; R. de Plinval de Guillebon, *Porcelain de Paris 1770-1850*, Fribourg 1972, pp. 246-248 & stamped mark 137; Baer & Lack, *op.cit.*, 1979, pp. 52-65, figs. 55, 57-59, 61, 63-65

16 J. G. Schadow, *Kunst-Werke und Kunst-Ansichten*, Berlin 1849, p. XVII; G. Kolbe, *Geschichte der Königlichen Porcellanmanufaktur zu Berlin*, Berlin 1863, pp. 201, 215; S. Grandjean, *Inventaire après décès de l'Impératrice Joséphine à Malmaison*, Paris s.d., p. 85; E. Köllmann, *Berliner Porzellan 1763-1963*, Braunschweig 1966, vol. I, p. 223; *idem*, 'Ein Berliner Teller für Kaiserin Joséphine', *Keramos*, 1970, no. 48, pp. 47-48; H. W. Lack & W. Baer, 'Ein «botanisches» Porzellanservice aus Berlin für Kaiserin Joséphine', *Willdenowia 8*, pp. 235-259; Baer & Lack, *op.cit.*, 1979, pp. 64-76 & figs. 73, 75, 79, 81, 82, 91, 98, 100, 101, 108-110 & pl. 3; *Pierre-Joseph Redouté. Le 'Raphaël des Fleurs' 1759-1840*, cat. Centre d'Action Culturelle de la Communauté d'Expression francaise (CACEF) et du Centre Culturel de la Comunauté française de Belgique à Paris, Paris 1982, cat. no. 7, 9, 11 (Les Porcelaines)

17 H. Börsch-Supan (ed.), *Die Kataloge der Berliner Akademie-Ausstellungen 1786-1850*, Berlin 1971, vol. I, no. 467-468

18 H. W. Lack & W. Baer, 'Pflanzen aus Kew auf Porzellan aus Berlin', *Willdenowia 16* (1986), pp. 285-312; G. Himmelheber, *Kunst des Biedermeier 1815-1835*, cat. Bayerisches Nationalmuseum, Munich 1988, cat. no. 143, fig. & pl. p. 119; *idem, Biedermeier 1815-1835*, Munich 1989, cat. no. 143, fig. & pl. p. 119

19 A. V. Sidorov, *Pawlowsk. Putevoditel po pawlowskomu dvorzu i parku*, Leningrad 1936, pp. 74-75, A. Kuchumov, *Pavlovsk, Palace & Park*,

Leningrad 1975, pp. 293-294; Baer & Lack, *op.cit.*, 1979, pp. 83-86, figs. 131, 133, 135, 137, 139 & 132, 138, 140

20 W. Wehrlin, 'Mon Musée Russe', *Connaissance des Arts*, August 1964, p. 45, fig. 18 (three plates dated 1822); L. Nikiforova, *Russian Porcelain in the Hermitage Collection*, Leningrad 1973 (one plate dated 1827); *Sotheby Parke Bernet & Co.*, Los Angeles, 6.-9.3.1978, lot 812 (12 plates dated 1827 and provided with number of volume and page); Baer & Lack, *op.cit.*, 1979, pp. 86-87, figs. 144,145; V.H. Taylor, *Russian Art at Hillwood*, Hillwood Museum (USA), 1988, fig. 112 (dish decorated with a rose and a different border, dated 1826)

21 Baer & Lack, *op.cit.*, 1979, pp. 80-82, figs. 127-130

22 *Ibid.*, pp. 90-102, figs. 150, 160, 168-170, 174, 181, 189, 203, 207, 208, 213, 214, 219-221

23 *Ibid.*, pp. 104-114, figs. 229-231, 250, 251, 253, 254, 261, 280, 282, 283 & pl. 4

24 Cf., J. Knapp, *Jacquins Denkmal. Ein naturwissenschaftliches Huldigungsbild von 1822*, Vienna 1976 (Bildheft 1 der Österreichischen Galerie, Schloss Belvedere)

25 Baer & Lack, *op.cit.*, 1979, pp. 119-124, figs. 324, 331, 332

26 Cf., *Sotheby's. Later English and Continental Ceramics*, 20.3.1990, London, lot 5 (ill.) (all of them marked with their botanical name); cf., Baer & Lack, *op.cit.*, 1979, pp. 88-89, fig. 146; *Sotheby's. Later English and Continental Ceramics*, 7.3.1989, London, lot 50 (ill.)

27 Cf., D. G. Rice, *The Illustrated Guide to Rockingham Pottery and Porcelain*, London 1971, pl. 95

28 *Sotheby's. Later European Ceramics*, 15.3.1988, London, lot 69 (ill.)

29 Cf., *Christie's Review of the Season*, Oxford 1987, col. pl. p. 377 (top)

30 Cf., *Sotheby's, op.cit.*, 1988, lot 161 (ill.) (no name indicated)

31 Cf., *Sotheby's, op.cit.*, 1989, lot 109 (col. pl.) (no name indicated)

Peter Wagner
Icones Florae Danicae

pp. 93-100

1 Kgl. resolution of 6 May 1754. Chatollkassens memorialbog pro 1754, p. 27 ff., appendix no. 3. The National Archive, Copenhagen

2 Kgl. resolution of 3 Oct. 1752. Chatollkassens memorialbog pro 1752, p. 50 ff., appendix no. 186. The National Archive, Copenhagen

3 Pro Memoria for de resp. Herrer Professorer ved det Kongl. Sculptur og Maler Academie i København. 28 Nov. 1753 fra A. G. Moltke. Concept in Bregentved Archive

4 Jens Petersen Lund (ca. 1725-1793)

5 Statement signed by L. A. Leclerc, C. G. Pilo, J. M. Preisler, I. C. Petzold and S. C Stanley. 8 Dec. 1753. Bregentved Archive

6 Letter from Eigtved addressed to Moltke, 9 Dec. 1753. Bregentved Archive

7 Letter from von Berger and Wohlert addressed to Moltke, 14 Jan. 1754. Bregentved Archive

8 Letter from I. G. Zinn addressed to Oeder, 25 March 1754. Abstract in Bregentved Archive

9 Cf., note 1

10 Wilfrid Blunt, *The Art of Botanical Illustration*, London 1950, p. 146

11 'A Memoir of Georg Dionysius Ehret' (written by himself, and translated, with notes, by E. S. Barton), *Proceedings of the Linnean Society of London 1894-95*, pp. 41-58, espec. pp. 55-56

12 Chatollkassens memorialbog pro 1755, 31 May, pp. 46-47, appendix no. 155. The National Archive, Copenhagen

13 A. von Halem, *Andenken an Oeder*, Altona 1793, pp. 30-31

14 Letter from Oeder addressed to Moltke, 2 Sept. 1761 and from Moltke addressed to Oeder, 21 Sept. 1761. Bregentved Archive

15 H. D. Schepelern, 'Danske konkyliesamlere', *Konkylien og Mennesket*, Vibeke Woldbye & Bettina von Meyenburg (ed.), cat. Kunstindustrimuseet, Copenhagen 1983, p. 44

16 Letter from Oeder addressed to Moltke, 25 Nov. 1761. Bregentved Archive

17 Letter from Oeder to Bishop Gunnerus, 5 March 1763. Ove Dahl, 'Biskop Gunnereus' Virksomhed fornemmelig som Botaniker tilligemed en Oversigt over Botanikens Tilstand i Danmark og Norge indtil hans Død', III, *Det kgl. norske Videnskabers Selskabs Skrifter 1897*, no. 4., Brev no. 504, pp. 6-9

18 Blunt, *op.cit.*, p. 153

19 August Johan Rösel von Rosenhof, *Der monatlich-herausgegebenen Insekten-Belustigung 1-4 Theil... sauber illuminirten Kupfern, nach dem Leben abgebildet...*, Nuremberg 1746-61

20 Pro memoria 31 Dec. 1761. Bregentved Archive

21 Chatollkassens memorialbog pro 1762, pp. 20, 158, appendix no. 52; with a summary of the meeting at the Royal Danish Academy 3. Febr. 1762 and 'kgl. resolution af 27.ejusdem'. The National Archive, Copenhagen

22 *Icones plantarum... florae Danicae*, fasc. 7, Copenhagen 1768, p. 10. Kaltenhofer executed 29 plates for *Flora Danica*

23 I. W. Hornemann, 'Historisk-kritiske Bemærkninger over Flora Danica', *Det skandinaviske Litteraturselskabs Skrifter*, vol. 5, Copenhagen 1809, p. 327

24 Jean Anker, 'Billedfremstilling til *Flora Danica* i det attende Aarhundrede', *Philobiblon 2*, Copenhagen 1949, p. 123

25 *Ibid.*, pp. 123-124

26 *Ibid.*, p. 125

Jørgen Hein
Fashions in floral enamels

pp. 101-106

1 Jørgen Hein, 'Goldemail des Manierismus und Frühbarocks', *Kunst & Antiquitäten*, vol. 2, Munich 1988, pp. 26-37

2 Ismail Ünal, 'Cin Porselenleri Üzerindeki Türk Târsiâti', *Türk San'ate tarihi Araztirma ve Jncelemeleri*, Istanbul 1963, vol. 1, pp. 676-711

3 Note 1: figs. 9-11, 15; *idem*, 'Christian

IV's skatte', no. 604, *Christian IV and Europe*, Steffen Heiberg (ed.), cat., Copenhagen 1988

4 Jørgen Hein, 'Der dänische Krönungsdegen', *Kunst & Antiquitäten*, IV, Munich 1989, pp. 62-64

5 Erik Lassen, 'En dansk prinsesses guldkande', *Det danske Kunstindustrimuseum. Virksomhed 1959-1964*, Copenhagen 1964, pp. 40-47

6 Gudmund Boesen, *Danmarks Riges Regalier*, Copenhagen 1986, p. 90 ff.; Jørgen Hein, 'Frederik III's kroning og regalier', *Historisk tidsskrift*, 1990, no. 1, pp. 78-79

7 Covered goblet attributed to the turner Jacob Jensen Nordmand, who does not, however, give the enameler's name. Cf., Mogens Bencard, 'Two 17th-century Eskimos at Rosenborg Palace', *Meddelelser om Grønland*, (Man & Society 12), 1989, pp. 47-55. A replica of Paul Prieur's miniature (inv. 5.84) shown in Jørgen Hein, *Sophie Amalie*, cat. Rosenborg, Copenhagen 1986, no. 34. The miniature from 1663 is unusually large and was probably – like the goblet – made for the elector of Saxony's visit the same year, when he became engaged to Frederik III's oldest daughter

Charlotte Christensen
The flowers' metamorphoses

pp. 107-115

1 Quotations from Ovid from the *Metamorphoses*, translated by A.E. Watts, Berkeley 1954

2 Richard E. Spear, 'The Literary Sources of Poussin's Realm of Flora', *Burlington Magazine*, vol. 107, Nov. 1965, pp. 563 ff.; with references to earlier sources dealing with the painting. Spear discusses the poem *La Rose* by Poussin's friend Cavaliere Marino as a further source for the Dresden picture, and claims that Flora might be Venus instead. The usual title is attributed to Bellori; the picture was previously refered to as *giardino di Fiori* and *Primavera*

3 For Grandville, cf., *Grandville. Dessins originaux*, cat. Musée des Beaux-Arts Nancy, Cabinet des dessins, Nancy 1986. Grandville lost his will to live after his wife and three little children died, one after another. He had composed his own epitaph with these words: 'Il anima tout, et, après Dieu, fit tout vivre, parler, ou marcher; Seul, il ne sut pas faire son chemin.' Grandville's first woman-flower analogy is from ca. 1828; *ibid.*, cat. no. 106. The museum in Nancy possesses excellent flower studies made form nature for *Les fleurs animées*

4 *H. C. Andersens breve til Carl B. Lorck*, H. Topsøe-Jensen (ed.), Odense 1969, p. 291. Thanks are due to Hanne Westergaard for the reference. The tableaux are described in greater detail in 'Brev til Henriette Wulff, 7.1.1854', *H. C. Andersen og Henriette Wulff. En Brevveksling*, H. Topsøe-Jensen (ed.), Odense 1959, vol. 2, pp. 155-156. *Ibid.*, vol. 3, p. 266, has the text for the Grandville bouquet. The letter shows that Ida Wulff, married to the architect Jørgen Hansen Koch, had lent the book. The flowers were: rose, pansy, forget-me-not, camomile, and cornflower

5 Hanne Westergaard was the first person to point out Vilhelm Pedersen's quotation from Grandville. Quoted in Erik Dal, *H. C. Andersen-illustrationer 1835-1975*, Copenhagen 1975, pp. 31-32

6 Walter Crane, *On the decorative Illustrations of Books Old and New*, London 1896, pp. 154-155. For Walter Crane cf., Isobel Spencer, *Walter Crane*, London 1975, with lists of all of Crane's hand-drawn flower books and printed volumes. Note the reference on p. 131 to the strange painting *The Mower* from 1901, in which death with his scythe is about to cut the heads off of daisy-people (Staatliche Kunsthalle, Karlsruhe), the most extreme image of life's brevity, symbolized by flowers. In addition to the books by Crane with illustrations of flower-people mentioned in the text, he published *A Floral Fantasy in an Old English Garden* (1899), *The Flower Wedding* (1905), *Flowers from Shakespeare's Garden* (1906), and illustrations to Margaret Deland, *Old Gardens and Other Verses* (1893)

7 Walter Crane, 'The Work of Walter Crane', *The Art Journal*, 1898, p. 10

8 Stina Hammar, *Elsa Beskow*, Stockholm 1958. For the Crane exhibition, pp. 169-170: '«But how Walter Crane's excellent and splendid art could give inspiration to something as diametrically opposed as the tale of the itsy, bitsy old woman, is something I have never understood to this very day,» explained Elsa Beskow.' On p. 174, she describes Elsa Beskow's own intimate relationship with flowers, which she characterizes as both speaking and demanding her attention – 'Just like insistant children!'.
The last flower books in Elsa Beskow's oeuvre are *Gørans bok* from 1916 and *Lasse liten i trädgården* from 1920.
For Ottilia Adelborg, cf., *Ottilia Adelborg*, cat. Nationalmuseum Stockholm, Uddevalla 1986. In general about animals and flowers in children's books, cf., Eva von Zweigberk, *Bilderboken*, cat. Nationalmuseum Stockholm, 1971

9 Frida Strindberg, *Strindbergs andet Ægteskab*, Copenhagen 1937, p. 263

10 *Ibid.*, p. 302

11 *Gads religionshistoriske tekster*, Copenhagen 1984, p. 57. According to legend, Ra emerged from a lotus

Charlotte Paludan
A beguiling similarity

pp. 116-126

1 O. J. Rawert, 'Blomster', *Almindeligt Varelexicon...*, Copenhagen 1831

2 H. C. Lund, *Anvisning til at forfærdige de smukkeste kunstige Blomster*, Copenhagen 1827

3 'Fleurs artificielles', *La grande Encyclopédie*, Paris s.d.

4 Else Østergaard, 'Tekstilfragmenter fra Jarlen af Bothwells kiste i Faarevejle Kirke', *Alle Tiders Odsherred*, 1985

5 Aileen Ribeiro, '«A Paradice of Flowers». Flowers in English Dress in the late sixteenth and early seventeenth Centuries', *The Connoisseur*, vol. 200, 1974, pp. 110-117

6 'Fiori artificali', *Enciclopedia Italiana di Scienze, Lettere ed Arti*, Treves 1932-40

7 C. Vecellio, *Dagli Habiti antichi et moderni*, Venice 1590

8 'Fiori artificali', *op.cit.*

9 'Fleurs artificielles', *op.cit.*

10 Henry Havard, 'Fleurs', *Dictionnaire de l'Ameublement et de la Décoration . . .*, Paris s.d.

11 Mogens Bencard, 'Med en dyne nedrevet', *Skalk*, 1981, no. 6, s.p.

12 Jacques Savary des Bruslons et Philemon-Louis Savary, 'Fleurs', *Dictionnaire universelle de commerce, d'histoire naturelle et des arts & metiers*, Copenhagen 1760

13 *Kjøbenhavns Adresse Contoirs Efterretninger*, (= Adresseavisen), 1760, no. 41

14 Thomas Georg Münster, *Fruentimmerets Ven. Oversat efter det Parisiske Oplag*, Copenhagen 1761

15 Bruslons, *op. cit.*

16 S. Brun Juul, *Blomster, Naturhistorisk, oeconomisk og technologisk Handels- og Varelexicon*, Copenhagen 1807

17 *Ibid.*

18 *Adresseavisen, op.cit.*, 1760, no. 94; *ibid.*, 1761, no. 37

19 *Ibid.*, 1761, no. 71; *ibid.*, 1768, no. 52

20 *Ibid.*, 1761, no. 76, gentages in no. 82. Georg Meis, living 1767 in Gothersgade, Copenhagen, was a manufacturer of ribbons, plain and floral-patterned. (*Dannemarks Speil*, Sorøe 1767)

21 *Adresseavisen, op.cit.*, 1761, no. 83

22 Kommercekollegiet. 1735-71, Da.no.sekr. Concessioner og Privilegier 1750 no. 53 + Journ. E no. 2. The National Archive, Copenhagen

23 Kommercekollegiet. Da.no.sekr.no. 59, Concessioner og Privilegier, D 1764-69, no. 25 + Journ. L 1765-67 no. 189. The National Archive, Copenhagen

24 Lars N. Henningsen, 'Et «Flittigt og oeconomisk» folk', *Sønderjyske Årbøger 1989*, p. 150. Thanks are due to Lars N. Henningsen for his willingness to make available his transcripts on the subject from the court records of the City of Haderslev in the regional archives in Aabenraa

25 Bruslons, *op.cit.*

26 *Penia*, 1806, p. 28; Kommercekollegiet, Privatarkiver. Generalkommisær Ewalds Papirer, vol. 9, no. 91. The National Archive, Copenhagen

27 *Penia*, 1809, no. 21

28 *Københavns Vejviser*, 1810-30

29 *Almanac de Gotha*, Paris 1778, pp. 114-116

30 Kommercekollegiet. Industri og Fabrikfaget efter 1816. Privilegieprotokol. The National Archive, Copenhagen

31 *Udsigt over Industriforeningens foranstaltede Udstilling 1844*, Copenhagen 1845, p. 129

32 Thione Rath, *Die Geschichte des Seidenblumen*, Hannover 1981

33 *Ibid.*

Index to articles

Photographic acknowledgements

Fig.: photograph in the articles
Cat.: photograph in the catalogue

AFP, Polfoto, Copenhagen: fig. 69
Fonds Albertina, Österreichische Nationalbibliothek, Vienna: fig. 108
Jörg P. Anders, Museum Dahlem, Berlin: fig. 79, 81, 82, 83
Richard Avedon, New York, copyright 1967: fig. 70
Blauel/Gnamm, Arthotek, Peissenberg: fig. 32
Museum Boymans-van Beuningen, Rotterdam: fig. 46; cat. 215, 241
Sally Andersen Bruce, Connecticut: cat. 338
Burghley House, Stamford, Lincolnshire: cat. 7, 238
Jes Buusmann, Copenhagen: cat. 124
Galerie Börjeson, Malmö: cat. 351
The Trustees of the Chatsworth Settlement: cat. 142
M. Clavel, Musée des Tissus de Lyon, Lyon: fig. 64
Courtauld Institute of Art, London: figs. 16, 99
Alexis Daflos, Statens Konstmuseer, Stockholm: cat. 101
Jos Fielmich, Amsterdam: cat. 266
S. Franses Ltd., London: cat. 270, 271
Germanisches Nationalmuseum, Nuremberg: fig. 33
Hubert de Givenchy, Paris: cat. 335
Tom Haartsen, Rotterdam: fig. 48; cat. 107
Frans Halsmuseum, Haarlem: fig. 50
The Harvard University Art Museums, Cambridge, Massachusetts: fig. 53
B. P. Keiser, Herzog Anton Ulrich-Museum, Braunschweig: fig. 42
Lennart Larsen, Nationalmuseet, Copenhagen: figs. 11, 21, 41, 77, 78, 91, 92, 93, 94, 96, 97, 109, 112; cat. 90, 91, 204, 226, 233, 343
Collections of the Prince of Liechtenstein, Vaduz Castle, Liechtenstein: fig. 34
Linnémuseet, Uppsala: fig. 75
Manchester City Art Galleries, Manchester: fig. 29
Bent Mann Fotografi, Copenhagen: fig. 24
Nationalmuseet, Copenhagen: fig. 107
Fotostudio Otto, Vienna: fig. 62
Thomas Pedersen og Poul Pedersen, Aarhus: cat. 26
Per-Magnus Persson, Statens Konstmuseer, Stockholm: cat. 98, 99, 100
Hans Petersen, Statens Museum for Kunst, Copenhagen: figs. 9, 18, 20, 22, 23, 27, 36, 38, 43, 63, 102; cat. 6, 19, 30, 52
The National Archive, Copenhagen: figs. 84, 85, 86, 87
Rijksmuseum, Amsterdam: cat. 275
The Royal Collections, Rosenborg Palace, Copenhagen: cat. 234
Walter Schmidt, Karlsruhe: fig. 80
Jørgen Schytte, Billedhuset, Copenhagen: fig. 68
Christine Smith, The Trustees of the Victoria & Albert Museum, London: fig. 76; cat. 181, 186, 188
Sir John Soane's Museum, London: fig. 19
Jørgen Sperling, Politikens Pressefoto, Copenhagen: fig. 65
Statens Konstmuseer, Stockholm: figs. 17, 25, 40, 111; cat. 102, 208, 262, 332
Aage Strüwing Foto Aps, Birkerød: fig. 66
Studio Image, Nancy: fig. 60
Otto Stupakoff, New York: fig. 71
L. Sully-Jaulmes, Musée des Arts Décoratifs, Paris: cat. 173, 174, 258, 260
Hans Thorwid, Statens Konstmuseer, Stockholm: cat. 150, 165, 169, 180, 197, 198, 210, 211, 212
The Trustees of the Victoria & Albert Museum, London: cat. 183, 191
Elke Walford, Fotowerkstatt Hamburger Kunsthalle/Altbau, Hamburg: fig. 39
Whitworth Art Gallery, Manchester: fig. 59
Ole Woldbye, Kunstindustrimuseet, Copenhagen: cover, figs. 1, 2, 3, 4, 5, 6, 7, 8, 10, 12, 13, 14, 15, 26, 28, 30, 31, 35, 44, 47, 49, 51, 54, 55, 56, 61, 67, 72, 73, 88, 89, 90, 95, 101, 110, 113, 114; cat. 43, 53, 57, 59, 87, 93, 94, 108, 111, 114, 136, 140, 143, 144, 146, 154, 155, 172, 237, 239, 265, 269, 295, 311, 321, 325-326, 328, 339-340
Österreichische Nationalbibliothek, Vienna: fig. 100